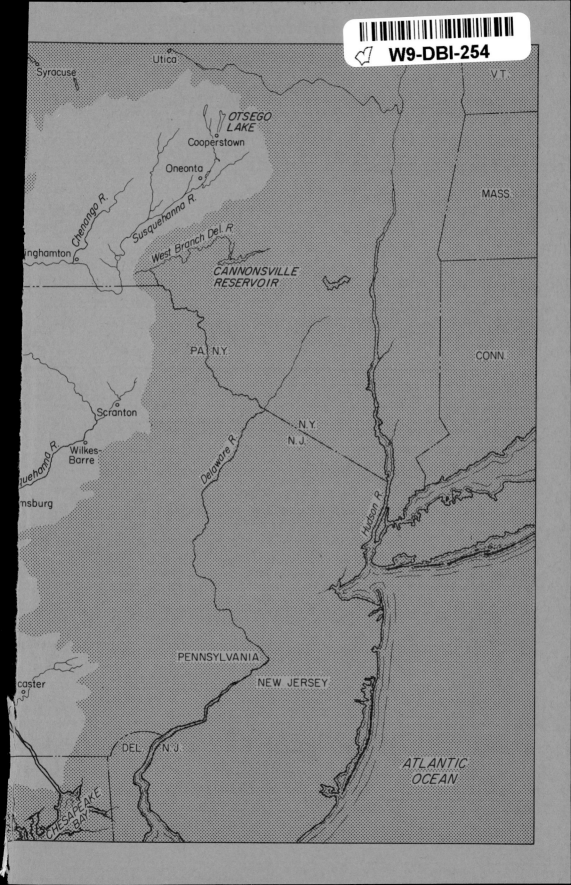

Syracuse

Utica

VT.

OTSEGO
LAKE

Cooperstown

MASS.

Oneonta

Chenango R.

Susquehanna R.

West Branch Del. R.

inghamton

CANNONSVILLE
RESERVOIR

PA. N.Y.

CONN.

Scranton

N.Y.

N.J.

Susquehanna R.

Wilkes-
Barre

Delaware R.

Hudson R.

msburg

caster

PENNSYLVANIA

NEW JERSEY

DEL.

N.J.

ATLANTIC
OCEAN

CHESAPEAKE
BAY

to the continuing usefulness of the river to its own people.

Mr. Voigt was executive director of the Interstate Advisory Committee on the Susquehanna River Basin from its activation by the basin states in 1963 until 1968. In this time the compact was drafted and enabling legislation put through the three legislatures. Mr. Voigt covers the entire history of the compact: how the quasi-official body was established by the basin states for the purpose of drafting the compact; the provisions of the compact, how they were arrived at, and how it resembles and differs from its lone predecessor, the Delaware Compact; how the public was informed; who were the supporters and how they were encouraged, and how the opposition was countered. He reports on how the legislative action was accomplished in each state and on the at times delicate, often frustrating negotiations with the federal government. In December, 1970, in the closing days of the 91st Congress, federal legislation satisfactory to the states was passed and signed by the President.

The author was deeply committed to the cause he was serving professionally and his book combines the technical approach of the specialist with the zeal of the dedicated conservationist. He describes an exciting and promising new approach to water resources management, and shows how one important and complex piece of major legislation was guided to passage by three individualistic state governing bodies and the federal Congress.

The full text of the Susquehanna River Basin Compact is given in an appendix, as are brief biographies of major figures in its creation.

The West Branch, bottom left, joins the Susquehanna at Northumberland, Pennsylvania.

THE
SUSQUEHANNA COMPACT

Guardian of the River's Future

WILLIAM VOIGT, JR.

RUTGERS UNIVERSITY PRESS

New Brunswick, New Jersey

To the people who live in or are influenced by the water resources of the Susquehanna River and its tributaries, who stand to gain or lose most by how thoughtfully and well they are conserved and managed

Preface

This book has a split personality. It is partly a narrative of things that were accomplished, partly an account of why and how they were done. It is somewhat autobiographical, since the central subject matter and the writing, in combination, consumed much of nearly a decade of my life.

It should be said at the beginning, as it was of Baumhoff's *The Damned Missouri Valley*, that it "is essentially a journalistic report, not the treatise of an economist, an engineer, or a political scientist." Yet all these readers and, I hope, many others will find it of interest, may even detect something of substance only half hidden between the lines here and there.

Historians and critics of historical writing should read with a mental caution signal working, for this is a subjective book, written by a partisan; I recognize I am practically a zealot where my concept of the meaning and intent of the Susquehanna River Basin Compact are concerned. Its drafting and advocacy became a consuming interest; I had a part in both.

In one sense this manuscript should not perhaps have been necessary, or at most have been written as a shorter monograph, for the compact it describes and whose course it follows to enactment into law does not constitute a first. The Delaware River Basin Compact was the pioneer of its sort, and any who were associated with the writing and support of the Susquehanna Compact will gladly recognize the Delaware as its parent, the prototype of the genus. Someone should have written a case study of the conception and the birthing of the Delaware Compact while they were fresh in the minds of the leading participants, for that would have had all the elements of history in the making—but no one did. My book does not describe in detail the evolution of that first multiple-purpose, administrative–regulatory federal–interstate water resources compact, though it is referred to in numerous places. Rather, it is the first detailed telling of the story of the next such in the line of evolution—the origin of the idea, and what occurred thereafter until the compact became both state law in New York, Pennsylvania, and Maryland (the Susquehanna basin states) and federal law, with the government of the United States a signatory party and active participant.

In recent years I have been asked why a compact such as this was needed to guide the destiny of the Susquehanna for the next century and more. I have tried to provide the answer in the text. Those who may want at least a partial reply now will find much of it in words I am freely filching from a memorandum written by one who had much to do with this compact from drafting stage to enactment. He is Dr. Mitchell Wendell, a Washington attorney who has specialized in intergovernmental affairs. I am paraphrasing his words in the next three paragraphs.

Since the Susquehanna is the last major river in the Northeast–Middle Atlantic region of our country that is relatively underdeveloped, *it is particularly in need of a federal–interstate coordinating mechanism to lead the conservation, development, and administration of its resources in a manner that will preserve and enhance its value as a scenic and recreational asset for the tens of millions who live within the basin's area of influence.*

Fine as the individual programs of many federal agencies may be, and valuable as the efforts of the three states and their resources departments, a comprehensive and coordinated governmental management instrument is by far the best hope of safeguarding and maximizing the usefulness of the Susquehanna in a way that will accord proper recognition and give effect to the state, regional, and national interests involved. Because the extreme population pressures ringing the basin already are bound to accelerate the existing trend toward fragmented, duplicative, and unplanned development, an overall, combined mechanism for the legal and administrative harmonization of federal and state activity is urgent. The dangers of fragmentation arise on the one hand from the separatism of federal agencies, and on the other from the individuality of state programs.

The Susquehanna River Basin Compact provides a means for attempting to overcome these difficulties. With its enactment by the three basin states and by Congress the compact has become both state and federal law. Now all the governments and agencies working in any part of the basin have been brought within one legal framework for specific purposes. The Susquehanna Commission, composed of the very topmost level of state responsibility (the governors or their personal designees) and a direct representative of the President, was ordained by the enactment of the compact. While the commission is to function as an administrative body in its own right, the compact contains specific safeguards against its displacing existing agencies—federal, state, or local. Coordination is expected, while all existing talents and facilities will be permitted to be employed.

I believe the compact and its administration are destined to influence significantly if not actually to be a chief determinant of the water-related economic and cultural future of the basin and its people. This prediction is qualified only to the extent that any such performance depends ultimately on the ability, courage, dedication, and perseverance of the chief performers, the Susquehanna River Basin Commission and the key members of its staff.

Shortly after the federal phase of compact legislating ended, the chairman of the task force that drafted the agreement, Professor Frederick L. Zimmermann, chairman emeritus of the Political Science Department at Hunter College in New York, wrote me as part of an exchange of mutual congratulations. He recalled that when the Delaware River Basin Compact was enacted Stewart L. Udall, then Secretary of the Interior, had referred to it as "oddball" and declared it should not be considered a precedent. (He later supported the Delaware Compact strongly.) Yet the affected states and the Congress have now enacted another, one very much like that for the Delaware. Zimmermann called this type of compact a markedly innovative step in river basin resources management. The device, he wrote, had now moved to the Delaware's adjoining basin, the Susquehanna, and was under serious consideration in the nearby Potomac valley. What the future holds remains to be seen. In contrast, Zimmermann reminded, the Tennessee Valley Authority approach, which had been advocated strongly for the Delaware, has not been duplicated in any other river basin "despite many efforts and almost total laudatory worship by political scientists."

In this narrative I have attempted a logical progression. The first two parts of the book present an overview of the basin and of some of the conditions, problems, and opportunities that set it apart from other rivers with which I am familiar. An account is given of how the administrative–regulatory type of federal–interstate compact came into being, and how it came to be applied to the Susquehanna. The compact drafting stage comprises Part III. In the fourth segment we take the draft to the public, discover friends, answer critics, and I—for one—observe with awe and at times trepidation the seemingly endless obstacles and uncertainties that can and do arise as a major piece of legislation moves through three state assemblies. Part V tells of discussions of the Interstate Advisory Committee on the Susquehanna River Basin—the impressively labeled quasi-official tristate body formed to draft and advocate enactment of the compact—with the agencies of the executive branch in Washington seeking federal reservations acceptable to all, and of final enactment by Congress after a variety of delays and frustrations that occasionally appeared to exceed what had been experienced in the states. The account closes with the signing into law by the President of the federal form of the legislation.

I cannot move casually into that part of a preface which an average reader might consider perfunctory, my acknowledgements of help of all sorts before the manuscript was completed. Many persons lent a hand, not only as the writing went forward, but through the years that passed as the compact was taking form and moving on its uncertain, even stormy at times, course to legislative passage. Some are named in text or in footnotes. A special thank-you is due Chairman Maurice K. Goddard and the other members and alternate members of the Interstate Advisory Committee; to the drafting task force; to Zimmermann by all means, and the committee's chief consultants, Dr. Wendell and Charles F. Schwan, Jr.; to my secretary, Mrs. Mildred I. LeVan; and to my wife Billie, who not only did much of the final typing but offered excellent criticism. Working through the years with these and literally hundreds of others in the three states and in Washington has been a joy. They eased many a headache while I was actively involved, shared both setbacks and achievements, large and small, and ultimately made possible the reality of a Susquehanna River Basin Compact with the promise it holds for the people of that often abused but still lovely valley of New York, Pennsylvania, and Maryland.

WILLIAM VOIGT, JR.

Mechanicsburg, Pennsylvania
August, 1971

Contents

William Voigt, Jr. was a journalist from 1925 to 1942, working for several large newspapers and for six years with the Associated Press. Throughout World War II he was a historical writer for the Army Ordnance Department and thereafter he was associated with the Isaac Walton League of America and the Pennsylvania Fish Commission.

From 1963 to 1968 Mr. Voigt was executive director of the Interstate Advisory Committee on the Susquehanna River Basin and his experiences in that position are detailed in this volume. Now semiretired, he divides his time between homes near Mechanicsburg, Pennsylvania, and Blackshear, Georgia, and is engaged chiefly in writing and consulting.

Mr. Voigt is the author of *National Fishing Guide* (1946), he has served as editor of *Outdoor America* and editorial director of *Pennsylvania Angler,* and he has contributed articles to a number of nature and field sports periodicals.

Part I

Something to Start With

Chapter 1

The Rocks and Rills Tell a Story

In its journey from source to mouth the Susquehanna River makes a series of twists and turns that at first look strange on the map. It starts on its way from Otsego Lake at Cooperstown, New York, its official birthplace, flowing a bit west of south, turns farther toward the southwest at Oneonta, New York, shifts southward at Nineveh, New York, and crosses into Susquehanna County, Pennsylvania. There it makes a 90-degree turn to the west, then angles northwestward to flow through Binghamton, New York, whence it shifts to a course south of west before bending sharply southward to enter Pennsylvania again near Sayre in Bradford County. After a short southerly reach it loops its way southeastward for close to fifty miles through what is locally known as the Endless Mountains country. Just above Pittston, where the Lackawanna enters from the northeast, the Susquehanna makes another abrupt turn, to the southwest. It continues on this general course to its junction with the West Branch at Northumberland, then flows a little west of south to its confluence with the tributary Juniata River, from which point it runs a relatively straight southeasterly line to Chesapeake Bay.

What a crazy way to run a river! To find the answers to the question of why the Susquehanna flows as it does, we must take a short journey into prehistoric times and borrow information from the realm of geomorphology, the study of the river's origin, its characteristics, and the development of its land forms. We will find clues to the reasons for some of the water-related conditions that led to the writing of a still new and unusual type of statutory agreement between the basin states and the federal government for the purpose of solving problems that stem from those conditions.

The map in the end papers, adapted from maps obtained from the U.S. Geological Survey, gives a general idea of the shape of the basin in our modern times; it graphically discloses the many changes in course of our river, it hints at the places where it traverses or makes end runs around numerous ridges that stand in its path as though they had tried unsuccessfully to block its flow to the sea.

The Long, Crooked River, by Richmond E. Myers, contains an enlightening chapter on the geomorphology of the river.[1] It tells the story accepted by many physical geographers of the origins of the present Susquehanna basin. The author points out that it is not uncommon for rivers of today to be far different from those that existed earlier in the multiplied millions of years in which the earth was taking its present surface form. A seismic cataclysm could result in massive changes, and bring overnight modification in the relief pattern of a sizable region. A minor one occurred only a few years ago just west of Yellowstone National Park, in the upper Madison River Basin of Montana, where a slippage of higher elevation surface blocked the valley and created what is now known as Earthquake Lake. However, such events appear not to have occurred in historic times in our basin. The changes have been so gradual as to go relatively unnoticed, and their ultimate magnitude may not become apparent for additional millions of years.

The theory accepted by Myers and others is that in the Paleozoic Era, from 230 to 600 millions of years ago, give or take a few, either a large land mass existed near the edge of the present Atlantic Coast, or was part of the present coastal region. To its west and southwest lay a vast trough containing a long narrow sea. This included the approximate region where the Susquehanna now flows. The land mass has been named the original Appalachia, and it towered no one knows how high above the level of the trough. Weathering is with us constantly, and as the years trooped past, million after million, the heights were worn down and the trough filled to a depth of about 30,000 feet. Another source[2] gives the possible thickness of the layered limestone, sandstone, and shale in what had been the trough as perhaps 40,000 feet.

The coal seams in the basin, which have had so great a part in the industrial–economic development of Pennsylvania and the nation, were laid down in this era, chiefly in the Mississippian and Pennsylvanian Periods.[3] The mining of coal has brought such severe surface scars that at first sight their ugliness leaves the viewer incredulous, sometimes even nauseated. And the acidulated waters draining from the mines have left hundreds of miles of perennial streams biologically dead. This is discussed more fully in succeeding chapters.

The erosion of the earliest Appalachia was followed by a dramatic reversal of roles. What had been the trough uplifted to alpine heights and what Myers calls the "ancestral" Appalachia simply "ceased to exist and the waters of the sea took its place." Now the persistent forces of erosion began working on the new Appalachian highlands, at a time estimated at about the end of the Paleozoic Era, and after the passage of another vast aggregation of years the new mountains themselves were worn down to the semblance of a plain, with few constrasting features. The gentle slope was toward the east or southeast. While the surface showed little change, just beneath lay rock formations folded into anticlines (upthrusts) and synclines (downward slopes of rock masses), which played decisive parts in the formation of the Susquehanna basin into its present configuration. These folds and thrusts also dictate the pitch and other characteristics of the coal seams and of exposed and buried strata of earth material in general.

Myers believes today's Susquehanna and other southeastward-flowing rivers had their beginnings in the Mesozoic Era, when the peneplane was the dominant land form of this part of the continent. It is postulated that there was a slow but gradual uplifting force at the western edge of the peneplane, tilting the surface so the streams flowed with greater force along steeper gradients, digging valleys in the process. These were wider where the rock formations were less resistant, narrower where the opposite was the case. The widths and slopes of the valleys had decisive roles in guiding, if not ordering, where man—when he came along—would put his dwellings, his roads and other utilities, his industries, his sacred houses, the places where he buried his dead.

Streams are would-be empire builders, in a sense. The headwaters constantly dig away at the high ground of their sources, working ever upward toward the tops of the divides that separate them from the streams that flow on the other side, either on parallel courses or in other directions. This process is called headwater erosion, or heading. In time, a strong stream will erode its way to the crest and cut downward through the divide area until it intercepts the neighboring stream and captures its flow. From that time on—at least until some stronger, more vigorous stream works its own thieving way to the area and itself turns captor—the original pirate stream takes the entire upper flow of the captured watercourse as its own, and its basin is enlarged to the extent of the acreage or square mileage tributary to the captive at the point where the piracy occurred.

In this generalized way the Susquehanna lost a bit and gained a bit and eventually assumed its present zigzag course. Our river may at one time have drained a part of the New York Adirondacks when they were much higher mountains than now. The Hudson is believed to have captured early Susquehanna headwaters with the aid of its tributary Mohawk River. The Delaware's east and west branches may have belonged to the Susquehanna once upon a time. On its part, the Susquehanna took unto itself the Unadilla, Chenango, and Tioughnioga, and headed for Pennsylvania, picking up the Chemung at some point in time and geography.

As the relatively gentle uplift occurred, accompanied by the inevitable erosion, the wearing away process disclosed folds and thrusts of various degrees of hardness. The erosion left the landscape in sharper relief, with numerous ridges where the more resistant rock formations stood, and valleys where the underlying material was more amenable to the winds and water relentlessly demanding change. Myers noted that there were breaks in the ridges here and there, or soft spots that eroded more easily than the material to right or left, eventually permitting streams to flow through gaps or corridors. At other places the ridges simply failed to continue, and streams could flow around them into what otherwise would have been adjacent valleys. And each stream was eternally changing in character; all were either captors or captives, actual or potential. They were always working—just as they are working today. The process is the same; the less than snail's pace keeps it from being obvious to the eye of the casual beholder. In the process of erosion many large and small streams cut downward through coal seams, exposing them so that, when their time in history arrived, they were visible and available for their conflicting roles of hero and villian in the Susquehanna story.

The coming of the various glacier ages in the Pleistocene or Recent time is not believed to have greatly altered the course of the Susquehanna, but the increased flows that were caused by the melting icecaps as the glaciers retreated toward the north no doubt did affect the rate of erosion effected by the river and its tributaries; Myers says the relatively deep gorges in the Susquehanna Piedmont have been attributed by some to accentuated erosive action when the ice fronts were moving northward.

Chesapeake Bay is often referred to as the sunken bed of the lower

View of the Chemung River in the New York portion of the Susquehanna River Basin. *Ted Jones, Stuart Finley Films*

Susquehanna. The mouth of the river was once as far south as the Virginia Capes, and the stream meandered between low banks in an extended flood plain that lay only a few feet above the level of the river and the ocean. As the glaciers built up and crept southward from the polar cap, sea levels declined and the earth seemed to rise as it surfaced above the waters. Then, when the glaciers melted, freeing more water to raise the level of the ocean, more of the flood plain was covered. Meantime, the forces of erosion continued, and deposits of silt as well as heavier earth material were laid down as river flow merged with the tides of the ocean. By the time the Wisconsin, last of the great glaciers, gave way, the flood plain had been built by succeeding periods of sedimentation to a point where the sea covered only that portion of the Susquehanna's ancient valley that is now the rich estuary we call Chesapeake Bay.

So much for how the Susquehanna is believed to have obtained its present form. Geographers say the basin lies in parts of four physiographic regions—the Allegheny Plateau, the Appalachian Mountains, the Ridge and Valley area, and the Piedmont—with only a smidgen of Coastal Plain where the flow of the river unites with the estuarine tides of the Chesapeake.

Above the mouth of the Lackawanna River in Pennsylvania the basin lies in the Allegheny Plateau, where much of it has been sharply marked by glacial action. The main valleys have been deepened by scour and refilled; rock usually is relatively far below present flood plain surfaces.

The upper West Branch subbasin also is in the plateau region, but in an unglaciated part where streams are steeper and valleys narrow with more precipitous walls. The lower West Branch and part of the main stem below the mouth of the Lackawanna lie in the Appalachian region, which forms a belt of mountainous terrain traversing the basin. The Juniata rises in this region, where the highest ridges reach 2,900 feet above sea level and the majority of the crests are at or above 2,000 feet.

The Ridge and Valley region, found in central Pennsylvania and embracing not only the main stem but the lower reaches of the Juniata, is marked by numerous water corridors through the ridges and easily recognized places where streams have run around ridges that came to more or less abrupt stops.

Elevations are relatively low in the Piedmont, with few above 1,000 feet, but the river falls rapidly in a short distance. It drops more than 200 feet in little more than fifty miles to the negligible coastal plain.

The character of the terrain in these provinces had its effect on man from the beginning of his occupancy of the basin. His earliest footpaths followed the stream banks, and these became the forerunners of modern man's roads and railroads. Early man's villages in the flood plain evolved into today's river-edge towns and cities. The occupancy and use of the bottomlands was convenient, and first costs were relatively low. Over time, however, man's tendency to build in and cling to his holdings in the flood plains has been an expensive luxury in terms of flood

One of the Susquehanna's marvels, a corridor it has cut through a mountain a few miles upstream from Harrisburg. The stratification matches, and can be easily traced, from the elevation across the river to the one behind the photographer's vantage point. The National Park Service in 1969 listed this series of gaps or corridors in its register of American Natural Areas. *Ted Jones, Stuart Finley Films*

losses and the price in tax dollars of damage reduction works. We tend to blame losses and costs on conditions of terrain and conveniently overlook or ignore our sins of commission and omission. We cannot escape the fact, though, that terrain as carved through geologic ages has so shaped the basin as to lead to the kinds of situations and problems that made the Susquehanna Compact socially desirable and politically feasible.

If a line is drawn around the perimeter of the New York portion of the basin it takes little imagination to see in it the distorted outlines of the head and antlers of a giant moose. The head faces westward and encompasses the New York segment of the Chemung River subbasin. To the east, where the river proper rises, are the roughly fan-shaped "antlers." Two sizable tributaries are picked up by the Susquehanna in this region, the Unadilla and the Chenango; and the Tioughnioga, itself a substantial stream, feeds the Chenango.

The generally southward course of these and other tributaries of the "antlers" area is in striking contrast to the seemingly erratic flows of other Susquehanna feeders. Two streams large enough to be labeled rivers—the Cowanesque and Tioga—run north from Pennsylvania's Potter and Tioga counties to join New York's Canisteo and the Cohocton which comes from the northwest. Together they all become the Chemung, which continues southeastward to merge with the main river in the northern part of Bradford County, Pennsylvania.

The West Branch runs north, northeast, southeast, east, and south in its winding course to unite with the Susquehanna at Northumberland. The Juniata, its Raystown Branch in particular, seems even more unusual over much of its length. In Bedford and Huntingdon Counties, Pennsylvania, this branch looks as though it might have been cut by a giant bulldozer piloted by a drunken driver. It heads toward nearly every point of the compass between its source springs and its junction with the Frankstown Branch to form the main Juniata about eighty stream miles above its confluence with the Susquehanna.

All of which is to say that the Susquehanna basin in its entirety is one of numerous unusual geographic parts, individual and fascinating in their separate ways, and helps make clear—when seen on a relief map or with the human eye—the story of its origins as told by the physical geographer. They also, when studied discerningly, help toward understanding why the Susquehanna River Basin Compact was written and enacted into law.

Chapter 2

Water Quality in the Basin

The main line of the Susquehanna runs erratically southward from its source in Otsego Lake, Cooperstown, New York, to the head of Chesapeake Bay at Havre de Grace and Perryville, Maryland. Statistically the Susquehanna ranks twelfth among the rivers of the United States in average flow, at 35,800 cubic feet per second (cfs) at Marietta, Pennsylvania, the government gauging station nearest its lower end. It is sixteenth in drainage area, at 27,500 square miles, and nineteenth in length, traveling 444 zigzagging miles from headwaters to mouth.[1]

Between top and bottom, and from uppermost source springs of feeder streams to the main stem, the Susquehanna basin contains commonly recognized water resource conditions, problems, and challenges to perhaps as encompassing an extent as any other in eastern America. Some of these are massive, some in miniature; some are universally present, some spottily or sporadically so; but they are there. The basin differs from its nearer neighbors, though, in a major way: Generally speaking, its waters have not yet been fully utilized and exploited. They have been grossly degraded in places, overdrawn in others, and haphazardly managed as we use the term in America today, but not yet fully overworked or progressively maltreated.

This fortunate condition is not likely to continue indefinitely, for exploitative pressures seem sure to rise rather than fall. Since the tendency in this country has been to use water to the utmost, misusing and abusing it in the process, and only then to take belated steps to try to atone for damage done, the opportunity still remaining in much of the Susquehanna basin for coordinated planning and carefully programmed action is unusual. In few other respects does this appear to be as vital to the basin's future as in the field of water quality management, which I prefer to call pollution abatement and control.

The quality of water appears to be the most pressing aspect of the total subject of water in many regions of the United States, and it presently dominates the scene in the Susquehanna basin, but with a difference. This is one of the important ways in which this basin is dissimilar from nearby river systems such as the Delaware, Hudson, and Potomac, which grow more and more soiled as they approach the sea. It is hard to visualize worse pollution situations than those prevailing in certain parts of the Susquehanna valley from the standpoint of present and prospective human uses. I have especially in mind the tandem Lackawanna and Wyoming valleys in Lackawanna and Luzerne Counties, Pennsylvania, where domestic, industrial, and coal mine pollutants have combined to do almost unbelievably dirty work. I refer to the upper portions of the West Branch and several of its sizable tributaries that have been biologically dead for generations as a result of coal mine drainage impregnated with sulfuric acid, iron, manganese, and other contaminants.

Lesser river reaches, and fouled tributary streams, too, are problems to authorities and others. Specific examples: The Susquehanna and its tributary Chenango River, which join in the heart of Binghamton, New York, were closed to water-contact sports in September, 1968, because of polluted water conditions. York, Pennsylvania, has been mandated to go to advanced waste treatment processes or to pipe-line secondarily treated waste waters to the nearby main line of the Susquehanna because of the gross pollution of Codorus Creek. Spring Creek, in Centre County, Pennsylvania, is a classic example of how pollution, in this instance from a rapidly growing university-based urban complex, can kill off high quality recreation and related uses of a receiving stream. The Pennsylvania Fish Commission for years had some of its principal trout-rearing facilities on Spring Creek. Its chief research facility is there. A reach above Bellefonte was officially, if tritely, designated "Fisherman's Paradise." In the late 1930s when I first came to know Spring Creek its waters ran clear. Early in the fishing season shadflies matured and rose from the surface in uncounted millions while trout churned the surface everywhere gobbling up those that didn't get away to fulfill nature's reproductive plan in their short adult life stage.

Today "Fisherman's Paradise" is closed as such. The water is a dirty gray and unwanted vegetation from its excessive enrichment grows profusely. The Fish Commission has phased out all hatchery facilities dependent entirely on creek water except one raceway, and it utilizes more desirable waters that flow from limestone springs for reduced fish production. The technologists at the research station have had to become more selective in their use of available water, relying more and more on that flowing from Benner Spring and abandoning the creek as a source except to a limited extent in a single experimental pond. The former "Fisherman's Paradise" stretch, which the commission seeks to maintain as a fish-for-fun project, must now be laboriously stripped with hand tools of choking aquatic vegetation so anglers will have open water in which to cast their lures.[2] The state has ordered tertiary treatment for all community wastes in Spring Creek valley, and the equivalent for industrial wastes. Let it be said of The Pennsylvania State University and the municipality of State College that after a reluctant start they are making strenuous efforts to improve conditions. One experimental effort involves spraying treated effluent over nearby land so the filtering action of the soil may cleanse it further before it emerges as seeps and springs.

It is obvious to even the most casual observer that cleansing efforts of the past and those under way at this moment have not yet brought desired results in the basin; indeed, they likely will not do so for a long time to come since there is so much catching up to do. In the jargon of the sanitary engineer, too many people are still thinking primary waste treatment when they should be practicing either secondary or tertiary treatment. Nevertheless, long stream reaches are yet relatively clean, and an extraordinary situation still exists over the lower seventy-five miles of the main stem. From its confluence with the West Branch to its mouth a combination of vital factors makes it possible to say that in comparison with neighboring rivers the Susquehanna unites with the salt of the ocean in its estuary relatively clean by today's realities.

All the way from the point where the two branches meet, the Susquehanna varies from a half-mile to a mile wide. It is not deep or still anywhere along this run except in four downstream places where it has been impounded behind power dams; throughout its free-flowing course it runs over, about, and between rock ledges, boulders, and riffles, and it swirls around numerous large and small islands. The water becomes supersaturated with oxygen, and the result is a fantastic capacity to assimilate organic matter. The mineral input that comes from coal country and other sources is not reduced by oxidation; it remains and gives the water on its way to the head of the bay a degree of hardness and other qualities that water supply people would rather not have to cope with, but excessive organic loads have rarely entered the Chesa-

Islands stud the Susquehanna downstream from its confluence with the West Branch. *Ted Jones, Stuart Finley Films*

peake from the Susquehanna up to now. Those words "up to now" should perhaps be emphasized, as will be made clear shortly. The importance of the assimilative capacity of the lower seventy-five miles is hard to overestimate as far as southern Pennsylvania and Maryland are concerned—especially Maryland. The bay is Maryland's greatest natural resource. It supports a large commercial fish and shellfish industry and is one of the eastern seaboard's most prolific spawning areas for such migratory fish species as striped bass. The bay's quality is a factor in Baltimore's water-borne commerce. It is used heavily for many kinds of water-based outdoor activity including fishing for food and sport. It has helped mold the culture of a considerable region. Maryland has long looked anxiously upriver, not knowing what New York or Pennsylvania might send down into her precious bay. Of course, Maryland has had certain avenues she could travel toward correction of wrongs tied to the river. She could say "please don't," and if the offending neighbor refused to "please" Maryland could take it to court or, under certain circumstances, could appeal to federal agencies having jurisdiction.[3] All three courses are uncertain and the likelihood is that in a majority of instances the most favorable result securable would be long in coming.

The coal mine drainage referred to earlier must have considerable added description, because it is so widespread and deadly, and because the future is so clouded. Pollution from coal mines originates only in Pennsylvania portions of the basin. These are located in two principal areas, and a few smaller regions, with one of the bigger consisting exclusively of anthracite, the rest bituminous. The anthracite or hard coal is found in three belts: The larger crosses the Lackawanna–Wyoming valleys and the two smaller ones are to the south, east of the river. The middle belt straddles the divide between the Susquehanna and the Lehigh drainages and contaminates both, but the upper and lower are entirely in the Susquehanna basin. (One very small detached anthracite area was discovered in the headwaters of the Loyalsock Creek subbasin, Sullivan County.)

Dependable records are few but it appears probable that the "black rock that burns" was known to the Susquehannock Indians, and may have been to other primitives before their time. Early white settlers learned to burn it in fireplace grates and stoves, and for industrial purposes; it began to be mined commercially in 1769.[4] Since then, in excess of five billion tons have come from the hard coal fields of Pennsylvania, a significant factor in the evolution of the nation's industrial and economic might. But as the coal was mined, deplorable things happened to the streams into which mine waters drained. The flows became acidic and killed off aquatic life. They became impregnated with iron and other minerals and grew hard. As iron oxides were precipitated they gave the sides and bottoms of the streams a bright brown coating that came to be called "yellowboy." Analysis also often discloses manganese, aluminum, and sometimes other minerals in solution in these streams. The yellowboy is unsightly, and the other minerals have their adverse aspects, but the chief killer of the lot has been the sulfuric acid.

Students long puzzled over the fact that waters draining from coal

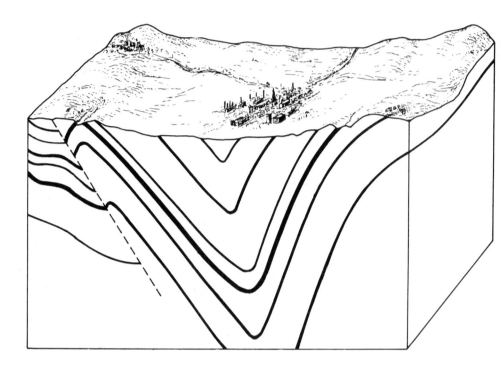

Figure 1. Graphic representation of the folding and faulting in the anthracite coal belt centered within the tandem Lackawanna and Wyoming Valleys of Pennsylvania.

mines were deadly. Late in the nineteenth or early in the twentieth century evidence collected over the years began falling into place and technologists started publishing papers in scientific journals on how the acid was formed. They deduced it was from the interaction of water, air, and the sulfur found in association with coal seams.[5] Reaching tenable conclusions on the formation of acid was one thing; discovering feasible techniques of coping with the acid quite another. The basic antipollution law of Pennsylvania, that of 1937,[6] excluded coal mine drainage from any state enforcement efforts; the lawmakers were persuaded there was nothing that could be done about pollution from that source. By 1945 the state had secured technological evidence indicating that the pollution of streams could be prevented by operators of active mines, and the law was amended to give the state authority to prevent contamination of what were then considered clean streams; however, it still excluded action against operators whose workings drained into streams classified as acid polluted.[7] It was not until 1965 that the Commonwealth of Pennsylvania moved purposefully to halt the discharge of acid from all active coal mines.[8] Even this strong step forward is so far meaningless as regards hundreds of streams and streamlets, for officialdom has only made a beginning toward the immensely difficult task of abating and controlling flows from mines that have been worked out or abandoned for other reasons.

Contaminated drainage is a baffling, frustrating thing nearly everywhere coal has been discovered and mined; hard coal or soft coal—it makes no real difference. Figure 1[9] is a diagram representing the anthracite region, showing how folded and faulted strata lie, but it does not purport to indicate the total number or location of coal seams found there. The Pennsylvania coals were deposited in densely grown coastal swamps which flourished across the state ahead of advancing seas eons ago. In each swamp a layer of coal-forming peat accumulated. The layer was then buried by mud and sand. This happened again and again as the uneasy Paleozoic landscape rose and fell and rose again, and over time the layers of peat became coal and the covering sediments hardened into sandstone, shale, and limestone. The final result was a sequence of strata some 2,000 feet thick consisting of widespread layers of coal separated by other rock types. "Roughly it resembled a thick book with every twentieth page made of black paper to represent the coal seams."[10]

The faulting and folding represented by Figure 1 leads to an extension of the theme in Figure 2, which represents mine interconnections resulting from two centuries of hard coal mining in the Lackawanna and Wyoming valleys. Beneath the earth's surface is a fantastic maze of rooms and corridors that came with the digging and removing of the coal. Some are deep, some very near the surface. Coal beds slope from higher ground toward and dip under the two rivers. A Knox Mine Company tunnel was cut so near the bed of the river above Wilkes-Barre that, in a time of high water early in 1959, the tunnel ceiling gave way. Several lives were lost. A costly program of filling old tunnels has been

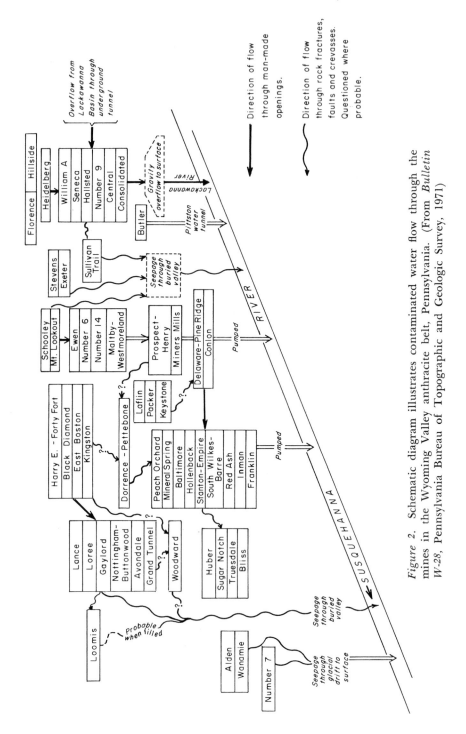

Figure 2. Schematic diagram illustrates contaminated water flow through the mines in the Wyoming Valley anthracite belt, Pennsylvania. (From *Bulletin W-28*, Pennsylvania Bureau of Topographic and Geologic Survey, 1971)

under way in areas where houses, streets, and other properties have broken through or shifted and become a hazard. Subsurface fires burn in several places in the anthracite region.

Where coal cropped out the operators' tunnels followed the seams to the next property line—which presumably runs vertically down to the center of the earth—and where they pitched downward the coal was mined as deep as man could go and profitably keep ahead of inflowing waters with pumps. Where coal was known to be present but did not crop out, shafts were sunk or tunnels drilled to intercept it, and the miners worked it out until they, too, were blocked by somebody else's property or by depth and water problems. In the process ownership and lease boundaries were broken through in hundreds of places. So there came to be hundreds of interconnections—vertical, horizontal, and sloping. Water percolated from the surface and poured into the man-made voids. It leached sulfur and other solubles from the coal measures and overriding strata, and acidic waters resulted. The hills to the east of the two valleys rise more than 1,400 feet higher than the bed of the Susquehanna, those to the west more than 600 feet; as a consequence of the filling of the subsurface openings with water plus the addition of new infiltration every time it rained or snow melted (the annual precipitation averages about 35 inches), hydrostatic pressures built up to a point where permissible pumping was unable to keep them under control.

A multimillion-dollar federal–state program was begun in 1956 with a two-avenue approach to anthracite mine drainage problems. One was to pump mines dry enough so they could be worked safely. The other was a preventive program of diverting surface flows so they would not enter subsurface workings. Through the years the emphasis was on pumping, which was a direct economic aid to the mine operators and their employes. Little more than lip service was paid to diversion intended to reduce contamination over the long term. In recent years the volume of acid water that might be pumped to the river has been regulated by the state and varies with the flow of water in the Susquehanna.

In the summer of 1961 subsurface water pressures in the Lackawanna valley increased so greatly there had to be a blowout somewhere, and it came in the flood plain of that small river at the downstream edge of the Borough of Duryea. It looks like a gigantic spring, as it flows at a rate of about 20,000 gallons a minute, but has officially been dubbed the "Duryea Gravity Outfall." In October, 1962, a valve-controlled borehole capable of drawing off a similar volume was completed at the stream's edge in Old Forge, the adjoining upstream community. This was in-

The pipe in the foreground carries untreated wastes from a residence. In background is the valve chamber of the bore hole built by the Commonwealth of Pennsylvania to draw off polluted subsurface coal mine waters to prevent subsidence and basement flooding. The stream, just off the picture at right, is the Lackawanna River. *Ted Jones, Stuart Finley Films*

tended to provide sufficient pressure relief to keep cellars dry and prevent the surface from subsiding in the vicinity. Contaminated water enters the Lackawanna and the Susquehanna from other openings;[11] no one knows how many breaks and seeps exist in the bed and lower banks of the river in this area. A half-dozen of the larger feeder streams that drain the two southerly hard coal belts are acid polluted.

Soft coal has been mined commercially, contaminating the water in the valley of the Tioga River, which flows northward into New York State to become part of the Chemung River system upstream from

What looks like a nice rocky stretch of rural stream is the dirty Lackawanna River at Old Forge—and that stuff in the middle distance, on the bank, is rubbish from an unregulated dump.

Corning. It has been mined in the drainage areas of several tributaries of the West Branch in Tioga and Lycoming Counties. It has been mined in headwater portions of the Juniata subbasin. These, however, are insignificant pockets compared with the rich bituminous measures found in upper reaches of the West Branch and along a number of its major feeder streams. This region embraces all or parts of six central Pennsylvania counties: Cambria, Cameron, Centre, Clearfield, Clinton, and Elk. In some West Branch subbasins—that of Moshannon Creek in Clearfield County comes to mind—underground interconnections are similar, on a smaller scale, to those in the Lackawanna and Wyoming valleys. The upper main stem of the West Branch, Bennett's Branch of Sinnemahoning Creek, and Anderson, Clearfield, Moshannon, and Chest Creeks are the most grossly polluted in the West Branch headwater region.

Dealing with pollution from coal mine drainage seems without question to be the largest and most difficult task presently facing water managers in the Susquehanna basin. Since the passage of the 1965 Pennsylvania law prohibiting all acid discharges from active coal mines, new acidic loadings of streams should be pretty generally prevented, except from accidental spills caused by such things as breaks in holding basins or failure of treatment equipment, or from deliberate violations. This is fine, except that active mines are not the majority of offenders and haven't been for years. The overwhelming bulk of the polluting flow comes from mines closed out or abandoned long ago. Their owners are dead or departed, no longer where they can be served with summonses and prosecuted or otherwise held accountable for conditions they left behind. Pollution from abandoned mines is not somebody's business; it has become everybody's business, which means the costly correction that must be carried out has to be paid for from everybody's pocketbook, that is the taxpayers of the state or nation, or both. We are long past the time when preventive measures might have been applied, even if they had been known or had been officially determined to be economically feasible.

That question of economic feasibility has from the start been a factor strongly influencing the attitudes of operators, government agencies, and the courts; it is as true today as it was in 1885 when the Pennsylvania Supreme Court held in effect that it was the inalienable right of the operator to get his coal out of the ground regardless of the effect his mine's drainage might have on the receiving stream and downstream riparian owners.[12] That was considered no more than a "trifling inconvenience" by comparison with "the necessities of a great community"; furthermore, coal mine pollution was "an injury for which the law provides no redress." The upper riparian owner could deal with the waters of his property any way he wanted to for "the improvement or better enjoyment" of his land; that right was "almost unquestionable." Couple this then realistically hard judicial line with the woeful lack of technology and it is not difficult to understand how it could take more than three-fourths of a century for the legislators of Pennsylvania to be persuaded that enough progress had been made so the operators could be required to recover their coal without adversely affecting the streams.

An understanding of these historic and technologic factors is necessary if we are to recognize or admit that we are faced with a *fait accompli*, that the after effects will long linger and plague all who are directly or indirectly affected, and then proceed boldly in concert to correct what can be corrected as rapidly and on as widespread a geographic scale as possible. It won't be easy, and it is likely that Pennsylvania and her taxpayers alone will prove unequal to the task.

In the less concentrated bituminous operations of the West Branch and Juniata subbasins, segments physically separated from other sources of mine drainage can be found and treated in one fashion or another. Here the problems differ in certain aspects from those in the anthracite belts. The coal measures don't pitch as steeply, for one thing, and many of them are close enough to the surface to be worked with modern stripping equipment. This method of mining can be carried out with less danger of contaminating drainage, as a rule, by preventing the accumulation of water in the presence of sulfur and air for a long enough time for acid to form, and by appropriate backfilling. Old strip mine spoil banks can be and are being "reclaimed," as the common expression goes, and being planted to grasses, legumes, and trees. Virtually all of these can in time be dealt with satisfactorily, though expensively. The flow from worked-out or abandoned deep mines is a tougher nut to crack, and where present the problem more nearly resembles that gigantic headache that exists in the anthracite regions.

There the owners of the remaining active operations say they should not be held accountable for contaminated water ⸱that merely flows through their mines, that originates in mines long shut down and that runs or has to be pumped from their pits in order to keep them dry enough to be worked. They say it is physically impossible to segregate and measure the water their mines produce from that which seeps or pours in from the others. No doubt a judgment value of some sort could be reached through negotiation but it would be no more than that; scientific accuracy would be out of the question. One of the largest of all the hard-coal mining companies of former years (the Blue Coal Company, formerly Glen Alden) is now down to a fraction of its earlier pace, and has attributed its shutting down of other workings to the cost of waste-water treatment.[13]

A start has been made by the Commonwealth toward high-degree treatment of a substantial flow of anthracite coal mine water from one of numerous sources, but at this stage it can be designated little more than a beginning. For example, at the so-called Buttonwood discharge, which flows from 16 to 20 MGD of highly acid water, the Commonwealth in 1969 let a contract for construction of a 5-MGD flash distillation plant that is expected to eliminate nearly all contaminants and reduce hardness to a range of 10 to 20 parts per million (ppm or milligrams per liter). Dr. David Maneval of the Pennsylvania Department of Mines and. Mineral Industries, characterized this in a personal communication as "only a drop in the bucket" by comparison with the total input of acid water to the river, "but it is a start." Plans are flexible and gallonage increases are anticipated. Its successful and economic, even self-sustaining operation (from the sale of water) would probably result in extension of the technique to other acid discharge areas. The Mine Drainage Section, Department of Health, hesitated to estimate the total flow of acid water into the Susquehanna in the Wyoming-Lackawanna region because of fluctuations and various unknowns.

It would be fine to discover that a single universal and inexpensive type of treatment plant could be installed in all kinds of streams for discharges from mines, but such has not been developed. A type of lime treatment plant, semiautomatic and much simpler, which neutralizes in-steam acidic flows, has been under experimental operation elsewhere and gives promise of being capable of improving conditions measurably in relatively small watercourses in both hard and soft coal areas. The prototype, installed by the Department of Mines and Mineral Industries in 1968 in western Pennsylvania, has been reported functioning satisfactorily. The liming increases the hardness of the water.

Mine sealing can be done with success in certain types of abandoned deep mines; the most perplexing problems arise when sealing is attempted at mines where the coal seam pitched upward from the outcrop. This, of course, was the kind of seam the operators looked for. As they progressed with their mining they hauled empty buggies up to the coal face and, loaded, these could be brought down to the adit by the force of gravity. Ordinary sealing by means of plugs of earth or concrete set in the openings are useless in that sort of mine because hydrostatic pressure will either cause the water to force out the plug or detour around it and break loose somewhere else.

Considerable space has been devoted to coal mine drainage pollution in the Pennsylvania part of the Susquehanna basin; deliberately so because it is so devastating and so difficult and costly to eradicate. At the moment I can foresee only one other broad type of water pollution that has the capability of causing more trouble, and the full effects of it are still in the future whereas the mine drainage is with us now. I refer to

accelerated eutrophication traceable to excessive and unnatural enrichment of the basin's waters, which is both a technological and a population problem. It has reached massive proportions only spottily in the
basin so far, and then, generally speaking, in smaller waters. This is not
a fully understood condition and problem as yet, and it will be approached with due caution in this discussion.

Part of it is associated with municipal pollution. The condition of the
river at Binghamton and vicinity in the late summer of 1968 was mentioned earlier in this chapter. New York, working with a billion-dollar
bond issue with which the state is assisting its communities to upgrade
treatment facilities, is moving to bring a considerable degree of correction. Factors of federal grants and municipal dollar capability will affect
the pace of improvement, not only at Binghamton but at virtually all
other sewered communities in the New York segment of the basin.

There is even more to be done, quantitatively and qualitatively
speaking, in Pennsylvania. For example, the City of Scranton, which had
a 1970 population of 103,000, is on the Lackawanna in a reach where the
stream averages about twenty feet wide and a very few inches deep. The
city had just begun construction of a primary treatment plant in April,
1969, changed design to secondary, and put the facility in operation late
in 1970. Chances are, if growth continues, it will be asked before long to
give its wastes tertiary treatment. Wilkes-Barre, not much smaller than
Scranton, joined with about twenty of its neighbors in and near the
Wyoming Valley after dragging its feet all the way to the state Superior
Court over the question of whether it should have to treat its wastes at
all. A primary treatment plant for the Wyoming Valley metropolitan
complex went into operation in the late summer of 1969, but no treatment more advanced than secondary was in sight there at the end of
August, 1971. In fact, no community of consequence on the main stem,
the West Branch, or the Juniata had installed more than primary treatment facilities at the end of the calendar year 1971.[14]

The federal Water Quality Act of 1965[15] and later laws are expected
to result in betterment of effluents from main stem and other interstate
portions of the basin over time. What the impatient citizen must but
doesn't always like to remember is that there is an inevitable time lag
between the signing of a law or the passing of a bond issue and the
flipping of a switch to signify that a high-degree treatment plant has
been put in operation.

Pennsylvania, due to geographic realities, has a far greater number of
sewered communities on tributary streams, not affected presently by

federal law, than either New York or Maryland, so comment on that aspect of our total municipal wastes subject will be concentrated there. The conditions of Codorus Creek in York County, of Spring Creek in Centre County, and the Lackawanna have been mentioned. They are not alone in their misery caused by municipal pollution. The Conestoga below the City of Lancaster, and two creeks, the Conodoguinet and Yellow Breeches—whose difficulties may be traced in good part to the fact that their valleys serve as bedroom areas for people whose livelihood is based on the Greater Harrisburg urban complex—are becoming increasingly contaminated. The place I now call my summer home has overlooked the Yellow Breeches since 1955; through the years I have observed a marked deterioration which is made evident by the stream's telltale gray appearance and the increase in aquatic vegetation.

Out along the tributaries, where state law now rules, it looks as though officials will continue to consider assimilative capacity of the receiving stream as a chief criterion when the degree of treatment to be accorded municipal waste waters is up for determination. In some parts of the basin—not all of which were named earlier—that capacity has long since been exceeded, even when treatment was at secondary level. Tertiary treatment seems inevitable for a number of communities, and the equivalent for industrial plants.

Agricultural pollution—manures, pesticides that get out of control or are used excessively or unwisely, and soluble nutrients such as phosphorus and nitrogen that leach or are washed into waterways—has proved baffling. Its adverse effects have not yet been satisfactorily measured in most areas and under varying conditions, yet they are indubitably present, perhaps in larger degree than is commonly realized. There was so little said until recently in high quarters which would guarantee public attention that there was temptation to think perhaps some of our rural leaders believed if they kept quiet it would eventually go away— which isn't the case. (Strong public statements made in 1968 and thereafter by such ranking officials in the U. S. Department of Agriculture as Hollis Williams, assistant administrator of the Soil Conservation Service, in which emphasis has been put on organic pollution from livestock operations such as feedlots, may be considered exceptions.) The richest agricultural lands in the Susquehanna basin are those in south central Pennsylvania—in Cumberland, Dauphin, Lancaster, Lebanon, and York Counties—though this is not to say that highly fertile farmlands aren't found elsewhere. Indeed, Hollis Hatfield, Pennsylvania spokesman for the Farm Bureau affiliate and one of the adamant opponents of the Susquehanna River Basin Compact in 1966 and 1967, emphasized in writings and speeches that fully 70 percent of Pennsylvania's crop and pasture land in USDA capability classes I, II, and III lay within the Commonwealth's portion of the basin, though the basin comprised only 46 percent of the total area of the state.[16] However that may be, the farmlands in the named southern Pennsylvania counties drain into the main stem of the river in the last fifty or so miles of its course. It seems significant that in the late summer of 1968 algal blooms were detected in Conowingo Reservoir, which straddles the Pennsylvania-Maryland border. Were they caused by the leaching of nutrients from farmlands? Did they come mostly from the inert bases used in household detergents? Were there other primary sources? Or was the incident a result of a combination of causes? If the last named, how and where and when do we start to sort out and separate the causes so each may be dealt with effectively in the most appropriate manner by the most appropriate people? Did the algal bloom in Conowingo originate in one or several of Pennsylvania's southerly counties or was it a cumulative thing? Are the nutrients building up from New York State areas all the way down to the bay, with, of course, variations in the curve due to local situations? Is upper Chesapeake Bay's already rich aquatic pasture to be next to see an algal bloom as a commonplace or annual affair?

Overenrichment put an abrupt stop to swimming in the vicinity of Binghamton in 1968. It has destroyed most of the beauty and recreational use of a stream once considered a "Fisherman's Paradise." Houses along the Conodoguinet and Yellow Breeches are feeding them too rich a diet through their septic systems and in leachings from dairy herd wastes and crop fertilizers. The Conestoga below Lancaster on any hot summer day gives forth a septic stench at the lower sewage treatment plant outfall. And the list can be extended; these have been mentioned by name only because they are the most familiar to me.

In time overenrichment is likely to become as great a threat and a challenge as coal mine acid is now. One of the state agencies most intimately concerned with coping with coal mine pollution once suggested that a Susquehanna River Basin Commission be given specific authority to move into that field. Will the time come when dealing with the interstate aspects of overenrichment and resultant eutrophication will be put in the same category?

Thus far we have considered only the bad aspects of the water quality situation in the basin: existing and potential pollution significant enough to warrant attention on an interstate or federal–interstate basis.

A placid reach of the Susquehanna River in the Endless Mountains near Towanda, Pennsylvania. *Ted Jones, Stuart Finley Films*

The New York portion of the basin may be considered fortunate that its
two major urban centers—Binghamton and Elmira—are on sizable
rivers, Binghamton on the main line of the Susquehanna and Elmira on
the Chemung. Consequently, the absence of completely adequate waste
disposal systems has had a severe adverse effect on only comparatively
short stretches of the upper basin's streams. Except for the incipient
problem of overenrichment, most of the waters of the New York segment
are not in bad overall condition. In the much larger Pennsylvania part
of the basin the good to excellent quality areas are proportionately

sizable. The Endless Mountains stretch of more than sixty river miles, from the New York line to the mouth of the Lackawanna, has not so far experienced a fish kill attributable to municipal pollution. The focus in the West Branch has been on acid tributaries but it has many clean ones: the First Fork and Driftwood Branch of the Sinnemahoning, the Black Moshannon, Kettle, Young Woman's, Bald Eagle, Pine (except for its Babb Creek feeder), Lycoming, Loyalsock, and Muncy Creeks, and others less well known. Farther down, Penn's Creek and others tributary to the still excellent lower main stem are noteworthy for their good quality, and Maryland's chief feeder, Deer Creek, is good enough to be a favorite spawning ground for anadromous fish of Chesapeake Bay. In July, 1969, the Pennsylvania Fish Commission announced that the investigations of its biologists had shown a number of mountain streams, including numerous basin brooks, were of sufficient quality to maintain fishable trout populations without annual stockings of catchables—that is, trout of legal length or larger.

The point attempted, if it isn't already clear, is that despite the reckless destructiveness of the past, with its lingering effects, there remains a base for constructive water resources activity over much of the basin. Not all of the water quality effort must be devoted to reclamation and restoration; a good deal can go into conservation, development, and protection against future unwise exploitation.

Chapter 3

Water Uses, Present and Future

Granted that the problems of water quality in the Susquehanna basin can and will be solved, what of water supply for municipalities, industry, irrigation, and recreation? These are the principal uses in the basin, and present no insurmountable obstacles at this time. In 1968 the federal Water Resources Council found the upper portion of the valley to be characterized generally by a surplus of water.[1] The council wasn't quite as sanguine as regards abundance in the lower portion, and it provided no dividing line to tell where it considered the upper stopped and the lower began. A general statement based on personal observation and knowledge would have to note that in the lower half of the basin there is a surplus under ordinary circumstances, except in several tributary areas where water requirements of an expanding population have outstripped local sources of supply, of which more later. It may facilitate understanding if we set forth a few statistics first.

The Susquehanna must be called a large river. The U.S. Geological Survey in cooperation with the Pennsylvania Department of Forests and Waters reported[2] that the average daily flow at its farthest downstream gauging station—Marietta, Pennsylvania, about forty airline miles from Chesapeake Bay—is 35,800 cubic feet per second (cfs), each of which equals 646,000 gallons a day. This is approximately 23 billion gallons a day (BGD). The highest flow of record was 787,000 cfs, or more than 508 BGD. The lowest sustained flow for a 24-hour period was 1,380 cfs, or less than 900 million gallons a day (MGD). If all was "average," which often is meaningless in terms of practicalities, something like 84,413 billion gallons of water would flow past Marietta in the course of a year.

Quite frequently the minimum flows of record are determining factors for both plant and animal life. Minimum flows, connoting drought and the insidious effects of drought, may over time be fully as destructive as the generally more spectacular opposite condition, flood. Flood destruction comes as a relatively swift wiping out, knocking down, or breaking up. Drought damage manifests itself in failure of natural processes to achieve fruition of the magnitude considered "normal" over an "average" growing season. As an academician might put it, drought results in underachievement. Perhaps it is because of its highly visible nature and its ability to wreak havoc rapidly that so much more public attention has been given to coping with flood by comparison with that accorded drought. Seeking ways to tame the flood monster has permitted the erection of massive earthen and concrete monuments to the technological genius of man. These are more eye-catching than sprinkler systems fed by wells or tiny ponds near patches of cropland. As a people we tend to favor that which is heroic in concept and stature; drought relief measures seldom are. But let's get back to statistics. What depleting uses do the people of the Susquehanna basin now make of its comparatively large average flow? The consumptive use, use that does not result in a substantial return flow, is fairly low in relation to total gallonage.

The New York Water Resources Commission estimates that in 1963 in the New York portion of the basin approximately 98 MGD were withdrawn for use by municipalities and industry, 55 MGD for water service areas of all sizes and 43 MGD for industrial processes and cooling.[3] This totals approximately 35.77 billion gallons a year.

Pennsylvania Department of Commerce figures show that in 1966 industrial water used in basin counties from other than municipal supply lines was 526.2 MGD and municipal withdrawals aggregated about 268 MGD, for a combined total of 289.9 billion gallons over the year.[4]

Maryland's withdrawals are small. Baltimore diverts from Conowingo and is the state's largest user of Susquehanna River water, by far. In 1966 the city pumped an average of 57.5 MGD or a total of 21 billion gallons.[5] Other Maryland use of basin water probably didn't exceed 6.5 MGD, or less than 2.4 billion gallons, in a comparable year.[6]

No differentiation has been made between surface and ground water sources in the above. The grand total utilized is considerably less than 1 BGD, with the takings scattered the length and breadth of the basin and, with the exception of Baltimore's case, from 80 to 90 percent comes back to the river in return flow after use. It is generally degraded in quality at each outfall, but not wholly consumed in the using. In some cases industrial consumption is greater than municipal, but water-consuming factories are not present in large numbers.

Agricultural irrigation consumes a far greater percentage of the water withdrawn, some 70 percent or more usually going into the crops watered or being lost through evaporation. At times return flow to a stream after spray irrigation may be zero. Yet figures furnished by the Harrisburg office of the U.S. Soil Conservation Service show present irrigation use is comparatively small. Basin farmers were taking about 24,200 acre-feet of water in the growing seasons of the late 1960s, from ground and surface sources. New York farmers used 3,100 acre-feet, Pennsylvanians 21,000, and Marylanders the rest. Three acre-feet are almost a million gallons; therefore, the total was on the order of 8 billion gallons a year.

On the basis of figures such as the above it is accurate to say the Susquehanna now has much more water than is used, for which plans may be made and additional beneficial uses projected, but at this point we run into complicating factors. First, to which we will return later, is the question eternally in official Maryland minds of whether there is in fact any present surplus if the optimum health, productivity, and uses of Chesapeake Bay are properly considered. Other complexities are disclosed by the minimum flow reported and by projections of future use in the basin as the towns and cities grow, as industries increase in number, as their per-unit water requirements change, and as the demand for more fruits of the soil for human and animal consumption forces farmers to increase irrigation withdrawals.

The Soil Conservation Service forecasts a ten-fold increase in irrigation use by the year 2020, to some 84 billion gallons per growing season. Figures furnished by the Pennsylvania Department of Forests and Waters and attributed by it to the Federal Water Pollution Control Administration[7] indicate that by 2020 the aggregate withdrawals in the basin for municipal and industrial purposes will be on the order of 2,408.6 MGD, or in excess of 878 billion gallons a year. These are large figures, but nothing like the 84,413 billion gallons expected to pass Marietta in an average year. They should prove useful as general guides to planning, but should not be considered absolutes until actual values in the target year show them to be so.

Because of flow statistics cited I am not unduly concerned about water supply in the basin in coming years, with the exception of the impact of possible diversions, to be discussed shortly. If this optimism is to be justified, water quality must be brought to and held at a high level in the municipal and industrial fields and upgrading of water must go on apace in the coal areas. It is likely that additional storage will be required here and there to sustain flows in dry years, to assure that water is where it is needed when it is needed, and probably to knock some of the tops off high waters in flood times. More communities likely will have to go to the river for municipal water, and so will industries, when present tributary sources or wells prove inadequate. Some users will be situated off the river proper, even off major tributaries. Older communities were located where they are partly because their founders did not or could not know they would outgrow their normal or ordinary water sources.

Scranton is one example. In the dry year 1966 I saw Scranton's water supply reservoirs when they were dangerously low, some almost dry. York is another. In 1966, before a sizable new reserve reservoir was completed, a parade of tank trucks hauled water eleven miles from the Susquehanna for rationed use by residents; and that wasn't the first year emergency measures had been required at York. Lancaster is now pipelining water from the river, a dozen or so miles to its west, and in time probably will ask permission to take more. There already is controversy between the city and farmers up the tributary streams above Lancaster, over which should have preferred use of the available surface supply. Meantime, Lancaster County fishermen and swimmers seem to side with the city as they plead that more water, to support their respective sports, be allowed to flow in creek channels all the way from source areas to the river. Altoona has special problems. It is situated near the heads of small tributaries of the Juniata, and mine drainage has contaminated a series of three of its reservoirs nestled in the famed Horseshoe Curve of the Penn-Central Railroad. Harrisburg is located in the flood plain as are so many other basin communities, where floods can hit them hard; a filtration plant on City Island, shut down some years ago, was reactivated for a while in 1966 when Harrisburg's principal source on a tributary creek got too low for municipal comfort. These are types of situations the federal Water Resources Council probably had in mind when it said one of the problems confronting the lower Susquehanna basin was "the expansion of metropolitan water systems,"[8] but I would not say they are representative of the entire lower basin.

Agricultural water should not be excessively difficult to obtain in

Drought can be as damaging as flood. Corn, stunted by drought, in the valley of Yellow Breeches Creek, a tributary of the Susquehanna, York County, Pennsylvania, 1966. *Ted Jones, Stuart Finley Films*

desired quantity in most of the basin's farming country. The most critical situation likely is that in Lancaster County. Studies have been carried out by the county planning commission and proposals call for reservoirs on small streams considered adequate to care for projected needs into the twenty-first century, which is no longer very far in the future. River water may prove the ultimate answer, if the taking can be made acceptable to downriver interests. One of the perplexing irrigation questions involves the farmer who owns land of excellent quality but so high or far away that pumping from the nearest stream isn't economically

Dry stream bed in central Pennsylvania, 1966. Ordinary flow waters stock and irrigates row crops. In this condition it won't even carry away waste waters.

feasible; this is made doubly troublesome if the land lies so or otherwise isn't suited to the construction of a pond. His chief hope at present is that he may be able to tap a good aquifer with a shallow well. Another irrigation problem that is sure to arise time and again stems from the fact that the farmer's need is still great after streams have begun their usual summer decline from springtime highs. The lower main stem often shows a substantial flow from basinwide runoff in July and August, when crops are topping off their season's growth and productivity, but smaller tributaries here and there may by then have shrunk so low as to be of little or no use to the farms they are expected to serve. Fortunately, well water is available and economically feasible for irrigation in many parts of the basin.

Future increases in in-basin use will bring their problems; no one can seriously doubt this. However, they are likely to be small by comparison when Megalopolis moves in, as it is sure to do, and begins to claim Susquehanna's allegedly "surplus" waters.

Diversion, which in the present context means water coming into or going out of the basin, has not yet reached major proportions. Water in substantial volume is brought into the basin in dry years near Wilkes-Barre, where industrial users may import certain of their requirements from a federal reservoir on Bear Creek, high in the Lehigh valley.[9] Water is exported, however, at a number of points. Susquehanna flow helps feed the New York State barge canal system via relatively small transfer reservoirs in headwater regions. It goes into the Allegheny River drainage from a sewer outfall at DuBois in the upper West Branch subbasin. It flows into the Lehigh valley from an outfall at Hazleton, Pennsylvania. The City of Chester, on the banks of the Delaware, takes Susquehanna water from both Octoraro Creek and the lower main stem. And Baltimore City diverts from Conowingo. The last two named are the largest. The Chester Water Authority has Pennsylvania permits for up to 55 MGD, and Baltimore has Maryland authority to take up to 250 MGD. Aberdeen Proving Ground, situated on Chesapeake Bay, diverts about 2.4 MGD from Deer Creek.

Uncertainties over future requests for diversion of Susquehanna basin water pertain to timing and volume, not to whether the requests—or demands—will come at all. The New York metropolitan area already is looking speculatively toward the upper Susquehanna River as a likely supplemental water source. Whether New York goes first to the Hudson to fill its extra wants doubtless will depend partly on how successful state and federal authorities are in persuading upstate communities and industries to treat their wastes to a degree high enough to satisfy the city's quality requirements. Next in downstream progression, if not in timing, come northern and central New Jersey; northern Jersey now slakes part of its thirst from the Delaware, as does New York City. Then there is Philadelphia, whose municipal waters presently come from the Delaware and its tributary Schuylkill. Wilmington, Delaware, is a potential future applicant. Baltimore has already filed notice through a State Planning Department study previously noted that its needs from Conowingo will rise sharply by the year 2000.[10] Greater Washington must be deemed a prospect in connection with possible future requests for Susquehanna water; it is using about all it can take from the Potomac and leave that river a live stream.[11] The sprawling and rapidly growing suburban areas tributary to the cities may not be overlooked as prospective applicants, either on their own or in conjunction with their closer urban centers.

In-basin increases in use plus out-of-basin requests will bring a procession of perplexing questions, and providing good answers will tax the wisdom of the decision makers. If all the requests that can be anticipated are made and complied with, it is entirely possible that severe water shortages could develop within the basin. This is true even if the diversions should be coupled with upstream storage to the practical limits of terrain to catch spring rains and snow-melt. Because of this, I am confident the basin states will scrutinize every request for diversion of Susquehanna water with utmost caution and wariness.

Logical areas from which to divert water to the regions most likely to clamor for it are not hard to find. Metropolitan New York probably would think in terms of shifting water from above Binghamton to its existing reservoirs in the upper Delaware and then transferring it to the municipal network. (A suggested reservoir near Oneonta isn't far from New York's Cannonsville impoundment, and is at a higher elevation, allowing lower-cost gravity flow.) Northern and central New Jersey also could be expected to look first to the Susquehanna above Binghamton. The diverted water would flow down the Delaware until it was intercepted to be siphoned off or pumped to the east and southeast. Philadelphia could consider a similar take-off point or points, or seek diversion downstream to either the Lehigh or Schuylkill and thence into its treatment and distribution system. Baltimore City's diversion point is already staked out on Conowingo, and the Mason-Dixon proposal (see footnote 11) would make one of the downstream power reservoirs the source for at least part of what both Wilmington and Washington might desire. Wilmington, however, could prefer to plump for river water from below Conowingo dam or even pursue the idea of a dam across the nonsaline head of Chesapeake Bay as proposed by the late Brig. Gen. Norman Lack. Gen. Lack was for several years the alternate member from the State of Delaware on the Delaware River Basin Commission. At one time he envisioned a series of inflatable dams to be built across the upper end of Chesapeake Bay, from Turkey Point to Spesutie Island, with locks to pass watercraft. The dams would create a huge fresh-water reservoir to be used by such communities as Wilmington, Baltimore, and

Washington. The proposal was referred to the Baltimore District Office of the Corps of Engineers, but no definitive study of its merits has come to my attention.

Let's examine these prospects somewhat more closely, with attention to the reception each seems likely to get.

First must be New York City, which is a sizable power in the state Assembly and also has influence in the executive branch. However, Binghamton is no small power itself as a component of that loose and sporadic but nevertheless potent amalgamation of urban and rural interests collectively known as Upstate New York. If future New York City requirements appear to threaten those of Binghamton, it is not difficult to foresee a tug-of-war between the great metropolis at one end of the rope and Binghamton and its upstate allies at the other.

Binghamton's location makes it a logical contestant if New Jersey's demands involve water from the upper basin. In fact, all New York might unite in an effort to prevail against New Jersey's pleas. The same would apply if Philadelphia coveted water from above Binghamton.

New York communities would seem less logical opponents of requests for water from the river by communities proposing to divert from points downstream from the state line. By then they would already have had their chance to use it and what they hadn't utilized would have traveled far below their intakes. Their interests, privileges, and opportunities to exploit the water would not be involved. The same is not true of Pennsylvania. The Commonwealth may be expected to join with Binghamton if diversion of upstream water to New York City or New Jersey is in prospect. It would have a more ambivalent view in the case of Philadelphia, for that city is fully as influential in the Pennsylvania General Assembly and executive branch as New York City is in Albany. The chief conflict to be resolved in Harrisburg would seem to be the issue of just where Philadelphia wanted to start removing Susquehanna basin water. There are several possible diversion points inside the borders of the state. If Wilkes-Barre industrialists can pump water over the divide from a Lehigh tributary it would seem feasible to pump it in the other direction, except that although the distance is indeed short, the water might have to be lifted to an undesirably high elevation, which would change the economics of the situation. On-stream communities probably would object if Philadelphia wanted a lot of Susquehanna water that otherwise would flow past their doors. Farther down, diversion via the Schuylkill probably could be physically accomplished by reviving the old original Union Canal route, built by the Commonwealth in the first quarter of the nineteenth century, and soon rendered obsolete by the coming of the railroad. This route involved the Schuyl-kill east of a low divide and Swatara Creek westward to its confluence with the river downstream from Harrisburg. In case the flow of the Swatara itself couldn't meet local needs plus those claimed by Philadel-phia, water probably could be pipe-lined along easy gradients from the main stem of the Susquehanna a short distance above Harrisburg to a regulating reservoir in the Swatara valley. It appears safe to forecast that a diversion point downriver from Harrisburg would bring only a muted Pennsylvania outcry against the water wants of Philadelphia. And Har-risburg probably couldn't care less about water requests from Wilming-ton, Baltimore, or Washington.

But what of Maryland through all this? The extent and power of the pressures brought to bear by basin interests in New York and Pennsyl-vania conceivably could vary considerably, depending on a multitude of factors, most of them tied to how the prospective diversion would affect individuals, industries, and communities below the point of taking. There is no question about the magnitude or unanimity of Maryland's concern. Its watchful and jealous eye likely will be upon all the peti-tioners, with the possible exception of Baltimore and Washington. Bal-timore's influence in state matters is great; the governor maintains an office and staff in Baltimore as well as in Annapolis. Furthermore, most of the municipal water taken from the lower river by Baltimore would flow, after use, into the Chesapeake Bay no more than forty miles below Havre de Grace. And the interests of the huddle of suburban communi-ties in Maryland just outside the District of Columbia could militate against energetic opposition by Maryland to the diversion of Susque-hanna River water to the nation's capital, since the suburbs would benefit.

It remains to be seen whether time will bring more affirmative atten-tion to the Norman Lack idea of a huge impoundment in the fresh upper reaches of the bay. If achieved and if as felicitous as its originator believed, it might fill the extra water needs of Wilmington, Baltimore, Washington, and even southeastern Pennsylvania areas for a century or more. The Lack concept could have a considerable impact on official Maryland attitudes. But let Megalopolis, from the Mason-Dixon line north and northeast, be warned that Maryland will be vigilant around the clock and calendar in the matter of diversions that could diminish below a proper minimum the flow into Chesapeake Bay.[12] Of course, what constitutes "a proper minimum" has not yet been resolved but

Fine angling waters stretch sixty miles or more below the New York State line into Pennsylvania. Hard coal and municipal pollution appear downstream, but as of 1971, in this long reach there had never been a recorded fish kill caused by man-made pollution. *Ted Jones, Stuart Finley Films*

Maryland undoubtedly will want it to be a yearly gallonage figure high enough to guarantee no diminution of the bay's quality and usefulness.[13]

No mention has been made in the above of possible alignments and combinations of influential interests in the basin states, but it is elementary that they are almost infinite and could be of most unexpected and complex composition.

Long-time friends in certain niches of the conservation movement probably have wondered when I'd get around to specifics on the subject

Officially this is all wrong, for the water is the coal mine acid-polluted Bennett Branch of Sinnemahoning Creek, Pennsylvania. Unofficially, ten-year-olds couldn't care less. *Ted Jones, Stuart Finley Films*

of water-based outdoor recreation. Let them be reassured; the time is now. They will recognize that the preceding chapter on water quality was closely allied to recreation; they know that much hinges on how soon and how adequately the dirty waters of the basin are cleansed enough to be recreationally useful, and they know beneficial change comes slowly. Industrial polluters will probably continue to utilize every delaying device invented by ingenious counselors under the broad due process clause of the Constitution. Municipalities will drag their feet in the future as they have in the past until some genius creates a sewage disposal plant that looks like a monument and smells like a rose. If that happy day arrives every mayor in America will work like hell to put such a plant in operation in his term of office so he can lead a parade past it on the Fourth of July. Until it does, securing and assuring clean water for all human purposes will be occasion for endless sweat and strain by those concerned, and it is an odds-on gamble that the leaders in the conservation movement will be the most vociferous and persistent in its advocacy. They know their outdoor recreation is at minimum a welcome by-product of all the other good things that flow from clean water, and on occasion a primary benefit.

Water for outdoor recreation, a nonconsumptive use, comes in most of the standard and well-known forms in the Susquehanna basin. It consists of lakes and streams for fishing, for waterfowling, for the trapping of fur bearers, for pleasure boating and water skiing where there's enough elbow room (and at some times and places where there isn't), for swimming where the water is clean enough (and occasionally without official sanction where it isn't), and just for looking at and being near. To hear water-loving recreationists tell it, and some state and federal officials as well, there isn't enough water to meet today's recreational demand. This is true if we are speaking of sufficient good water to suit all recreational uses in close proximity to all users. It is not necessarily so if we consider the tendency of today's recreation seeker to pursue his sport wherever he has to go for it or to make do with what he can find or improvise nearby. I doubt not that more recreation water can be used now and that a great deal more will be required to satisfy everybody's wants in years ahead. Nevertheless, the Susquehanna basin today must be considered a "have" rather than a "have not" recreational region; it has a tremendous capacity for accommodating more users without deterioration of quality, provided the spirit of *laissez faire* is avoided and the entrepreneur who says, "To hell with the future; I want mine today," can be kept out or under control.

Natural lakes left behind from the Great Glaciers are found in the headwater area of the basin in New York, and in five of its Pennsylvania counties, Lackawanna, Luzerne, Sullivan, Susquehanna, and Wyoming. A few water supply reservoirs are open to recreationists, and more should be. The flood damage reduction reservoirs of the Corps of Engineers and the Commonwealth of Pennsylvania and certain impoundments built by the Soil Conservation Service are used by recreation seekers. The state agencies concerned with water-based recreation and fish have bought or built lakes for public use. New York State has for

Late stage of construction of a flood-damage reducing impoundment on the West Branch, Susquehanna River. *Ted Jones, Stuart Finley Films*

some years been purchasing public fishing rights on trout streams, and some of these are in the basin. Stream reaches officially declared navigable are all open to public use if they can be reached, and all three Susquehanna states have programs for acquisition, development, and maintenance of access areas on these and other waters. Most state parks have bodies of water as their central attraction, and are of course open to public use. The streams that flow in state forest lands and through Pennsylvania state game lands are available to the public, but some bodies of shallow water managed by the Game Commission for water-

The completed impoundment. The water is polluted by acids and other impurities from bituminous coal mines, but is safe for swimming and boating. *Ted Jones, Stuart Finley Films*

fowl are closed to fishing. The hydroelectric reservoirs in the basin are open to public fishing and other recreational use. All three states consult and cultivate the good will of owners of streamside property in a continuing effort to prevent posting; this program includes enforcement of antinuisance laws of various kinds. The mouth of the river is, of course, adjacent to the broad upper expanses of Chesapeake Bay.

Most of the larger flood-retarding structures still to be built in the basin by federal and state agencies will have recreational water. There are places where such structures could be built but shouldn't; in my opinion, most of the remaining free-running water ought to be left that way. This includes all the main line from Otsego Lake to the existing downriver power reservoirs, especially the excellent and accessible Endless Mountains stretch in northern Pennsylvania. It includes a large number of clear mountain brooks in New York and Pennsylvania's north central counties. Much of the latter region already is in public ownership and its most beneficial future use seems to me to be as tension-relieving hinterland where a visiting man or woman can still find a modicum of solitude and near-wilderness in which to refresh and renew the spirit before returning to Megalopolis. The managers of the forests and game lands, in whatever parts of the basin they may lie, have a magnificent opportunity to analyze in depth the qualities of the public holdings, to determine areas that lend themselves to reversion to wilderness, to let portions become miniature wildernesses over time instead of lumber factories, and seek laws to guarantee that they will be held inviolate until crowding future generations decide mundane needs outweigh human requirements for cells of natural beauty. This will take some doing; it won't come if all who have influence allow political pragmatism or strict economic efficiency to rule. There is a growing interest in the preservation or reclamation of environmental quality in federal resource agencies; it deserves encouragement. More, it deserves emulation and enlargement at all levels.

Here, in sketchy outline, present and future uses of and demand for Susquehanna water have been described as seen from this observation point. I see great opportunity in the basin's future, complicated largely by the pollution described in the preceding chapter and by the question of diversion delineated above. The first must be attacked with vigor; the second should be approached with caution and with full knowledge of the consequences to the basin and to the receiving waters of Chesapeake Bay of whatever actions are taken.

It seems obvious that both the development and the degradation found in the basin today have evolved over time and have come haphazardly. The outlook for the future is for more of the same so long as institutional arrangements for water management remain unchanged. For decades the waters of the basin have been subject to the duplicating, overlapping, uncoordinated, and in some cases conflicting jurisdiction and administration of a large number of federal, state, and local agencies. These exercise a multiplicity of powers and there has been a

Patches of snow remain amid the hemlocks, but the bottom and rim ice is gone and soon trout fishermen will be dunking worms and whipping flies on this tributary of the West Branch of the Susquehanna in north central Pennsylvania. *Ted Jones, Stuart Finley Films*

splintering of authority and responsibility.[14] The situation has long cried out for attention, especially in regard to planning and programming for cleaner water. The need is scarcely less urgent if the optimum number and variety of water uses are to be appropriately met; it is hard to overemphasize the importance of coordinated approaches, based on fullest practical information, to the coming questions of water diversion. All that has been named or implied calls for something that until now did not exist in the basin, for interstate effects are there over which no one of the three states can claim jurisdiction; and whereas in some fields

A shallow-draft air boat is a handy gadget when a Pennsylvania waterways patrolman wants to run up riffle water in the Susquehanna to check out anglers. This scene is below Towanda, Pennsylvania. *Ted Jones, Stuart Finley Films*

federal action is beneficial, there are and will be cases where it should be held in restraint. The times and conditions indicated something new for the Susquehanna, an intergovernmental mechanism that would allow coordinated planning and programming of water resources activities and the making of decisions appropriate to the region and acceptable to its people.

Such a mechanism had initially been brought into existence upon the enactment of the Delaware River Basin Compact in 1961[15] which created the Delaware River Basin Commission. That was the stimulus needed for what was to require years of work in the Susquehanna valley with the objective of bringing a similar compact and commission into being. The rest of this narrative has to do with the evolution of the concept of a compact involving a federal–interstate partnership, and the case history of the writing and enactment of such an instrumentality for the Susquehanna.

Part II

From Concept to Specifics

Chapter 1

The Evolution of the Federal—
Interstate Concept

A catalog of conditions that cause intergovernmental problems probably would contain more specifics under the general heading of water resources than any other subject, largely due to the simple fact that water runs downhill, disregarding politically determined boundaries. In crossing borders, water can and does at various times bring both benefit and harm. Which it may be in a particular case depends on natural conditions as well as those caused by man; the latter seem to be increasing both in whole numbers and percentages.

Reason leads to the assumption that where benefits result from the interstate flow of water, the inclination of the benefited people would be to leave the situation in *status quo,* to avoid the diminishing of a good thing. An exception might be an instance where the doing of certain things above the border could increase the benefits to the downstream neighbor and would therefore be advocated.

The same reasoning would make it logical to assume that where demonstrable and substantial harm was being wrought or appeared imminent by reason of actions or conditions upstream beyond the state line, the downstream neighbor would be unhappy and would seek redress, correction, or preventive measures.

This has indeed been the general situation through the years. Whether the damaged party is an individual, a state, or a state's subdivision, ordinary avenues of recourse are restricted. This is true universally in the United States, but the present discussion is directed to the easterly states where the riparian doctrine prevails. Here, if a riparian property owner claims damages against another as an outgrowth of actions that have taken place or are occurring in an upstream state he can bring civil suit in Federal District Court. However, the burden of proof is on the plaintiff in nearly all instances. Clear proof of guilt may be difficult to establish. To this must be added the problem of determining standards with which to measure specific loss or deprivation. A nonriparian downstream owner has no legal recourse at all. If the aggrieved party is a state and sues the upstream state the case may go directly to the United States Supreme Court, but the burden of proof likely would be as heavy as that upon an individual. Evidence would be taken by a master appointed by the court, after which lawyers would argue the merits of the matter from both viewpoints, and in time a decision would ensue. There are some exceptions to the rule. If degraded water quality was the issue, the offended state could request a conference conducted by the Federal Water Quality Control Administration, which went in the Environmental Protection Agency (EPA) in 1970. Under existing law the EPA would in due course become the prosecutor if the conference disclosed a cause and a condition or attitude requiring court action in pursuit of correction, and such an action would be had in federal court. Questions involving nuclear wastes could be raised directly with the federal agency having jurisdiction; in such a situation the granting, lifting, modification, or suspension of a federal license might be deliberated. Under certain circumstances prevailing statutes permit the administrative authority of the Federal Power Commission to be invoked. Rulings by any of these agencies often end in litigation. Even though in specific instances judicial or administrative relief can be sought, going to court usually is a chancy thing and the administrative route may prove long, tortuous, and frustrating. More satisfactory and faster avenues of travel seem preferable.

Other kinds of situations have arisen in the past and can arise at any time to cause unhappiness in areas where interstate streams flow. The contention may be over action or inaction by a federal agency. In these cases the individual can write a letter to his congressman, which may or may not bring more than a perfunctory response. And the dissatisfied state can (1) write to its entire delegation in Congress; (2) consult with the offending agency in hopes it will come around to the state's viewpoint; or (3) go directly to the White House with its complaint. So long as the activity complained of lies within the lines drawn by the laws passed by Congress, the state or individual would have little reason to hope that a determined agency would change its mind once its course was set, although it is quite true that in recent years some of the old arbitrary attitude has gone out of parts of the federal establishment. I have had opportunity to observe federal attitudes in process of change here in the eastern United States in recent years. The modifications, whose extent and permanence cannot yet be foreseen, have not come without resistance and pain. One well-placed and long-time Corps of Engineers official commented privately on this in my presence:

"Now we're expected to take the public in our confidence and ask if we may do something," he said. "We used to tell them, and that was that."

If the negative has been stressed so far in this chapter it was in recognition of a long-standing human habit of forgetting benefits. This is the "What have you done for me lately?" syndrome attributed to a former supporter some years ago by Vice-President Alben C. Barkley. Older avenues open to beneficial alteration of water resource activities and operations where an interstate effect could be anticipated have been narrow and limited.

Over the years the compact has proved superior to court action and what is usually long-distance dickering in bringing about more equitable treatment of problems—positive or negative in their consequences— arising from the use, misuse, or excessive use of water. This seems true whether individuals or units of government are the ones most directly concerned. The compact route is not a new one. Compacts were entered into the Colonial era to seek adjustment of boundaries. The Constitution itself may be termed a compact among the several states. Since the Constitution was ratified, approximately two hundred compacts have been entered into by two or more states.[1] The Supreme Court has advocated the use of the compact to deal with interstate problems, saying in one case[2] that interstate "controversies may appropriately be composed by negotiation and agreement, pursuant to the compact clause of the Federal Constitution," adding that "such mutual accommodations and agreement should, if possible, be the medium of settlement, instead of invocation of our adjudicatory power."

Interstate compacts dealing with water have fallen most frequently into two broad categories. In the drier western states they have tended to be concerned with the equitable sharing of a scarce commodity. In the more humid East the most common objective has been improved water quality, the abatement and control of pollution. In recent years a number of other subjects have been added to the list, including flood control, fisheries, construction or acquisition of bridges over border streams, questions arising where port waters lap the shores of more than one state, the recreational management of border waters, planning, and economic development. Up to the time of the enactment of the Delaware River Basin Compact[3] all had been single-purpose in official scope. They have varied greatly in the composition of the agency intended to administer the compact, and in the authority given to that agency. Some have had no prerogatives other than to study and make suggestions which may or may not receive favorable attention and subsequent action.[4] A few have had real power, reposing in the background, with provision of one sort or another to exhaust other alternatives before invoking agency authority.[5] Federal participation of one kind or fashion, generally but not exclusively advisory, has been a feature of others.[6] None, until the Delaware Compact came into being, had been multiple-purpose, administrative–regulatory, and federal–interstate, all in one package.

It is with this type of new and—prior to the coming of the Delaware— untried compact that this narrative treats. And as we moved toward the enactment of such a compact for the Susquehanna River Basin we had the assistance of two persons credited with leading roles in formulating the general concept, though they did not themselves inaugurate it. They were Frederick L. Zimmermann, professor of political science at Hunter College, New York City, and Dr. Mitchell Wendell, the Washington-based intergovernmental specialist of the Council of State Governments. Zimmermann was chairman of the task force that drafted the Susquehanna compact; Wendell was our chief drafting consultant. (He left the council in 1968 to enter private consulting in association with Charles F. Schwan, Jr.)

It is relevant at this point to look into some aspects of the evolution of the multipurpose, administrative–regulatory, federal–interstate compact, and the roles played through the years by Zimmermann and Wendell, as their career activities have been quite closely linked to it.[7] Zimmermann's interest goes back to the 1930s when, shortly before ending six terms in the New York State Assembly, he was approached to assist in the formation of the Council of State Governments.[8] A legislative liaison group was needed. Zimmermann introduced a resolution in Assembly for the creation of a New York Joint Legislative Committee on Interstate Cooperation. The committee thus formed remains to the present as the chief mechanism of New York's lawmakers for approaching and dealing with matters of intergovernmental relations. When Zimmermann in 1936 began teaching political science at Hunter College

Frederick L. Zimmermann, chairman of the task force that drafted the Susquehanna River Basin Compact. *Ted Jones, Stuart Finley Films*

he was asked to serve the committee as research director, a position he held for twenty-seven years. During that period it was natural, even necessary, that he remain in close communication with the Council of State Governments. (The joint legislative committee and the eastern staff of the council share office space in New York City.) From the late 1930s into the first half of the 1960s these two organizations were potent primary bases for Zimmermann's increasing absorption in and attention to the compact and its potential for greater breadth and scope. Wendell came on the scene as a college undergraduate in the early 1940s when he went to Zimmermann seeking information on compacts for his senior paper. In the next few years the two worked on occasion on a variety of intergovernmental matters, and in 1953 Wendell became a consultant to the joint committee with the title of assistant research director. Their paths have converged and separated somewhat at various times since then, and their respective activities have varied from instance to instance, yet their primary concern in many of these was a compact and, more specifically, the coordination, management, and conservation of interstate water resources via the compact route.

It is not intended as derogatory to say that a noticeable Zimmermann trait is a degree of impatience that stems in large part from his eagerness to get on with a job. Wendell, though he has rapid mental processes and can move swiftly when there is need, is of a more philosophical turn; he will more readily resign himself to the need to wait for another opportunity tomorrow if the deed does not prove capable of accomplishment today. In the 1940s Zimmermann's flair for getting on with it led him to resort to an existing ingenious device that in essence, regardless of intent, did serve to short-cut the generally more pedestrian legislative process. The device was called "Articles of Organization." Zimmermann's first use of the tool was in collaboration with the other states of the Delaware basin in the 1940s to form the old Interstate Commission on the Delaware River Basin (INCODEL). The technique is to assemble a gathering of people who hold official positions but are without authority to commit their states to such things as the expenditure of public funds without additional or confirming action. In conference assembled they adopt impressively phrased Articles, which they know at the time do not have any standing in law. These are given quasi-legitimacy if the legislatures of the states subsequently appropriate funds with which to operate the organization the Articles are intended to create[9] or give them statute status.

They were to be used afterward when drafting a compact for the Susquehanna was planned, and later the Potomac, but no such Articles were needed as the initial multipurpose federal–interstate compact concept progressed in turn from a blob of intellectual protoplasm to a seminal stage and then to a pair of aborted fetuses before—with different official parenthood—the prototype saw life in the Delaware River Basin in 1961. The originals in this field were pure Zimmermann and Wendell.

Three of the compacts mentioned earlier—the Upper Colorado, Interstate Sanitation, and ORSANCO[10]—caught Zimmermann's eye and are credited by him with stimulating his and Wendell's thinking in various ways thereafter. The two were together often and their conversations were interlarded with discussion of what they considered the as yet unrealized capabilities of the compact. The authoritative "Compact Clause of the Constitution" by Frankfurter and Landis,[11] which discussed the use and operation of the compact from Colonial days to 1925, was well-thumbed and stimulated further mental exploration. The question forming was how great an extension of limited past accomplishment seemed possible and defendable under the Constitution's compact clause.[12] Zimmermann and Wendell were frankly searching for practical ways to prevent further deterioration of states' rights and prerogatives in an age of advancing federalism. They believed the waves of influence flowing outward from the federal executive branch, and the alluring inducements available to be used by it, were so overpowering that the roles of the states would in time become intolerably submerged and degraded. Signs and omens indicating a subtle change now in process were noted earlier. The emphasis placed upon "environmental quality" as one alternative to "economic efficiency" in gauging the desirability of water development proposed for the Susquehanna basin in the study ended in 1970 is indicative of the trend. To this must be coupled the open solicitation—much more than mere tolerance—of state participation as the study progressed, and the careful attention given to state comments and suggestions concerning specific projects.[13] A generation ago, however, such an attitude would have been rare; even the traditional holding of public hearings would at times seem little more than a bow to habit or custom.

It is immaterial for present purposes whether Zimmermann and Wendell asked for the assignment or received it on the initiative of others. The fact remains that in 1950 they were writing for the Council of State Governments a treatise that would discuss developments in the compact field that had come about since the Frankfurter–Landis study. It was printed by the council in 1951 under the title of *The Interstate Compact Since 1925* (the year the Frankfurter–Landis review was published) .[14] This assignment provided the authors with what may be termed a lectern, and the manual's publication gave them a built-in audience to whom to propound the thoughts that had been taking shape. Zimmermann considers their specific contributions of significance were (1) to make compacts multiple-purpose in scope; and (2) to make active, responsible, voting membership by the federal government routine where appropriate to the issues.[15] They recognized the importance of making any reservations necessary to preserve constitutionality and to set the conditions under which Congress would have the federal executive branch participate, but putting them outside the compact proper was another's idea (See Part V, Chapter 3).

The authors of the manual recognized that compacts had fallen somewhat into disrepute among a considerable body of political scientists and others. Their view was that this came about through no fault of the mechanism itself but due to the limited and unimaginative manner in which it had been employed in times past. They were in fact of the opinion that compacts could have "unexpected versatility"[16] if given the opportunity, that they had a "real potentiality . . . of uniting the powers of the national government with those of a group of states through a single legal mechanism" to deal with delineated subjects both administratively and regulatorily.[17] They pointedly directed the attention of the reader to water by saying that ". . . through national membership as a party . . . it would be entirely possible to establish a joint national, multistate commission for planning and administration of a river basin development itself or to coordinate the work of existing national and state agencies."[18]

The time was propitious for the testing of this concept, though the initial efforts failed. An expression commonly used in Washington and other places where efforts are made to advance new statutory ideas is that it usually takes at least ten years to achieve acceptance and enactment by Congress. In this instance the elapsed time was about double that.

Nevertheless, in Washington and elsewhere—perhaps particularly elsewhere—there was dissatisfaction with existing institutional arrangements for dealing with water resources. This unrest manifested itself in such ways as the testing of public sentiment to determine if a Tennessee Valley Authority type of federal corporation might be acceptable in the Missouri and Columbia River basins. There also came into vogue in that era the use of interagency committees to try to coordinate basin activities that often overlapped, duplicated, or conflicted.

Part of the uneasiness doubtless was born of the tremendous surge of federal spending for river basin projects and programs in the years following World War II. More money than had been dreamed of for public works, even in the relatively lavish prewar Roosevelt era, was being poured into the hinterlands, mostly the western half of the country. It was inevitable that ambitious men would want ever bigger shares to be spent by their agencies, and that states would wish a larger voice in decision making. Many persons saw the need for coordinating the activities of the agencies; the difficult question was how this should be accomplished.

The Missouri basin was in especially high ferment in the 1940s. In that decade had come the so-called "shotgun wedding" of the Corps of Engineers' Pick Plan and the Bureau of Reclamation's Sloan Plan for water resources development in the basin.[19] An interagency committee had been formed, with participation by the states through a committee of governors. The goal was coordination of thought and action. It was only partly successful. Baumhoff wrote that "you could count on the fingers of one hand specific issues that have been settled by Interagency." On the other hand, he added, it probably was true that the existence and influence of the group had prevented conflicts from coming to a head or at least had kept them from reaching the public.[20]

Notable events occurred in rapid order, sometimes simultaneously, in those years and it is both difficult and unnecessary for present purposes to sort them all out and say positively that this came before or after that. When someone proposed a Missouri Valley Authority patterned after the TVA the governors weren't at all sure they wanted such a monolithic federal entity operating in their jurisdictions. Governor Val Peterson of Nebraska, chairman of the Missouri Basin States Committee, in 1949 wrote the Council of State Governments and asked for a study, with analysis and evaluation of the development "of the administrative machinery for the operation of the Missouri Basin's water resources facilities," and to suggest an operating mechanism for effective management.[21] In 1950, at a meeting in North Platte, Nebraska, council staff described to the governors' committee "every kind of plan that the states might use." At that meeting the governors decided they wanted a "compact" plan: "the kind of plan where the states would be partners with the United States of America." This led to the creation of a compact drafting committee and Zimmermann and Wendell became its drafting consultants.[22]

A prestigious President's Water Resources Policy Commission had been appointed in 1950 and its report, printed a year later, recommended the setting up of federal commissions to operate in all the country's major river basins.[23] These would have recommendatory powers only, and the states could take part in the planning process. Doubtless this was no more pleasing to the states than had been the basin authority scheme, since it relegated them to a subsidiary role. In 1952 another presidential study group, called the Missouri Basin Survey Commission, was appointed and in 1953 it suggested still a different institutional arrangement, a planning commission in which the states would have no more than membership in an advisory committee.[24] This all-federal agency could produce a water resources plan for the basin and keep it current, but the recommendation ignored the substantial activities of the states in water resources matters, and it had what were considered other serious defects.[25] Again the states were unhappy.

The completion of *The Interstate Compact Since 1925* and the writing of the Missouri basin compact draft paralleled much of the activity of the federal study commissions. When the decision was made to try for a compact it was doubtless the newness of the concept that caused this first effort of its kind to follow the coordination route rather than the stronger administrative–regulatory road. The states were ambivalent about the whole thing. They wanted those multiplied millions of federal tax dollars spent in their jurisdictions but wanted to help the federal construction agencies determine where, in what order of priority, and in what volume the money would be spent. Nominally, the governors could consult with their delegations in Congress, which had the authorizing and appropriating power; but it was the engineers of the agencies who had the technological expertise, and they had influential supporters of the views they put forth. The governors doubtless wanted to go as far as they felt they dared toward assuring that their views would have weight, but not so far as to antagonize the powerful agencies with which they would deal. As a consequence, the Missouri basin compact draft presented to the governors was quite mild, almost innocuous by today's standards.

The governors were given a preliminary draft in August, 1952, which was approved with minor modifications in December of the same year. A revised draft was then published by the Council of State Governments in January, 1953.[26]

The commission created would have no real powers. It would not be allowed "to engage in any regulatory or operational activities"; it would be "prohibited from drawing specific construction plans for particular projects and from engaging in any construction works," all of which were "to be carried on by other agencies of the participating governments." Its authority would be limited to formulating "over-all" plans— a term discarded by drafters in later years in favor of "comprehensive" plans; to reviewing proposed construction and operational plans; and then reviewing operations themselves to determine whether approved plans were actually being carried out as approved. Further, the reviewing would be restricted to cases where there was "substantial effect on interstate relations in the use of water."[27] The commission could do no more than complain and protest publicly if its over-all plans were not followed, or if the constructing and operating agencies—the Corps and Reclamation primarily—should choose to thumb their noses at the commission in constructing or operating phases of the basin program. Indeed, even this complaining might have to be done privately by the state people, for the memberships and voting arrangements were such that the federal participants, by standing together, could veto any action wanted by the basin states; and the aggregate federal vote would in all cases equal the aggregate state votes,[28] and a tie vote under usual parliamentary procedures would fail.

Weak though the compact was, the federal people still would have none of it. The huge construction agencies considered it could lead to interference in their spending and building and operating. They didn't want any combination of state and federal officials looking over their shoulders at any stage. Zimmermann wrote me that "the setup on the Missouri between Reclamation and Army Engineers was so powerful in economic terms that they were able to kill [the compact proposal] very quietly."[29]

The other proposals for the Missouri likewise got no further than the federal–interstate compact suggestion. The construction agencies had a relatively free hand to do much as they pleased from that time forward.

The locus of this narrative now moves to New England, where in the early and middle 1950s the Corps of Engineers led a federal survey of the water resources of New England and New York: It resulted in the publication in 1957 of the NENYIAC (New England-New York Inter-Agency Committee) report consisting of forty-six volumes of water-related information.[30] While this study was proceeding, an organization of state officials called the Northeastern Resources Committee held meetings from time to time, and as an outgrowth of the New York interest Zimmermann and Wendell were, in effect, put on loan to the committee to help draft a Northeastern Compact.[31]

This time a long legislative step forward was taken, but again the compact language presented to the states and to Congress was no particular improvement on that in the ill-fated Missouri experience, though all this apparently was not the fault of Zimmermann and Wendell. My correspondence indicates they had proposed that the federal government have only one vote, the same as each of the signatory states. The state resources officials liked the idea and it advanced to the semifinal draft of the proposal. Then, at a meeting neither Zimmermann nor Wendell could attend, for reasons now unimportant, federal observers taking part in the discussions brought about a revision providing for seven federal votes—as many as the six New England states plus New York would muster.[32] If enacted, the Northeastern Compact would put the states in no stronger position than the one previously written for the Missouri.

Four New England state legislatures passed this compact: Connecticut, Massachusetts, New Hampshire, and Rhode Island. Maine and Vermont held back. Under the compact's terms passage by only three would have been enough to send the agreement to Congress for action.[33]

The chief bill was introduced in the House under excellent auspices. Its sponsor was Representative John W. McCormack, then majority leader, later speaker. When hearings were held, federal agency statements, to the astonishment of McCormack, opposed the compact and expressed fear that the government might under its terms "be committed by the votes of its representatives," who would be second- or third-echelon civil servants. Further, they suspected the commission as constituted could in some way "interfere with the jurisdiction of the United States and the powers and prerogatives of . . . federal agencies."

McCormack chided the agencies in his testimony, saying "to see . . . them take the bland position they do is an amazing phenomenon to me, showing they have lost their vision so far as an appreciation of the significance of regional compacts in the life of America today and tomorrow is concerned." He appealed to the committee to disregard the position of the agencies and report the bill favorably, which it did. It did not come to a vote in that session but was reintroduced in the 87th Congress, where it was passed by the House and died in the Senate.[34]

The rejection of the New England compact is astounding in the light of what occurred in the same year affecting the Delaware basin. A minor miracle was achieved by the enactment of the much stronger and decidedly different Delaware River Basin Compact by the legislatures of the four states and by the Congress in a total elapsed time of only ten months.[35] Further research would be needed to confirm or deny the assumption, which appears plausible at present, that the inclusion of a separate set of federal reservations, correctly phrased and sufficiently inclusive, might have allayed the agencies' fears and made the ill-fated federal–interstate Northeastern Compact the first enacted in the multiple-purpose category.

This is not a detailed history of the Delaware Compact; that must be written by others. However, reference to it and the manner in which it came into being is pertinent here in that the Susquehanna Compact follows it so closely. In fact, many comparable passages are identical except for the difference in names, and the Delaware will be referred to often in later chapters.

Conflict and contention had for many years characterized attempts to manage and control the waters of the Delaware basin. Water quality was—and still is—of prime concern there, and is related to a controversy of importance involving water supply. This had to do with supplemental municipal water for New York City. The Hudson River was badly polluted by upstream municipalities and industries, and New York considered it would be less costly and provide better quality water to build holding reservoirs, conduits, pumping stations, and other appurtenances so as to tap the much cleaner headwaters of the Delaware. New Jersey resisted, and Pennsylvania sided with Jersey. Nevertheless, in two decisions, the U.S. Supreme Court in 1931 and 1954 allotted New York City first 400 MGD, then 800 MGD from the upper Delaware.[36] Meanwhile, through the informal Delaware interstate commission (INCODEL), representatives of the basin states repeatedly tried to produce an instrument that would facilitate efforts toward accommodation of differing wants and viewpoints without resort to the judiciary.

In the course of time no fewer than three futile efforts had been made to draft an acceptable compact. Unimpressed by the record of the interstate compact as it had existed and performed to that time, the political leaderships in the affected states tended to push INCODEL into the background. The third draft of a compact for the Delaware was written by Zimmermann in the 1950s. It was to be strictly an interstate affair, with no federal membership. This time it came close to succeeding. It was passed by New York, New Jersey, and Delaware, and by the Pennsylvania House, but it got bogged down in the Senate.[37]

Shortly thereafter nature took a hand in Delaware basin affairs. Hurricane Diane swept across New Jersey and Pennsylvania and on into New York State in the summer of 1955, causing devastating flash floods and loss of life. Much of the damage was centered in northeastern Pennsylvania's Pocono Mountains resort country, where cottages and camps had been built in flood plains perilously close to creek banks. The flood was followed quickly by authorization for a flood control-oriented Delaware basin survey headed by the Corps of Engineers.

The Delaware's other problems, especially those caused by pollution, didn't improve, and the combination of the lot gave the proponents of coordinated interstate action another chance. In 1956 the basin states' governors formed a Delaware River Basin Advisory Committee with John P. Robin of Philadelphia, chairman of the Pennsylvania State Planning Board, as its chairman. The mission of the advisory committee was clear and unmistakable. A simple directive was signed by the four governors instructing the committee to undertake the preparation of a suitable coordinating mechanism; that is, to draft the basin compact. There were no "articles of organization" in this case.

Here a gap in the documented record must be bridged by fallible human memory. INCODEL was disbanded when the Delaware River Basin Commission was created in 1961. As this chapter was written in 1969 the INCODEL archives were not available for inspection.[38] It is known that a long and close friendship existed between Robin and the late Francis A. Pitkin, for many years executive director of the Pennsylvania State Planning Board and concurrently chairman of INCODEL. The two had been prime movers in earlier efforts to resolve Delaware problems. As the storm-spurred events began to pick up momentum Pitkin asked Zimmermann to draft a federal–interstate compact for the Delaware, which he did with the assistance of Wendell. It was on the order of the Northeastern Compact, with Missouri compact overtones. This was shown to INCODEL members and discussed by them.

Meantime, the new advisory committee had set up for business under the executive directorship of Walter Phillips, a Philadelphia attorney. In 1957 a research group was formalized, and plans were evolved for a citizens organization to stimulate a cooperative attitude on the part of influential Delaware basin residents and friends.[39] This was to be a go-for-broke attempt to overcome obstacles that had confronted previous efforts to harmonize water resources planning, development, use, and conservation in the basin. The research group obtained a Ford Foundation grant to finance a study of administrative alternatives. This was entrusted to a Syracuse University team headed by Dr. Roscoe C. Martin, and the advisory committee awaited its report with restrained impatience. The report was published in 1960 under the title *River Basin Administration and the Delaware*.[40]

The Martin report recommended a two-phase administrative development. First would come a federal corporation similar to TVA, with which Martin had been associated for twenty years. This new entity would be called the Delaware River Agency for Water (DRAW). At some indefinite future time, if, as, or when the states considered themselves ready for the transition, or were so considered, a federal–interstate compact with broad administrative–regulatory powers might be enacted into law.[41] It does not require a great deal of cynicism, just observation of the habit of "temporary" federal establishments to linger on and on and on and to grow ever more entrenched, to gauge how much real chance the second stage suggested by Martin, *et al.*, would have had of enactment and realization.

The Delaware basin governors, it seems, were no more favorably inclined to monolithic federalism in 1960 than their counterparts in the Missouri valley had been in 1950. They desired a more definitive role in how, where, and to what extent federal funds would be spent in the basin, and didn't want to be forced to the long, tedious, and uncertain court route to a decision in a time of interstate dispute. They rejected the TVA-like device and staked the future of the basin on the enactment of the compact. It worked, as was indicated previously, being enacted into law in 1961, the same year the much less meaningful Northeastern Compact failed to emerge from a Senate committee.

Having selected the compact as their vehicle, they chose a drafting team headed by Attorney William Miller of Princeton, New Jersey, to construct it. Zimmermann and Wendell did not take direct part in the drafting. As Zimmermann recalls it, "We were too closely identified with INCODEL; they wanted the job done by people who had not been associated in the public mind with what had been attempted before."[42] Zimmermann was, however, still counseling New York on interstate matters and was a consultant to the Delaware advisory committee, 1956-1960, while Wendell served as a member of its legal and legislative affairs committee, 1957-1961. Both have asked me to make it clear that the essential language of the Delaware Compact is not theirs but was produced entirely by Miller and his drafting associates.

The architects of Delaware Compact enactment were many. The citizens association joined with the advisory committee in a strong, well-conceived and executed campaign of enlightening the public and—of much importance—helped enlist and inform leading members of Congress from the basin states. The eight senators acted as an informal committee of support, and all joined in sponsoring compact legislation when it had been passed by the states and was ready to go to Congress. It likewise had the enthusiastic support of Representative Francis E. Walter, chairman of a House Judiciary subcommittee, who was from Easton, Pennsylvania, at the confluence of the Delaware and its tributary Lehigh River. David L. Lawrence, who had succeeded George M. Leader as governor of Pennsylvania, had been instrumental in swinging his state to John F. Kennedy in the 1960 presidential election and was

very much *persona grata* at the White House. Kennedy had designated
Stewart L. Udall, Secretary of the Interior, as spokesman for the executive branch in matters of water legislation. In that capacity Udall presented to the Senate Committee on Public Works a statement that was a
composite of federal agency views on the compact bill when it was at
hearing stage. The statement was favorable in all respects but one.
Under law[43] public bodies such as cities and rural electric cooperatives
had enjoyed preferred status for the purchase and use of power gener-
ated at federal hydroelectric facilities. Udall stated the federal view that
a similar preference clause should be in the Delaware Compact. The
inference was that since the Delaware commission would have the authority to build and operate hydropower plants, however remote the
possibility of its doing so might be, the clause should be inserted. Udall
did not press the point and the preference clause stayed out.[44] The most
significant passage in his presentation probably was the following:

> The agreement between the states, which has been ratified by the states,
> was drafted very wisely in such fashion that in agreeing to the compact the
> Congress could enact legislation and attach conditions and reservations to
> the congressional approval. . . . In other words, the proposals that we have
> submitted as federal reservations or conditions to protect the federal inter-
> est can be attached, and once this enabling legislation is passed we have the
> package all put together and we are ready to go.

Probably no single feature of the compact legislation served more to
secure federal agreement to participate than the one thus described by
Udall. It wiped away objections based on constitutional grounds since
in this relatively simple manner all strictly federal rights and prerogatives under the Constitution were retained or specifically fixed. Also,
putting the reservations in a separate place obviated the necessity of
sending the legislation back to the four states for concurrence. No tricky
question of a state being in position to override an act of Congress by
failing to concur would have been involved, only the loss of valuable
time in setting in train the beneficial elements of planning and programming for the basin's water resources.

A noteworthy departure from previous compacts was the proposal, by
Robin, that the states' members be the governors and the federal member an appointee representing the President. In earlier compacts the
members had been heads or other personnel of various departments of
government, legislators, technologists from institutions possessing expertise of a specialized nature, or laymen chosen for any of a variety of

reasons. These persons might or might not be able to speak with authority or to commit fully the jurisdictions they represented. It could be a long and arduous journey from their respective places in government to the more elevated regions where decisions were actually made. Not so in the case of the Delaware. The membership provisions clothed the compact commission with an aura of state and federal authority and responsibility of the highest order.

Whether another compact similar to the Delaware might ever become law was then moot. Udall's statement at the hearings, and occasional offhand comments overheard afterward, made it clear the federal establishment did not then accept it as a precedent. In private conversations high federal officials had been overheard to characterize the Delaware Compact in such terms as "oddball." The success of the Delaware Compact to the present must be considered impressive enough to give its general format the status of a precedent, and Udall's later comments, while attending meetings of the Delaware commission, indicated he had a complete change of heart as to its efficacy in its several fields of endeavor.

Nevertheless, there was no general body of opinion in Washington supporting the concept; almost the contrary prevailed. The federal Water Resources Planning Act of 1965 was in the making; it authorized multiple-purpose federal–state planning commissions for interstate basins anywhere in the nation.[45] We who were even then drafting the Susquehanna Compact—and some had helped draft the new federal law—began wondering if the Delaware would become the only one of its kind, as TVA has been the country's only basinwide water authority, and our labors wasted. Clairvoyance would have been a great help, then and on other occasions yet to be described.

Chapter 2

Origins of the Susquehanna Compact

Coincidence can play a role in the affairs of river basins as well as those of men. It did so in the case of the Susquehanna River Basin Compact.

In the winter of 1960-1961 the Council of State Governments sponsored an interstate conference in Chicago. Fred Zimmermann attended as a representative of the New York Joint Legislative Committee on Interstate Cooperation, in his capacity of research director. One of those present from Pennsylvania was Harris G. Breth, member of the House of Representatives and chairman of the Joint State Government Commission, research arm of the Pennsylvania General Assembly. The two met, and Zimmermann turned the conversation to the Delaware River Basin Compact, which was in process of being placed before the legislatures of the states of that basin for enactment. Zimmermann suggested the Susquehanna basin should logically be considered a candidate for administration under a federal–interstate agreement similar to that for the Delaware.[1]

Even casual examination of the basins discloses similarities as well as significant differences. The Susquehanna flows through two of the states party to the Delaware compact. It is not a border river, as the Delaware is for most of its length; hence water conditions expected to have an interstate effect and thus be subject to commission attention may not be quite as numerous at the outset as in the case of the Delaware. Nevertheless, existing and potential situations are present that transcend state borders and make it apparent that intergovernmental collaboration and a coordinated approach should be mutually beneficial. There are degrees of imbalance in the impact of the Susquehanna upon the states, which in part parallel the Delaware situation but are more pronounced. By far the greater part of the Susquehanna basin—some 76 percent—is in Pennsylvania. New York has 23 percent, Maryland 1 percent. The upstream Delaware basin states—New York, New Jersey, and Pennsylvania—also have most of that watershed within their borders, the State of Delaware only a small fraction. This put Maryland and Delaware in similar situations, each the smaller partner and both looking to their upstream neighbors for protection of vital waterways against a variety of ills, eternally fearing the worst and hoping for the best. No one could say truthfully that the downstream states with the smallest shares of the geography of their respective basins had smaller stakes in the appropriate management of their waters than did the upstream states. In Pennsylvania, faulty reasoning in this regard did crop up later, as is detailed in Part IV.

The Delaware compact came along after much of the water of the basin had been committed to human use. It furnished domestic, commercial, and industrial supplies to two of the nation's largest cities and to other parts of our eastern Megalopolis, as well as lesser volumes for irrigation and other agricultural use. True, considerable water ran off in spring freshets and other high-water times, and there was opportunity for working constructively toward assurance of dependable inbasin supplies. The task of the Delaware commission was in considerable part to increase the potential for use of what there was to work with. The commission also had to plan as best it could for betterment of water quality in an effort to prevent further deterioration of a commodity that was progressively degraded following each successive use on its course toward the sea.

The waters of the larger Susquehanna, on the other hand, served a much smaller population—about 3.5 million persons as of 1960 as compared with the 20-plus million dependent in whole or in part upon the Delaware. There was a fully adequate flow nearly everywhere in the Susquehanna basin except in cases of extreme drought and along specific tributaries. Severe quality problems were present, but scattered internally rather than increasing progressively down the main stem. It may be said that the Susquehanna was certainly in as favorable a condition as any major stream in the United States, in the sense that there was still time for forward thinking, time in which to plan for both development and conservation.

Zimmermann in effect led Breth to the top of the mountain to show him the opportunity to carry out coordinated planning, which could then be followed by timely programming to assure the appropriate utilization of the waters of the river and its tributaries for the benefit of the basin's people. The conversations made a deep impression upon Breth. He discussed the subject with a fellow legislator as they returned from Chicago, and concluded that doing something in behalf of the Susquehanna had merit. A third legislator was enlisted, to give the effort a bipartisan flavor, and the three introduced a resolution in the Pennsylvania House to authorize the Joint State Government Commission to undertake a study of Susquehanna basin matters.[2]

Coincidence appeared again about this time, in the form of congressional resolutions authorizing the Corps of Engineers, with help from other federal agencies as well as the states, to conduct a survey of the basin's water and related resources.[3] This made the timing right for two entirely separate activities involving the same basin to be carried forward on roughly parallel courses.

Under authority of the Pennsylvania resolution, a task force of the Joint State Government Commission conducted two public hearings, one in January, 1962, at Wilkes-Barre, the other the following March, at Huntingdon.[4] The concept of a Susquehanna compact received little specific attention at these hearings. I testified as a private citizen at Wilkes-Barre and advocated that something be done similar to that which was getting started over east in the Delaware basin. This, too, was coincidence, for at that time I knew only a few details of the Delaware Compact, and the name Zimmermann meant absolutely nothing to me. I simply regarded the Delaware Compact as beneficial, and suggested that we who were interested in the Susquehanna basin should move in the same general direction. Many of those testifying did so narrowly. Their concern was the desirability, or otherwise, of a purely local project proposal, or endorsement of the federal survey and the spending of federal tax dollars for water projects in the basin.[5] Nevertheless, the hearings provided Breth and his legislative associates the support they required in order to maintain and stimulate communication with Zimmermann.

By phone and letter, and in face-to-face meetings, Zimmermann and Breth kept in close touch through 1961 and in the early months of 1962. Breth became convinced—Zimmermann had envisioned it all along—that a vigorous temporary instrumentality of the three basin states must be brought into existence if the compact concept was to get anywhere. Both talked with resource and planning leaders in their respective states. Zimmermann persuaded Senator Elisha T. Barrett, chairman of the New York joint committee, of the desirability of such a mechanism.

He consulted with New York State water resource officials, especially Dr. Harold G. Wilm, conservation commissioner, who in turn discussed the matter with his immediate associates and with Governor Nelson A. Rockefeller, who approved. Breth talked it over with such Pennsylvania officials as Francis A. Pitkin, executive director of the Pennsylvania State Planning Board and chairman of INCODEL, Dr. Maurice K. Goddard, Secretary of Forests and Waters, and Governor David L. Lawrence—and they approved. To this point Maryland had not yet been consulted, but the time had arrived. Breth asked Pitkin to draft a letter addressed to Governor J. Millard Tawes of Maryland to be signed by Governor Lawrence, seeking to establish an official Maryland interest in having the three states do something collectively about the Susquehanna basin. Governor Tawes consulted James J. O'Donnell, director of the Maryland State Planning Department, and O'Donnell in turn communicated with the Maryland legislative leadership. All agreed that Maryland's stake was so great she could not afford to pass up this opportunity to stimulate joint action.[6]

At Zimmermann's suggestion, Senator Barrett agreed that New York should be the host state for a full-dress meeting, to be held at Binghamtion, chief metropolis of upstate New York's southern tier of counties, which stood at the confluence of the Susquehanna with its tributary Chenango River just north of the Pennsylvania border. Jean Storey, staff assistant in Barrett's office, took over many of the details. Miss Storey had assisted Zimmermann and Wendell in the early years of the evolution of the concept of a federal–interstate compact, and she plunged enthusiastically into setting up the program and arrangements. There would be a full day of speechmaking by dignitaries representing all the interested federal agencies, and by spokesmen for the basin states. Zimmermann wrote Articles of Organization for an Interstate Advisory Committee, patterned after those he had earlier written for INCODEL,[7] and these were circulated to executive and legislative leaders for approval. Those officials who could attend the meeting would constitute a steering committee to pass finally upon the language of the Articles of Organization.[8]

It often happens that there are slips between the conception and the culmination of a grand idea, but not in this instance. Everything went off as scheduled and on schedule.

The verbatim record of that meeting, published with the minutes of two succeeding meetings,[9] discloses (1) that the federal people generally confined their remarks to stereotyped accounts of their existing and contemplated activities in the basin, while (2) the state officials centered their spoken thoughts upon the budding opportunity for interstate co-operation and the conditions that might confront whatever intergovernmental instrumentality might eventuate. Examples of the last named:

Barrett [who presided and commented at intervals between formal presentations]: [The purpose of the meeting is] to initiate intergovernmental coordination in planning the management of the water-related resources of the Susquehanna River Basin. . . . The problem we seek to solve is [that] of underdevelopment. This problem is underlined by the need for utilizing and developing water resources, and the major [objective] is the maximum of recreational and economic growth . . . of the basin. The problem of underdevelopment is paralleled by problems of abuse, pollution, erosion, floods, etc. The general problems of improper utilization of water . . . resources are characteristic of many of our river basins. We need to plan and to program; we need a comprehensive water plan [that includes] flood control, water supply, recreation, water quality control, irrigation, and all the other uses that should be included in any comprehensive plan. *Our basic need then is also a major opportunity, an opportunity that is greater in that the water problems of the Susquehanna have not yet reached a critical stage.* This makes planning of maximum effectiveness possible. . . . We must secure governmental coordination among the three states and the Federal Government . . . [emphasis added].[10]

Pitkin [speaking directly of the organization of an Interstate Advisory Committee]: A . . . level of organization is needed which brings together representatives of the legislative and the executive branches of each state government. This would be an advisory [group] charged with preparing the legislation necessary to create an eventual river basin commission. . . . It would . . . be the organization instrumental in securing passage of the necessary interstate compact.

Wilm [obviously bearing in mind the practicalities of state water resources administration]: Our great [water] problem is going to be one of control of rate, so that you hold it back when you have too much, for the time when you have too little; and distribution, so that you move it from the place of abundance to the place of shortage; plus, of course, the problem of cleaning it up and cooling it down. That is our big problem in the Northeast.

Goddard: People have pointed out here today that [the Susquehanna] is a relatively undeveloped basin in terms of population density. . . . We do have a real opportunity. We have referred to [this river] in our state as a water reserve area. . . . Nevertheless, we have some serious problems, and I agree with Dr. Wilm that perhaps the most important problem is . . .

pollution abatement. . . . There is a map . . . which indicates the [coal mine] acid-contaminated streams and . . . you [can] relate the economic problems of the basin to the acid-contaminated streams; Mr. Voigt . . . has pointed out that they almost exactly coincide.[11]

John P. Robin, Chairman, Pennsylvania State Planning Board and chairman of the interstate committee that had produced the Delaware basin compact: "We've heard . . . able people . . . talk about many aspects of the physical planning of the Susquehanna. Flood control, water quality, recreation, fish and wildlife, soil conservation are all vital. But essentially, to accomplish these, . . . we must find a framework of political organization, of governmental organization, which will make a program become possible. I would like to separate in your minds, if I may, the framework of governmental organization from the framework of the Susquehanna River plan and the development of the river. . . . Those things are properly separable; . . . we ought not let the one hang upon the other. . . . I think we are anxious, most of us, to come to grips with the total problem and then trust the agency which is created to work out the . . . methodology of getting [things] done. . . . What the [Delaware] compact . . . does is to create the mechanism to guide the development of that river for a hundred years and likely through the perpetuities of our civilization, because a compact . . . is a very serious undertaking. . . . As to whether this compact fits the Susquehanna I can't pretend to say; we don't know. I think it would be a useful thing and I hope the result of this conference will be that the three states will . . . appoint a . . . group to determine . . . what type of governmental organization should be recommended for the Susquehanna. . . . The governmental organization is a means of carrying out a [continually updated master] plan. It is not the plan. And the plans to be developed by the Corps of Engineers; the plans developed by the several states; the plans to be developed by a score of agencies, or whatever—in order to effect them, in order to execute them, some new governmental organization in all likelihood is not a necessity, but is a tremendous expeditor and a source of true accomplishment.

It seems obvious, on reading the record, that the speakers' line of march had been carefully planned, and that Robin had been saved for the last in the conviction that his prestige as the chief architect of the Delaware basin compact production effort, and his commendatory comments, would bring those present to the desired pitch of enthusiasm, the proper readiness to accept what the steering committee had produced as a foundation for the tasks ahead.

When Robin left the platform, Barrett called Breth to the lectern. Breth produced the Articles of Organization of the Interstate Advisory

Maurice K. Goddard, Secretary, Pennsylvania Department of Forests and Waters (later renamed and incorporated into the Department of Environmental Resources). He served as chairman of the Interstate Advisory Committee on the Susquehanna River Basin.

Committee on the Susquehanna River Basin (IAC/SRB), and to much applause announced they had been adopted unanimously by the steering group in behalf of the executive and legislative branches of the three states.

I sat in the audience at Binghamton, but took no active part in the meeting. I had met Wilm and knew most of the Pennsylvanians there, and some of the federal people. All I then knew of Elisha (June) Barrett was what followed his name in the printed program. More than two years would pass before I'd meet Zimmermann, at the get-acquainted meeting of our drafting task force in June 1964. At the time of the Binghamton affair I didn't dream that I would have a consequential part in the undertaking then being launched. I sensed the significance of the day, but claim no prescience. I expected to and did do volunteer work as a member in a Susquehanna River Basin Association, a citizens group that did not draw support and quietly died about two years later, but more than a year would pass before my involvement in the compact effort.

Meantime, those directly concerned with the formation of the Interstate Advisory Committee pushed forward with determination. In August delegates representing the executive and legislative branches of the governments of the three states, as provided in the Articles, met in Harrisburg and formally organized.[12] Goddard was chosen permanent chairman; Wilm of New York and O'Donnell of Maryland were elected vice-chairmen. They also were to comprise an executive committee, with authority to hire a staff and to take interim action for reference later to the committee at formal meetings. Breth was elected treasurer. The committee itself was to consist of four members from each state: two chosen by the Governor, one appointed by the presiding officer of each house of the state legislature. Each was entitled to an alternate, who was privileged to attend all meetings, obtain all information pertinent to the work of the committee, and to vote in the absence of the member.[13]

One of those political quirks that have to be expected occurred to change the membership situation in the fall of 1962. Breth was defeated for re-election to the Pennsylvania lower house, and was replaced early in 1963 by Representative Orville E. Snare of Huntingdon, who subsequently was made the IAC secretary-treasurer. (This and other changes in the committee membership are indicated in Appendix A.)

In November the committee met in Baltimore, where a budget of $60,000 a year was decided upon as adequate for at least the earlier years of activity, apportioned on a basis of 60 percent from Pennsylvania and 20 percent each from the other states. The prorating was justified on the ground that doubtless more staff or staff-related attention would have to be paid to Pennsylvania matters in the formative years than to those involving New York and Maryland, and this did prove to be the case.[14] Holding that meeting in November, 1962, gave the executive branch people time to put their share of the committee budget in departmental appropriation proposals to be presented to the respective assemblies in January, 1963.

The money was voted without difficulty in each basin state, and in the summer of 1963 the executive committee—Goddard, Wilm, and O'Donnell—was ready to cast about for candidates for the executive directorship. Meanwhile, the federal basin survey was being funded by Congress, and the initial meeting of a Susquehanna River Basin Study Coordinating Committee was scheduled for June 27 in the Harrisburg area. I had been informed of the coordinating committee session, for I was on numerous official mailing lists, and arranged to attend. Coincidence made Goddard, Wilm, and O'Donnell the appointees of their respective governors to the coordinating committee, and Goddard called an IAC executive committee meeting the evening of June 27; Goddard and

O'Donnell were there; Francis W. Montanari, Wilm's assistant commissioner for water resources and his alternate, both on the coordinating committee and the Interstate Advisory Committee, attended in his stead.

In the course of the afternoon, Goddard called me aside and asked if I would serve as executive director of the IAC if asked to do so. I may have deliberated for as much as five seconds, or some such decent interval, before admitting that I could be persuaded. My recollection is that I tried not to appear overeager—just willing. He telephoned me at my home that night, where my wife and I were entertaining some of the visiting officials, to say I could go to work for the Interstate Advisory Committee on the Susquehanna River Basin as of August 1, 1963. Again I must rely on recollection, for I kept no written record of the incident, but I am sure the remainder of the evening I was half exuberant, half soberly thoughtful in contemplation of what lay ahead.

Chapter 3

Getting Started

How does one who had never before done it go about being the executive director of an Interstate Advisory Committee such as ours? The administrative routine should present no particular problem; details would have to be worked out that were compatible with customary procedures of, or at least were not offensive to, the states. I anticipated no great difficulty in getting along with the members and alternates. True, they were a large group—twelve of each at full strength—but ordinary tact should bring response; they were reasonable men, knowledgeable people who appeared eager for the undertaking to succeed.

Certainly I would have to look inward for guidance as well as outward where guidelines were few, and draw on earlier experience for whatever help it could provide. The main thing at the start was to busy myself with the mundane matters of getting an office opened, furnished, and staffed, to begin accumulating a library of useful references, and to get on with other more obvious tasks. Time and my superiors would dictate the course thereafter, as would the dynamics of helping write the compact and following approved courses of action pursuant to the enactment of legislation in a not fully charted field.

The committee agreed early that the office would be in Harrisburg. It was the capital of Pennsylvania, situated beside the river, and most basin points to which the staff might be expected to travel were reasonably accessible. While the office should be fairly close to state government buildings, it should not be physically located in one; that could lead to misunderstandings and other complications.

Finding appropriate office space, furnishings, equipment, and supplies was time consuming but not strenuous. It would be nice to have the office near the river, somewhere on Harrisburg's Front Street. There mansions of wealthy families who had died or moved to the suburbs were being converted into offices or razed to make way for modern structures. The office of the Interstate Advisory Committee went into one of the latter, and stayed there until no longer needed.

Finding a competent secretary took four weeks, but certainly was worth the wait. Mrs. Peter LeVan (Millie) joined me at the end of August, 1963, and soon became not only secretary but chief and only file clerk, librarian, bookkeeper, superintendent of the supply cabinet, receptionist, and principal answerer of the telephone. In time we changed her title to administrative assistant. Millie remained on the committee staff to the end, a loyal and capable helper. For about eighteen months Dr. Eleanor E. Hanlon, a professional grographer, was with us as technical assistant. She was succeeded by Peter M. Coleman, whose experience had been in news writing and dissemination, skills we were to need in abundance. He left in December, 1967, for state public service. The staff never numbered more than three. I resigned at the end of 1968. The compact had been written and passed by the legislatures of the three basin states. The focus of attention had shifted from state level to national level. The action from that point forward was to be centered in Washington, and it was time to put more emphasis at that end of the line. In August, 1968, we had engaged the services of Wendell, who by then had left the Council of State Governments and had set up a consulting business. Before I departed, I assisted in the transfer of most of my functions to Wendell and his associate, Charles F. Schwan, Jr. This left Millie as the sole staff member in Harrisburg. In May, 1969, notice was given to the owners of the building where the offices were housed that the lease would be terminated as of the end of November, 1969.

After a short stay in a windowless interior room, we moved to more attractive space on the third floor, front, where large picture windows let us look out upon the Susquehanna. The broad stream—eight-tenths of a mile wide at that point—is dotted with wooded islands, and at low stages rock ledges, boulders, and gravelly shallows vary the view. Our first January there, in 1964, we watched the last fast water near our bank close over with ice. One minute the stream still flowed visibly at a riffle, though solid ice extended for more than three-fourths of a mile to the west bank. Two or three minutes later surface movement was stilled; and a pair of mallards that apparently had lingered too long for their own good swept past on their way to Chesapeake Bay or more southerly points.

Some of these blocks of ice weighed more than a ton. Rising waters from early spring rains and snowmelt lifted and broke up the ice jam that had existed since January and the forces unleashed hurled these blocks high enough and far enough so some of them rested on the curbing of Front Street in Harrisburg. *Ted Jones, Stuart Finley Films*

In March of one year, when spring rains came and upcountry snow melted in a concurrent thaw, we watched thick ice buckle and break, saw chunks that weighed a ton or more tossed about. Much of the city is in the flood plain, and some blocks of ice were thrown far up the sloping bank, about to the edge of our street. Slabs of ice slid upon and rode down young trees on the islands, bending them so firmly it took most of the growing months that followed before they straightened again. We saw migratory waterfowl of many kinds in temporary residence, including intent egrets and herons poised for pray in the shallows. One memorable spring afternoon a flock of hundreds of snow geese settled in for a day of rest before continuing northward toward nesting grounds.

We called the splendid river view our "fringe benefit"; and did so only partly in jest for, although we enjoyed the same holidays and vacation privileges accorded Pennsylvania state employes, we had no retirement plan, not even federal Social Security, during the first four years of our operation. Then a district administrator who seemed eager for us to be paying that particular tax, discovered a niche into which he could fit us, one his predecessors had overlooked. A branch of the Pennsylvania Department of Labor and Industry agreed to accept us as a unit of state government for the specific purpose of receiving our F.I.C.A. taxes and remitting them to the Social Security Administration. After that came the painful business of having an extra sum deducted from checks each payday to reimburse the committee, which had advanced our shares of the taxes for the full term. (In Washington the late Alvin (Shorty) Watson, executive director of the Potomac basin advisory committee, ran into a similar problem but he was smarter than I; he held Social Security taxes in escrow until he and his staff were covered).

When the office was opened the states had not yet been billed for their agreed-upon shares of committee operating funds. This administrative routine took several weeks to complete. Meantime my personal checks paid Mrs. LeVan's salary, and I watched each incoming mail eagerly, hoping money would arrive from one of the states before I reached the bottom of my bank account. It did.

At the outset we borrowed temporarily a few pieces of surplus furniture from the Pennsylvania state warehouse through friends in the department headed by our committee chairman. We established credit and chose desks, chairs, a couple of typewriters, a duplicating machine, a small calculator, and the customary miscellaneous supplies needed in the operation of any office. Eventually we furnished a reception area near the door. For a letterhead I drew on my memory of a triangular design I had used in a business that no longer existed. The names of the states went into narrow triangles in source-to-mouth order, New York at the top, Pennsylvania in the center, and Maryland at the bottom. The Pennsylvania triangle was slightly longer than the others, to accommodate the longer name. As drawn the triangles, whose points converged, somewhat resembled an Indian arrowhead, which was appropriate to the name of our river. The triangles were grouped off center at the top left of the paper, pointing at our committee name and other needed letterhead information. The names of the states were printed in black on a basic blue inside the triangles; the blue, of course, was intended to hint at the traditional concept of the color of clean, clear water. I will swear under oath that the combination of black and blue was not chosen in anticipation of political or other bruises.

In those early months I tried with only partial success to secure wall decorations symbolic of our member states. Maryland, produced a great seal, which we had framed for hanging. However, neither New York nor Pennsylvania could furnish anything comparable, so instead of seeming to play favorites, Maryland was tucked away out of prominent view. Later, near the end of 1968, we purchased flags of the three states to be hung on the walls. In the early era we secured from New York an enlarged photograph of Otsego Lake at Cooperstown, the source of our river, and from Maryland a large picture of a scene near the river's mouth. These went on the wall in the reception area. We felt that since our picture windows framed the living stream in Pennsylvania a photo probably would not improve upon the real thing and therefore wasn't needed.

Physically, we were in business, and psychologically we were ready to go—but go where? Through the late summer, fall, and winter of 1963-1964 the staff was largely on its own as far as work projects were concerned. Did our executive committee use these months as what the Navy might call a shakedown cruise for the staff, to be sure things were shipshape before the main task was to begin? I didn't ask.

Late in July, 1963, a few days before the office was to be opened—actually, before I was officially employed—I drove to a Philadelphia suburb to visit Walter Phillips, attorney, who had been executive director of the Delaware River Basin Advisory Committee. When drafting began on the Susquehanna Compact, the Delaware no doubt would be used as a starting point. Phillips had pioneered my type of job. Perhaps he would give me the benefit of his observations and experience. We had a cordial chat, and he outlined the course he and his associates had followed. However, even as we talked, I recalled the words of Heraclitus that "you cannot walk in the same river twice for fresh waters are ever flowing upon you." If that was true as to one river, how much more so it would be of two separate rivers. So, pleasant though our visit was, for me at least, its chief benefit was to convince me that although we could profit from the Delaware experience, we would likely have to follow a course of our own choosing for the Susquehanna.

Drafting the compact would be our principal initial undertaking, but the committee, not I, would decide who should do the drafting and when it should begin. As a new employe I was not about to use a cattle prod on my superiors. Instead, I pored over the Articles of Organization to see what they said the staff could or should do when we were not working on something directly related to the compact.

At first reading it could be surmised that the Articles of Organization were written by people who were a bit uncertain as to what the committee might eventually be called upon to do and wanted to cover as many possibilities as they could. This was at least partly the motivation. As indicated in Chapter 1 of this part, the Articles were by Zimmermann, who told me they were based largely upon the articles he had written in the 1940s for the Interstate Commission on the Delaware River Basin. He was himself unsure of the eventual scope of the Interstate Advisory Committee's activities. It was entirely possible they might be limited exclusively to the drafting and the advocacy of a federal–interstate compact. On the other hand, if the committee members decided to go further, and secured appropriations for more extensive activities, Articles of Organization written broadly would cover and there would be no need for amendment. Preliminary organization had been initiated at the Binghamton meeting of May, 1962, when the Articles were put in force, but there was no way then of being sure the members would be content to let an advisory committee carry on the work without more secure statutory standing; it was possible that legislation relating to the place in government of the committee might be introduced in the assemblies of the basin states.

By common consent the members let the informal committee status stand, and the position of the IAC in Susquehanna basin matters was not questioned during its active life. The assemblies annually made available the needed operating funds, which, by the way, did not exceed the original $60,000 estimate; in fact, at our request they were cut in half for the fiscal year 1968-1969, and no appropriations at all had to be requested after that year. We of the staff were accepted at face value from the beginning in official places.

A cursory reading of the Articles of Organization indicates the wide latitude given the committee. First, it could promote, coordinate, cooperate in, and where necessary undertake studies. Conducting studies was something we could do pending the time drafting would start, so we pounced upon it. Of course, we had to bear in mind that virtually all the water-oriented agencies of the three states and of the federal government were constantly engaged in studies and that these had grown broader and more numerous with the commencement of the comprehensive survey of the basin. It would be easy to undertake something before discovering we were duplicating studies already going on elsewhere. We therefore canvassed the field, and wrote proposals for ten studies not already under way that we laid before the committee.[2] Several were started, and the information sought out was of value from time to time later, but only one actually was completed and published. This was done in part to set forth the responsibilities of federal and state agencies in water resources in our part of the country, and to chart or otherwise indicate the channels of communication being used or available. This study also was intended to clarify the separateness of the Interstate Advisory Committee from the then ongoing federal survey and the federal–state coordinating committee organized as the survey got under way.[3] The parallel courses being followed in the matter of timing, the fact that many of the same state officials were participating also in various phases of the federal survey, and my own involvement in the work of the coordinating committee and its subcommittees and work groups, all were bound to confuse people not intimately informed and close to the action. Figure 3 is from the published study, and indicates the comparatively close relations between our committee and its staff and others connected with the comprehensive survey. Almost from the beginning I had been given membership on the coordinating committee subcommittees and work groups, and by 1965 was accepted as an "ex officio" member of the coordinating committee itself. It should be obvious that this was helpful to me in numerous ways; I valued it especially because it gave me the equivalent of an extended course of instruction in aspects of water resources development, management, utilization, and conservation that otherwise may not have come my way.

It soon became obvious that I needed more information about the basin if I was to do my job right, and many hours were spent poring over documents of various kinds accumulating in our library (including several hundred volumes Eleanor Hanlon brought with her and made available until we shipped them out upon her departure), making extended use of the contents and facilities of the excellent Pennsylvania State Library in Harrisburg, bombarding knowledgeable persons, in government and out, with questions, and traveling up and down the basin to observe conditions and problem areas.

The second key paragraph of the Articles of Organization permitted the committee to assist in the formulation and implementation of plans.

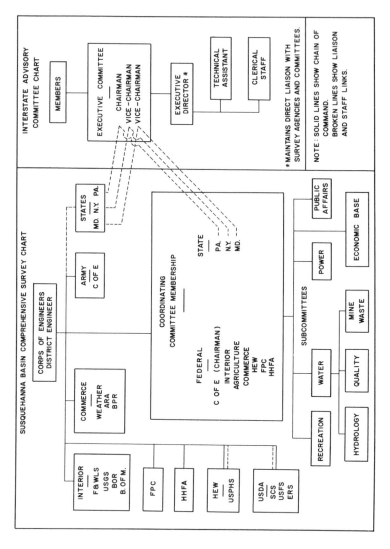

Figure 3. There was much confusion among laymen in the Susquehanna basin over the responsibilities of the coordinating commitee and the Interstate Advisory Committee. This chart was drawn for clarification and enlightenment.

The third allowed it to seek to coordinate the activities of state and federal agencies. Next, it might encourage appropriate policies in the three states and the enactment of state laws for their effectuation.

As a body the committee did not get into plan formulation involving the three states, nor in the implementation of plans. The committee, as such, took no formal action toward coordination of state and federal agency activities. This is not to say, though, that individual committee members, acting as state officials, did not engage in these kinds of undertakings. What I am saying is that the permission granted in the two clauses may have been useful under other circumstances, but appear to have been superfluous in our specific case. This certainly was true with regard to the staff.

The last of the above group of authorizations to the committee—the encouragement of appropriate policies and enactment of state laws for their effectuation—leads to an exercise in semantics. The fact that various action articles of the Susquehanna Compact were written as they were could be considered as indicating a direction of travel advocated by the committee and thus encourage what the committee believed to be appropriate policies for agencies responsible for water resources management. Similarly, the fact that legislative members of the committee, assisted by information supplied by the staff, worked assiduously toward the enactment of the compact by the assemblies of the basin states may be called furtherance of the second action clause in the sentence, for the compact was to become the law of each state and of the United States.

Finally, the Articles of Organization instructed the committee to study and recommend legislation for the creation of a permanent intergovernmental agency to have administrative–regulatory powers in connection with the basin's water resources. The task force that would draft the compact language the committee would study and recommend for enactment into law would be appointed in May, 1964, as it turned out, and would hold its get-acquainted meeting late in June. The details of drafting activity are the substance of Part III of this narrative, and are mentioned here only to fix them properly in their niche in time.

In retrospect, time appeared to hang heavy on staff hands for only a short while in the late summer and fall of 1963. People early began to ask us for information, often information we were in no position to supply. The simple fact that a basin committee had been formed gave rise to the erroneous belief on the part of some persons that a formal organization to manage and control the water situation throughout the valley had been born and was ready to pass miracles, especially with regard to waters polluted by municipalities, industry—including coal mines—and agriculture. All inquiries had to be answered, diplomatically of course. We took pains to give fully and freely whatever information was available, and to give inquirers the names and addresses of agencies and individuals having primary responsibility; on occasion we forwarded the inquiries to the latter with copies of our letters of acknowledgment.

Time was taken to visit Albany, Baltimore, and Annapolis to try to absorb what the executive branch members and alternates there, and their staffs, could show and tell that was relevant to our mission. Most water-oriented Pennsylvania agencies likewise were visited, and revisited.

It became clear in short order that making speeches would be a routine part of the job. This phase of the work was undertaken gladly; the groups wanting to hear what we were doing were among our publics, with whom we should be communicating freely, and they had every right to know. It should come as no surprise to the reader that among the first to ask questions and invite statements was the League of Women Voters. A little more than a year earlier, with what I regard as characteristic foresight and initiative, the League in Pennsylvania had published a twenty-six page report of its own study of the Susquehanna River Basin, a report to which I referred time and again from 1963 through 1968. It was well done. The League also fashioned its own interstate organization to follow what was happening concerning the water resources of the basin. This was called the Susquehanna Inter-League Council (SILC) and consisted of delegates from league chapters in the basin in New York, Pennsylvania, and Maryland. At my first confrontation with SILC members, in the fall of 1963, I confess they probably had at the tips of their tongues more physical and economic details concerning the basin than I had. Those women could, and did, ask some tough questions! Other meetings with segments of the League of Women Voters were held in months that followed, and they became convinced we were traveling in what they believed to be the right direction. At no time did we have support from other citizen groups comparable to that given by SILC and other LWV leaders. Working with them was an exhilarating, a gratifying experience.

Writing magazine articles has no particular hardship. Through all my adult career I've had a typewriter on my desk or near it. I did not intend to abandon the habit when this work began; and here was a fresh subject, one crying to be put on paper.

And there were meetings to attend. I'd rather not dig through old calendars to add up their number, and jog my memory of others that were not recorded but nevertheless took place when someone phoned and asked if I could leave my desk then and there, or an hour or so later, to go to some hastily called session on a water-related subject. Figure 3 indicates the number of subcommittees and work groups appointed to serve the federal–state coordinating committee as the comprehensive survey progressed. In the earlier years it seemed that all of them wanted to meet at least once a month. In addition, an advisory committee to the Pennsylvania Sanitary Water Board had been formed and asked to recommend courses of action to reduce or otherwise alleviate the problem of contaminated water draining from the network of active and abandoned mines in the anthracite coal country. I became chairman of a work group assigned to write the report and recommendations of that committee.

And there were visitors. It seemed that every federal and state agency with the remotest interest in water resources was curious about this new advisory committee. A few in those earlier months tried to press upon us their particular point of view for one reason or another, but mostly the visitors simply wanted to get acquainted, to wish us well, even to offer assistance in the form of information from their office files and libraries. We welcomed all, and most of the initial communications were followed by cordial relationships and frequent exchanges of information, a pleasant situation that endured.

I suppose each day in the eleven months between the opening of the office and the holding of the initial meeting of the drafting task force had its usual quota of hours. In retrospect, they seem to have marched at double time. When the task force first met, on June 22, 1964, I was there as the staff representative instructed to serve it as secretary. Considering the make-up of the task force, I probably was the least informed person at the conference table on the subject of a federal–interstate compact for the Susquehanna River Basin. The months that followed were illuminating in many respects, for they gave me the opportunity to watch in action, and work with as well as for, a group of professionals who appeared to me to be always in top form in their relentless pursuit of their assigned objective: a workable administrative–regulatory, multiple-purpose water resources compact for the Susquehanna River Basin.

Part III

Labors of the Drafting Task Force

Chapter 1

The Compact's Contents

The language of interstate or interstate–federal compacts may vary widely according to their purposes, as well as to the writing styles and idiosyncrasies of the authors. In nearly all instances, though, the proponents consider it essential to produce a preamble—by whatever name it may be called—in which at least some of the reasons that the agreement is considered necessary are set forth. It is the one place in the legislation where the drafters feel they can let themselves go, write with a flourish and use a lot of superlatives intended to point up the importance of and the beneficence to result from, the mundane statutory language that follows. We conformed to this custom, but our preamble contained little original language. It was modified from the preamble previously written by the drafters of the Delaware River Basin Compact and took the form of a conventional resolution. Following the "whereas" were ten numbered "reasons why" paragraphs and a "now, therefore" closing declaration that indicated our hope that the prospective signatory parties would "covenant and agree with each other" to do beneficial things to, with, and about the basin's water resources.

Thereafter the compact consists of fifteen articles that contain 117 sections; many of these are divided into subsections, and there are a few subsubsections. Each article is titled, and the sections are subtitled. The latter are specific as to section content; in the cases of some of the articles we could do little more than write a headline or generalized label. Naturally, the headlines could not be all-inclusive; in a number of articles the label tells only a fraction of the story and it takes some digging to discover the full scope of the labeled contents.

For example, Article 1 is headed "Short Title, Definitions, Purposes, and Limitations." It contains passages on all four of those subjects. It also reserves to Congress certain powers Congress has, including its right to withdraw the federal government as a member at any time, and sets forth both the duration of the compact and the method of determining how any assets the Susquehanna commission may own are to be distributed among the signatories if or when the compact should be voided.

It was appropriate that Article 2, then, should declare the Susquehanna commission created, prescribe commission membership, lay down voting rules, provide for commission organization, and indicate the geographic area in which the commission might exercise whatever powers the compact gives it.

A highly significant article on the commission's general, ancillary, and regulatory powers and duties comes next. Its scope is broad and underscores the desire of the compact's proponents to give the commission considerable background authority and influence. This statement is not at all negated by the whittling down of commission prerogatives in later sections of this article, and in other compact clauses. It is probable that the ultimate extent of Susquehanna commission power may not be fully delineated until after one or more court tests. Fine distinctions between what the commission may or may not do and the things it must do or has the discretionary power to do, are discussed later. It is enough for present purposes to note that beyond the granting of considerable power, Article 3 contains no fewer than ten specific limitations and restraints upon commission authority, and declares its determinations subject to court review.

Seven succeeding articles—4 through 10—relate to specific fields of water resources activity or concern in which the commission is empowered to act in its own name. We tried to assure that the nature of permitted action in each was clearly expressed, and to state with equal clarity the limits beyond which the commission may not go, the conditions that must prevail before it can act, the preliminary steps it must take before acting, and so on.[1] The fields covered in these articles are water supply, water quality, flood protection including flood plains management, watershed management including fish and wildlife habitat, water-based recreation in general, natural beauty, and hydroelectric power and energy. The natural beauty article, Article 9, consists of a very limited and inconclusive venture into the amenities that, weak as it is, nevertheless does commit the signatory parties to consideration of cultural and kindred factors before the basin's water resources are manipulated.

Article 11 is regulatory, and relates to commission powers in the event of drought or the occurrence of a natural or man-made disaster or catastrophe.

The degree of control the commission may exercise over federal and state water resources activities and operations is detailed in Article 12.

Articles 13 and 15 are concerned mostly with financial and housekeeping matters, respectively, although Article 15 also contains passages relating to what are termed general powers, one example of which is the right of eminent domain, or condemnation.

Article 14 particularizes the formulation and continuous updating of the basinwide comprehensive plan, and the development of relatively short-term action programs based on the plan. It also outlines the very important budgetary procedure precedent to appropriation of funds for commission activities.

This brief resume of some of the principal contents of the compact was written rapidly and with relative ease. Not so the final language. That required toil by the drafting task force, the Interstate Advisory Committee, and staff; it also required some soul searching—and thirty-two months of time.[2]

Chapter 2

Drafting the Compact

Upon looking back across more than five years of intermittently close association with the task force that wrote the Susquehanna River Basin Compact, my outstanding recollection is of a group of men with varied backgrounds and personalities working together in extraordinary harmony, imbued with a determination to bring forth a creditable product.[1] Some were strangers to the others at the outset, untested for specific capability and compatibility. Possibly the intimacy of the small conference table brought irritability or impatience to one or another now and then, but if so it generally was well concealed, subordinated to the pursuit of the common objective. I recall only one minor explosion —and this came about as a result of an error by me in a mailing of meeting notes. One of my many 'bosses'' gave me oral hell at the time but that was the end of it.

At the close of the drafting segment of the total effort I think a poll would have shown a combination of mutual respect for integrity, of belief in each member's sincerity of purpose, and admiration for the broad sweep of talent brought to the work table. When the compact was at last passed by Pennsylvania in the summer of 1968, completing legislative action at state level, Dr. Carl N. Everstine of Annapolis, director of the Maryland Department of Legislative Reference and the statutory language stylist of the task force, wrote me that our group should not be disbanded without ceremony to mark its passing. He said that since Chesapeake Bay is the last stop for the flow of the Susquehanna in the fresh water stages of the hydrologic cycle, the victory celebration and phasing out party should be held on or near the bay. This is still listed on my books as imperative unfinished business.

Our job was attacked with vigor and purpose. We tape-recorded task force meetings, and these later were transcribed—roughly so at my request, since a perfect verbatim transcript was both unnecessary and impossible. The many places where Mrs. LeVan could not transcribe from the tapes because, as she put it, "all talking at once" indicate the enthusiasm of the group at our meetings.

Seriousness was as necessary as enthusiasm, but there might be danger that needed seriousness could degenerate into pedantry, pomposity, or even a messianic attitude. We quickly began grasping opportunities for levity, occasionally ribaldry, that opened as we drafted, and I believe the moments of badinage that interspersed the hours of solemn discussion helped speed the overall production. All participated in these lighter interludes. On one occasion we were deep in a discussion of judicial review of determinations that would be made by the commission created by the compact. Robert J. Trace of Camp Hill, assistant attorney general of Pennsylvania, and Francis W. Montanari of Albany, assistant commissioner of conservation and director of the New York Water Resources Commission, had the floor:

> *Trace:* There is nothing more enchanting to a lawyer than to have a question go to the Supreme Court for a solvent client.
> *Montanari:* How would you describe the ideal client?
> *Trace:* A wealthy man badly scared.
> *Montanari:* Or a wealthy woman?
> *Trace:* That would be a treasure chest.

A news story in March, 1964, quoted Chairman Goddard as indicating the task force would consist largely of lawyers chosen by the attorneys general of the three states, who would be assisted by "technical experts." This concept of task force composition changed as the matter was given more consideration. Legal assistance was vital, but should it be dominant? The concensus was that at least equal emphasis should be put on water technology coupled with experience in water resources administration. The purpose of the compact, and the operations of the commission to be created by it, would primarily affect the activities of water agencies of the signatory parties, in which technology and administration were prime considerations. As a consequence of this line of reasoning, the task force actually appointed included two state water agency administrators and one specialist in water resource legislation and administrative coordination. The administrators were Montanari of Al-

bany, and Paul W. McKee of Annapolis, director of the Maryland Department of Water Resources; the third specialist was Alan J. Sommerville of Camp Hill, Water Resources Development Engineer (later titled
Water Resources Coordinator) of the Pennsylvania Department of Forests and Waters. Sommerville's duties were chiefly advisory to Secretary
Goddard of that department in water resource legislation and related
policy matters. All three were experienced in working with federal water
agencies, and Montanari and Sommerville also served as technological
assistants to their superiors in the workings of the Delaware River Basin
Commission. Expertise contributed by this trio was matched in other
fields by the rest of the task force, who all had varying degrees of experience in water matters. Trace, for example, had been solicitor for the
Pennsylvania Sanitary Water Board for ten years prior to moving over
to the Department of Forests and Waters in 1963. Everstine also served
as Secretary of the Maryland Legislative Council, a bipartisan interim
body that studied all manner of legislative proposals between sessions of
the General Assembly, water legislation included, and recommended
action thereon at the start of each lawmaking session. Zimmermann's
talents have been indicated in earlier chapters. So have Wendell's, who
joined us in late October, 1964. Without the thoroughgoing knowledge
of water resources compact philosophy that Zimmermann and Wendell
had helped so greatly to originate and establish, the job before us probably would have been completed more or less satisfactorily in time, but
whether it would have been as professional and workable a final product
is a question. It should be added that all task force members were
knowledgeable in matters of intergovernmental relations.

Zimmermann, of course, had an excellent grasp of the drafting problems ahead as we came to our first meeting, held at the New York
regional office of the Council of State Governments, on June 25, 1964.
Sommerville had taken part in Delaware Compact discussions, though
not in its drafting. Montanari had been on the staff of ORSANCO
(Ohio River Valley Water Sanitation Commission) before going to the
New York Department of Conservation, and also was familiar with the
workings of the Delaware Compact and commission. The rest of us
lacked such explicit experience and entered the meeting room on that
first occasion with wary anticipation, willing and eager but wondering
what course drafting events would take. One of the chief attributes each
member possessed was a keen sensitivity to the political realities in his
state; they all had learned about how far their lawmakers might be
expected to go in the fields covered by the Susquehanna compact.

The task force chairman moved purposefully from the start. He permitted, even encouraged, wide-open discussion in which all members, and I as secretary, might take part freely. His mind was open to new ideas or to improvements on the precedents we had to go on, but at the outset he nailed down the core issue before us as being water management, including but by no means limited to water quality. Many other essentials had to be written—sometimes rewritten many times before being mutually agreed upon—as well as lesser but still necessary housekeeping and other passages. However, water management and the powers relating to water management to be granted to the hoped-for Susquehanna River Basin Commission, powers to be exercised responsibly where actual or potential interstate effect was concerned, would be uppermost in his mind and consequently in ours for the duration.

It was inevitable that copies of the Delaware Compact would be on the table before us as we worked. The Delaware had been the pioneer administrative–regulatory multiple-purpose federal–interstate compact. It was the only one of its scope that actually had been enacted into law and was in operation. The earlier kindred efforts in this field—the draft for the Missouri basin and that written for New England, referred to earlier—had aborted. The Delaware Compact had been in existence for two and a half years as our writing got under way, not long enough to prove its long term worth but enough to indicate the significant role such an agreement could have in water resources planning and management in the public interest. The wisdom of our following the Delaware pattern in general and in numerous particulars seemed justified later when the Delaware Compact successfully met a series of crises and challenges, and demonstrated its workability in conclusive fashion. (The most significant short-term accomplishment of the Delaware commission may have been its resolution of drought conflicts in the middle 1960s, as a result of which New York City's faucets did not go dry and salt water did not flow through those of Philadelphia.)

The realities thus had already set a number of guidelines for us. We would follow the Delaware Compact so far as practical because (1) it appeared to be workable; (2) sharp deviation without defendable reason might be viewed with suspicion by legislators, administrators, and others; and (3) it made our task easier than if we started afresh. We were quite frankly concerned about deviating from the Delaware without substantive cause; it lay on our subconscious mental processes at all times, and in hindsight perhaps it did so more than was necessary. Those most familiar with it recognized that the Delaware was not a perfect instrument of its sort. It was, however, the first effort in its field, and we could not forget that it had been enacted into law by the legislatures of its four basin states and by the Congress, all in record time and by overwhelming majorities. Beyond that, in its short life span the Delaware commission had begun to give promise of what it would show that it could deliver in specific circumstances. We determined to mold and adapt the Delaware to fit the characteristics and realities of our river basin, and to improve upon it as we felt we could without deviating so greatly as to raise legislative and administrative eyebrows in the affected jurisdictions.

Other fundamentals surfaced early in our drafting era. We recognized that we shouldn't attempt to foresee each last detail of every question that might conceivably come before the Susquehanna commission for resolution and try to provide neat answers in advance. There were pragmatic practicing public servants on the task force. They knew approximately how fast a coordinating–administrative water resource body could travel in exercising planning and directing leadership without experiencing setbacks at the hands of the elected officials of the signatories. They conceived our task to be to write a compact that not only would allow necessary planning and programming to be successfully accomplished but that also could be expected to be enacted into law without extreme difficulty by all four of the sovereignties involved. We wanted to assure that the Susquehanna commission would have the required authority, without unduly arousing fears that the powers granted would be wrongfully or improperly exercised. One task force member wanted commission powers brushed in with broad strokes only, saying, "If you're too specific you hamper rather than help." Another commented that if we wrote the compact in language that wouldn't pass the legislatures, ". . . we won't have to worry about the commission's exercising any authority, ever." The rest of us accepted these attitudes.

The subcommittee was overly optimistic about the rapidity with which the draft could be completed. (We thought it would go much faster than it did.) Zimmermann, in particular, wanted as much speed as was prudent. He feared the impact on the compact that might result from legislative reapportionment, which was a matter of much public concern in each of the basin states at the time. An extreme situation existed in New York State; there Assembly elections were to be held in three consecutive years, which could cause problems incident to continuity of leadership in the Assembly and what one draftsman called "lawmaking savvy." Because of reapportionment, and for the simple reason that he was eager to get the job finished, to see enacted into law as quickly as possible a compact of the type he had envisioned for years and of which he would be a principal author, Zimmermann pushed his workers rapidly in those first months. We joined him enthusiastically. We hoped the compact could be drafted, approved by the parent Interstate Advisory Committee, and laid before the legislatures of the basin states early in 1965. Events proved this to be a hopeless goal; our first draft was published in June, 1966, nearly two years after our initial task force meeting, and final polishing consumed eight months more. It only required sixty days each for the Maryland and New York legislatures to pass the compact as it was modified and printed in January, 1967; Pennsylvania dawdled and fussed from April, 1967, to the end of July, 1968.

We met ten times in the last six months of 1964, with seldom an absentee. Two were two-day meetings, with a work session the first night on each occasion. This schedule may not appear rigorous to some readers. It will be considered an accomplishment by those who have experienced the difficulty of setting up acceptable dates for seven busy and widely separated persons. The five state officials were mandated to attend meetings and carry out other activities fixed by statute or long custom. Zimmermann had classroom conflicts and other consulting commitments. Wendell was often on the go for the Council of State Governments. It was, of course, even more complex to fix meeting dates for the Interstate Advisory Committee for it had a larger membership whose composition came from state cabinet level positions as well as from the state legislatures. In 1964 I made up a chart to indicate the set meeting dates of the twelve members from the executive branch. It disclosed that the fourth Thursday was the only day of each month all members were free of regularly scheduled meetings of one kind or another. The upshot was that one or more members usually had to miss another meeting in order to attend an Interstate Advisory Committee meeting or vice versa. Occasionally we'd get a break when the calendar showed a free working day or two beyond the fourth week of the month. Finding satisfactory dates was complicated when the legislatures were in session. William S. James of Bel Air was president of the Maryland Senate. Delegate Marvin Mandel of Baltimore (who was to become governor of Maryland when Spiro T. Agnew was elected Vice-President) was speaker of the Maryland House. Senator Z. H. Confair of Williamsport, and Representative Orville E. Snare of Huntingdon, were chairmen of committees of their respective houses of the Pennsylvania

General Assembly. Prior to his death, Senator Elisha T. Barrett of Bay Shore had been the long-time chairman of the New York Joint Legislative Committee on Interstate Cooperation. And so on. They found it hard to break away from legislative duties to travel to IAC meetings. There were a few times—fortunately not many—when last-minute complications prevented attendance by one or more who previously had planned to come, with the result that we wound up without a quorum. In order that the cost and effort of those who arrived for the meeting might not be a total waste, on those occasions we informally discussed agenda items so as to shorten the time needed to cover them at the next session which, we hoped, would be better attended.

Normal drafting procedure at the beginning was to work from the Delaware Compact as from a basic guide. We studied its provisions much as a student would a text, but we did not at any time conclude that its language was sacrosanct. We accepted Delaware provisions that we considered unassailable from a Susquehanna viewpoint. Others we worked over, occasionally many times. When we had at last plodded through the Delaware Compact from start to finish and began reassessment—a painstaking, line-by-line review—we depended less and less on the Delaware and worked more from our own typed preliminary drafts of articles and sections, polishing and tightening; we turned to the Delaware Compact only for specific reference or comparison.

The task force first met with the parent committee in mid-September, 1964, about two and a half months after drafting began, and Zimmermann made a brief progress report. Thereafter we asked the IAC to meet to review our work as often as we felt necessary, but tried not to burden the members without genuine cause. At the IAC meetings the task force presented new or modified language, and defended its work when questioned or opposed. In most instances there was no serious contention, but this is not to say the Interstate Advisory Committee members did not question the task force—and each other—incisively, at length, and with spirit. A few would cheerfully admit they didn't know a great deal about federal–interstate water compacts when they were appointed to the committee, but those who remained all the way or attended regularly had no excuse for ignorance on the subject at the end. A number of the members and alternates were well informed specialists; some had more than a little knowledge of the generality of the subject being tackled, others had expertise in other fields upon which our particular subject impinged. Each in his way contributed to the end result. The biographical sketches of the committee leaders and others in

Appendix A give career highlights and at least hint at the total breadth and scope of experience and knowledge brought to the task.

The staff work was considerable, but I prided myself on being capable of fairly rapid journeyman-quality work under pressure, and Mrs. LeVan was indefatigable at the typewriter and the duplicating machine. Our goal was to put draft material in the hands of the task force far enough ahead of a meeting so the members could familiarize themselves with it by assembly time. (This was common practice, too, with respect to material to be before members of the parent committee when it met.) The volume of staff work rose as the tempo of drafting increased, and even minor modification of a single sentence often entailed a change sheet for a complete section or article. Penciling corrections or new language in old sheets had its limitations. Before the end of 1964 the task force had completed its first consideration and modification of Delaware's contents, and had added one new article relative to the preservation of natural beauty. As of January 12, 1965, staff had reproduced the task force's product and bound it for easy comparison reading with twenty-odd pages of explanatory information and Zimmermann's covering letter to the Interstate Advisory Committee. On the cover of each numbered copy we stamped the word CONFIDENTIAL in bold capital letters, and on the inside the words "Draft" and "For Internal Use Only" were prominently stamped. We wanted all concerned—IAC members, their alternates, the task force, committee staff, and staff aids of IAC members who had access to the rough draft—to know without question that this was still in work-sheet form and was not to be discussed outside the group.

We were criticized in some quarters for what was termed our secrecy, but we felt that tentative material, incomplete and subject to extensive revision, should not be made public. Our attitude was that language prematurely disclosed would result in reaction to only a part of the instrument and perhaps an imperfect part at that. We considered it better to keep its contents to ourselves until we could turn out a complete document that we were willing to discuss and debate publicly. At that time we would distribute the first public draft widely in all three states and to selected people in Washington, and be prepared to talk over any aspect of it with all who wished to do so.[2]

After the first in-house draft had been circulated the task force obtained agreement from the IAC that the latter would not attempt to draft compact language from the floor, so to speak. Instead, when the committee agreed upon contents of a particular portion of the compact,

The drafters at work. Clockwise, Trace, Sommerville, McKee, Zimmermann, Voigt, Everstine, Wendell, and Montanari. *Ted Jones, Stuart Finley Films*

large or small—whether that portion was new or merely different from previous language produced by the task force—it would instruct the task force as to what was wanted, after which it was incumbent upon the task force to put the committee's wishes into acceptable words. As changes were reduced to writing by the task force, change sheets had to be put in proper form and distributed to authorized holders of the in-house draft.

By January, 1966, so many alterations had been made that the draft was more confusing than enlightening, and in that month we did the whole job anew, delivering clean copies to all. Months before this time, though, the drafting had advanced to the point that we were largely working on bits and pieces that seemed to need tidying up or nailing down, such as seeking to assure a necessary minimum flow from the river into Chesapeake Bay, or polishing the definition of "diversion," or coming to a determination as to the power the commission might have over the occupancy and use of flood plains, and so on.

On March 9, 1966, after nearly a full day of such final touching up, Zimmermann leaned back in his chair, sighed as with relief, and said, "Well, fellows, that's it; we are through."

Through, yes, with the initial drafting. There remained a meeting of the IAC on April 14, 1966, at which it gave approval for us to print the first official committee draft, which we took to the public on June 8, 1966.

Chapter 3

Powers Granted; Powers Withheld

The heart of a compact such as we were writing for the Susquehanna River Basin consists of the powers granted, and those denied or circumscribed. At no time was there a serious question in the minds of the drafters as to whether the commission created by our compact should carry authority. Trace put the issue succinctly at one of our earlier meetings when he said "if the compact is worded so the commission is allowed to do no more than advise and recommend, we are wasting our time."

Two of our number were heads of state water resources agencies that would be affected by the degree of power written into the charter of the Susquehanna River Basin Commission, and would in some respects be subservient to a commission strongly constituted, yet they agreed with Trace. So did the rest of the task force. As indicated in an earlier chapter, one of our group spoke out in favor of providing clearly defined guidelines for the agency and leaving it to the discretion of responsible officials to assure that the trust placed in them was not misused. There was no disagreement among our group. A considerable majority of our parent Interstate Advisory Committee felt the same way. This is not to say, however, that there were no debates on the subject and no compromising of opposing views. The IAC frequently settled differences by the use of alternate phrasing which, in a few significant areas of commission activity to be recounted shortly, left its authority at a level far below that which the task force had initially proposed. There were a few occasions when the debates over commission powers grew spirited, but they were all conducted on a high level, without any oral slugging or gutter tactics.

(On one occasion, in October, 1966, one of our number spoke out publicly in opposition to the compact, taking a position counter to that of the member to whom he was alternate. This brought a passing flurry but no lasting harm to the cause of the compact.)

After Trace's comment, when the task force talked of commission authority, discussion usually centered on the adequacy of the powers we were putting on paper to meet needs we conceived of arising. We gave concurrent—and equal—attention to the inclusion of restrictions sufficient to prevent empire building or the superseding without cause of state or federal prerogatives. A remark by Trace at one of our meetings brought a chuckle. He said, "This is language I'd like to see in the compact if I were the attorney for the commission, but if I represented a corporation operating in the basin I'd pound the table and cry out against usurpation of power by hungry bureaucrats." None of us had any desire to create a superagency. On the contrary, we made every effort to give existing agencies opportunity to do all in their statutory power to achieve optimum conservation and appropriate use of the basin's water resources. It would be when they could not act by reason of those interposed state borders, or when they failed to act on matters with present or prospective interstate consequences, that the commission would be allowed to step in and take charge. Likewise, the commission would be given authority to review and approve water resources projects only (1) when the interstate effect was obvious; (2) where it could be claimed on a cumulative-effect basis; or (3) where the comprehensive plan for the basin was involved.

It is necessary to an understanding of the Susquehanna Compact and of the powers granted to or withheld from the commission to make certain mental separations in regard to the several kinds of authority found in the agreement. The simplest is, of course, the authority exercised over in-house affairs. This is essential to any administrative agency at any level of government. Although regulatory authority is inherent in the Susquehanna commission, the compact also provides for the commission to exercise purely recommendatory power; here its muscle would be far from absolute, and it may merely advise, encourage, coordinate, and promote in several phases of water resources activities and operations. It may conduct research, and may pick the brains and reference files found in water agencies of state and federal government. It is in two other areas, however, that Susquehanna commission powers impinge upon and are expected to have their greatest influence on the course of conservation, management, development, and utilization of the water resources of the basin. The first of these is the nature and degree of control that may be exercised over the activities and operations of others. Second is the power granted to the commission to enter into a variety of water-related activities in its name or on its initiative. This chapter tells of the simpler type of powers first, then the more complex and authoritative passages.

Since housekeeping powers are more or less standard among administrative agencies and are written into most administrative codes, we picked up nearly all of the provisions in the corresponding article of the Delaware Compact.[1] Our Section 15.1 permits the commission to enter into contracts and to sue and be sued; to accept funds as appropriations, as gifts, or as otherwise may properly come to it; to provide for plans and specifications for its projects and facilities, if any; to regulate the use of owned facilities; to acquire, hold, and dispose of real and personal property; and to exercise whatever corporate powers are essential to its mission. The same section makes it mandatory for the commission to serve as the agency's governing body; rule on the nature and amount of obligations incurred in the commission's name; provide for internal organization and administration; appoint principal officers and allocate duties; create or abolish staff jobs as necessary or desirable; and let and execute contracts. Section 15.2 gives the commission power to make and enforce rules and regulations as needed to carry out provisions of the compact.[2] Other commission powers that seem to relate to this category are:

1. To fix rates and charges for the use of any facilities it may own or operate, or for services or products furnished.[3]

2. To constitute and empower advisory committees.[4]

3. To issue bonds,[5] which is meaningless unless the commission has assured income with which to pay interest and retire principal when due. The passages governing the bonding process are extensive, detailed, and written to comply with statutory requirements at state and federal levels. This, too, is almost verbatim Delaware Compact language.

One power in Article 15 would not be characterized as purely administrative, however. Section 15.14 lets the commission exercise the right of eminent domain, or condemnation, over real estate needed for its activities and operations. This would be done under state law if one is applicable; otherwise federal law would prevail.

The second category of powers—those advisory, recommendatory, coordinating, or otherwise intended to further the technology and practice of water resources management in a major river basin—is found in earlier sections of Article 3, the general article on commission powers and duties, and Article 7, which deals with watershed management. These passages caused few headaches. They came to us in all except comparatively minor substance direct from the Delaware Compact; our main discussions had to do with their placement in the line of march according to our concept of what was appropriate, and niceties of phraseology. Nevertheless, they should be itemized to some extent. For example, the commission is authorized to:

1. Establish standards of planning, design, and operation of water projects.[6] Without standards set uniformly for the basin, water developments would indeed be haphazard, "subject . . . to duplicating, overlapping, and uncoordinated administration" by agencies and entities exercising "a multiplicity of powers resulting in a splintering of authority and responsibility."[7] This is not written to disparage standards in the rule books and procedure manuals of existing agencies and others but is principally intended to emphasize that they do differ; we believed uniform standards should apply in Susquehanna water matters.

2. Conduct and sponsor water resources research,[8] which seems self-explanatory.

3. Collect, compile, coordinate, interpret, and disseminate surface and ground water data.[9] This appears clear, and subject to little question.

4. Conduct whatever surface and ground water tests may be needed in formulating and administering the comprehensive plan for the basin's water resources.[10] A necessary corollary, which was provided for, is the compilation of data following the tests.

5. Prepare, publish, and disseminate information concerning water resources conditions and problems in the basin.[11] In other words, *communicate* with the commission's several publics—an activity I consider essential. There is likelihood that some of the communicating will be self-serving; the historical record shows clearly that this occurs whenever and wherever the practice of public relations is carried out.[12] However, I consider it no more out of line than the work done in behalf of his client by an attorney.

6. Negotiate loans, grants, gifts, services, and other aids "as may be lawfully available."[13]

7. Adopt, amend, and repeal rules and regulations to implement the compact.[14]

8. "Promote and aid the coordination of the activities and programs" of all concerned with water resources administration in the basin.[15]

Neither the task force nor the parent committee had any qualms about the all-inclusive subsection 3.4-1, which lumps in a single sentence what on the surface appear to be vast powers to be wielded at will by the Susquehanna commission. It was to cause problems later, when we went to the public and to the Pennsylvania legislature with our compact, for it does have an ominous ring to those conservatively disposed who don't take the time and trouble to read and digest the passages in the compact that qualify the exercise of those powers. It declares the commission may "plan, design, acquire, construct, reconstruct, complete, own, improve, extend, develop, operate, and maintain any and all projects, facilities, properties, activities, and services which are determined by the commission to be necessary, convenient, or useful for the purposes of this compact." Persons who singled this one sentence out of context and read no further could—and did—scream in righteous alarm. They seemed especially perturbed by the fact that the doing of any or all these things rested on determinations made by the commission and, further, that there didn't even have to be a finding of necessity but they could be done if the commission found them either "convenient" or "useful." (Fuller details are in Part IV.) At drafting time, we didn't discuss this aspect at great length; we felt the numerous restraints scattered through the compact could and would hold even the most ambitious set of commissioners and staff in check.

Nor did we hesitate over the language of Section 3.4-8, which also aroused what we felt to be needless fears in Pennsylvania. This subsection allows the commission to "exercise such other and different powers as may be delegated to it by this compact or otherwise pursuant to law, and have and exercise all powers necessary or convenient to carry out its express powers and other powers which may reasonably be implied therefrom"—which we copied from the Delaware compact and interpreted to mean the commission had the authority to do what the compact or other law said or implied it could do. It was a compressed reiteration and confirmation, nothing more.

Although the development of a comprehensive plan and of a water resources program for the basin[16] are properly definable as duties, there is a close relation between them and the powers of the commission, especially its authority over government agencies and private enterprise active in the water resources field.

Who builds or conducts or carries out water projects? Government agencies do, of course. At federal levels they are presently built in the Susquehanna basin by the Corps of Engineers, the Soil Conservation

Service, and the Bureau of Sport Fisheries and Wildlife. State agencies doing so usually are those concerned with fisheries and wildlife, parks, and flood damage reduction. Local units of government ordinarily move in matters of water supply, waste water treatment, and water-based recreation. Private enterprise is most likely to act in such things as hydroelectric power and energy, process or cooling water, public water supply (usually as contractor to a municipality), fish production, privately operated parks containing natural or man-made lakes, real estate development associated with adjacent water, or agricultural irrigation.

Any or all of these could qualify for inclusion in the comprehensive plan, and it is mandatory that state and federal projects do so.[17] The others would qualify in the event they should fall into one or more of the categories of water projects the commission is authorized to review and approve. Section 3.10 contains the controlling language—and also provides for judicial review of commission determinations, which is a strong deterrent to the unrestrained exercise of power. Section 3.10-2 makes commission approval mandatory for these types of undertakings:

1. Projects on or crossing the boundary between signatory states. These are inherently interstate in character and effect.

2. Any project involving the diversion of water; that is, either its exportation from the basin or its importation into the basin. Here the commission is to be informed about and have a determining voice regarding quantities allowed to leave or come into the basin. It is safe to say it will be as interested in the quality of water imported as in the quantity, both of which it will have the right to look into prior to granting or withholding approval.

3. A project wholly within the borders of one signatory state but so large or otherwise significant as to have an appreciable effect on the water resources of another signatory state. This appears self-explanatory and requires no comment other than that neither the task force nor the IAC could find a way to avoid the use of the indeterminate word "significant."

4. Any project included by the commission in the comprehensive plan or that would have a significant—here's that word again!—effect on the plan.

With water plans of several kinds constantly being made by many agencies and private enterprise in various parts of the basin—and in Washington or by a controlling federal agency suboffice physically situated outside the basin—a mechanism was necessary to assure that the commission would be apprised of what was going on. Section 3.10-1 provides that up to a point existing agency practices continue in effect in the signatory states. These states have long had laws requiring certain procedures before the first earth is to be moved or other action taken in a water project. Usually they provide that plans and specifications be submitted to a named board or other agency. An impounding structure must be approved, except for those the statutes define as too small to matter. So must a waste-water disposal system. Section 3.10-1 requires the sponsors to continue to submit proposals for water projects to the state agency set up by law to receive and pass on them. As we envisioned the operation of this section the state agency, after acting on an application, would send the commission word as to the action taken, with or without auxiliary information, depending on the nature of the project or as agreed upon by the agency and the commission. Notification to the commission could be sent in the form of the minutes of periodic meetings of the regulatory state agencies, or otherwise. After receiving definitive word, the commission staff would have a look at the proposal, following which the commission would accept staff recommendations or take such other action as the situation warranted. If no agency of a signatory party had statutory jurisdiction over a particular kind of water project considered reviewable the commission could set up its own procedure for sponsors to follow en route to commission review and approval.

It has been noted that projects proposed by state and federal agencies require commission approval.[18] Section 12.1, which relates to federal projects, and Section 12.2, which is concerned with projects of state agencies, specify that the powers granted to the commission in those regards are "for the purposes of avoiding conflicts of jurisdiction and of giving full effect to the commission as a regional agency of the signatory parties." Thereafter a subsection declares that in the case of federal agencies water projects may not be considered authorized prior to their inclusion in the comprehensive plan by the commission, and equally restrictive conditions apply to projects of state agencies. This article is virtually the same as its counterpart in the Delaware Compact[19] and little time was put into its drafting. That was not the case with our Article 3. The latter contains much Delaware language but also much that is new and wholly Susquehanna, particularly our long Section 3.10, which has seven subsections; 3.10-1 and 3.10-2 have been described. These and Section 3.10-3 were largely the work of Sommerville, who wrote the basic draft and set the pattern. Thereafter the task force modified and refined but did not deviate greatly from the Sommerville fundamentals. Students of water resources compacts may wonder why we changed our review and approval section so greatly from that found in the Delaware Compact,[20] since we had committed ourselves to follow it so far as practical. We considered the Delaware language susceptible to misinterpretation and misuse. We thought it too broad, too sweeping, too all-encompassing. It could be read as giving the commission control over so minute a matter as whether a water or sewer line might be extended as little as a city block—at least so we believed. We wanted to make as sure as we could that the commission and staff would concern themselves with water matters of a proved substantial nature. We wanted limitations on the power to review and approve. We wanted interstate effect, actual or truly potential, to be the governing consideration. This is why Section 3.10-2 was so specific as to the categories of projects that required review and approval, and why Section 3.10-3 exempted from review projects so small or insignificant that the states themselves didn't bother to exercise statutory control. Beyond that, we gave the commission discretionary power to extend the exemption to additional categories of projects that time and experience might prove to have no demonstrable interstate effect. Our overall intention was to put a restraining hand on the commission, to encourage it and its staff to concentrate their energies and attention on larger water resources matters, not the picayune. We must leave it to time to judge whether or how well we succeeded.

This leaves to be described one more important regulatory field entrusted to the commission: the rationing of water in time of drought and the control of water use in a disaster area. Article 11 of the Susquehanna Compact applies. Section 11.1 allows the commission to take action in its own name or to delegate power to one or more of the signatory parties. The article divides drought into two categories. The lesser may be limited in severity or area, or both. In such case the commission may delineate a "protected" region[21] and with the consent of the affected state or states may regulate the quantities of water allowed to be used.[22]

In two types of more significant situations the commission may tighten its control of water use. The first is a severe and widespread drought. Before a drought emergency area may be declared the commission must hold a public hearing and the affirmative vote must be unanimous.[23] The character of drought had a bearing on the requirement of a public hearing. It is insidious in that it usually proceeds inconspicuously and its grave effects become apparent only over an extended period; thus there is time for witnesses to testify as to the growing gravity of the situation before the drastic step of rationing water is taken and the ordinary and customary processes and dictates of other agencies of government are superseded. In the case of "a disaster or catastrophe other than drought, natural or manmade," there may not be time for a public hearing. Conditions could call for immediate action to restrict or forbid water use, or require use from alternate sources until the disaster had been overcome or the danger had passed. Section 11.4 (b) permits the commission to "impose direct controls on the use of water." This power is expected to be invoked in any of a variety of situations, such as the dumping of critical quantities of a poisonous substance in the river or one of its tributaries, deliberately or as a result of an accident or storm damage. Again, however, just as in the case of a drought emergency, the vote must be unanimous.

It seems appropriate that water supply[24] should be the first of the specialty fields dealt with in the compact, since it is so essential to human survival. We didn't originate the idea of giving water supply precedence; credit for that goes to the writers of the Delaware Compact. In fact, we followed the Delaware order of precedence in all the several compact articles that allow the Susquehanna commission to undertake projects of its own volition. As was done in the Delaware, we gave the Susquehanna commission authority to "develop, implement, and effectuate" plans and projects for the use of the water of the basin for domestic, agricultural, and industrial supply.[25] To that end the commission may do what it considers necessary both along basin streams and at off-river sites, but it may not engage "in the business of distributing water";[26] it is to be a wholesaler, not a retailer. The article's deterrent to indiscriminate commission action is in Section 4.4, which directs the commission to consider the "rights, plans, and programs" of others and to hold public hearings before proceeding in its own name.

Other deterrents to commission action in this and other water project fields may be appropriately singled out at this point. The principal one is Section 1.3-6 which forbids the commission to undertake a project unless it is "necessary to the execution of the comprehensive plan and no other competent agency is in a position to act or such agency fails to act." This is a powerful and explicit prohibition, a forthright expression of the intent of the compact proponents that the commission was to be created primarily to lead or guide others, not to do itself what they can and should do themselves. The restriction is treated in more detail in Part IV, in the chapter on the subject of criticisms and how we answered our critics. Another deterrent that comes particularly to mind in this context, one not contained in the compact at all, is the pride and ambition of those others referred to in Section 1.3-6 who are competent to undertake a water project that, lacking their action, would fall to the commission's lot. It is inconceivable to me that any administrator— other than perhaps a coasting political hack or other incompetent— would willingly allow the commission to move physically into his field of statutory responsibility and prerogative. That is totally alien to the thinking and attitudes of all state, federal, and local agency administrators I have encountered in long years of rubbing elbows with them, even being one of their number for a time. A third, which should not be tossed aside lightly, is the probable reluctance of the legislatures of the signatory parties to appropriate funds for commission action in a field previously allotted by statute to an existing state or federal agency. It is true, as critics have held, that the commission could issue bonds to get money for construction and operation of a project, provided the project was of such a nature that it would be reasonably sure to return enough revenue to retire the bonds with interest. Giving traditional projects of this sort a probability value in the Susquehanna basin today is difficult. Hydroelectric sites of consequence have long since been pre-empted by the investor-owned utilities, and few other types of revenue-producing water projects that would seem attractive to the commission or to bond buyers come to mind.

But it is time to return to the subject of water supply, from which I deviated in order to emphasize that the commission will be operating under powerful restraints and limitations despite the undenied authority it does possess for specific purposes.

Section 4.2 (a) grants the commission the right to "acquire, construct, operate, and control" projects and facilities for increasing low-water flows in the streams of the basin, but I am confident the emphasis here rests in the word "control" rather than "acquire," "construct," and "operate." Flow augmentation is a statutory function of Corps of Engineers impoundments, and in fact has been written into the plans for the federal Raystown Reservoir in the Juniata subbasin, Huntingdon County, Pennsylvania, where construction contracts were let late in 1968, and in certain other proposed reservoirs. Flow augmentation to improve downstream quality, likely to be wanted in a drought, may be nonreimbursable under federal law, which means costs come from the generality of the taxpayer without specific sharing by downstream beneficiaries. If the commission should seek to construct and operate in its own name a flow augmenting structure it would have to do so with funds appropriated by one or more of the signatories or through the sale of bonds. It could not sell bonds without a repayment schedule for principal plus interest, and it is unrealistic to believe prospective beneficiaries would willingly pay the commission for augmented flow if they could get it through the Corps without special taxation or assessment. On this reasoning it appears safe to assert that flow augmentation action by the commission would most likely be collaboration with the federal agency to assure water releases to alleviate drought conditions when and where the need appeared greatest, rather than a costly and elaborate undertaking of its own.[27]

It is easy to second-guess someone else's effort. This applies to compact drafters as much as to "Monday morning quarterbacks" in football or to the drama critic of a metropolitan newspaper. At every step of our way we were judging whether we could improve on what the writers of the Delaware Compact had produced, just as those who later began drafting the Potomac River Basin Compact attempted to do better than both their predecessors. The Potomac Compact writers dared to go further in substantive changes than we did, for various reasons. We had what may almost be called an obsession about deviating substantively, largely because we were so committed to the opinion that legislators and others of influence would closely compare our compact with the Delaware when lawmaking time came. I am of the opinion now that we were unduly concerned about this, at least with respect to the state lawmakers. Regardless of whether that opinion is valid, it is true we wanted to keep the substance of the Delaware Compact's water quality article in our draft but were unhappy with the Delaware's arrangement of words. As a result, we neither added to nor subtracted from commission powers to any appreciable extent, but we did substantially alter the order of the article's contents, as a comparison reading of the Delaware and Susquehanna Articles 5 will disclose. We bowed deferentially toward states' rights in our Section of 5.2 (b), and deleted a Delaware passage requiring the evocation of police powers through state agencies,[28] but made no other important change. We stated vigorously that our commission would (a) build and operate waste treatment plants if effectuating the provisions of the compact made it necessary to do so;[29] (b) encourage state and local people to act constructively so as not to force the commission into a treatment program;[30] (c) recommend water quality standards to the signatories and suggest uniform enforcement programs and

The Susquehanna at flood stage, March, 1964. And this wasn't even a big one! *Allied Pix Service, Inc.*

policies where these appeared desirable;[31] and, (d) assume jurisdiction itself if cajoling and recommending failed to result in needed quality improvement.[32] Further, if all else proved fruitless, the commission could institute a court action in its own name to compel compliance.

In drafting Article 6, on flood protection, we veered sharply from our rule against substantial deviation from Delaware language; flood plain use and occupancy caused us to do so. The Delaware law is toothless in the matter of preventing unwise utilization of flood plains, as it can

High waters at Harrisburg. The municipal stadium, other recreational facilities, and the city's auxiliary waterworks, as well as a huge parking lot, are on City Island. *Allied Pix Service, Inc.*

delineate and is authorized to identify areas subject to inundation, but it cannot compel compliance with orders as to their use. Our drafting task force determined to try for more for the Susquehanna.

Initially we borrowed the Delaware Compact's all-inclusive Section 6.1, granting our commission permission to build flood-retarding structures, but we then dropped the subject of flood damage reduction through structural measures and concentrated on flood plain control. We believed it was better to keep man's door away from high water than to try to keep high water away from man's door. The record shows we

Flood plain use planning by staff of the Broome County Planning Commission, Binghamton. The Chenango, to which the man in the photo is pointing, joins the Susquehanna in downtown Binghamton. *Ted Jones, Stuart Finley Films*

discussed one or more aspects of the subject in seven of the first twelve months of compact drafting. When we were ready to submit a draft to the IAC we had prescribed that (1) the commission could describe flood-prone areas and write standards of use for those areas—which was a repetition of Delaware provisions;[33] and (2) in consideration of the effects of specific flood plain uses "on the health and safety of persons and property," it could *"regulate the use of particular flood plains in the manner and degree it finds necessary"*[34] (emphasis added). The task force draft exempted existing structures from requirements of removal or demolition without "just compensation,"[35] confident that time and normal wear and tear would take care of them over the long term, and carefully noted that flood plain regulation was clearly within the police powers of the compact parties, hence restrictive control might not be deemed a taking of land for which the owners should be paid.[36]

We thought then—and I'm sure the task force still does—that the drafting had been well done, but it appeared that we had gone further than the parent committee believed politically prudent. Zoning, which is what the draft amounted to, had long been in local hands. All members were fully aware of the potency of local government in legislative matters. County committeemen and other locally influential politicians figure largely in election of state lawmakers. Our legislative members were sensitive to this fact of their political lives, and our executive branch members and alternates were just as keenly cognizant of all the implications. In addition, certain members of the IAC were charged by law with seeking to improve the economies of their states, and one of the major ways they tried to do this was to bring in more commerce and industry. Stream bottomlands often are considered desirable for such establishments; among other reasons they are near water if it is needed for processing or cooling, and cost and construction factors may be more favorable there than elsewhere from the viewpoint of the management of a corporation. I'm sure these, and doubtless other aspects of the matter, were racing through the minds of the committeemen as our draft was put before them. They didn't speak as bluntly as I have written, but didn't have to; each knew what the others were thinking. One member spoke the convictions of several others, I'm sure, when he said that if the controls weren't softened he'd be forced to oppose the compact when he got back home.[37] He said he wasn't arguing whether it was right or wrong but knew "local determination of land use is a sacred cow"; to grant full zoning authority to the commission would surely result in the consolidated opposition of all local government units and the associations that lobby in their behalf.

In a short time the task force members realized the alternatives were a strategic retreat or disaster. At one point in the discussion the provision of a gubernatorial or state veto had been suggested, and the state veto supporters prevailed. As finally approved, the key sentence read that the commission could regulate flood plain use, "but only with the consent of the affected state."[38] Further, the same subsection declared the commission should "suspend such regulation when and so long as the signatory party or parties or political subdivision possessing jurisdiction have in

There are societies in several states dedicated to the preservation of the few remaining covered bridges. They or someone failed to prevent this one from being desecrated by the Great American Litterbug, sometimes known as *Homo Swinus Americanus*. *Ted Jones, Stuart Finley Films*

force applicable laws which the commission finds give adequate protection." Everyone concerned recognized how much the article was being weakened by the change but saw it as an "or else" situation; the weaker language could be accepted or the expectation should be that the entire compact would die.

A few more provisions—taken from Delaware—were added, such as permission to acquire flood plain property so as to raze a structure or otherwise reduce or eliminate a flood hazard, the inclusion of a provision that the signatories would cooperate in flood plain use control, and agreement that the signatories and their subdivisions could, if they wished, exercise more stringent control than the compact provided. Then, at the very end of the article, we tacked on an antilitterbug section that seemed to fit there as well as anywhere else in the agreement.[39]

I indicated earlier that Article 7, on watershed management, was more a matter of coaxing than ordering anyone about or of the commission doing things of its own accord. Neither it nor Article 8, on recreation, gave the task force or the IAC any problems. Each would let the commission take affirmative action, but each also reiterated the all-inclusive strictures of Section 1.3-6 by specifying that action could be taken by the commission only if "no other suitable unit or agency of government" was available or in position to act.[40] The principal intent of Article 7 is to promote and encourage soil conservation and sound forest land management because of the beneficial effect they would have on water resources. Somewhat strangely, to my thinking, "projects and facilities for the maintenance and improvement of fish and wildlife habitat related to the resources of the basin" are included in this article on watershed management.[41] I would be inclined to put fish and wildlife with water-based recreation, in Article 8, since in the Susquehanna basin these resources are so closely related to outdoor recreation aspects of modern living.

The Susquehanna Compact's Article 9 relates to another area of control in which the task force took a beating, in that the Interstate Advisory Committee struck down the passages that would have put the commission deeper than it felt we should go in the battle then raging nationwide over the preservation and enhancement of natural beauty. Zimmermann drafted the article, and disclosed his own uncertainty as to the kind of reception it might receive by titling it "Other Public Values." His original draft, approved by the task force, would have given the commission several powers of consequence. It could (1) consult with the signatory parties to assure that their water projects would be compatible with "values inherent in the historic and the scenic and other natural amenities of the . . . basin for the enjoyment and enrichment of future generations"; (2) set up a basinwide "conservancy fund" to receive land, water, and other things of value with which to acquire and safeguard scenic, historic, and other cultural values endangered by water projects; (3) acquire or control property "to achieve the preservation through limitation of future use of open spaces, historic sites, and open areas for public use and enjoyment"; and (4) through acquisition and dedication, set aside water-related land areas for park purposes.

The task force debated the article draft chiefly with respect to the reception the parent committee might give it. There were misgivings, since it was then novel if not downright radical to propose that a river basin commission should go so deeply into the natural beauty or amenities business. We were doubtful of the attitude to be expected of the IAC, and still more so of that of the legislators who might be asked to enact it into law. Remember, this occurred many months before the administration in Washington sought to popularize the natural beauty preservation concept through the May, 1965, White House Conference and other activities. Our doubts were justified. The IAC weakened the article to the point of emasculation. These were its chief points:

1. We could be accused of intruding into territory traditionally occupied by museum and historical commissions.

2. We were violating our professed intent to steer commission jurisdiction away from "related land."[42]

3. The commission would be required to hire and maintain a specialized staff to administer the activity properly and operating costs could be expected to rise, particularly so if dollar grants or donations didn't materialize.

The task force and the IAC debated "Other Public Values" long and earnestly, but the latter approved only a fragment of Zimmermann's original draft. This was the passage providing that the "compatibility" of water projects with the amenities must be "considered" by the signatory parties, their agencies and subdivisions, and the commission.[43] Beyond this the article provides that the commission may recommend desired action—or inaction, for that matter—to applicable units of government in the form of suggested minimum standards "and such other protective measures" as the commission may deem desirable.[44] It may also suggest model ordinances to the legislative bodies of local units of government with the intention of providing some measure of protection to natural beauty or other culturally valuable areas.[45]

The most significant aspect of "Other Public Values"—regardless of its emasculation—was that the inclusion of the article at all put the compacting parties on record as recognizing that there is value in such things as natural beauty. Section 9.1 asserts that the contracting parties "agree that it is a purpose of this compact . . . to preserve and promote" these values. The task force was disappointed that the whole package did not survive, but we consoled ourselves that the battle did not end in total defeat. When the Champlain and Potomac basin compacts were written, each had much stronger language relating to the preservation and enhancement of natural beauty. (Zimmermann had had an effective hand in drafting both these compacts.) We were solaced by remembering that in our time and way we were moving at least one significant step in what we considered the right direction, that we were planting the thought in law that in river basin management and conservation "other public values" were not entirely worthless. We knew well that we were walking in the footsteps of many others who had long and often effectively worked on one or another aspect of the subject, at local, state, and national levels of action. Our arena was an eastern interstate river basin, and our tool a document intended to become law.

It is probable that when the Delaware Compact was drafted its article giving its commission the right to build and operate plants to produce hydroelectric power and energy[46] was included with some foreboding. Public utilities could be expected to fight the creation of another potential public power producing and distributing bureaucracy, and their lobbies were influential. These fears proved unfounded, so we breezed through the corresponding Article 10 of our compact, changing nothing but the section numbers and the name of the river basin involved. In brief, the article would let the waters of the basin be impounded and used for power purposes "by or under the authority of the commission."[47] The commission could if necessary transmit the power and energy produced at its facilities or facilities authorized by it,[48] and execute development contracts.[49] For whatever it may do under the permissive clauses of the article, the commission may charge fees for power produced that are "reasonable, nondiscriminatory, and just."[50] The only question raised when the Delaware compact was moving smoothly through the congressional process in 1961 was whether public power bodies, such as REA co-ops and municipal authorities, should have preferential treatment.[51] When our compact was made public in draft form one of the largest of the investor-owned utilities operating in our basin, the Pennsylvania Power and Light Company, issued a special "position paper" to its employes, stockholders, the members of the General Assembly, and others approving the Susquehanna compact. The network of utilities serving the basin and adjacent regions had formed a "steering committee" to study such matters as our compact and other things with a governmental flavor. I was informally told that our compact had received close scrutiny and the group would not oppose its passage, nor did it. At one time during the last half of 1966, when our first printed draft was being looked over by everyone interested, a few suggestions for relatively minor revision were received from a Maryland-based utility; these were reviewed by the IAC, but no action was taken for their inclusion.

As a matter of practicality, the utilities really had little to fear in the way of power producing competition from a water resources commission in the Susquehanna River Basin. As noted earlier in this chapter, the basin's conventional hydropower possibilities had been thoroughly explored and exploited long years before our compact became a gleam in Zimmermann's eye.[52] In more recent years the Corps believed it could justify the addition of power generating facilities to its Raystown Reservoir project in Juniata subbasin, previously referred to. Likewise, the Corps had at one time thought power would make feasible a high dam on the main line of the river above Pittston at the very edge of the anthracite coal region; and wouldn't that have been an interesting thing to watch from the viewpoint of a very sick King Coal! (This does seem ironic, but in fact an official of one of the larger mining companies told me in private conversation that the dam, if built, might provide "cheap electricity to pump our pits dry enough to work.") Neither of the two proposals gained acceptance. A few more pumped storage sites may be located in the basin—two have been found and one of them is in operation[53]—but the utilities may be expected to seize upon any locations that are considered economically feasible long before the commission should one day decide it was a good idea to get into the business itself.

References to standards, the peg upon which orders and instructions must hang in so many respects, are scattered here and there in the compact or are implied or inherent in the language employed. One vital passage, Section 3.4-2, referred to earlier in this chapter, permits the commission to set standards of planning, design, and operation of water projects. Another, Section 3.5-1, orders the commission to "adopt, promote, and coordinate policies and standards for water resources conservation, control, utilization, and management." Between the two—the permissive 3.4-2 and the mandatory 3.5-1—they cover most of the water front.

Doubtless the standards that already have been set or that may be formulated in years ahead by responsible federal and state water agencies will be so high that no additional requirements by the commission may be called for. However, the authority is there to be exercised by the commission in the event standards set by some agency of government, or by private enterprise, do not provide the margin of safety or the excellence required in any particular situation. Of course, the commission would have to defend against attack any standards it sets; they dare not be capricious or arbitrary, and must be backed by sound reasons and reasoning.

In addition to the above references to standards, others found in the compact are:

1. Section 5.2 (c) instructs the commission to recommend water quality standards, and under 5.2 (d) the commission shall encourage cooperation and uniform enforcement programs and policies by the signatories to the end that standards established in the comprehensive plan shall be met. Note that this implies that standards shall be set in the formulation of the comprehensive plan, even though the word "standards" as such is not found in the section—14.1—that gives instructions as to how comprehensive planning shall be done.

2. Section 6.2 (a), also mentioned earlier, permits the commission to set standards to be met in the use and occupancy of flood plains, though the setting of the standards may be meaningless in specific instances if an affected state exercises its veto.

3. In Sections 8.3-1, pertaining to recreation and 9.3, relating to natural beauty and other cultural values, the standard setting specified in the compact is recommendatory only.

4. Permission to set standards is implied in Section 11.5, which refers to the granting, modifying, or denying of permits to deplete basin streams at a time when "protected" status has been ordered in the wake of a limited drought.

5. Additional far-reaching authority is granted in Section 12.4, the first sentence of which reads: "The commission shall establish uniform standards and procedures for the evaluation, determination of benefits, and cost allocations of projects affecting the basin, and for the determination of project priorities, pursuant to the requirements of the comprehensive plan and its water resources program."

Here the drafting task force and the parent IAC were swayed by the long standing "economic efficiency" policy of the Corps of Engineers, more commonly known as the benefit/cost ratio, for judging the feasibility of a water project. As we were drafting our compact the "regional development" philosophy, which evolved in the program for improving the economy of that loosely defined area known as Appalachia, was just being born; this philosophy dictated that projects be recommended for authorization even when the benefit/cost ratio was negative, if there was a good chance the economy of the affected region would be sustantially improved. And it was only after the Susquehanna Compact had been passed by the three basin state legislatures that federal thinking moved tentatively in the direction of recommending projects that would improve "environmental quality" regardless of the benefit/cost ratio.

In the unlikely event that I should take part in drafting another river basin compact similar to that for the Susquehanna I'd lean toward approaching this matter of powers granted and withheld somewhat differently. In hindsight it seems to me it might be appropriate to say something in the preamble, or certainly not further along than the first article, regarding the kinds of powers in the document, and to assert plainly then and there that limitation on power would be spelled out clearly and in needed detail. Perhaps an alternative would be a descriptive section on the varieties of power granted. I'd look into the desirability of grouping all regulatory powers in one article under a master title, and of grouping under another title the various kinds of authority given the commission to enter into physical acts affecting water resources. Most if not all the rest of the passages could be lumped in a catch-all third segment, title, or part. Clearly labeled compartments containing the major subdivisions of a river basin compact would seem to me to make it easier for the layman—and the legislator, who often is a layman who happened to run for office and get elected—to understand the contents. It is tempting to toy with the thought of one day rewriting the Susquehanna Compact along the suggested lines, purely as an academic exercise, but right now the rest of this narrative must be completed.

Chapter 4

The Comprehensive Plan

The contents of a number of other articles of the compact remain to be described, including that on Susquehanna commission composition and voting, but they must wait. The comprehensive plan for the basin has been mentioned in preceding chapters but up to now its scope and significance have not been sufficiently emphasized. The comprehensive plan is intimately related to the regulatory and the physical or self-initiating action powers given to the commission. Indeed, it was the need for coordinated planning and programming on a basinwide scale that led to the evolution of the Delaware Compact, of which that for the Susquehanna is a lineal descendant.

As one of our task force once put it, planning is a continuing process and responsibility, whereas the comprehensive plan is something specific adopted or promulgated which then must be conformed to or followed as a guide, even by the commission itself when or if it may possibly become the constructor or operator of a water project. It includes not only physical things but also objectives to be met that cannot always be defined as projects, for example, water quality or flood plain use stand-ards. The central feature of the Susquehanna commission's work under the compact is to be the initial formulation and the continuous updat-ing of the comprehensive plan for the basin's water resources. "Compre-hensive multiple purpose planning," says subparagraph 1 of the com-pact's preamble, is expected to bring "the greatest benefits and produce the most efficient service in the public interest." Thereafter comprehen-sive planning and the comprehensive plan are referred to frequently by name in the compact and are elsewhere invoked by implication or in the context of a power, duty, or function.

With so many references to the comprehensive plan in the body of the compact the term would seem to call for a paragraph in the section devoted to definitions.[1] The Delaware Compact contains what amounts to a definition in the section that orders its commission to formulate and adopt a comprehensive plan.[2] It does so by specifying what the plan should include, which is declared to be "all public and private projects and facilities which are required, in the judgment of the commission, for the optimum planning, development, conservation, utilization, management, and control of the water resources of the basin to meet present and future needs." Our task force debated whether this was sufficient for our Susquehanna purposes and saw no reason to make changes or to put it up front in the definitions section. We considered the language flexible enough to embrace aspects of water resources management, use, control, and conservation that did not in themselves involve either projects or facilities as defined.

While the language of our comprehensive plan section,[3] almost a duplicate of the Delaware passage, tells what aspects of water resources management, control, and so on are to be included in the plan, it says nothing about the form the plan is to take. There is no particular reason why it should—indeed, its inclusion could constitute excessive and unduly binding statutory detail—but its absence has caused confusion and misunderstanding, as is described further in Part IV, in the chapters on legislative action by Pennsylvania. By its nature the plan is not and cannot be a static or one-time thing. It does not fit neatly in a pretty blue binder or between hard covers and then go on a seldom consulted reference shelf. It may be likened to a jigsaw puzzle, some of whose pieces may be deemed already in position, a puzzle whose limits extend to the basin's boundary, and even these can be stretched under special conditions for limited purposes.[4] Also, the shapes and purposes of individual pieces of the whole can be altered from time to time as need arises or as greater efficiency, utility, or conformance to societal requirements can be demonstrated.

The parts already in place are certain types of water projects completed or under construction at the time of enactment of the compact. They include federal and state projects of all descriptions as well as others of various kinds under diverse sponsorship that fit into comprehensive plan categories delineated in the agreement. In these instances the commission will have little choice. It will be faced with accomplished facts. The projects exist, and won't go away. It does not matter that they might be planned and executed better if done over. They are there and they meet comprehensive plan specifications; they fit into one of the four categories outlined in Section 3.10-2, or qualify for inclusion under other compact language. The agreement is not and cannot be retroactive. The commission cannot decree that existing projects be started anew. It is in the realm of significant water projects of the future that the commission can exercise discretionary power, can relate this water activity to that, and in its regulatory role or in its own behalf coordinate, guide, lead, or do, as the case may be or as need dictates. It is in this field that the promise envisioned in the concept of comprehensive planning, for the future of a basin that has been in civilized hands for more than three centuries, is expected to be kept.

In the end the comprehensive plan becomes a collection of open file folders of approved projects and activities that meet commission-formulated standards or criteria, rather than a single closed report or other document. Even the word "comprehensive" will be misleading and inaccurate for a considerable period after the actual start of commission activities. The commission will have submitted to it a "laundry list" of projects completed or under construction by federal and state agencies. Projects that have been completed or started under private auspices and that qualify for inclusion will be added. So will municipally sponsored projects. It is probable that these, or a comparable compilation, will become the nucleus of the Susquehanna comprehensive plan. To them will be added each new project properly brought before the commission and approved by it. As the commission from time to time comes to determinations regarding standards to be met and criteria to be followed—in water quality and in flood plain occupancy and use for the most part—these, too, become part of the comprehensive plan.

Over the years a number of water projects has been authorized by Congress for federal construction, but money has not yet been appropriated for final planning, designing, and construction. These do not appear to fall into the category of projects that will require commission approval. Section 12.1-2 reads, "No expenditure or commitment shall be made for or on account of the construction, acquisition, or operation of any project or facility nor shall it be deemed authorized, unless it shall have first been included by the commission in the comprehensive plan." However, since the compact is not retroactive, those federal projects previously authorized seemingly would fall outside the commission's review-and-approve prerogatives. The commission nevertheless would seem to have the power to rule on the adequacy of the standards of planning, design, and operation followed, as set forth in Section 3.4-2.

Questions have been asked at times by interested individuals as to whether the inclusion of federal projects will be automatic, a rubber stamp operation. This will, of course, be a matter for decision by the commission and I certainly am not in position to speak for it, but am quite confident the drafting task force and the IAC proceeded on the assumption that federal projects, as much so as any other, would have to conform to the commission's concept of need and desirability, and meet its standards, in order to be approved for inclusion in the comprehensive plan. As I see it, this means the commission would be in position to return a federal proposal to its sponsors with a request that it be amended, modified, or altered to fit the commission's view of what is best for the basin and its people; indeed the presumption seemingly must be that the commission has the power to send a federal proposal back stamped "disapproved," and to make the ruling stick if its facts are straight as they should be, and if specific federal reservations are not adversely involved.

After the initial input of *faits accompli* the commission can expect a more or less steady monthly budget of action proposals to come before it for consideration. They will consist of:

1. Federal agency projects, in conformance to Section 12.1-2;

2. State agency projects, which Section 12.2-2 says may not be started prior to inclusion in the comprehensive plan; and

3. Projects sponsored by municipalities or other lesser governmental units, and by private enterprise, that qualify for comprehensive plan status under one or more paragraphs of Section 3.10-2. This, of course, includes all requests for permission to divert water.

To these will be added lists of orders by state and federal regulatory agencies to municipalities, industries, and others relative to water use and treatment, all of which the commission must weigh and evaluate in terms of compact provisions. Out of all these types of things—even more —the comprehensive plan will evolve and grow more inclusive with the passage of time.

Finally, the commission will put into the plan its determinations on such subjects as the occupancy and use of specified flood plain areas, water quality standards to be achieved in named stream reaches, and whatever other water-related matters are appropriate under the compact.

There is little reason to fear the commission will lack advice in the process of formulating the plan. The compact declares in Section 14.1

that "before the adoption of the plan or any other part or revision thereof the commission shall consult with water users and interested public bodies and public utilities and shall consider and give due regard to the findings and recommendations of the various agencies of the signatory parties, their political subdivisions, and interested groups." Presumably much of the advice given the commission will be at public hearings to be held prior to the adoption of the initial plan and "any part or revision thereof"—except insignificant additions—but it also is likely that there will be frequent communication of other kinds between the commission and the many agencies and private entities it must deal with. The "interested groups" was a Susquehanna addition to the list of official consultants that we borrowed from the Delaware Compact; we saw no reason that they shouldn't be included in a blanket category.[5]

From this era forward most of the large water impounding projects to be put in the Susquehanna comprehensive plan are likely to be of federal origin or sponsorship. The electric utilities acquired and used the best downriver sites for hydroelectric plants years ago.[6] The sites most feasible under the federal benefit/cost formula for sizable flood damage reduction and other statute-approved categories of projects had been sought out by the Corps of Engineers in prior years and construction had been completed or initiated on a number of them before the compact was enacted.[7] Over the long pull it seems probable that the contents of the filing cabinets containing the comprehensive plan will be swelled more by the accretion of smaller projects and activities having a cumulative effect than by single projects of massive proportions. Moreover, many of the smaller types—that is, less costly when considered separately—may be expected to relate to water quality management. I say this because waste water treatment today, other than in the most exceptional instance, leaves a substantial volume or percentage of pollutants in the effluent. At some point in time, a point whose date I won't attempt to guess, the degree of treatment provided by even the most remote of basin villages will have to be judged by the cumulative effect of its effluent joined with that of other communities, which is highly technical—and controversial.

Water diversion is the likeliest competitor of water quality for long-term effect on the nature and content of the comprehensive plan. The Corps of Engineers in a study being carried out in the states from Maine to Virginia under Title 1 of the Rivers and Harbors Act of 1965,[8] had already identified a number of water-short subregions by late 1967.[9]

These lay mostly northeastward of the midsection of the Susquehanna basin, extending as far as Boston. This must be added to what has already been written on the subject of diversion in Part I, Chapter 3, as bolstering the likelihood of requests, if not demands, of the Megalopolitan East for Susquehanna water. Some of the water-short areas are growing faster than the basin. Some may find it feasible to meet genuine needs for additional water from New England surface sources—the Lake Champlain basin and Maine come to mind—but for others an inter-basin network of structural works and suitable pumping stations may lead them directly or via more or less elaborate interchanges to the Susquehanna. It is true that pumps can be reversible and might be installed in such a network so water could be pumped into the Susquehanna as well as out of it. However, except in a few tributary reaches and in areas where coal mine and other pollution have rendered existing supplies unusable, the Susquehanna in general is not presently water-short. Certainly no portion of the main stem nor of major tributaries is now being overdrawn. If or when diversion is allowed the pumps probably will send water out, not bring it in, and before the first pump is authorized we can expect plenty of fur to fly. I believe the most bitterly debated question, the most critically examined proposition, to come before the Susquehanna commission will come not in regard to water quality but when that first request is made for water to be exported to some other basin.

Water quality problems are here now, have been for years, and facing up to them, with varying measures of success, is already a familiar, and ever-present thing to everyone concerned. Meeting increasingly serious quality situations is largely a matter of hardening attitudes and intensifying actions that are well known to officialdom and those of the public who care. On the other hand, diversion will be something relatively new in most of this area even though it has become commonplace and accepted in the adjoining Delaware basin to the east.[10] It seems probable from geographic and water quality reasons that the area most likely to be eyed covetously first in the Susquehanna basin is that lying upstream from Binghamton. Here the water quality is comparatively high, and the distances that would have to be traversed by pipelines are fairly short. It is conceivable that Greater New York, northern New Jersey, and metropolitan Philadelphia may one day be joined in a race to see which can put its case for diversion first and strongest before the Susquehanna commission. Signs pointing to the coming demands have been clear and legible for years. In 1957 David C. Coyle[11] wrote the following:

> Twenty years from now, with another 50 million people in the country and fewer of them living in houses without plumbing, we can expect a real strain on the household water supplies in the eastern part of the U. S. as well as in the West. After that, if the population goes on growing, lack of water can be expected to be more and more the factor that limits where people can live.

Irving K. Fox has asserted that today ". . . scientific advance and technology permit us to manipulate demand as well as supply. If we do the job we are capable of doing, in the future river basin planning will be as much concerned with minimizing the amount of water used as with increasing the supply of water for use.[12]

The quoted statments are both pertinent to the prospect of requests for water to be diverted from the Susquehanna. So is a statement I presented in Wilkes-Barre, Pennsylvania, on April 13, 1967, at a public hearing relative to the water supply study referred to earlier in this chapter, conducted by the New York Division Engineer, Corps of Engineers. The gist of it was that the foreseeable needs of each basin in the study area, which includes the Susquehanna, must be cared for first, before consideration is given to the exporting of any of its water to another basin.[13]

It seems inconceivable that the commission will fail to consider Fox's premise that demand can be manipulated as well as supply, and to insist that this be done before coming to the Susquehanna with hand and pipeline extended, requesting that diversion be permitted and made a part of the comprehensive plan. Regardless of whether that is done, I am quite confident that the basin states will seek guarantees that their legitimate requirements are first met before any diversion is approved.

For this record it should be noted that both New York and Pennsylvania members went along willingly when Maryland asked that the comprehensive plan should "take into consideration the effect of the plan or any part thereof on the receiving waters of Chesapeake Bay."[14] They knew the insistence was pointed fully as much toward questions of diversion as toward matters of water quality. They likewise approved without quibble or argument a compact provision drafted by the Maryland delegation to allow a signatory party to appeal directly to the U. S. Supreme Court any commission-approved diversion that would reduce "below a proper minimum" the flow of water from an upstream neighbor or neighbors.[15]

As it happens, the compact does not define "a proper minimum." This is one of the queazy terms we found so hard to avoid in writing a statute as lengthy and as complex as the Susquehanna compact. But defined it doubtless will be, either by agreement between contending parties or by the courts, and when decision is reached—for an interim period or a longer term—the outcome will become part of the comprehensive plan. I suspect it will be termed a landmark ruling.

Chapter 5

And So to the End

At an early stage in the writing of the Susquehanna Compact I was asked to draft certain passages for consideration by the task force and let myself go, rhetorically speaking. Convinced the job had been done well, I began reading at the next meeting; and all my "fine writing" was methodically knocked to bits, phrase by phrase. Wendell put things in perspective, as teacher to student:

"In preparing this sort of material," he said, "whatever is written in extremely dull language gets you an 'A.' If it is only ordinarily dull you rate a 'B.' Anything prettier than that and you flunk. We are drafting the bare bones of a statute, not making a speech to a jury."

In some respects this, then, will be an "A" or "B" chapter, quite dull, for it deals in large part with what may be termed the nuts and bolts intended to hold our river basin mechanism together and help it work. It contains information on routine housekeeping articles, sections that guide administrative and financing activities. Passages on these subjects must be in any compact or other legislation that has administrative connotations or concerns the handling of public funds. Most of this language is relatively standard, and we borrowed freely from the Delaware Compact.

In other respects this chapter has to do with matters of critical importance, such as the composition of the commission and the voting rules.

Our preamble differs from the Delaware's chiefly in that, as we wrote it, it becomes an integral part of the compact instead of a preliminary listing of conditions and existing water management realities. Ours was viewed as a sort of declaration of legislative intent, especially our numbered paragraphs 1 and 2.

Our definitions were not out of the ordinary except in one respect. We differentiated between water withdrawals and water diversion; the first was a taking or removal of water from any source within the basin for use therein, whereas the second was defined as "the transfer of water into or from the basin."[1] What has been said earlier regarding the keen scrutiny likely to be given to requests for the exportation of water from the Susquehanna to Megalopolis, or elsewhere, caused us to make this differentation between diversions and withdrawals.

In the first article we wanted it clearly asserted that the foundation of our federal–interstate agreement would be comprehensive planning and a programming of action under the comprehensive plan, and that the commission created would be a directing agency instead of merely a recommendatory coordinating instrumentality. We therefore repeated some of the declarations in the preamble, saying that ". . . increasing economies and efficiencies in the use and reuse of water resources . . . can be brought about only by comprehensive planning, programming, and management under the direction of a single agency." We stated unequivocally that the basin's water resources were "functionally interrelated" and their uses were "interdependent." These passages recognize inseparability of the various uses to which man puts water resources, the inevitable conflicts between users over uses, and the fact that there will be times when a need for choosing between or rationing will arise.[2] The question of why we repeated preamble passages is valid. We did so for two reasons. The terminology in both places is markedly similar to the Delaware, in which it was necessary to repeat because its preamble was not incorporated in the body of the compact. We could therefore have omitted it without taking away from our agreement, but as discussed elsewhere we were fearful of departing substantively from Delaware language without obvious reason; this came up repeatedly in our drafting sessions. Omission of the passage likely could have been explained without too much difficulty, but the repetition did put emphasis on a very important aspect of the entire endeavor. The subsections referred to, taken in context with Section 1.3-5, on general purposes, went to the heart of the reasons and reasoning behind the enterprise.

Late in the drafting—when we were revising the first printed draft, after it had been exhaustively reviewed and commented upon in each of the three basin states—we became convinced that this section should contain a disclaimer that would serve both as a guide to the commission and as reassurance to persons fearful that a superagency in the project construction field was being created. The disclaimer—Section 1.3-6—

stated simply that the commission would build and operate a water project itself only if it was essential to the comprehensive plan and there was no other competent agency ready and willing to undertake it.

Article 1, far toward the front of the document, was of course the appropriate place to state the constitutionally obvious fact that Congress has the power to withdraw the United States as a signatory party any time it chooses to do so. This declaration became Section 1.4, which also noted that Congress reserved to itself its powers and prerogatives relating to navigable waters and to interstate and foreign commerce. We subscribed to the view that while other needed federal reservations could be put in enabling sections, these should be forthrightly stated and made a part of the body of the compact.

We considered it possible that the commission might in time accumulate assets jointly owned by the contracting parties, and a question could thereafter arise as to their disposition in the event the compact should be terminated. Consequently, in the same section that declared the compact should last at least a hundred years—Section 1.5—we added a paragraph setting forth a formula for prorating assets in the event of dissolution.

No part of the compact caused more debate, wrangling, and dispute in Pennsylvania than the portions of Article 2 setting up the composition of the commission and providing a basic rule of voting on issues not decided by common consent.[3] The drafters agreed early that this was something to be resolved by the parent committee. We wanted the Delaware formula of one signatory, one vote, but Sommerville relayed word that Chairman Goddard was not at all sure Governor Scranton and other Pennsylvania leaders would go along. We discussed the matter informally at some length but made no firm recommendations. The IAC, then, postponed determinative action until its very last meeting prior to the printing and distribution of our first draft in June, 1966. The argument that later developed in Pennsylvania arose from the accident of geography, when boundary lines, run in the early years of colonial America, put 76 percent of the basin in what became the Commonwealth. New York drew 23 percent and Maryland a bare 1 percent. Many Pennsylvanians simply could not see the situation in any way other than that the Susquehanna was mostly a Pennsylvania river and, by golly, Pennsylvania should have a dominant voice in commission deliberations and voting. They could not and would not see that water was not fixed in place, as are land and buildings, but is transient and that Pennsylvania people, broadly speaking, had no ownership in it.

They declared that since Pennsylvania had three-fourths of the basin in her borders, she should have three-fourths of the say-so about what should be done with Susquehanna's water. It did little good to point out that the United States was to be a member and, theoretically at least, could demand dominant voting rights over any basin state. Further, it would be totally unrealistic to believe the federal government would allow itself to be outvoted by any one state. However, I am getting ahead of my narrative. These sticky aspects of the matter of memberships and voting which arose later are touched upon here only to emphasize why the language of relevant sections of Article 2 had to be bucked to the parent committee from the outset.

Other than the matters of commission composition and voting, Article 2 posed no particular problems. It declared the commission a body politic and corporate, an agency and instrumentality of the governments of the signatory parties; it would be an integral part of each of the four governments and of all of them, serving all in its specialized jurisdiction. Commissioners and alternates could be compensated by the appointing government but would only be paid reasonable and necessary expenses by the commission. Each commissioner could have an adviser, if desired. The adviser might be a water resources specialist competent to assist the member, who could be a layman without prior water experience. The commission would organize itself annually by the election of a chairman and vice-chairman, and would set the rules for the conduct of its meetings. The closing section fixed the basin's boundary as the limit of commission jurisdiction, but reserved to it the right to act outside the basin if that proved necessary to implement its responsibilities within the basin. Where essential, taking action outside the basin would be subject to the consent of the affected state or states. Our compact did not spell out reasons for the last-named clause but in the comparable Delaware section it was contemplated that the commission might at some time "sell or dispose of water, hydroelectric power or other water resources within or without the basin."[4]

Many of the powers and duties of the commission detailed in Article 3 were treated in the preceding chapter. Section 3.2 declared it to be the policy of the commission to "preserve and utilize the functions, powers, and duties of the existing offices and agencies of government to the extent consistent with this compact" and directed the commission to do so. This gave added assurance to the existing agencies that there was no intention for the Susquehanna commission to move in and usurp their prerogatives or to pirate their powers and functions. It also was intended as an instruction to the commission to seek needed expertise from existing units of government instead of needlessly building a bureaucratic empire of technicians or specialists.

In Section 3.4, since we knew one legislative body cannot bind succeeding legislatures to a course of statutory action, we merely provided that each signatory would "seek" enactment of whatever new or amendatory laws were deemed necessary or desirable so its agencies might more effectively do their duty under the terms of the compact. A subsection allows any signatory to enact laws with more stringent or restrictive provisions than those found in the compact or in rules and regulations promulgated thereunder.

The more significant passages in the succeeding articles—that is, those dealing with the powers and prerogatives of the commission and the limits of its authority—have been described in a preceding chapter, up to the closing section of Article 14. It, Section 14.3, relates to the commission's current expense and capital budgets. A major decision was to retain the Delaware Compact's requirement of a unanimous vote by the commission in arriving at current expense budget figures to be presented to the signatories for appropriation. Pennsylvania's delegation welcomed it as an answer to critics of the one party, one vote clause in Article 2. Although the compact constitutes a solemn contract or covenant, the threat or possibility of a budget veto by a signatory would always be present regardless of whether it ever would be exercised. In the event this occurred the commission would be out of business for all practical purposes. No budget, no money; no money, no office, no staff, no activities of any kind. The compact would be no more than a scrap of paper even though the commission, in theory, would still exist.

Unanimity also would rule in capital budgets. In the event the commission should undertake construction of a water project in its own name, or any other capital budget item for that matter, the affected signatories would have to agree to a cost-sharing formula. The furnishing of a disproportionate segment of the total cost by any one party could not be forced upon it by the other three.

The commission would be expected to defend the budget when it was presented to the signatories for scrutiny and when it was in process of being acted upon by the appropriating authority, which is to say the legislatures. However, the defense in the vast majority of instances would be conducted in the several jurisdictions by the respective members rather than staff; the latter presumably would be called upon by the members for background information where needed but ordinarily would not appear before a signatory's budget officer or a legislative appropriations committee except possibly in an advisory capacity to the member. New York and Pennsylvania put procedural instructions regarding the budgetary process in the enabling sections of their compact legislation prior to final passage.

Article 15, part of which was touched upon in a preceding chapter, is in many respects a catchall, since its contents range widely across commission rights, prerogatives, duties, and functions. The sections that grant or withhold powers will not be gone over again here. It is in Article 15 that such miscellaneous matters as the following are covered:

1. Appointment by the commission of a chief executive officer who shall then have authority to choose other officers and employees; he shall also have the authority to dismiss.

2. Inclusion of a nondiscrimination clause in regard to employment, and provision for the immediate dismissal of any staff official who violates it.

3. Oath of office, surety bond (paid by the commission), and the usual "behave yourself; stay honest" clauses.

4. Instructions to staff on purchases, providing for sealed bids and contract letting to the lowest and best bidder except in emergencies or where only one supplier is known; purchases of items costing less than $5,000 do not require sealed bids. This figure, though twice as much as in the Delaware compact, surely will prove unrealistic in a relatively few years if present inflationary forces are not checked.

Other standard sections cover insurance (the commission may self-insure if it wishes); an annual independent audit of commission books, which must be open to inspection by appropriate officials of each party; authority to issue reports on a variety of subjects, including accounts of commission activities and operations addressed to the legislative bodies of the signatories; approval for the commission to accept grants, gifts, loans, and payments by states or their subdivisions; permission to convey real or personal property of the commission; authority to relocate public facilities at commission expense in case operations should require relocation; permission to acquire and maintain needed rights of way; provision for the commission to prosecute violators of the compact and have any fines levied deposited in its treasury; making the commission responsible for payment of claims against it arising from acts of negligence or omission by its officers or agents; saving to the signatories their laws concerning riparian rights; and specification that the compact may be amended upon the initiative of any signatory concurred in by the others.

The article closed with a section on construction and severability, preserving the remainder of the compact if any part should be held unconstitutional, and another making the compact effective "thirty days after the enactment of concurring legislation by the federal government, the states of New York and Maryland, and the Commonwealth of Pennsylvania."

When the finishing touches had been applied, the last "t" crossed and "i" dotted by Everstine, our stylist, we were ready to go to the public with what had been produced.

Part IV

Moving at State Level

Chapter 1

Going to the Public

Introducing the compact draft to the public was planned with considerable care and executed with attention to detail. Whether it is appropriate to insert a chapter on what can be termed public relations in a book of this nature may be questioned by those who will; we were convinced that our efforts would be an exercise in futility unless the compact won support from a majority of those who constituted our several publics, and so proceeded to map a course of action with that in view.

I felt competent to prepare and carry out a public information program by reason of past experience. One who has carried the title of executive director of an association or a state agency knows that public affairs will command the greater part of each working day, and he must be reasonably skilled in public relations. Competent help is, however, essential in any sizable public affairs program. Consequently, when a staff vacancy occurred in 1965 I cast about for a technical assistant with a feeling for the public pulse, some knowledge of basic political processes, and writing skill. Pete Coleman filled that part of the bill of particulars. He knew little of water resources and none of the finer points of natural resources conservation, development, use, and management or control. When he joined the staff at the beginning of 1966 his orders were to spend the next sixty to ninety days with his feet on his desk if he wished them to be there, and his nose buried in books and papers selected with an eye to giving him a cram course in water matters. My door was always open, and when any point or factor raised a question, or when he was puzzled by contradictions stemming from differences of condition, motive, opinion, or conviction, he was to pop in and I'd try to give him satisfactory answers. Coleman proved a willing student and a good questions asker; we had many an hour of solid debate, and he stimulated teacher fully as much as teacher stimulated pupil—of that I am certain. The skills he brought with him added considerably to our staff stock, and came in very handy during the almost two years he was with us. Thus as we approached the time to go to the publics who should understand and approve, there was increasingly competent staff help available.

I have used the plural advisedly in talking of going to the "publics" with our compact. We recognized several, each with its individual viewpoints and area of influence. Among them were (1) elected state officials including the legislators; (2) the heads and certain personnel of state departments, boards, and commissions with an interest in water resources; (3) planners and other officials in local government whose activities and operations could be affected; (4) the people of the news media, both press and broadcast, particularly the executives who determined what editorial position would be taken; (5) interested organizations and societies of various kinds, especially their elected leaders and those holding top staff positions; (6) several segments of official Washington; and (7) the lay or general public. These publics or audiences obviously had significant differences. Their viewpoints would be influenced by differing aspects of the total subject. They should be approached differently. And in this regard it should be remembered that we considered our mission to be not only to write our compact but to interpret its contents so as to further its enactment into law. We were more than drafters; we also were information specialists conducting a communications campaign we hoped would lead others to support that which we recommended. Each of us concerned with the success of the undertaking wore several hats, sometimes simultaneously. When other duties permitted, members and alternate members of the IAC freely discussed the compact subject in general, and of course staff did so, too. However, we had nothing specific to talk about before the spring of 1966. Until that time we had been writing, rewriting, polishing, and refining what eventually became an approximately 17,000-word piece of prospective legislation. Information taken to one or more of our audiences was an occasional news release, speech, magazine article, or interview but none of these could or did disclose draft contents prior to the public announcement date in June.

However, despite the press of drafting and related matters, time was spent in preparation for the public affairs program we knew was to come. Members of the IAC discussed the subject at some length at an informal meeting (so labeled because late conflicts prevented a quorum) on February 8, 1965. An outline of a program proposal was prepared in March[1] to be laid before the committee at an April 9 meeting. In it the IAC was asked to come to determination on the following:

First is the purpose of the program. What is its goal?

Next, what publics are to be reached and informed?

Third, is it necessary or desirable to set priorities for informing these publics? If so, what are they?

Fourth, the tools and techniques to be used must be chosen, and guidelines set for their employment.

The final step is, of course, the carrying out of the program decided upon, and what that entails.

The memo then listed the publics identified earlier as being important to our success. In the outline, state administration leaders and water-related state agencies were given high priority. "A major effort should be made to inform them and to enlist their support . . . after a compact draft has been given your [IAC] approval." Then, "the other publics indicated should be provided with a steady flow of information, . . . some of it patterned to fit their specific interests." And, "the program should be flexible as to timing, nature, and the extent of information activity, and it should have astute supervision tailored to conditions in each state and in Washington."

The outline continued,

[a] rather sharp line should be drawn to separate those who consist of elected and appointed officials from other publics named, and the techniques of informing them. In connection with the officials, there may be numerous times when a telephone call or informal visit would be more beneficial in behalf of the compact than all the motion pictures, brochures, and news releases that could be produced in a year. For informing lawmakers and administrators, films, folders, and the press and broadcast media should be considered as more or less incidental.

The proposal was favorably received by the committee, and although it was not followed in meticulous detail as our campaigning progressed —it did remain "flexible" to the end—it formed a sound base and good starting point for our subsequent course of action.

Our most ambitious 1965 public affairs undertaking had been the making of a twenty-one-minute, 16mm sound and color picture, titled *Renaissance of a River,* which was planned and filmed to portray general reasons why a compact seemed desirable, but it did not go into compact specifics. Some forty-five prints of this film were made available without charge to agencies of the basin states that maintained libraries of films for distribution to groups of various kinds, including schools.

At times in the fall and winter the public affairs program was discussed either with the full committee or with the chairman and other individual members, and in March, 1966, as the first compact draft neared completion, a formal program outline with timetable of accomplishment was prepared for the IAC.[2] It was in four parts, the first of which outlined activities of staff and members from then until the draft would be made public in June. The second described how we proposed to present the compact, which was to be done simultaneously in each state. The third phase took us from the time of public disclosure through the general election in November, 1966, but in order not to invite too close attention to the importance we attached to the outcome of the voting, the date written into this part of the proposal was November 15, which fell about a week after election day. The presentation closed with a brief and indeterminate Part IV, to be filled in after we had had time to gauge the effect the outcome of the elections might have on our chances for enactment, but by then we were too busy to do so; from that time forward we worked without a formal script.

Our first film *Renaissance,* had been well received. Several agencies requested and received additional prints to meet demand and the Pennsylvania Power and Light Company purchased two prints for its circulating library. We determined late in 1965 to have another made. We hoped it might be ready in time for premiere showings at the announcement luncheon meetings to be held in June, but delays were encountered in script preparation and that could not be done. In all, four different scripts were written and rewritten before shooting began on what we called *A Horseshoe Nail.* The title was a ploy to liken the compact to the horseshoe nail of the seventeenth-century English doggerel that Benjamin Franklin, in *Poor Richard's Almanac,* expanded to hint that the nail might have prevented the loss of a war and a kingdom. No fewer than sixty-eight prints of this eighteen-minute film were made and distributed by us to state agencies having film libraries, to the Pennsylvania parochial school film library, and to the Pennsylvania Power and Light Company. Later the Department of Housing and Urban Development asked where a print could be obtained to be put in the Lyndon B. Johnson Memorial Library. The ultimate impact of our two films cannot be measured with any degree of accuracy, nor can other of our separate efforts, of course, but we do know that a good many thousands of adults and students at elementary and intermediate levels were exposed to the messages they carried.

The announcement luncheons were to be held on June 8, 1966, in Binghamton, Harrisburg, and Baltimore, and our office was a scene of considerable to-do and stirring about. Coleman and I were hunched over our typewriters much of the time, and there was telephoning, and consulting with our printers, who came through handsomely, sometimes on quite short notice. At the announcement luncheons we would have double folders with pockets in which we would put the printed compact draft, a news release giving the gist of the compact's contents, a legalistically phrased summary of the compact's major provisions in leaflet form, a simple map of the basin, and a pamphlet entitled *For a Basin and Its People* describing the compact and how it came into existence. At the meetings we would also have in the information kits mimeographed statements to be read by the governors if they could attend, or by the ranking IAC member if the governors had conflicting engagements. The compact, the leaflet, and the pamphlet were printed for us in lots of 10,000, as we anticipated a considerable demand. (This material had an element of timelessness, and was used on into 1969. At the end of 1968 fewer than 500 copies of each remained.) We also prepared and had printed tens of thousands of copies of simple folders of information to be made available to attendees at showings of our two films. Additional material was to be printed or mimeographed by the thousands in the aggregate before the campaigning at state level would come to a close, but details of that activity come later. The compact draft, leaflet, and pamphlet were to be our chief information pieces for the time being.

We planned a series of three special preannouncement luncheon meetings for news media executives, to be held in the early part of May in the Pennsylvania portion of the basin. Two—at Lock Haven in the West Branch subbasin, and at Harrisburg—were well attended; the third, at Wilkes-Barre, must in candor be called a failure, for only two of our expected guests showed up, and we were stuck with a luncheon bill for twenty since the hotel kitchen had prepared for that many. At the others, top level people from each medium attended from strategic communities. Coleman and I presented them with a simple on-the-record mimeo of background facts, and in off-the-record discussion outlined the essential features of the compact and of our conception of how the commission to be created would operate. Questions were many and the discussions lively.

As June approached, we wrote special news releases for the daily press, for the weekly press, and for broadcast. With the release date of "AMs, June 9, 1966, and thereafter" showing at the top of the first page, these were mailed, along with a copy of the compact draft, to all the daily press and broadcast media in the three states, and to all less-often-than-daily papers in basin counties. The mimeographing was an undertaking in itself, what with the collating and stapling to be done in our limited work space. Mrs. LeVan was priceless help on that as on many other occasions, doggedly and rapidly completing each task only to find a batch of new work on her desk before the last one could be completed. We wanted as nearly all the mail as possible to go out the same day so it would arrive at least a day ahead of Announcement Date but not so far in advance that it might be mislaid or overlooked. Mrs. LeVan enlisted her husband and two of her daughters for a weekend of envelope stuffing.

Before the announcement luncheons were held there was an important bit of preliminary work to be done in Washington. The Water Resources Planning Act had become law in 1965,[3] and Henry Caulfield, Jr., had been moved from a post in the Interior Department to the executive directorship of the new federal Water Resources Council. Secretary Stewart L. Udall of Interior was the council chairman. Goddard made a date with Udall for June 6, 1966, two days ahead of our plans for public disclosure, so he and Caulfield could be briefed off-the-record ahead of announcement time. Goddard, Lawrence,[4] O'Donnell, and I went to Washington and met with Udall and Caulfield for about an hour. Udall was familiar with the Delaware Compact, was in fact the official federal member although he was represented by his alternate at all but "summit" meetings. Goddard was our spokesman and he outlined briefly the chief ways in which our compact differed from Delaware. I write from memory, for we took no notes at the meeting itself; my recollection is that Udall told us he would issue a news release as chairman of the council shortly after our announcement was made, in which he would endorse the compact in principle. When the news release was issued, however, it merely commended the IAC for having "worked hard" and said the council would "study the proposal in depth and make our recommendations."[5] I remember a slight sinking feeling when I read the news release a few days afterward, but as the four of us left the Interior Department building before noon on June 6, 1966, we were elated and hopeful of swift federal approval.

The luncheon meetings went off almost as scheduled. Vice-Chairman Lawrence presided at the Binghamton luncheon, where he read a very complimentary statement sent by Governor Rockefeller. Vice-Chairman O'Donnell was in the chair at Baltimore, where Governor Tawes came in person to present his statement approving the compact and urging public support for its enactment. Both meetings were well attended.

At Harrisburg we encountered what I have ruefully come to conclude must have been predestined obstacles. Governor Scranton sent word to Chairman Goddard that he did not believe he would be able to attend, and he wanted Goddard to read a statement for him. Then several busloads of people came to the capital from the Philadelphia area to put on a demonstration over something not related to the compact, and that happening seriously reduced attendance from the capital press corps and key members of the general assembly. Then, as Goddard was on his feet, opening his comments, an aide to Scranton raced in tripping over the extension cord connected to our tape recorder as he did so and pulling it from the wall socket, which we didn't discover until the meeting was over. He told us the governor was in the lobby and would deliver his statement in person. Goddard, of course, interrupted his speech and the governor was escorted into the room.

All would have been topnotch from our viewpoint, except that Scranton said at the outset of his statement that he "had some reservations concerning some specifics of the compact." He didn't give the newsmen present a chance to ask questions then and there, but hastened back to his executive offices; however, they didn't forget the "reservations" and were laying for him at his next news conference. What did he mean by those words? He answered that he didn't especially like to see Pennsylvania, with her overwhelming proportion of the basin's land and water area, in a position where the other three compact members could "gang up" on the Commonwealth and outvote her.

Shortly afterward, through Goddard's persuasiveness or as a result of his own second thoughts, Scranton changed his mind and in the closing months of his administration tried to make amends for his off-the-cuff fears that the other signatories might gang up on Pennsylvania. However, the damage had been done. His unfortunate phrase had made the headlines and the television screen, and beat against eardrums all across Pennsylvania from countless radios. No amount of retraction or correction could entirely kill first impressions. The words were to haunt us from the moment they were spoken until July 15, 1968, when the General Assembly at last officially made Pennsylvania a party to the compact.

In this fashion June 8, 1966, came and went. Now it was time to put into effect Part II of our public affairs program, to take our compact and our story to as many segments as possible of our group of publics, to hear comments and suggestions, to listen to criticism, to provide answers, and to look and listen warily for signs and portents as general election campaign oratory time approached and passed. As it turned out, the election returns in New York and Maryland apparently had little effect either way on the chances for passage of the compact; in Pennsylvania the overall impact, on balance, must be declared adverse. (See Part IV, Chapters 4 and 5.)

Chapter 2

Compact Critics and Friends

We had hardly begun to bounce back from the initial blow by Governor Scranton on compact voting arrangements before we faced overt and covert criticism from leaders of rural Pennsylvania, one of whom was the principal U. S. Department of Agriculture official for Susquehanna basin survey matters. They were provided an excellent—though I believe unintentional—forum for the purpose by the leadership of the survey. The occasion was the tenth meeting of the Susquehanna River Basin Study Coordinating Committee, at Wellsboro, Tioga County, Pennsylvania. These meetings were held three times annually in the earlier survey years, once in each basin state. Meeting themes were determined months in advance to give speakers preparation time, to facilitate making arrangements, and provide prospective attendees adequate notice. It was Pennsylvania's turn, and the theme related to agriculture in the basin. It was happenstance that the compact draft was made public in time to become a target. It would be interesting but academic to speculate on what might have been said and done at Wellsboro and thereafter if we had delayed our public announcement by one month.

The leadoff speaker was Ivan McKeever, administrator in Pennsylvania of the Soil Conservation Service, who had been in that position for many years and whose views were respected throughout the Commonwealth. At the beginning of the survey he was appointed chairman of the USDA's field committee, which included the Forest Service and the Economic Research Service, and his authority for survey purposes extended across state lines into the basin portions of New York and Maryland.

McKeever and I first got acquainted in 1955, when I became executive director of the Pennsylvania Fish Commission, and for the four years of that experience we had collaborated closely on a number of projects and programs, developing a warm, harmonious relationship between the two agencies. One of my first acts when joining the IAC staff was to visit McKeever. A year later we collaborated on planning and carrying out a two-day "show me" float trip for upward of forty federal and state officials, assisted by local people, in the scenic Endless Mountains segment of the Susquehanna in northern Pennsylvania. A few months afterward on another visit to McKeever's office, he was cool and distant; the reason given was that he was not being consulted in the drafting of the compact. He was told the IAC drafting rules, and that no other federal agencies were being consulted either, nor were state agencies, but he was not placated. Thereafter the phone calls were few, and there were no visits, but he was not considered unfriendly to the compact.

At Wellsboro we of the IAC attending listened in disbelief and dismay as McKeever ignored the compact in his speech and plumped enthusiastically for a strictly recommendatory and advisory commission to be set up under the 1965 federal Water Resources Planning Act.[1] He urged that a prepackaged water resources development plan emerge from the basin survey, to be adopted *in toto* by the planning commission. The speech read as though it had been cautiously framed. Only two weeks earlier he had been sent copies of the first printed draft of the compact by special messenger, and it appeared to us that courtesy would have prompted him to mention the Interstate Advisory Committee and its work, even if he disapproved of how it was accomplished and of what it consisted.

John Scott, master of the State Grange,[2] was next, and at the time he put the Grange tentatively on the opposing side. He noted that the West Branch and Juniata tributaries flowed from headwaters to the main stem entirely in Pennsylvania, and wondered whether it was necessary to set up an interstate administration to guide their progress. This questioning attitude was maintained for only a short while by the Grange, and when the legislative battle was joined in Pennsylvania Scott helped us mightily; few individuals worked harder for compact passage than Scott, but at that particular moment we couldn't know this would be the case. We feared things might turn out just the opposite.

Hard on Scott's heels came Hollis Hatfield, Farm Bureau Federation spokesman in Pennsylvania, who made his objections to the compact abundantly clear, then and later. His message was shrewdly phrased, for he was a master of the indirect stroke. He feared the compact contained "discrepancies" with "agriculture's" objectives, which he did not define. He was leary of the "all-encompassing" powers given the commission, which he hinted could encroach upon "the private enterprise sector of our economy." He asked—and left the question dangling as he did others then and in coming times—whether the commission might not even have the authority to supersede soil and water conservation districts, which was patently absurd. And, wasn't the Susquehanna a Pennsylvania river with whose governance the other basin states should have no say? Then came more myths and misrepresentations, as I construed them, including a suggestion that the one man, one vote decision of the United States Supreme Court[3] was applicable and meant Pennsylvania should dominate any commission created.

Donald Stephens, president of the Pennsylvania Association of Soil Conservation District Directors, dissented to the voting arrangement; he thought it should be proportionate to basin area. But his organization, in the footsteps of the Grange, also came to our support later when the compact was in its life-or-death stages in the Pennsylvania General Assembly. The Soil Conservation Service goes to considerable lengths to assure the public that it does not influence the districts organization, but I believe it is worth noting that the latter was silent until after McKeever retired at the end of 1967, and came to the support of the compact only after that occurred.

In four speeches that came one right after the other, we had been given what we then considered four blows. True, two were light taps and one should be called a snub, and only the fourth was forthrightly negative. It put us on notice as to what we might expect from a legislatively strong portion of organized agriculture in Pennsylvania. Nor could we know at the time that opposition from this source would reach its apex in Pennsylvania and be negligible in the other two states; we feared we might be in trouble with the farmers all over the basin. It was especially disconcerting to have McKeever advocate something other than the compact. We did not underestimate his influence. So far as I have been able to determine he did not at any time overtly condemn the compact, and IAC files do not even disclose clippings to indicate that his Wellsboro speech was distributed to the papers of the day. In his further defense, it must be said that McKeever may have avoided mention of the IAC and the compact in the belief that he could not then be said to have taken a position on it one way or the other. It appears at this point in time, long after the event, that a single innocuous paragraph to the effect that an Interstate Advisory Committee had produced a draft of a basin compact for study would have covered him in this respect, if indeed this was the purpose he had in mind. Be that as it may, he at no time publicly veered from his advocacy of a federally dominated commission whose powers would be limited to planning, and this clouded the rural picture in Pennsylvania for the duration.

Immediately after the four speeches, Goddard asked for and got the floor for an extemporaneous rebuttal, but again the initial damage had been done; the initiative had gone to the opposition and once more we were on the defensive. Nevertheless, our quick and positive reaction to the attack brought an unusual aftermath that night. Coleman was approached by the information specialist of the SCS in Pennsylvania and the technical liaison officer—which in Pentagonese means information specialist—of the office of the District Engineer in Baltimore,[4] for assistance in drafting a news release based on the afternoon's happenings. The Hatfield attack and the McKeever speech were to constitute the lead, or first, paragraph. Coleman came to my room for consultation, after which he returned to the others to say that if any of the attack material went out Goddard's rebuttal had to be given equal rank; otherwise we would get in touch with the wire services and give our own version of what occurred. Coleman obviously performed nobly for our side, for the upshot of it was that no one sent out any story that night. Since the meeting was in an off-the-beaten-path area—good deer, bear, and turkey hunting amid lots of fishable trout streams, but without sizable communities and not even one daily paper in the county—no reporter for a metropolitan daily was on hand nor was there a knowledgeable string correspondent for The Associated Press or United Press International.

The result was that the Wellsboro events did not become highly visible, for which we were grateful. That, however, was but a temporary respite. McKeever's speech seemingly died on the spot, but Hatfield distributed widely the material in his talk and from then on used it freely against the compact. When I returned to the office a memo was sent to our people to tell them what had occurred.[5] Copies of the four speeches were sent to forewarn them of possible coming events in the other two states. (As the import of the speeches became clear Coleman had gone to the table in the lobby and secured enough copies so we could send them to all IAC members and alternates and to other friends to alert them of the potential danger to the compact—and it is possible some persons present who may have wanted copies failed to find them.)

The memo also told that two weeks ahead of the Wellsboro meeting arrangements had been made for Goddard, Sommerville, Coleman, and me to meet on August 4 with top officials of the Pennsylvania Department of Agriculture and all the Wellsboro speakers except McKeever, to discuss the compact in detail. The memo added that the Wellsboro speakers "seem to have taken advantage of an opportunity to sound off prematurely, perhaps mainly for the benefit of their predominantly rural audiences."

The August 4 meeting was one of eight we held with leaders of Pennsylvania state departments and commissions, starting as early as June 15. This was one of the basics of our public affairs program. We wanted the water agencies to be informed of the compact's contents and to answer any questions they might have, to allay any fears that their statutory prerogatives would suffer unduly. In somewhat different ways our committee leaders in New York and Maryland saw to it that influential people in the water-related agencies of their states were consulted. No opposition of consequence arose in New York State. That in Maryland was more nearly concerned with the legislative action in 1967, and is discussed in a later chapter.

The Pennsylvania consultations generally went off well. Good questions were asked and answered. The State Planning Board echoed the governor's early anxiety about voting but appeared satisfied with our elucidation of how and why the one party–one vote formula had been reached. Health wondered if its prerogatives were adequately protected. That department's spokesmen would have liked to see language in the compact making it mandatory that the Susquehanna commission accept whatever the department approved or promulgated concerning water quality control and management. This would have been contrary to the concept of an interstate–federal agency with policing powers over the agencies of the signatories, and the IAC turned it down. The department also wanted the commission to have specific authority to attack the coal mine drainage problem, which would, of course, have shifted a good part of one of its most baffling responsibilities to the basinwide agency. This, too, was refused, though the IAC recognized that at some future time the commission might be asked by the signatories to undertake some effort in this direction for the good of all. Despite refusal of its requests, Health did not overtly oppose the compact when it was moving through the Pennsylvania legislature. The few questions raised by other Pennsylvania agencies were of no great import.[9] It should be said, too, that except for the McKeever episode I know of no other federal official whose public statements could be construed as anticompact—or pro-compact for that matter—while the agreement was approaching and going through state legislative processes. If they mentioned it at all it was in strictly neutral terms.

When August 4 arrived, the date for our meeting with the Department of Agriculture, we felt seasoned and ready. This meeting differed from the others already held, which were attended only by state officials, administrators and their assistants. As earlier indicated, the farm organizations wanted to sit in on the Agriculture Department meeting. So did the editor and managing editor of a weekly magazine for farmers. We felt that in view of the Wellsboro experience this meeting would be more difficult than the others, but seeing no good reason to refuse the department's request to let these people take part we promptly acceded. As it developed, it could not be said there was a single "other" side at the conference table. It soon became obvious that several viewpoints were held by those with whom we met. The department leadership had an open mind, and later officially approved the compact. The Grange was still doubtful on some points; so was the soil and water conservation district leadership. Both seemed sincerely trying to be constructive in their questioning, seeking satisfactory solutions to what they considered problem areas affecting the people for whom they spoke. They wanted to be in position to assure their local leaders that they had nothing to fear from the compact, but they needed first to be themselves convinced. It became clear before the meeting ended that the Farm Bureau would be our chief antagonist in the rural sector. The editor of the magazine sided with the Farm Bureau man, and we never did convince him to the contrary; he frequently wrote critical editorials in which he followed the thoughts so often expressed by Hatfield.

It also was demonstrated at this meeting that opinion had not solidified in the editorial staff of the magazine. Richard Denison, the managing editor, contributed the thought that caused us to write and insert the "last resort" clause in Article 1. If it was truly intended that the commission would coordinate and lead others rather than become a mammoth construction agency in its own right, he asked, why didn't we say so frankly and prominently instead of half concealing the prohibitions deep in the body of the action articles? He had read the compact carefully, and understood that limitations and restraints were there, but "why make everybody read every word of every section of every article before they can be found?" We added his suggestion to the list we were compiling as an outgrowth of the meetings with agencies, and the conversations and consultations we had with others. To anticipate a little, the IAC agreed that his thought was sound and did insert a disclaimer section, putting it as far up front in the compact as we could find what looked like a logical place for it; it became a part of the third section of the first article.[6] Thereafter, without contradicting his superior, the managing editor frequently wrote and published objective, straightforward news stories about the compact. On one occasion he sent me a group of twenty-five questions he wanted answered. I did so, and he published most of them and the replies. Shortly afterward Coleman and I departmentalized this material, supplementing where we believed desirable to round out the whole, and published it as a "Q. and A." pamphlet of advocacy for the compact. At least 10,000 were printed and distributed before midsummer of 1968.[7]

I have gone into this meeting with agriculture's representatives and spokesmen in some detail because it was conservative rural Pennsylvania that needed reassurance and was the place where our hardest campaigning would have to be done. Much of metropolitan Pennsylvania didn't seem to care much either way, generally speaking. Pittsburgh, the population center of western Pennsylvania, apparently considered itself a long way from the Susquehanna and should concern itself with conditions and problems closer to home. Erie was silent on the subject. In Philadelphhia, where close attention was paid to the Delaware basin commission's activities and accomplishments, we found an editorial friend in the afternoon *Bulletin*. It twice exhorted the legislature to enact the compact, which it deemed a good thing for the entire Commonwealth. The press in the basin showed more interest. The morning *Intelligencer-Journal* of Lancaster was a strong ally throughout, more so than its afternoon companion, *The New Era*, whose farm editor appeared to take pleasure in using whatever of an adverse nature came across his desk. In Williamsport both the local *Sun-Gazette* and the peppery nationally distributed weekly *Grit* were firm editorial supporters. So were the *Clearfield Progress* in the upper West Branch region, and the Centre *Daily Times* at State College. Tom Cauley, a wide-ranging columnist for the Binghamton *Press*, which has considerable circulation in northern Pennsylvania, gave the compact several assists. The Harrisburg papers? The jointly operated morning *Patriot* and *Evening News* helped editorially late in the day, when the compact was in what appeared to be its death throes in the Pennsylvania General Assembly. Prior to that time almost the only compact news they used was an occasional wire service story that surely would be picked up by competing papers in areas where they had circulation. I have seldom had a colder reception than when on an appointed visit to the executive editor of these papers while we were campaigning. The atmosphere appeared hung with icicles. He read things on other subjects as I talked, and showed me out of his office less than three minutes after my arrival. In Scranton, the *Times* was friendly. Little if any self-generated help came from other basin news media. If it was there we saw little evidence of it. The Altoona *Mirror* and Lewistown *Sentinel* opposed the compact editorially.

The League of Women Voters proved to be supporters of the compact in a very solid and comforting way, after their leaders had given it their customary careful examination and pronounced it acceptable. The LWV helped through its state and local organizations in the basin, and also through its Susquehanna Inter-League Council. We met with LWV leaders, formally and informally, on a number of occasions. At all the meetings their attitude was one of friendly questioning. They knew how to cut through to the heart of an issue, and would have been quick to spot any evidence of evasiveness or floundering on our part. They learned that our practice was to answer straightforwardly if we knew the answer, and that if we didn't we'd say so and promise to furnish a reply as quickly as facts could be obtained. And you can bet we lost no time searching out what the League wanted to know and passing the word to them.

We felt we could count on the organized hunters and fishermen of Pennsylvania for approval of what we were doing, and got substantial help in our last-ditch legislative fight, but I was puzzled by what appeared to be apathy during the interim, those months when we were openly asking the organized and unorganized people of the Pennsylvania part of the basin to weigh the compact for adequacy and propriety of content, and some of their local clubs were influenced to oppose the compact. The Centre County sportsmen's federation was swayed by the Constitutional Party. So were a few influential members of the Lancaster County federation, though that organization itself escaped a re-examination of its favorable stance when its state leaders reiterated support late in March, 1968.

The one thing we could be certain of from the start was the determined opposition of the Farm Bureau affiliate. Its Pennsylvania spokesman seemed to us to be devoting almost as much time and attention to the compact as we were. At one point and for a brief time we almost believed the Farm Bureau opposition would end. On November 2, 1966,

Hatfield visited our office where, to my amazement, he presented only four objections he wanted to discuss. All were suggestions for change. He wanted (1) the appointment of advisory committees to be mandatory instead of permissive;[8] (2) a state equalization board to control any commission payments made in lieu of taxes;[9] (3) the condemnation by the commission of private property, if any, to be accomplished under state rather than federal law;[10] and (4) a change from "riparian rights" to "water rights" in a section that preserved state prerogatives.[11] The request regarding condemnation, which had previously been asked by the Pennsylvania State Grange, was considered reasonable and was followed. The "water rights" request was recognized as being tied to a then current attempt of the Farm Bureau to have the western doctrine of prior appropriation made law in Pennsylvania, and it and his other requests were turned down. The concession on condemnation wasn't enough for Hatfield. Nine days later his state organization, the Pennsylvania Farmers Association, adopted a policy declaration condemning the compact in much of the same language Hatfield had used at Wellsboro the previous June.

Hatfield visited my office once more, on January 30, 1967, when the revised form of the compact was already at the printer's, chiefly to ask that we specify that all commission hearings be "public" and "on due notice given." This was our intention all along but our language was not always specific. Goddard, Lawrence, and O'Donnell were consulted by phone and agreed this was a reasonable request, that references to hearings should be uniform throughout the document. We squeezed the change into the printed version of the compact as an end-of-the-book correction sheet, but Hatfield still wasn't satisfied. However, I'm getting ahead of the story. Back in October, 1966, the Bradford County, Pennsylvania, Farm Bureau adopted a resolution of opposition to the compact. The state president of the organization was quoted damagingly in the local paper under a double banner headline on page one; and our answer appeared several days later as a letter-to-the-editor on an inside page. When challenged by letter the state president had Hatfield reply, and he wrote that the president had said none of the things in the news story. However, they had to stem from some place, and the individual who had been saying such things and writing such things was Hatfield. After we got a copy of the Altooona resolutions we provided Hatfield— and our friends, too, of course—with an item-by-item response. It had no beneficial effect on Hatfield, for anti-compact speeches, letters, and publications flowed from his office in what seemed to us to be a steady stream. We considered that he had made up his mind to kill the compact if he could.

I have no love for Hatfield, but freely admit that he was energetic and at times an effective antagonist. His technique might have been anticipated, but even if it had been it would have been difficult to counter in advance. The compact was a long and complex document. After we scratched one series of his allegations relating to a half-dozen or so aspects of the compact, he could turn his attention to other phases and dredge up additional arguments, to which we then would have to address ourselves. While we were doing so he could ferret out still others to attack. The result was that we were kept busy rushing around with extinguishers putting out brush fires, and had that much less time for constructive activities. It was quite frustrating for most of the rest of his tenure in Pennsylvania—he was transferred to the home office late in 1967—and after effects of his anticompact campaigning kept turning up here and there until the final legislative vote sent the compact to the governor's desk. Perhaps it would have been better for our side if we had ignored his fulminations and pursued courses of our own choosing, but under the circumstances this was not practical. Attacks would occur in areas where the local legislator wanted us to respond, whether he was for us, undecided, or against us. Often the inquiries would be addressed to Goddard as IAC chairman. He in turn would buck them to me for reply, either over my signature or his. Similar situations led to answers in the form of news releases, letters to editors, and speeches at meetings promoted by our legislative members and alternates, or other friends.

Our experience with Hatfield illustrates how much difficulty can be caused by one person with imagination, an organizational base, adequate finances, and a desire to destroy something he opposes. The technique is basically simple and he certainly was not the first to employ it: Ask a few questions that raise doubts, and in the doing be at times direct, at times devious. Generally speaking, let the questions be broad in scope, but occasionally zero in on a small matter that is known to be considered significant by the person or persons addressed. After the proponents have answered the initial questions so as to satisfy the reasonable thinker or the person who still has an open mind, shift to other aspects of the total subject with a few more questions intended to bring adverse reaction. Don't abandon the old arguments entirely but change emphasis when they appear to be losing their punch. At all times seek to keep the proponents off balance, hoping they'll stub their toes by being inconsistent in their replies or—joy to the world!—even contradict themselves. Hatfield used the technique as though he was quite familiar with it, and did so in the earlier months of our set-to with considerable effect.

Through the fall and winter we pondered thoughtfully the problem of finding a way to run this particular fox to ground. Opportunity came in unexpected form late in 1966. The Cooperative Extension Service, also in the U. S. Department of Agriculture, had its state headquarters at the Pennsylvania State University, University Park (State College). A long-time friend, Robert Wingard, Extension Service wildlife expert, introduced me to William Carroll, public affairs specialist for the service. Carroll said he was interested in presenting both sides of the story to audiences brought together under the auspices of the Extension Service in several parts of the basin. He would set up debates between Hatfield and me, and I agreed. He secured Hatfield's concurrence, and the first of the confrontations took place on January 25, 1967, at Washingtonville, a village in largely rural Montour County, almost the center of the basin in Pennsylvania. I led off with a generalized talk on my favorite theme: Almost all our water problems could be traced to one or a combination of three conditions—too much, too little, and dirty; that is, flood, drought, and pollution—and that the compact could assist materially toward alleviation of all three. Moreover, it was the logical route to travel to that end, the Susquehanna being an interstate stream. Hatfield followed with many of his by now familiar allegations. He was beguiling as well, insisting he was not opposed to the generality of a compact, but had misgivings about this one, for such and such reasons. I obtained a copy of his Washingtonville speech—as I had of as many of his previous talks as possible—and while driving home that night an outline of what might be an effective stoppage of our antagonist began to take shape.

Next day at the office the copies of his speeches were spread on the desk and Coleman and I began methodically jotting down his points in argument, giving each an identifying label or headline, and number. Then to my typewriter to prepare answers to each. The wordage was held down as much as possible; in most cases the replies required less than one double-spaced typed page. When the drafts were completed Coleman and I went over them carefully, and a few technical and legal points were checked for accuracy with Sommerville and Trace. We believed Hatfield had nearly run out of "new" questionings by this time. The sheaf of answer material was catalogued under some thirty-odd headings, and we became convinced he would rely more and more on selection of points calculated to weigh most heavily with whatever audience was before him; we felt we had prepared the way to counter whatever he might now bring forth.

The preparation paid off at the second confrontation, in the small town of Wysox, Bradford County, on March 18, 1967. It will be remembered that this was the county where the local Farm Bureau unit had voted opposition to the compact the previous October. The debate consumed the afternoon of an all-day meeting, the remainder of which was on the general subject of planning. I led off as before, and in his opener Hatfield loosed the expected barrage of questions and allegations. As each point came up I pulled out the appropriate answer sheet. He was then given the full load, and in surrebuttal he said little more than that Voigt had "done his homework." Coleman and I agreed en route to Harrisburg that the advantage had swung our way this time, a conclusion that seemed substantiated shortly afterward when another group invited me alone to the same county to speak about the compact to people who had missed the debate. However, the local representative was adamant when the compact was up for passage in the House. He was a new man, chosen in an interim election; he listened to his friend, the Speaker, and voted "no"; nor did he change after the Speaker switched.

The two debaters met on the platform once more, in June, 1967, and the same procedure was followed as before, with me leading off and Hatfield following. It wasn't much, as debates go. I assumed he would produce ammunition similar to that used before, and my strategy was to defuse it before he could fire it. Much of his heavy artillery was spiked in this way, and when he was called to the lectern he spoke briefly and without much point for a couple of minutes and resumed his seat. While he appeared crushed at the moment, the likelihood is that Hatfield was convinced his behind-the-scenes maneuvers with legislators had ended all hope of the compact being passed by the Pennsylvania General Assembly and he saw no need to exert himself in debate with an already defeated opponent.

It is merely a statement of fact to say that the Pennsylvania Farmers' Association was ultraconservative in Hatfield's regime. His attitudes and arguments appealed to and were taken up by the equally conservative leaders of the Constitution Party in Pennsylvania led by Andrew Jackson Watson, who in the 1968 general election threw his organization's support behind the presidential candidacy of George C. Wallace of Alabama. Watson entered the compact conflict rather late, picking it up as a political gambit in the spring of 1967. His first upstate attack came on June 22, 1967, when he addressed an organization of borough (small city) officials of Columbia and Montour Counties, Pennsylvania. His talk was rather on the wild side, as it was reported in the Berwick *Enterprise,* and his chief points are itemized here principally to indicate the general pattern used in subsequent speechmaking by Watson and his followers. The compact, Watson declared, would "control" some forty-one Pennsylvania counties and the commission would have unlimited authority over "all streams and tributaries." It could displace state agencies at will in water matters, and could reach determinations right and left without accountability to anyone. Former Governor Scranton's fears that the other signatories would "gang up" on Pennsylvania were repeated. The borough officials promptly adopted a resolution opposing the compact. This tendency to take a position after hearing only one side of a controversy shows up again and again in the history of the compact campaign in Pennsylvania. It has been a common human failing throughout all history and by now should be expected but it is, nevertheless, a disconcerting and regrettable phenomenon. The mayor of the third largest town in Senator Preston Davis's district drafted this resolution and upbraided Davis for supporting the compact. All of Watson's points were answered in a letter to the editor, Ted Fenstermacher, who gave the reply as much prominence as he previously had given the report of Watson's speech. Later the local Grange at Light Street, a Columbia County borough, opened its hall for a public meeting where I gave a good-sized gathering answers to all of Watson's allegations.

Once Watson and his group discovered the compact, they used it wherever they could find similarly minded people in the Pennsylvania part of the basin, and out of the basin as well. Three incidents are fixed in my memory and pretty well tell the story of how they operated. All occurred in the early months of 1968, while the compact was stalemated in the Pennsylvania House of Representatives Appropriations Committee.

Huntingdon County was the home of Orville E. Snare, Pennsylvania House member of the IAC, who faced a stiff fight for renomination by his (Republican) party at the primary election to be held in May. In the fall of 1967, with what then seemed a rare talent for complicating situations, the Army Engineers had sent a core-drilling crew into Spruce Creek valley, in Huntingdon County, to check out foundation conditions at what was known as the Seven Stars dam site. Seven Stars was not on any authorized list of construction projects, and at the time the Susquehanna River Basin Study Coordinating Committee was at least

The city of Altoona, Pennsylvania, tried to keep coal mine acid out of one of its water supply reservoirs in the embrace of the famous Horseshoe Curve of the Pennsylvania Railroad by means of this interceptor canal, but it didn't work. This and two other reservoirs in the area are unusable. *Ted Jones, Stuart Finley Films*

two years away from a set of firm recommendations as to water resources activities in the basin. In private talks, we later learned that the only reason Seven Stars had been considered at all was for a possible supplemental water supply to be pipe-lined to the City of Altoona, which was plagued by coal mine contamination in three municipal reservoirs. But Spruce Creek was something special. Its valley was a fertile farming area, and the stream furnished good trout fishing to those who could gain access. President Eisenhower had whipped a fly over Spruce Creek in the years his brother Milton was president of Pennsylvania State University.

A number of fishing clubs and dozens of private cottages lined the banks. A local group sponsored by Watson's organization immediately tried to link the Corps of Engineers' *faux pax* with the compact and Snare. The Pomona Grange in the county set out to organize a public discussion in association with the League of Women Voters, and at a meeting to firm up plans they were confronted by the uninvited Watson group and the local Farm Bureau affiliate, each demanding equal time and an official part in the doings. The original sponsors found themselves in a position where they felt they had to agree, and the four-way meeting was held in February, 1968, with the opposition packed in the high school auditorium. Watson was there. So was Charles Ord, the Farm Bureau man who had succeeded Hatfield, and the conservative Republican state senator from the area who may or may not have recognized the extent to which he was being used to benefit the ultraright-wing Constitutional Party of Watson's making. On our side were Goddard, Snare, Grange Master Scott, and Edna (Mrs. Melvin) Isenberg of State College, water resources chairman of the Pennsylvania League of Women Voters. Questions were to be submitted in writing, and at the close of the meeting I obtained all of them, used or unused. Many were crude, even to the point of brutality and insult, and I, of course, had my own ideas as to their source.

The second incident occurred in Lancaster County in March, 1968. There the Constitutional Party was represented by a group that called itself "Pennsylvanians for Sovereign Rights." Chairman Goddard and I had recently received identical letters signed by the secretary of the group, virtually demanding that we appear and defend the compact at a "public forum" it had scheduled on the campus of Franklin and Marshall College. We refused. Shortly afterward the newly elected president of the Lancaster County Federation of Sportsmen's Clubs phoned to ask me to speak at a meeting sponsored by his organization to be held at the fire hall in the village of Penryn. On arrival I noticed one man huddling with three or four others, after which they scattered to separate places. The leader was later identified as the secretary of the Sovereign Righters, and a neighbor of the federation president. The speech was hardly ended before this man rose to ask a strongly leading question that seemed intended to condemn the compact no matter how it was answered. Nevertheless, he was given an answer, after which the others who had been seen with him prior to the meeting monopolized the floor for several minutes. When each had taken his turn the group leader tried to start a second round. Two members of the League of Women Voters, a reporter for the Lancaster *Intelligencer-Journal,* and others had been trying to get the floor, and I told the Sovereign Rights man I'd get back to him only after the others had been recognized. At the close of the rather tumultuous questions period the same group tried to persuade the sportsmen's organization to repudiate a previous endorsement of the compact. They didn't get that far, but did succeed in the passing of a motion for a reappraisal of the favorable position. It was shrewd strategy, worthy of a better cause, and it served an adverse purpose as far as compact publicity was concerned; it seemed natural for the reporter's lead paragraph to be on the restudy motion and the copy desk should not be faulted for basing the story headline on the restudy paragraph. To add to my discomfiture, the "Pennsylvanians for Sovereign Rights" had been forethoughted enough to write a letter to the *Intelligencer-Journal* editor in advance, timing it nicely so it would appear in the same issue of the paper as the story of the Penryn meeting. I can laugh now over being outsmarted but at the time it didn't seem funny. Three weeks later the State Federation of Sportsmen's Clubs, of which the Lancaster County organization was a part, voted to reiterate a previously stated support for the compact, so the restudy motion at Penryn proved meaningless.

In view of the political bravery Snare showed in the final days and nights of legislative battle over the compact I have forgiven him for getting me into the third of these set-tos with the Constitutional Party, but I was an unhappy individual the night of March 28, 1968, and Snare was the chief object of my anger. Wayne County is in the extreme northeastern sector of Pennsylvania, and only a fraction of it lies within the Lackawanna subbasin of the Susquehanna Valley. The member of the House from the district approached Snare about a public meeting in Honesdale, the county seat. Snare asked me to appear with him on the platform. I was given to understand that some of the people of Wayne County were complaining of something concerned with the Delaware Compact—most of the county is in the Delaware basin—but it wasn't anything for us to be disturbed about. The respected editor of the local paper would be the meeting "moderator," which at the time was interpreted as a synonym for "chairman." On the day of the meeting Snare telephoned to ask if I would go without him. There was nothing to do but agree. On arrival at the meeting place, who was present but Watson and the Sovereign Rights man from Lancaster County! Questions disclosed that the meeting had been requested of the Republican legislator by the Wayne County Chairman of the Constitutional Party. It obviously was a staged event similar in some ways to that at Penryn, and I would have walked out except that Watson and his associates could, and would, capitalize on it. My speech was first on the program. Next were the third-party leaders of the county, but instead of making speeches they began interrogating me as on cross-examination. Then came Watson. Finally, questions from the floor, and the first on his feet was the Sovereign Rights man from southern Pennsylvania. I told him in plain words that his questions had been answered at Penryn and this was Wayne County's night.

Before the evening was over I was ready and willing to use a bull whip on Snare for getting me into such a mess. What galled me more than anything else was that the Republican legislator, who had been the Constitutional Party's emissary, walked out of the meeting after introducing me, saying he wanted to be somewhere else. Furthermore, when the showdown came in the Pennsylvania House later in 1968 that worthy individual voted with Snare's opponents against the compact on every roll call. That seems to epitomize political friendship. Watson and his friends may recall that evening with appreciative chuckles, but it still doesn't seem funny to me.

By that time three rural groups were helping us enthusiastically in Harrisburg and elsewhere in Pennsylvania, and it is high time they were given some commendatory space.

Just before a public meeting at Williamsport in February, 1967, I was met in the hotel lobby by Kenneth Sorgen of Lock Haven, president of the Pennsylvania Vegetable Growers Association, a relatively small group that nevertheless included influential persons. Sorgen said his organization had previously gone on record as opposing the compact but had had a change of mind upon giving it closer study. They had recently met at State College, where they reversed their previous position, and they now wanted us to know they were ready to help in any way they could. This was pleasant news, and Sorgen and his organization did have a favorable effect on the outcome of the battle for compact passage.

In November, 1966, I made a breakfast talk before the Pennsylvania organization of Soil and Water Conservation District Directors. We had been deeply disturbed by the performance of McKeever at Wellsboro in June, as well as the less specific but still guarded comments of Donald Stephens, the district directors' now outgoing president. Consequently the breakfast speech was written with more than usual care. It mentioned that I had addressed two conventions of their national organization, had been a member of the Soil Conservation Society of America most of the time since 1946, and was the proud possessor of an honorary life membership in the West Virginia Association of Soil Conservation District Supervisors. I remember saying there were no callouses on my hands then from using farm tools and equipment but that in my younger years I could handle a team of mules and a walking plow better than a swivel chair and dictating machine now. Further I was a district cooperator in Pennsylvania and in my native state of Georgia. They were assured that because of my love for the earth and things earthy I would neither advocate nor support a Susquehanna compact that was not believed to be in the best interests of the rural parts and people of the basin. I like to think the speech, which was taken home by the delegates in considerable numbers, helped the organization make up its mind to back the compact when McKeever retired at the end of 1967, but really have no fixed illusions on that subject. It seems more probable that McKeever's stepping aside and his being succeeded by an official without such strong aversions had much greater influence and let sunshine and moisture reach dormant seeds of support so they could sprout and come to fruition.

Far more significant, though, from the standpoint of actual passage of the compact by the Pennsylvania General Assembly, was the help given by the state Grange after its initial opposition had been overcome. The state organization opposed the compact at its convention at Reading in October, 1966. A member from southern Lancaster County's Fulton Grange was identified as the author of the adverse resolution. Largely by coincidence I was invited to tell the Fulton Grange about the compact, and did so. By that time we had received and considered numerous suggestions as to changes in the compact's contents and the IAC had acted upon them. These were outlined that night and appeared to wipe away most if not all of the earlier fears. The upshot was that the state organization leadership shortly afterward reversed its position and came to our support. The convincing of the Fulton Grange leader may have had some effect but the personal conviction of State Master John Scott was much more significant. Coleman, who spent a good bit of time with Scott, was especially good at informal discussion. Their talks were fruitful. It does not detract from Scott's energetic efforts nor does it question his good faith to note in passing the spirited rivalry between the Grange and the Farm Bureau for the hearts of Pennsylvania's farmers. My belief is that this competition did spur both Scott and Hatfield to greater effort in behalf of their respective positions on this issue. After

Scott became personally convinced of the fundamental soundness of the compact, he worked about as hard as any other individual Pennsylvanian toward its acceptance and enactment. A bit more of the story of his efforts comes in a later chapter, but it should be said here that if the compact works as well as we believe it will, Scott can and should take a generous measure of credit for bringing it into being as Pennsylvania law.

If this chapter has read as though Coleman and I had the major roles in answering critics and swinging supporters to the compact's cause, it is unintentional and in error. We were instruments of the Interstate Advisory Committee, carrying out its instructions to follow the dictates of the Articles of Organization, though we did hit the self-starter button often when options were open to us. In their several capacities the members of the IAC worked in both affirmative and defensive fashion, speaking up positively on the merits of the compact, and countering adverse activities by its critics. This occurred in all three basin states but appears to have been far more necessary in Pennsylvania than either New York or Maryland because of the vigor of the attacks by the ultraconservative and opportunistic Farm Bureau and third political party. Goddard had much of the burden of explaining to Pennsylvanians the need for a compact for the Susquehanna basin. This stemmed from his cabinet position, which made him highly visible, as well as his chairmanship of the committee. Prior to his appointment as Secretary of Forests and Waters by Governor George M. Leader in 1955 no previous secretary had served longer than the four-year term of the governor who chose him. Goddard, however, was reappointed by each of Leader's three successors, Governors David L. Lawrence, William W. Scranton, and Raymond P. Shafer. This was unheard of, totally unprecedented. It is axiomatic that an appointed or elected official is never so popular as the day he is sworn in, for from that time forward much of his energy probably will be expended in fending off the importunate who want him to give something that probably should not be given. He must say no many times to many people. No matter how it is said it is still no, and no memory is longer than that of a politician—amateur or professional—who has been refused a favor. Goddard's combination of genius for accomplishment and devotion which resulted in his initial selection and his repeated reappointment to high state office meant nothing to those he had rebuffed—and he could be blunt—and over the years a sizable body of I-hate-Goddard sentiment had built up. If those who belonged to the hate club couldn't get at him through departmental responsibili-

ties they'd try it through the additional duties he was given to perform.

We probably will never know how much of the Pennsylvania opposition had a personal flavor, but it could have been what a Virginia-born
friend would call "right much." Goddard and his chief aides were frequently responding to inquiries about the compact and how commission
operations or activities under it might affect projects with which the department was officially concerned. On occasion the inquiries could be on
the belligerent side. We of the staff, too, inevitably became involved.
Our part took the form of drafting letters for Goddard's signature,
furnishing his staff information available to us, preparing special news
releases and letters to editors for his approval, writing statements and
speeches and doing other things of a communications nature. The load
on Goddard's shoulders grew heavier as we moved out of the first draft
stage and the compact began what became a long and arduous journey
through the Pennsylvania legislative process. There were times when he
seemed close to the point of leaving state government entirely. This
would have left the committee without effective leadership in the Commonwealth, for earnest as the other Pennsylvania members were, they
were not Maurice Goddards in the water resources compact field and
would readily agree that this is so.

There remains our relationship with the electric utilities to comment
on before closing out this chapter and going on to the lawmaking process in the basin states. The utilities that operate through an interconnected network of facilities in the Delaware basin also produce and sell
electricity in the valley of the Susquehanna. The group had been well
organized for many years, and each of the utilities is represented by one
or more observers at every public hearing or meeting of economic or
resource consequence or that in other ways might affect power company
operations. Corporate attitudes then crystalize on the basis of observer
reports plus a combination of formal or informal communications and
conferences. A number of network committees was set up at the start of
the federal survey of the Susquehanna basin, and those committees also
kept an alert eye on what we of the IAC were doing. The network had
an interest in whether a competitive situation might arise if the commission should at any time construct and operate hydropower plants,
and possibly sell on a preference basis the power and energy produced to
municipal authorities or REA cooperatives. After a thorough study of
the Delaware Compact the utilities supported it, and we considered it a
favorable omen for us when they indicated they would not oppose ours.

The chairman of an important committee for the group telephoned me from New York State to say there would be no opposition from the network. Indeed, the Pennsylvania Power and Light Company, serving much of the Pennsylvania portion of the basin, issued a strong "position paper" in support of the compact, as earlier noted.

References to the attitudes and activities of others of the corporate world properly should come, I believe, in the chapter on the lawmaking process in Pennsylvania, since they surfaced or occurred, as the case may be, in that critical era.

Chapter 3

Lawmaking at the Top and Bottom

Passage of compact legislation in the two states at the top and bottom of the Susquehanna River Basin had none of the lingering elements that came along afterward in Pennsylvania and Congress, but embodied certain cliff-hanging aspects that had us all holding our breath for a time. In Albany our problem was a last-minute rush of higher priority legislation in a session that had to be cut short so a New York State Constitutional Convention could take over legislative facilities on a given date. In Annapolis our people were contending with obstructive tactics by influential Baltimore City, whose opposition was based on faulty reasoning linked to what appeared to be procrastination in actually giving the compact attention and study.

The New York Experience

Preparatory work intended to lead to legislative determination of the issue in New York was a thorough going professional job. In the ordinary course of legislative events in Albany, our proponents would likely have secured the introduction of a "study" bill in one session of the Assembly, which bill then would hold over for a year while the legislators and others interested considered its merits and demerits. Our people were hopeful, however, that the compact could be passed by the legislatures of all three basin states in 1967, to be sent on to Washington before the end of the first session of the 90th Congress. In our naïveté some of us even dreamed of the compact progressing as far as committee hearings in Washington before the close of the congressional year. As a consequence of our hopefulness and eagerness to get on with it, the New York members of the Interstate Advisory Committee decided to short-cut the "study" bill route and try to achieve enactment at the 1967 session.

The executive branch members, Commissioner Ronald B. Peterson of the Department of Commerce, and Deputy Commissioner W. Mason Lawrence of the Department of Conservation, consulted with their then most active legislative members, Senator Dalwin Niles of Johnstown, and Assemblyman Francis J. Boland of Binghamton (an alternate), and with the leadership of the New York Joint Legislative Committee on Interstate Cooperation. This committee had initiated the action that resulted in the organization of the Interstate Advisory Committee, when Fred Zimmermann was on its staff under the chairmanship of the late Senator Elisha T. (June) Barrett. It was logical that the compact legislation should be introduced under its sponsorship. In preparation for the introduction, Zimmermann and the executive branch IAC members wrote a memorandum of legislative intent that appears to have thoroughly allayed any doubts on the part of the generality of the Assembly as to the desirability of the compact. The memorandum ran through the several available alternative institutional arrangements for water resources management, then continued, in part:

> As distinguished from a solely interstate compact where the federal government merely gives consent, the United States would be a full party to the Susquehanna agreement as it is to the Delaware River Basin Compact. Accordingly, the compact will be state law and federal law—the law of each of the compacting jurisdictions, Maryland, New York, Pennsylvania, and the United States. In other words, federal and state law will be welded into a single body of law for the management of the Susquehanna River Basin.
>
> The compact creates a regional interstate–federal administrative agency to act for and be responsible to the four governments in the planning, development, and management of the water resources of that basin. The Susquehanna River Basin Commission will be an agency not only of all the signatory parties, but of each of them, and all the party jurisdictions will have a voice in the determination of common policies. By providing a single agency for the basin that will be both multi-state and federal, and a single law for both the federal and state levels governing water administration in the valley, the agreement will avoid the growing difficulties of federal–state relations in water law and administration.
>
> Neither the Delaware nor Susquehanna commissions displace the existing agencies of government within their basins. Instead the confusion of overlapping jurisdictions is eliminated through integration of the activities of both the federal and state agencies. Possibly the major differences be-

tween the two agreements is the effort made in the Susquehanna to go even beyond the Delaware in emphasizing the primary role of the regular agencies of government.

The memorandum cited the so-called disclaimer passage, Section 1.3-6, as illustrative of this emphasis on action by existing agencies, and noted that Susquehanna's Section 3.10 was "expressly designed to give an even wider realm in [the review and approval] function to agencies of the signatory parties than has been the case in the Delaware."

The reason given for using language as near as possible to that of the Delaware Compact was "to avoid conflict and confusion with respect to water management administration in the two adjacent basins."

The compact was declared to represent "a major step toward the solution of the interjurisdictional problems of water resources management," and to provide "the opportunity of true partnership in the management of our water resources."

Zimmermann also assisted with the writing of the so-called enabling sections of the bill. These sections had no effect on the body of the compact, but were largely in the nature of instructions as to how the state would go about doing certain things bearing on its participation in the commission to be created. They provided (a) that the New York governor's designee to commission membership should be a member of the Water Resources Commission, (b) that whoever served New York on the commission should be reimbursed his expenses by the state, (c) that the members of the Water Resources Commission should serve the New York member as an advisory committee, (d) that in New York a "court of competent jurisdiction," as provided in the compact for review of commission determinations, meant the state supreme court except in specified instances, (e) that the budgetary practices of other New York state agencies of government would be followed in the submission and consideration of requests for funds to support the activities and operations of the Susquehanna commission—and so on.

The New York legislation was introduced in both houses on February 21, 1967. On August 13, 1968, an interview with Assemblyman Boland was tape-recorded in his Binghamton office regarding the legislative course the compact ran from introduction to passage, and the narrative that follows is based in part on the transcript of that recording.

Senator John J. Marchi of New York (Staten Island) had succeeded Barrett as chairman of the Joint Legislative Committee on Interstate Cooperation, and he and the ranking member on the House side, Assemblyman O. V. Maresca of New York City, sponsored the senate and house bills, with a number of others joining as cosponsors, Niles and Boland included. One public hearing was held by the committee on interstate cooperation, to consider this legislation and other bills involving interstate matters. Boland did not attend the hearing. The assumption is that there was no opposition of consequence, as the bills were released with favorable reports. The state senate acted promptly, passing the compact bill in mid-March on a "quick roll call"[1] vote without dissent and sending it over to the lower house. There a Rules Committee has powers similar to those of the Rules Committee of the lower house of Congress. That is, the committee decides what legislation the members of the Assembly shall consider and vote on, and its determinations are usually considered final. The truth seems to be that in the press of what appeared to be more important other matters the compact bill was overlooked until the session was almost at an end. Boland noted that the name of the chief house sponsor had appeared on the measure chiefly because of his position on the interstate cooperation committee and follow-through by the sponsor was missing.

The last official day of the 1967 session, Friday, March 31, approached with the compact bill still in the Rules Committee, and our people, in the Assembly and in the executive branch as well, awoke to realization that the chances of passage before adjournment were dwindling by the hour. Money bills involving in excess of a billion dollars each, and other legislation vital to more heavily populated areas, including New York City, were hanging fire. The Rules Committee could physically get around to only so much in the time remaining before the lawmakers were mandated to shut up shop and go home. In this extremity our legislative and executive members and alternates teamed nicely and, each working in his own way and through channels available to him, brought about the near-impossible.

Boland described how he secured last-minute cooperation from influential people in his area, and crossed political party lines for additional assistance. He is a Republican, and the Democrats were in the majority in the lower house; he talked with Thomas Conlon, chairman of the Broome County (Binghamton) Democratic Committee who, in turn, got on the phone to Albany and talked of the importance of the compact bill to the south central region of upstate New York. Simultaneously, Commissioner Peterson, a master practitioner of the art of the politically possible, was talking with people of influence in the legislature whom he knew best. So were our people in the Department of Conservation.

Boland phoned our office on March 31 and talked with Coleman. His news was ominous. Nothing that had been attempted seemed to be fully effective, and he was plainly worried. He had arranged with the secretary of the Rules Committee to be given the old familiar thumb signal— which dates at the latest from early Roman Empire days—when the Rules Committee came back to the chamber from its final meeting, hours after the clock had been stopped just short of midnight when adjournment must come. As the committee secretary entered he gave Boland the thumbs-up gesture, and the action thereafter was ordinary legislative routine. In the small hours of that last night the bill was called in its turn and passed unanimously. Governor Rockefeller signed it into law on May 2, 1967.[2]

Lawmaking in Maryland

From midsummer, 1966, until March 13, 1967, there appeared to be no likelihood of clouds on the Maryland legislative horizon. As soon as possible after our first printed draft had been made public a special task force of the Maryland Legislative Council, a bipartisan body consisting of ten senators and ten members of the House of Delegates, was appointed to study the compact. It met in a committeeroom at the capitol in Annapolis on July 26 to discuss the draft. Its composition was interesting. The chairman was Senator William S. James of Bel Air, President of the Maryland Senate and also Chairman of the Legislative Council as well as the senate member from Maryland of the Interstate Advisory Committee on the Susquehanna River Basin. Its other members were speaker Marvin Mandel of Baltimore, who also was the IAC House member from Maryland; Senator J. Albert Roney of Perryville, alternate to James; Delegate Frank Harris of Elkton, alternate to Member Thomas J. Hatem; and Delegate J. Frank Blair of Bel Air, the only one not connected with the IAC. Blair was Republican, the others Democrats. In the fall of 1966, Blair would run against James for his senate seat, and be defeated.

All of the task force members were on hand for the discussion except Speaker Mandel, who could not attend, and all were familiar with the compact and had had a hand in determining its contents; that is, except Blair. Others attending, in addition to two newsmen, were Wendell, Sommerville, Everstine, Coleman, and I. Blair asked some good questions, and was given equally sound replies. There is nothing of record that I have found to indicate that Blair was basically against the compact. Senator James showed me evidence that Blair criticised him in the fall of 1966 regarding his work on the compact, but dismissed it as just political campaign talk. For the sake of the council record we went over the compact at some length, paying particular attention to the passages that were intended to provide protection for Chesapeake Bay for obvious reasons.

In the fall the task force laid the compact bill before the rest of the council, the legislation at that time containing a simple two-section enabling or implementing addendum. The council approved it, and it was introduced in the Senate by James, in the House by Mandel—excellent sponsorship indeed—on February 21, 1967. At about the same time there was legislation to appropriate $50,000 for the use of the Susquehanna River Basin Commission as Maryland's share of operating funds for the first year of the commission's existence. This bill carried the customary reversionary connotation; that is, in the event the commission should not be created in time, or if all the appropriated funds were not expended by the commission, the unused money would revert to the Maryland general treasury. This appropriation was passed, and the fact that it did so helped us considerably in arguments in Pennsylvania, where fear had been expressed that Maryland, because of her scant portion of the Susquehanna basin, would seek to escape paying the cost of commission operations on a share-and-share-alike basis. Before the bill was introduced, I was asked to furnish an approximation of what the first annual budget of the commission might be, and estimated the total at somewhere between $200,000 and $250,000, depending on staff numbers and pay scales. Maryland took the minimum figure and divided by four, the number of commission signatories, to arrive at the appropriation figure of $50,000. The fact that Maryland actually passed the appropriation, whereas the other two states did not even introduce money legislation, was used by us in Pennsylvania later as tangible evidence that Maryland was quite willing to pay her way without quibbling.

On March 13, three weeks after the compact bills had been introduced, a joint hearing was held on them by the Senate Committee on Economic Affairs and the House Committee on Natural Resources. Everstine, as director of the Department of Legislative Reference, had written invitations to Wendell, Sommerville, and me to testify. As we visitors sat in Everstine's offices and waited for one of the houses to adjourn for the day, we heard corridor gossip to the effect that all would not necessarily be clear sailing, for Baltimore City had indicated it would interpose objections, based on an adverse report by a consultant. Maryland eyebrows went up and jaws dropped when the word got around that the objections were from Dr. Abel Wolman, professor emeritus of water resources at The Johns Hopkins University. Over the years Wolman had built a considerable reputation in his field, and was looked upon in the state as virtually infallible on water resource subjects. We just might be in for some difficulties.

At the hearing we proponents were heard first, as is customary, and O'Donnell, James, and Wendell, in particular, were well received. Sommerville and I took subordinate place, as was strategically proper. Favorable statements were presented by the Maryland League of Women Voters, and a conservation organization from the head of the bay area.

Then came the deputy solicitor of Baltimore City, Ambrose Hartman, who read a letter that Wolman had written in mid-December, 1966, in effect asking, "Why the rush?." Baltimore City certainly had been in no rush to act on the Wolman letter or even, for that matter, to assure that its spokesman at the hearing would be familiar with the compact's contents. To this day, so far as I have learned, there has been no explanation of almost a ninety-day time lag by Baltimore in letting Senator James know about the city's doubts concerning the compact. Wolman's letter to a city official was dated December 16, 1966. Mayor Theodore McKeldin sent it to James with a covering letter dated March 13, 1967, the day the joint hearing was held. This, of course, made it necessary for us to respond *ad lib*, without advance preparation. It is possible that the delay was an oversight. I suspected it could have been deliberate strategy intended to rock us back on our heels and, on the basis of the weight Wolman's word so often carried, swing the legislature against the compact.

The Baltimore attorney told the legislators he had seen a copy of the 17,000-word compact for the first time on Sunday, March 12, the day before the hearing; his oral statement reflected a lack of familiarity with its terms, as he made statements that I'm sure he would have himself recognized as not justified by the language of the bill if he had had time to give it further study. However, his statement was brief. He relied chiefly on Wolman to state the city's case, such as it was. In a letter of comment written to James on March 14, I noted that five of the seven specific objections by Wolman were matters of judgment in which he was pitting his opinion against those of all the members, alternates, and advisers of the Interstate Advisory Committee. James, Wendell, and Sommerville disputed the validity of the Wolman objections, and shortly afterward—following a statement objecting to the compact by

Boy Scouts at the end of a week-long camping trip on Conowingo Reservoir, on the lower Susquehanna. *Ted Jones, Stuart Finley Films*

the Maryland Farm Bureau affiliate, which utilized the Hatfield arguments heard so copiously in Pennsylvania—the hearing was adjourned.

Those on our side believed we had made a good showing, but we did not discount the towering reputation of Wolman. Of greater concern was the prospect that the legislative weight of the City of Baltimore would be thrown against us. The last named wasn't long showing up, for the Senate Committee on Economic Affairs on March 14 decided to pigeonhole the bill. A senatorial spokesman for Baltimore successfully urged the committee to say it would defer action for a year.[3]

Tied to the Baltimore opposition was the fact that the city had recently built a $40-million pipe line from Conowingo Reservoir to connect with its distribution system. Mayor McKeldin was fearful, he wrote, that the city's investment and its privilege of taking up to 250 MGD of Susquehanna water might be jeopardized by the compact's operation.[4]

James and O'Donnell came to the conclusion that a frontal assault on the mayor's fears and arguments was our best chance to forestall defeat. Time was rapidly running out, as the session was constitutionally limited to seventy legislative days, which would make adjournment mandatory at the end of March. The mayor was asked for a meeting in his office, and agreed.[5] He had Wolman, and Hartman and others of his staff, with him. On our side were James, O'Donnell, Wendell (who was brought from Washington by a state trooper), and possibly one or two others whose names do not show in available records.[6] The Wolman objections and the city's fears were gone over once more, in detail, and at the close the city's opposition did not appear to have been overcome. Wendell rode back to Annapolis with James and Everstine, and ideas for amendment to the enabling sections of the compact bill, to placate Baltimore, took shape as they talked over the situation. In Everstine's office, Wendell dictated a draft to Everstine's secretary, and next day Everstine put the material in legislative form.

Now a bit of statutorily legitimate legislative legerdemain was performed. The sticking point had been on the senate side of the capitol in Annapolis; the lower house had passed the compact bill without difficulty, but the Senate Committee on Economic Affairs was still holding up action and the calendar had already reached March 26. James met with the committee and presented the so-called Baltimore amendment. It was accepted. The committee reversed its previous vote to pigeonhole, and brought the bill to the floor, with the amendment to be tacked on at the end in open session.[7] The Baltimore *Sun* of March 28, 1967, carried a story from Annapolis saying the senate on the 27th had "shouted down a series of city amendments that would have rewritten sections of the proposed compact," and passed the bill carrying the harmless James amendment back in the enabler. Now the bill had to go back to the lower house for concurrence in the amendment. Normally that would have taken three legislative days, but under rules suspension, action can be had on a shorter time schedule. This occurred, and on the night of March 28, last of the session, the Annapolis correspondent of the *Sun* wrote that the Maryland General Assembly had passed the compact and cleared the way for its signature by the new governor, Spiro T. Agnew.[8]

The Baltimore amendment could now be passed over and forgotten, except that it was seized upon and used in southeastern Pennsylvania to try to build up opposition to the compact. Benjamin Reynolds, Chester County, Pennsylvania, representative, was the sponsor of what has been labeled the Mason-Dixon proposal to divert lower Susquehanna basin water into that of the Delaware, and elsewhere.[9] Reynolds appeared fearful that he might have less chance of gaining approval of the proposal under a compact than without a compact. He and his associates made statements to the effect that the Baltimore, or James, amendment had in fact amended the body of the compact. Here is exact language from the amendment, which was entirely outside the body of the compact, in the implementing portions of the Maryland bill:

> Sec. 2. *And be it further enacted.* That nothing in the Susquehanna River Basin Compact shall be construed to impair or to derogate from any power exercisable by the Mayor and City Council of Baltimore or in any way to diminish any right which the Mayor and City Council of Baltimore may have to the waters of the Susquehanna River Basin.

The amendment then went on to specify that the right of the city to construct and operate its own water facilities was confirmed.

Section 2 said, in effect, that Baltimore City has whatever rights Baltimore City has. The paraphrased passage simply indicated that the compact doesn't prevent the city from building and operating water works. It assumes that the city wouldn't build such facilities unless it had water to put in them.

Before the end of the legislative hassle in Pennsylvania we had been forced to get letters from Everstine, Wendell, and Trace, and distribute them widely in our effort to counter the false and misleading material being distributed by Reynolds or in his behalf by others who picked it up and made use of it.[10] The gist of the three letters was as outlined in the paragraph next above.

Lawmaking at the top of the basin, and at its lower end as well, had exciting and uncertain moments, but they were as nothing compared with the tensions, defeats, frustrations, and complications that preceded legislative victory in Pennsylvania.

Chapter 4

A Pennsylvania Pigeonhole

In the summer of 1967 information given to New York and Maryland members of the Interstate Advisory Committee and others oozed confidence that the Susquehanna Compact would be passed easily and quickly by the Pennslyvania General Assembly.

In the spring of 1968, more than nine months later—and ask any mother how long that can be!—my diary warned that "we can't call it a live baby until it has been spanked, and it cries."

In retrospect, indications of coming delay and difficulty seem plentiful. In those rose-colored earlier weeks we overlooked some and failed to recognize others, or underestimated their importance. The heady optimism seemed justified for a time. So, later on, did the pessimism.

The compact bills were introduced in April in both houses under excellent bipartisan sponsorship. Representative Snare, IAC member and treasurer since 1963, was chief sponsor of H. B. 729; Z. H. Confair, IAC Senate member just as long, was principal sponsor of S. 479. Snare was chairman of the House Committee on Conservation and Natural Resources. Confair chaired the Senate Committee on Forests and Waters, Fish and Game. It seemed certain the bills would be referred to their committees and would receive friendly treatment.

Unfortunately, on the House side about a fourth of the forty-eight sponsors eventually defected for one reason or another, and we also lost a few of the dozen senators whose names were on that bill. Some of these became aligned with our most adamant opponents while others merely backed away from involvement and eventually voted with the opposition. Unfortunate for us, too, was the fact that leading figures among both the House and Senate Republican majorities were either openly fighting the compact or were balanced in such uneasy equilibrium that they often appeared to incline toward the other side; they definitely were not *for* the compact and their assumed or professed neutrality wasn't convincing. Naturally, all this was not made manifest at the beginning, nor was the strategy to be pursued by the opposition. Actions taken by them and hints dropped from time to time might under some circumstances have brought different effort on our account, which may or may not have changed the outcome, and all of which is hindsight.

This is the skeletonized record:

On the House side Snare's committee readily reported out the bill in the latter part of May, 1967, and it was promptly recommitted to the Appropriations Committee where it eventually died.

On the Senate side the bill also was reported out favorably late in May, and in due course was passed by a comforting three-to-one majority.

When the Senate bill went over to the House it was dutifully given to Snare's Committee on Conservation and Natural Resources, which reported it favorably a few days later. Then it, too, was recommitted and joined the House bill in the Appropriations Committee pigeonhole.

Months later the Senate bill was reported to the House floor with seven proposed amendments, six of which we found objectionable, and the final decisive battles in both houses followed.

Now, to flesh out the skeleton.

When the Delaware Compact legislation was before the Pennsylvania lawmakers in 1961 public hearings were held in Harrisburg, Easton, and Philadelphia. Our leaders wanted to avoid going to places where a vociferous rural few might dominate. Even the word "hearing" was to be avoided, as that could lead to a belief that the body of the compact was subject to easy amendment. Consequently, what was termed a joint "public meeting" was held on May 2. In four preceding weeks Goddard was asked to meet in separate caucuses with the House Democrats and Republicans, to describe the compact and answer questions. Trace, Coleman, and I went with him. In June we met in caucus with the Senate Democrats, but were not invited by the GOP. It should be noted that the Republicans had slim majorities in both Houses, and Governor Shafer was Republican.

A short time earlier the Joint State Government Commission had asked us to make arrangements for a two-day bus tour of the lower Susquehanna and its power developments. The tour came in April, after the bills were introduced. Coleman and I went for the ride, and some of our Maryland friends met us at dinner in Aberdeen the first night, but I doubt if we converted any who weren't already supporters.

The May 2 meeting was well attended. It was chaired jointly by Confair and Snare. Goddard led off for us, and immediately was asked a series of critical questions by committeemen who were in opposition, and friendly questions by Confair and other supporters. He was followed by IAC Member Clifford L. Jones, speaking in his capacity as Secretary of Commerce, and more than a half-dozen others favoring passage, including the executive of an industrial development group, a former mayor of Wilkes-Barre, the master of the Pennsylvania State Grange, and the leadership of the League of Women Voters. The League was represented by Edna (Mrs. Melvin) Isenberg, water resources chairman of the state group, and Jeanne (Mrs. R. L.) Slobod, chairman of the Susquehanna Inter-League Council, both of State College. Former Mayor Frank Slattery of Wilkes-Barre had been the founder of a Susquehanna basin citizens organization that for various reasons failed to take root and grow. Favorable statements were presented for record in behalf of others, including the executive director of the Water Resources Association of the Delaware River Basin during the Delaware Compact's formative years.

Three statements in opposition were presented. These were by Hatfield for the Farm Bureau, by Watson for the third party, and by a man from southeastern Pennsylvania who spent more of his allotted time castigating Goddard then discussing the compact. In addition, the spokesman for the state association of second class townships—those least populated and generally quite conservative—told the legislators he wanted additional time and would send a statement later. When the League of Women Voters statements were being presented a former official of the townships group was heard to say "If they're for it I'm against it!." When it came, it was in opposition.

The opposing statements, including the subsequent townships arguments, could have been written in advance by any of us who had been through the experiences of the months between the first draft's publication and the compact's introduction; that is, they contained little that was new or different. In a response to Hatfield's statement prepared for submission by Goddard to the two legislative committees, it was noted that Hatfield's recommendations consisted of (1) philosophical declarations to which virtually the entire conservation movement subscribed; (2) ideas that may have sounded plausible but to us appeared fallacious and impractical; (3) suggestions that the compact should contain language that had been in it from the start; and (4) matters not relevant to the subject. The response commented on each at length. Hatfield also proposed several crippling amendments, including a spread of no fewer than five alternative arrangements to give Pennsylvania a voting advantage. They were: (1) That voting be in proportion to land area, which would let Pennsylvania dominate; (2) exclude the federal government as a member, which would lead to a weighted vote scheme; (3) unanimous vote on everything (which later caused Everstine to comment that the commission "couldn't even take a restroom break unless four voted in favor!"); (4) a veto for Pennsylvania; and (5) require the federal government to "vote with the minority." Hatfield urged that the commission be deprived of the power to reach any determination. He wanted the words "determined by the commission" stricken wherever they appeared. The result would be to kill or emasculate the compact. He wanted to chip away at the authority proposed for the commission, and either immobilize or entirely eliminate the federal government as a member. Watson's statement differed little from his later speeches and writings, which have been referred to previously.

When the townships' organization statement arrived our chief interest lay in its source. It had been written by a former judge of a Pennsylvania appellate court who, we learned, was then registered as lobbyist for the townships group. More significant was the fact that he had for years been closely identified with the Republican political leadership in central Pennsylvania. That leadership had lost some of its potency and could not deliver as solidly and completely as in the past, but at least on the Senate side of the capitol we found that old cronies still stood together and could even enlist an occasional maverick legislator. We noted with extra interest that a son of the townships' consultant was on the staff of the Senate majority leader. Hence, though the statement contained nothing new, we took pains to provide Confair and Snare with careful answers to all the points raised. Later, in July, the ex-judge was invited to and did meet in caucus with the Republican senators. Our informants felt he made a rather perfunctory presentation, raising no questions that hadn't been answered fully time and again.

At this stage the situation still appeared favorable. No one had produced any adverse material that we considered unanswerable with fact and logic. Others seemed to feel we were in good legislative shape, too. The capitol press corps has traditionally been cynical and wary, but quite knowledgeable. William Ecenbarger, statehouse reporter for United Press International, wrote for papers of May 28 of a few "pockets of opposition" to the compact but also of "support, crossing party lines, that would easily pass it in both chambers were the roll called today (*Harrisburg Sunday Patriot-News*)." However, when Speaker Kenneth Lee, at the beginning of the new week, recommitted Snare's bill to the Appropriations Committee we felt our first stirring of uneasiness, and later recognized it as a basic element of opposition strategy. There was no parliamentary reason why the bill should go to that committee since it was not a money-appropriating measure. Snare was told it was done because the bill, if passed, would entail future appropriations. The truth appears to be that Representative Alvin C. Bush, vice-chairman of the Appropriations Committee, who had volunteered or been chosen to lead the opposition, wanted the bill where he could keep an eye on it, and the chairman, while not seeming to care much either way, would do the bidding of the Speaker and his vice-chairman. Tucking the bill away in the committee's files, where it could be kept until or unless the opposition was willing to let it out, allowed our opponents ample time to try to sway more votes their way and to frame amendments that had not yet crystalized in language and form. They could control the timing of action, an important factor. When the bill did at last emerge the Assembly was believed near adjournment, an advantage to our opponents.

Trying to read another's mind is a chancy affair, but an effort must be made to indicate not only who the leaders of the legislative opposition were but also the best reasons I can furnish for their opposition.

The speaker of the House was from a rural district in the basin. At various times he communicated a fear that the commission would force the small communities he represented to install costly waste-water treatment works. This seemed to be a major factor as to his stance, but there was also the fact that a conservative rural element predominated in his district.

Bush appeared to have been motivated by a number of influences. A strong supporter in his district was a highly vocal state director of the Farm Bureau. There appeared to exist a personality clash where Confair, the senator from the same district, was concerned. Rivalry with Democratic Representative Robert G. Wise, the other House member from his county, may have been a factor. He may have sincerely believed he could improve upon the compact by advocating his version of it. Any number of other reasons may have been present.

Among the legislative opponents was Reynolds, the one who led the movement to have Susquehanna water diverted to a southeastern Pennsylvania. He appeared to fear the commission would prove an obstacle, or force the region in which he was interested to pay for water that he felt could be had without specific and obvious charge through storage initiated by the Corps of Engineers and paid for by all federal taxpayers. Another representative adamantly opposed letting the commission, under Section 15.2-2, hire an investigator or watchman with "the powers of a peace officer of the state" where he would perform. Present and impending water conditions and problems of the basin apparently meant little; what mattered was that there were just too darned many people running around with badges on their shirts and identification papers that labeled them officers of the law.

On the Senate side the leader of the opposition appeared to be George N. Wade, who with thirty-two years tenure was the dean of that body. He was friendly with the consultant for the rural townships group. He professed concern that the commission would commit the Common-wealth to spend untold millions on water projects, and said he feared the powers written into the compact. An associate had visions of the commission interfering with Harrisburg's long established permission to use the Susquehanna as a supplemental source of municipal water sup-ply. One of the two members who voted against the Delaware Compact in 1961 gave consistency as his reason for opposing.

These surely were not all the reasons for opposition to the compact, but were among those that were known or that surfaced. Doubtless some opponents were activitated by political debts—to be paid or collected—and this factor probably influenced legislators on both sides. A leading partisan on our team at one point quite frankly told me he expected votes from members of his house whom he had favored in like manner on other occasions. Overshadowing all reasons may have been simple conviction: on the one side that the compact was very much in the interest of the people of the basin and the rest of the state, and on the other that quite the opposite was true.

Whatever the motives or aggregation of motives, it now seems certain that the strategy of our opposition crystalized early in the legislative stage of the action; that is, in the spring of 1967. It will be remembered that on March 18 of that year Hatfield debated vigorously with me at Wysox. When we next faced each other in June, at Sunbury, after the House bill had been recommitted to Appropriations, his attitude was almost one of boredom, an I-couldn't-care-less sort of thing. As of now I believe he had become convinced the compact was a dead issue, that it would not get out of Appropriations or, if it did, would be in such emasculated form that New York, Maryland, and the federal government would refuse to accept it even if Pennsylvania did. Therefore, debating the merits of the compact was a waste of his time; he had come to the meeting only because he had previously agreed to do so. If this really was the case he was close to being right—damned close.

June, 1967, was marked by considerable activity, but it was of a subsidiary nature. Watson of the Constitutional Party used scare tactics to stir up the borough officials of Montour and Columbia Counties, part of the senatorial district of Preston Davis, our alternate member, as reported in an earlier chapter. One of Watson's publications of this era proclaimed that the commission would control the water used by farmers and by manufacturers of bologna and other products. Jack Seltzer of Lebanon, Chairman of the House Appropriations Committee, operated a bologna factory. Very subtle, this Watson! Coleman did some nose-counting on the Senate side and found only one or two Democrats were inclined to vote against the compact, whereas the Republicans were a more uncertain number. The majority leader there intimated to him that his side might try to amend the compact in several places and that one or more would have to do with the voting, perhaps provide for unanimous vote on every motion. Here was our first hint from an official source as to the principal proposition the legislators on our side would have to combat in months to come. It was to be repeated later, as will be related in due course. My present preoccupation with the matter is prompted by the question of whether it would have been possible to check it earlier if our proponents had then paid more attention to it. In retrospect it seems unlikely.

At the end of June Coleman went on vacation to the Pacific Northwest, and I moved into a Senate gallery observation post while he was away. July was a decisive month in that chamber, but the final vote was delayed until the 31st. We were plagued by "senatorial courtesy" and other postponements. Twice Senators who wanted to make speeches— one for us, one against us—had to be away on legislative days. The death and funeral of a senator brought another delay. At one point there was so much wrangling in Republcan caucus over a money bill that everyone emerged with nerves jangled, irritated, tired, and our people felt it best not to press for action under the circumstances.

On the 31st the senators began drifting in from caucus about 3 P.M., and a half hour later the session began. There were the usual preliminaries: the opening prayer, communications from the governor, messages from the House to be read and attended to, new bills introduced and referred, the methodical reading of the calendar and disposition of bills in earlier legislative stages, and finally arrival at bills on third reading and final passage. It was near five o'clock before S. 479, the compact bill, was called, and immediately Wade, with four Republican colleagues joining, offered a packet of six amendments. The principal ones would have given Pennsylvania extra votes and provided a veto by signatory states over any water action to be taken within their borders.

Much speechmaking followed. Wade was unalterably opposed to giving the commission "raw, naked power" that would make it "a law unto itself." He felt the legislature was being asked to "sell out" to a presumably irresponsible four-man commission. Thereafter a half-dozen more speakers for the amendments had their say; Davis, one other Republican, and two Democrats spoke for our side. Confair kept his seat, turning once to grin and wink at me. His attitude, as he put it later that evening, was "if you've got the votes, keep your mouth shut and let whoever wants to talk get it out of his system." When roll call time came the presiding officer declared that only those senators actually in their seats and voting would be counted. The call showed the amendments defeated by 29 to 11. Other amendments proposed were defeated by voice vote, and roll call on final passage followed. Additional members had entered the chamber, and a couple of those who had voted for the amendments switched sides; this time the call showed 32 senators voting for the bill, 10 against. Of the 10, nine were Republicans, which showed the compact had almost solid Democratic support.[1]

Earlier, Bush had requested me to present myself before a House Appropriations Committee task force for questioning, and on July 12 I was on the receiving end of pointed queries for two and a half hours. Bush presided, and had with him four Republican opponents of the compact. The Democratic side was represented by a staff aide who left before the meeting ended. Snare's was the only friendly face from among the House membership. And there was Hatfield, who acted as though he was right at home. Toward the end Bush asked Hatfield to state his rock-bottom qualifications for approving the compact, and he put them this way: First, he questioned whether there was then sufficient "protection" for Pennsylvania interests; second, he didn't want the federal government as a signatory party; and, third, he believed the amendment to the Maryland enabler concerning Baltimore's "rights" to Susquehanna water should in some way be countered. So this was what his thirteen months of campaigning against the compact appeared to boil down to! Bush at the time tossed out the Maryland matter as inconsequential and said he could "live with" federal participation, but wanted me to give written assurances that the compact's wording adequately "protected" Pennsylvania. First, however, I was to present the protective material to Hatfield and secure his approval. This was an extraordinary request and I would have none of it. Bush was told that a statement would be prepared and sent to him in his official capacity; what he did with it then was his business.[2] The material furnished Bush shortly afterward became a duplicated memorandum "To All Who Are Interested" in the compact, listing forty-odd restraints and limitations on commission power considered protective of the interests of Pennsylvania.[3] They were, of course, similarly restrictive as to the other states. This we distributed to all the legislators and to a considerable mailing list; it became one of our stock answers to questions about commission power.

In this same month, July, we began to hear rumbles that influential elements of Pennsylvania industry would oppose the compact or were already fighting it behind the scenes. We received evidence that one large corporation was putting pressure on legislators from Lancaster County in particular. The senator and four of the five representatives from that county voted against the compact. Representative Marvin Miller of the City of Lancaster, who favored the compact all the way, told me he had been subjected to heavy pressure to oppose it. Goddard invited an official of the company to a discussion of the compact, but no meeting was held.[4] Word came that the state association of petroleum producers and operators was fearful the commission would set excessively high standards for pipe-line crossings of streams. This resulted in another letter noting restraints and the recourse that could be had if some future commission should conceivably step beyond the bounds of reason.

Our jubilation over the Senate success was not long lived. On August 8 Snare's committee reported the Senate bill favorably. A week later Speaker Lee referred it to House Appropriations, and that was that until the following spring, so far as actual legislative action is concerned. Behind the scenes, at the capitol and elsewhere, however, the political and propaganda dance went on, improvised on this stage, choreographed on that. Coleman in mid-August sent me a memo addressed to "He Who Picks Right Time for Vacation," from which the following is an edited and censored excerpt:

Put my head down and headed for the capitol. Saw ——— who said he would talk with the Democratic leader in favor of the amendments. I asked what amendments, and he said, "why, these; they are all here." He handed me the book full of those *anti*-amendment speeches you'd written for ———. So I gulped and said I'd see him later. Didn't think I should be the one to straighten him out; could have caused scarlet cheeks. Went to ——— and asked him to take care of it, which he did.

Shortly afterward Coleman was invited to see Speaker Lee at his office, and did so. He was kept waiting an hour, during which he had visions, he wrote, of himself and the compact being tossed through the door or window. When Lee finally called him in, it was to discuss an entirely different matter. He offered Coleman a job on his staff!

Coleman's unofficial informers in back-room conversations and corridor conferences at the capitol often provided him with what proved to be reliable information. For example, Coleman wrote me that on Friday, August 18,

I ran into a fellow who told me for dead sure certain the compact would be amended in the House Appropriations Committee and that the amendment would call for a unanimous vote on all commission actions. I had to consider this a real good source, so I phoned Snare immediately. Orville was upset and said he would withhold his vote in the Appropriations Committee when the general fund budget came up for consideration Monday.

Snare did not do so. Nonetheless, it must be said to Snare's credit that after the lines of battle were drawn clearly and the last-ditch fight began he took a calculated political risk and fought his own party leadership stoutly—not an easy thing to do under conditions that prevail in political Pennsylvania. However, all efforts to rally strong Republican assistance in the House seemed failures; party discipline was too strong. This caused the compact's friends to turn more and more to the Democratic minority. Representative John Laudadio, Democrat, was also president of the state federated sportsmen, and he was an enthusiastic supporter. He told Coleman he was ready at an appropriate time to badger the House leadership with interrogations from the floor and in that way seek to force action of a decisive nature.

As summer drew to a close we kept on preparing material that our people might use to counter adverse eventualities. Through it all we had been in touch with Zimmermann and exchanged views about several of the ideas in that material. One thought had been that the executive branch members of the IAC in New York might ask Governor Rockefeller to urge Governor Shafer to press for early and favorable compact action. My information is that no such request was made of Rockefeller. Shafer favored the compact but at the time of which I write he was having genuine difficulties trying to get approval of his budget and tax proposals. One of his staff told me in utter frustration—which may have been momentary—that so long as these matters went unresolved Shafer would have to concentrate his efforts on them. Doubtless these were practical political realities, but they were sad news to me.

Zimmermann and I debated frequently, on the phone and otherwise, whether we should prepare to counter adverse amendments with amendments of our own that friendly legislators could try to have put back in the enabling portions of the bill and thus not alter the body of the compact. We didn't care much whether the enabler was changed. Our great concern throughout was to protect the language of the agreement itself from change; we didn't want delay, and if the compact had to go back to New York and Maryland for concurrence in Pennsylvania's changes, we would face a minimum of a year's postponement in going to Washington and the Congress. Ill-advised changes in the compact could be fatal to its hopes of passage by all. So from time to time Zimmermann and I drafted a variety of sections that might be of use in an extremity by our friends in the Pennsylvania Assembly. Since none was ever introduced it is pointless to reproduce them here, but they did cover a wide range of subjects that had been a matter of controversy between us and the Farm Bureau man, on which we assumed Appropriations Committee changes would be based. We went so far as to draft amendments, to be physically located in the enabling area, that could be moved into the body of the compact if the other parties should concur within a specified period of time. If they did not do so, or until they came to a decision one way or the other, Pennsylvania would serve as a full partner without the changes.

A Coleman note dated October 11 said Speaker Lee had told someone privately, "The compact will not go anywhere this session but will be held over until next year and then be amended." Coleman wrote: "Couple this with [previous rumors and reports] and it appears the GOP House leadership decided long ago not to move the compact this year. My thinking at this point is that they have decided to kill it."

One of the more frustrating aspects of a Pennsylvania legislative session is the system of meeting only parts of two or three of the first days of the week and of recessing frequently, for caucus meetings and for almost any other sort of reason. It was exasperating in the extreme to us, who were eager to get it over with. I was especially anxious, as the calendar showed that the Department of Health, Education and Welfare would soon declare me "socially secure" and I wanted to retire from a daily office stint. I was eager to remain until we were at least safely through the three state assemblies. We felt those strange and bewildering recess habits were losing us precious time; this was especially true in my case, but Coleman was feeling it, too. In an October 24 memo to me he wrote, "This assembly has more damn' recesses than a kindergarten class!"

It was a nail-chewing era for nearly everyone on our side, and desperation measures were considered. One was whether our friends should enter a recall motion on the floor of the House to try to pull the bill out of the Appropriations pigeonhole. A phone call to C. Edward Moore brought the word that in his forty years as parliamentarian of the House the only legislation successfully brought out on a recall motion was an anti-child-labor bill in the 1930s, during the Great Depression. We knew our compact couldn't compete with child labor in emotional appeal, and gave up the idea. This prompted me to tell my diary on November 29 that it was too bad the compact didn't have sex appeal or "tangibles that could be used to whip up public frenzy. Benefits are in the future, and diffused. It is hard, if not wholly impractical, to find ways to stir missionary zeal."

Hints dropped to indicate the bill would be reported out in 1968 raised an additional question, and the answer brought a modicum of hope. It was that 1967 bills would carry over into the 1968 session without change in status. This could not have been the case a year earlier. In May, 1967, Pennsylvania voters had ratified a constitutional amendment to allow the General Assembly to consider bills on any subject in any year. Previously, in even numbered years, when representatives are elected for two-year terms, the legislature was mandated to consider fiscal bills only, and bills not acted upon in any one year died. An Assembly ruling was made late in 1967 that bills still pending after the first year of the representatives' terms would be eligible for action in the session of the second year.

It was coincidence that caused three of the principals in the saga of the compact in Pennsylvania to be legislators from Lycoming County. They were Senator Confair and Representatives Bush and Wise. In the fall of 1967 Confair and Bush were quoted quite often in the Williamsport newspapers, the former pushing for early House action and Bush resisting. Soon the copy desk editors, seeking short, expressive words to use in limited headline space, began calling the Confair-Bush exchanges a "feud." This brought an appreciative chuckle, I'm sure, from Democrat Wise, but it made the county GOP leadership nervous, and word reached me privately but nevertheless authoritatively that local party officials pleaded with Confair and Bush to quit saying things that would let that awful word "feud" appear on the front pages.

The coming of December saw the going of Coleman. A constitutional convention had been called and, in the capitol newsroom jargon, he left us "to flack the con-con," that is, to handle the convention newsroom activity. It was intended only as an extended leave of absence, but in late April, after the constitutional convention ended, Coleman took a job with the Senate Democratic leadership.

Prior to Coleman's departure he had maintained much of our liaison with Scott of the Grange. It was only after Coleman left that I began to appreciate the full extent of Scott's efforts in behalf of the compact. He seemed to spend more time out of his office than in, and when he was away he usually was at the capitol, where he was registered officially as a lobbyist, or buttonholing legislators from rural districts in their home country. He wrote often about the compact in the legislative information he passed on to local and Pomona granges across the state. (Pomona is the name applied to a grange unit superior in rank to local granges in a given area. In Pennsylvania a Pomona Grange usually but not always covers a county.) He and Coleman were in almost daily contact during the work week, exchanging information and contriving strategy and tactics. When I took over Coleman's duties (we did not try to find a replacement at that late stage), visits with Scott were less frequent but no less cordial. We met once in a while in his office, and encountered each other in capitol corridors every now and then. He was always pressing, pressing, pressing for the compact, more so with legislators from rural areas than those from the bigger cities and towns, and he was effective. He helped especially with lawmakers from counties outside the basin, where the compact had less immediate meaning to the local people and their representatives in Harrisburg.

In a time of tension things can take on a distorted appearance, look out of perspective and focus, loom larger than they really are. A number of these came along in the early months of 1968. Some have been related in a previous chapter,[5] such as the hassle over Spruce Creek and the meeting in Huntingdon the night of February 16, my first confrontation with the Constitutional Party on March 7 at Penryn, and my second in Honesdale on March 28. Then, we were continually plagued by opponents' references to a Hudson River compact.[6] This compact was sponsored by New York State in an effort to preserve scenic, historic, and other cultural values on lands bordering the Hudson. As the compact was passed by the New York Assembly it would give that state nine votes, whereas New Jersey and the federal government, which were invited to join, would have only three votes each. This voting arrangement met a cold reception in Trenton and Washington, and neither took favorable action. By its nature it was far removed from valid comparison with the Susquehanna compact, but our opponents kept asserting that it was a precedent and its voting pattern should be followed in the case of our river, with Pennsylvania favored.

January brought an exasperating report addressed to the National Park Service by two State College-based consultants on an aspect of recreation in the basin. In it they advocated construction of a reservoir at the Seven Stars site on Spruce Creek, that most controversial of project proposals, which they presumably believed was still on the Corps of Engineers' list. The report apparently was made public by the consultants without prior approval of the Park Service, and neither my office nor Goddard's had any advance notice. We reacted fast. In fact, Goddard was just plain mad as hell. I wrote a news release that reflected his mood. One of his long-time departmental staff members later called it "the hottest news release I've ever seen come from his office." The Park Service, in effect, sat on the report, but the public damage had been done; it gave those Constitutional Party adherents in Huntingdon County more ammunition. (As of the end of 1970, the National Park Service had not publicly distributed the report. The study, by Burggraf and King, was a part of the NPS phase of the federal Susquehanna survey. Customary procedure would have been to send the report to the Corps office in Baltimore, from which it would have been circulated to coordinating committee members, and others. My information is that this was not done.)

A little later, in the spring, we learned that the influential Pennsylvania State Chamber of Commerce had some grave reservations about the compact. Goddard told me that if the state chamber formally and publicly opposed, we would be in deep trouble with the legislature. Thus we welcomed a meeting set up in March, 1968, in the office of Secretary of Commerce Clifford Jones with three members and the secretary of the chamber's Water Pollution Abatement Committee. Goddard asked me to go with him. William Tipton, the secretary, was principal spokesman for the state chamber people, and asked chiefly about the voting, the duration, and what seemed to us a new twisting of compact intent by the opposition; he asked whether the normal Pennsylvania legislative appropriating process could be circumvented by secret manipulation of funds allotted to a department such as Goddard's or to the governor's office. The answer, of course, was a flat no. Goddard responded to most of the questions, some at considerable length. Jones did so less often but no less vigorously.

Two weeks later, in early April, following up information given by a legislative friend, I phoned Tipton to ask if his people had as yet come to a firm conclusion. He replied that his committee had decided to take a "yes, but" stand, since the voting, duration, commission powers, and one or two other things still were disturbing. I phoned Goddard and asked if he could take a little more bad news—the day had seemed full of it—and he answered, "Not much; what is it, the state chamber?" I had to say that was it. Feeling we were at about as low a point as we were likely to get and that the road somehow had to start upward soon, we began working ourselves into climbing condition.[7] We visualized another coming-from-behind publicity situation—as we had experienced when former Governor Scranton had used that "gang-up" expression in 1966—if the chamber's news release opposing the compact should be allowed to follow the usual course; that is, it would get the initial play in the press and on the air while our response trailed it by one or more days. If that occurred the chamber's story likely would be printed on page one, and our counterattack would be put "back of classified," in the worst possible newspaper position from the standpoint of ready reader attention. So, we devised a somewhat unusual tactic. A news release of our own would be written in advance to answer the kind of attack expected on the basis of Tipton's comments in our phone talk, and it would be duplicated and ready to go ahead of time. We took a chance, of course, that in places we'd respond to attacks that did not materialize, and in that case we'd look a bit foolish. Arrangements were made for us to be notified quickly when the chamber story appeared in the capitol newsroom; a friend would tell us by phone. We'd hurriedly deliver our prepared release to the same place, and the capitol press corps, we believed, would then be under some compulsion to give our response approximately equal news treatment. Goddard approved, and we went through all the preliminaries. At the same time, we would make one more effort to prevent a damaging announcement by the chamber. A letter was written for Goddard's signature, addressed to the chamber's president, saying he felt it only fair that before an opposing statement was made public, he should have opportunity to meet with the group's board of directors. That didn't happen, but Goddard did have a couple of hours on April 30 with a large delegation from its pollution abatement committee, and asked me to go along. It appeared that the group was ready to oppose any sort of compact for the Susquehanna. They knew that in 1967 the Delaware commission had decreed, over the objection of the state of Delaware, which has influential industrial constituents, that waste waters in that basin should receive relatively high degrees of treatment. This seemed to chafe the business and industrial people at the meeting and make them fear the Susquehanna commission would be at least equally firm in its findings. They therefore held the mistaken opinion that the principal task of the Susquehanna commission would be to deal harshly with water polluters, with industry the primary target.

We left the room unsure that we had convinced them, and were right. However, when the chamber's anticipated statement came toward the end of June we had other things to preoccupy us and paid it practically no attention whatever.

It was in this fashion that the long months of waiting wore on, with skirmishes of patrol scale going on here and there but no decisive confrontation. That could not come until the compact bill was pulled out of that confounded Appropriations Committee pigeonhole and laid before the House for action.

My diary indicates great disappointment and discouragement. I wrote that I didn't know what to tell Coleman except to look hard at any good job offer before turning it down. Then: "Can't tell Millie [Mrs. Levan] yet; she has troubles enough with her husband in the hospital without having to face up to job hunting, too—although I don't think it would be difficult in her case to find another. Wonder what the office closing procedure should be" if we should find the compact defeated in Pennsylvania and, therefore, be faced with the need to phase out the committee undertaking.

Chapter 5

We Lose, and Win, in Pennsylvania

There was no way for us to know it, for we were not in the good graces of the Appropriations Committee of the Pennsylvania House, but as April gave way to May, 1968, we were "just before" seeing a strange and wondrous form of our compact emerge from the committee's piegonhole. It had been amended in seven places, six in the body of the compact, one in the enabling area. The amending was done somewhat high-handedly; Snare, though a member of the committee, apparently was not informed of what was going on until it was an accomplished fact. Be that as it may and whatever the uncertainties ahead, the bill was actu-ally out of committee, almost ten months after it had been recommitted. Bad as the amended bill was, our side at last had something tangible to contend with.

The first thing to do obviously was to get copies of the amended bill to find out exactly what the new language said, evaluate its effects, and draft comments that would be useful to our friends. The amendments were revealing, in what they omitted as well as what they contained. So, in chronological order:

The first would have required unanimous vote to approve any com-mission action,[1] exactly what had been hinted at in capitol corridors so many times. Some of our people were incredulous that Pennsylvania legislators would dream of such a thing. The reaction of the Maryland leadership in the Interstate Advisory Committee was that it was too good to be true. With such a provision in the contract Maryland would have an ironclad guarantee that her precious Chesapeake Bay would be protected—against undue pollution, against damaging diminution of inflow as a result of diversion, against anything else that might be deemed detrimental to Maryland's interests. Nevertheless, Maryland and New York both opposed the amendment, as will be detailed later. The ostensible purpose of the change was to protect the Commonwealth against conspiratorial action by the other three parties, but we believed the outcome could be far more detrimental than beneficial, since with most of the basin physically situated within Pennsylvania's borders, she would stand to lose most rather than gain most by giving any of the three other partners unlimited power to block water projects and other action.

The second amendment appeared to be little more than nitpicking. It affected Section 3.5-4, which gave the commission power to assume jurisdiction in water resource matters in case of extreme negligence or laxity by an administering agency. The section as we wrote it read that the commission "may" relinquish jurisdiction when shown the affected party will take needed action. The amendment would change "may" to "shall." The reason given was that the commission might refuse to give up jurisdiction even though the affected party was qualified and ready to do whatever was necessary. We held this was uncalled for because (a) if the commission refused to relinquish it could be hailed into court as acting arbitrarily and capriciously, whereupon the decision would hinge on the question of whether the affected party was in fact qualified and ready to act appropriately, and (b) it was too minute a matter to cause the compact to be sent back to the other two states for concurrence; they had found no fault with the original terminology.

The third also concerned a matter of little real consequence. It had to do with Section 12.5 on cooperative services, and would have mandated the commission to pay for assistance from another state or federal agency "at cost," which cost would have to be paid "not later than the fiscal period immediately following the fiscal period when services were rendered." We considered it self-evident that the contracting agencies would act as watchmen to make sure they were not underpaid for whatever technological services they were requested to furnish, and just as self-evident that in reviewing budgetary matters overcharges would be caught by auditing agencies of at least one of the signatories; surely all four would not overlook such a matter. Further, what was proposed might or might not fit customary processes and procedures of all the parties. We took the position that if Pennsylvania wanted this sort of thing in case a Pennsylvania agency was asked for special assistance, it should be put in an enabling section, not in the body of the compact.

Of much greater consequence was the fourth suggested change: It would completely alter Section 14.1, which detailed what the comprehensive plan should be and how it should be formulated. The amending language would have been laughable if it had not been presented under auspices that gave it a strong chance to be passed by the House. The proponents asserted they were amending to protect the interests of the people of the Commonwealth, yet in their drafting they eliminated entirely the compact's provisions for consultation with representatives of a wide variety of citizen and other interests, and even threw out the requirement of holding public hearings. It became evident after a first cursory reading of the amendment that its proponents had no correct conception of what a comprehensive plan, as set forth in the original language of Section 14.1, consisted of or how it would be arrived at. The amendment appeared to assume the comprehensive plan was no more than a listing of water projects to be constructed and operated by the commission, which was of course not the case at all. Beyond this, the amendment provided that "no action shall be taken by the commission in furtherance of this compact until the detailed comprehensive plan shall have been submitted to the legislative bodies of each of the signatory parties." When this was read to Maryland Vice-Chairman O'Donnell on the phone on May 7 he cut to the heart of the situation in a very few words: "How," he asked, "is the commission to prepare a comprehensive plan in the first place if this language is in the compact?" Further, the amending language could have caused a freeze of up to two years on water projects, regardless of sponsorship or need. This we held could result in critical shortages of municipal water, delay needed flood-retarding action—upstream or downstream[2]—and subject substantial areas to potential flood losses, bring hardship or even bankruptcy to contractors, and cause other undesirable consequences.

In the fifth amendment, the proponents would in effect have been in the position of advocating that Pennsylvania dictate budgetary processes to be followed in all four signatory jurisdictions. They held that Section 14.3 (c) did not protect the parties against fund manipulations outside the regular and customary appropriating processes. It will be recalled that this was one of the points raised in March by the state chamber. We believed the compact's original language, identical to that in the Delaware Compact on the same subject, where it had caused no difficulty of any kind, was amply protective in that it declared budgets submitted by the commission, after unanimous approval by that body, would go to the signatories and be "subject to such review and approval as may be required by their respective budgetary processes." How much clearer could a passage on that theme be? We noted that New York had put a section in its enabling legislation specifying the steps to be taken in that state after a budget had been approved by the commission,[3] and our reaction was that if Pennsylvania wanted a similar section in its enabler we would not object; however, it was improper for Pennsylvania to tell the others, including the federal government, what their budgetary processes should be.

Amendment No. 6, and the arguments used in its favor, seemed to us ridiculous. It would have stripped the commission of the authority to hire an investigator or watchman with the police power of a peace officer of the state in which he should be stationed. The commission, in Section 15.1, was given the responsibility of making and enforcing "rules and regulations for the effectuation, application, and enforcement" of the compact, but one of the essential elements of enforcement, Section 15.2, would then be stripped away and denied the commission. We were astounded when we learned later, from a position paper issued by the amendment proponents after we had begun our counterattack, that the great fear had been and still was that the commission might set up a force of officers who would go around the states harassing hunters and fishermen![4] This we interpreted as an appeal to fishermen and hunters to counteract the support being given the original form of the compact by the organized sportsmen, whose president that year, it will be remembered, was Representative Laudadio, a Democrat.

There was a seventh amendment, outside the compact body and to be made an enabling section, that we considered little short of incredible. It was written by or at the behest of the southeastern Pennsylvania representative, Benjamin Reynolds of Chester County, who wanted Susquehanna water diverted to his area, most of which would eventually go into the lower Delaware; none would return to the Susquehanna. This man was convinced firmly that the so-called Baltimore amendment to the Maryland enabler had real significance to Pennsylvania. So an amendment to the Pennsylvania enabler was written to declare that the body of the compact constituted the entire agreement and that material in enabling sections of the legislation as passed by any of the signatories would have no effect on the other signatories—specifically meaning Pennsylvania but not actually saying so—"without their specific concurrence." If it was not in fact meaningless it certainly was redundant in that all it did was state the obvious, but if he wanted it in and other Pennsylvania legislators did not strike it down, we would not object. Besides, its inclusion might please Reynolds enough so he'd vote for passage of the compact in its original form, but this was not to be the case; he voted against our position all the way.

It was quite an assemblage, and except for the unanimous vote amendment all of it was what might be called new material. Where were the many issues that had been trumpeted for so long by Hatfield and the Constitutional Party, which we believed Bush and his associates had adopted as their own? What happened to the objections to the 100-year duration? And all those powers given the commission? And the thirty-odd other questions that had been raised in the twenty-three months that had elapsed since we made public our first draft in June, 1966? They were gone, vanished, forgotten. Had they been abandoned and these new subjects chosen in the belief some of them might throw us off guard and catch us without convincing answers? Or were these several amendments drafted and inserted in the body of the compact in the hope that even if we beat down some of them we wouldn't be able to beat all, and the compact then would face long delay or death at the hands of the other signatories? Whatever the truth as to the why of it all, our immediate task was to produce answers we thought would convince those who had not already closed their minds to reason and logic. The answers would be reduced to writing in due course, but first we needed to know what hands to put them in, and here we were indeed caught short when the bill came out of committee.

Snare and those he could count on were a small minority of the majority party in the House, to which he belonged. He had few of his Republican colleagues on his side, and it looked as though whatever muscle could be mustered would have to come from the Democrats, including a floor manager when the compact legislation was being debated and voted on.

It seems logical, in hindsight, that the floor manager should have been Bob Wise, the Williamsport Democrat, but then he seemed to materialize from the blue. His selection doubtless had been made quite pragmatically by the Democratic leadership; it would be a shrewd move to confront Bush with his fellow member from Lycoming County, for if Wise was victorious it would strengthen his party there. Wise was an intelligent, up-and-coming young attorney who could take care of himself in the give-and-take of debate. Further, he was personally friendly with Confair, though of the opposing party, and could work in concert with him in matters that involved both houses of the Assembly. For example, Wise would not find it difficult to confer with Confair on

whether he believed specific enabling section language would be concurred in by the Senate.

Wise had been in the back of the room at a February 23, 1967, compact discussion in Williamsport, and we had met at a meeting of the
League of Women Voters in nearby Montoursville on September 27,
1967. He obviously was interested in the basin agreement but we did not
know how great or effective the interest would prove to be. However, it
was no surprise to find Wise among those present at a meeting of a small
group of House Democrats on May 8, 1968. I had been invited to this
meeting, at the suggestion of Coleman, who was by then on the staff of
the Senate Democratic leader. The amendments were discussed for
about two hours, quite objectively, I thought; indeed, there were times
when it looked to me as though some of those present were leaning
toward approval of certain of the suggested changes. Perhaps the point
had been reached when I was suspicious of everyone. With Wise were
two other representatives, Reid Bennett of Mercer County and Franklin
Kury of Northumberland County. A staff assistant to the Democratic
House leader and Coleman also attended. As we parted it was agreed
that I would put my comments on the proposed amendments in writing
and, since the lawmakers were adjourning for the rest of the week, mail
a memorandum to their homes to be studied before they returned the
following Monday, when floor action was expected. There seemed to be
all too little time to do what was needed.

On the 9th the memo was revised and sharpened, after a number of
consultations by phone. IAC leaders in New York and Maryland, Zimmermann, and Wendell were among those consulted, in addition to a
number of Pennsylvanians. Wendell's advice was wanted on legal points
and a call to Washington disclosed he was in Hawaii. He was located
there, but it wasn't easy. I was on the phone for twenty-five minutes as a
procession of operators traced him from point to point on Oahu, then to
Hilo and Maui, where he had just left the airport for an all-day tour of
education facilities. He finally returned my call about 10 P.M., EDT.
This was a minor detail of the whole campaign but indicative of what so
much of it consisted of. The result of the effort to reach Wendell eventually became one paragraph of a memorandum and a passing reference
in a House floor speech, but information he gave was needed *now* for
decision-making purposes, not several days later when he'd not be so far
away.

Typed copies of the memos were sent to IAC members in New York and Maryland, with copies of the bill containing the proposed ament-ments. Then, 400 copies of the memo, this time addressed "To All Who Are Interested in the Susquehanna Compact," were mimeographed by Mrs. LeVan, and arrangements were made with Snare to pick up packets on his way to the Statehouse the first of the week and have them put in the mailboxes of the members of both houses.

While the duplicating was going on, and all the rest of the week, including the weekend, my typewriter was clattering as numerous short bits and pieces of speech material were two-fingered to paper. Most of them were to be turned over to Wise for distribution to friendly legisla-tors as he and his associates saw fit. The intention was that they would be used on the floor during debate, which we expected either Monday the 13th, or 14th at the latest. In addition, one was written specifically for Snare as the principal House sponsor of the compact legislation. A good bit of the material was actually used, eventually, but by fewer speakers, and it was condensed here and supplemented there.

Zimmermann and Wendell, the latter by then back in Washing-ton, had both offered to come to Harrisburg if they were needed. Our legislators feared a backlash from the presence of nonresident advocates, and declined.

Wise stopped by on Monday morning, the 13th, and seemed pleased with the source material. Snare stopped, too, and picked up the speech draft prepared for him and the duplicated material to be distributed to the legislators. The diary entry indicates he wasn't sure how much GOP strength he could find and that he was relying largely on the governor's office to swing Republican votes in favor of the compact as we had written it. He seemed worried, preoccupied with the problems the situa-tion presented. Later Wise phoned that the Democrats, in caucus, de-cided to ask the majority for a week's delay in floor action, but had been brusquely told they could have only one day, until the 14th. Coleman advised in the afternoon that Snare had said he was sure he could count on twenty Republicans to vote with him, and we thought this comfort-ing if the promises given him were kept. Scott of the Grange also buoyed our hopes, saying he felt enough Republican votes could be had to kill the obnoxious amendments.

The 14th came and went, but nothing definitive occurred. The House, with me watching tensely from the gallery—which became standard procedure from then until the end—got into what my diary calls "a hassle, a real doozy, over a local-aid-to-higher-education bill," after which there was a recess so both sides could caucus, presumably on the subject of the compact bill, which was then on third reading. The Democrats came back first, and Wise brought the pleasing word that his side would vote almost solidly our way, with only two or three, all from conservative rural counties, against us. When the Republicans returned I was told the causus had disclosed a four-way division; (1) those against the compact in any form; (2) those who would vote for the compact with the amendments; (3) an undecided few; and (4) those who were for the compact without amendments. Further, the bill would not be called that evening, but would be held over, and the House would recess shortly until May 27. My reaction was that our opposition wanted time to twist political arms and try to gain more support for the amendments. Of course the delay gave lawmakers on our side time, too, to try to persuade a few who might be wavering. Scott of the Grange was pleased, as he now had opportunity to send another letter off to his people across the state urging them to talk with their home district legislators. Confair suggested and we held a strategy meeting attended by him, Snare, Goddard, and me at breakfast the morning of the 15th. Out of this came a promise from Snare that he would make up a caucus ballot sheet to show in which of the four categories referred to above he believed each Republican member should be listed. (Each party in each house used membership lists to ballot on controversial issues in caucus.) The outcome was an incomplete and only partly helpful listing.

Four weeks were to pass before the crucial voting would take place, not the two weeks between the recess and the reconvening. In the first half of this interval Wise was told that in the event the other side should be defeated on the proposed amendments and countered by offering a sheaf of others from the floor, I'd be in the gallery armed with source material for his use in counter-counterattack. Scott would be there, too —of this there would be no doubt—to do his part. It was in this period, the last half of May, that the state association of soil and water conservation district directors went on record as supporting our view, and made their position known to all legislators in a letter over the signature of their president. Too, a letter I'd written Representative George Gekas, Dauphin County Republican, assuring him Harrisburg had nothing to fear as to water supply from the compact, was reported by Snare to have brought a favorable reaction, and Gekas did indeed vote for our side throughout the House phase of the action.

The bill was not called the week of the 27th for a number of reasons; the members were preoccupied by various other controversial bills, and wanted to adjourn for the week on Tuesday night, so June arrived with the issue still unresolved. Friendly legislators spent the first few days of the month in deciding upon or refining strategy, and in tactical maneuvers. Wise and his company would first attempt by amendment to have the bill returned to its original language. If successful, sops would be offered the other side in the form of enabling sections intended to achieve there, for Pennsylvania only, commission actions and procedures that some of the offensive amendments would have put in the body of the compact. This, we hoped, would swing enough votes our way to provide the constitutional majority (102 votes) required for passage of a bill in the House.

After postponements on June 10 and 11, the bill was called on the 12th under severely adverse conditions. Ahead of it on the calendar were a half-dozen or so supplemental appropriations bills that brought on a good deal of debate. Next was a Delaware River Port Authority bill which would require Pennsylvania to help pay for port improvements at Chester, Pennsylvania, and at Camden, New Jersey, the first downstream, the second directly across the river from Philadelphia. Taxes paid by residents of Philadelphia would benefit its competitor cities. It was so hot an issue that a number of Philadelphia members, mostly Democrats expected to vote our way, absented themselves. The Republicans were under firm leadership control, and nearly all were in their seats. Tempers already were frayed by the acrimonious debate on the previous measures. Things definitely didn't look good, but there was nothing to do but drive ahead. The action to strike the obnoxious amendments and return the compact to its original form was first, as planned, and with it came the speeches.

Over on the Senate side of the capitol in 1967, as recounted earlier, Confair didn't bother to make a speech, sure he had the needed votes and questioning whether any minds would be changed. Speechmaking on the House side likely changed no minds, either. It may be questioned whether they were listened to by the majority of the members present. From my seat in the gallery at the rear of the chamber, which slopes downward to the well of the House as a theater slopes toward the orchestra pit, the members could be seen plainly, and few appeared to be listening. Many were reading newspapers, letters, and other papers. Others talked in whispers with their neighbors, walked out to the rest rooms or to telephone booths, or came back to the gallery to visit with constituents or others. Besides, the public address system of the House lacked something, or the acoustics were poor; at any rate, from the gallery area what was said often came through as little more than sounds

whose meaning had to be guessed or deduced from the occasional word
that could be heard distinctly.

Wise and other speakers for our side used most of the information
that had been supplied by our office after consultation with Goddard,
Sommerville, Trace, Wendell, Zimmermann, and others. What the opposition had to say was repetitious of the things previously expounded.
Bush had the leading floor role, and at the outset protested his earnest
wish for what he considered a workable Susquehanna compact. From
then on what he said could have been a playback on tape of an old
Hatfield speech though not of a blast by Watson. Bush engaged in
gentlemanly debate, not polemics or rabble-rousing. But he did play
upon fears that Pennsylvania could be wronged by a hostile commission,
and used familiar red-herring techniques. Were we giving away sovereign rights in not insisting upon a dominant position? Rectify it with
the unanimous vote provision. Was not Pennsylvania the "have" state of
the three and would not the other two, the "have nots," then conspire to
Pennsylvania's disadvantage? He said that, if so, they would only be
looking to the betterment of home state interests, and what was wrong
with doing the same for Pennsylvania? Wouldn't a year's or a few years'
delay be a small price to pay for amending the compact so as to make it
a more perfect instrument? One of Bush's colleagues, then, asserted he
thought it a compliment that the Appropriations Committee wanted to
amend the compact in only six places. As he said this my mind drifted
back across the long years the compact had been in the making, and the
effort so many thoughtful people had put into trying to assure that the
very passages these people were trying to change had been phrased properly in the first place. The speakers, one after another, droned on, but at
length talked themselves out and the vote was called for on the proposition of striking the committee's amendments. We lost, 98 to 82. Only
twelve Republicans voted with seventy Democrats to return the compact
to the original language; and twelve Democrats were among the temporarily victorious ninety-eight.

An attempt, then, to have a vote on final passage postponed was
objected to by Bush, and the Speaker ordered the roll called. This time
our team picked up a net of six votes for a total of eighty-eight, and only
ninety-four voted in favor of the bill with the amendments; it failed,
therefore, for lack of the needed constitutional majority.[5] My diary
entry next day began, "We lost a battle but the war goes on," for we still
had five legislative days to attempt to bring about reconsideration.

While Wise and his colleagues pondered strategy that might help us

over the hump, those of us outside the Assembly consulted among ourselves, by phone and otherwise. Observing that either side, at that stage,
would have a hard time winning, I asked Confair what he thought of a
possible meeting of Wise and Wendell with Bush and the Speaker. Not
a chance, he contended, saying Bush was floating on clouds "higher than
a steeple" and probably wouldn't even condescend to discuss the matter.

Zimmermann, on the phone, had a better idea. Why not try for a
conference in which IAC leaders, including legislators, from all three
states would discuss the differences with leaders of our opposition? His
reasoning was that if Bush and his associates were sincere in wanting a
compact, they should recognize the arbitrariness of one house of one of
the three state legislative bodies figuratively shoving amendments down
the throats of the others. The attempt must be made, he said, to reconcile differences before the irretraceable step was essayed by that one
house. He believed much harm had already been done our chances for
early passage of the compact by the Congress. Instead of divisiveness and
perhaps long-drawn-out bickering between the three states, we should
present a united front in Washington. Otherwise we'd be in a weak
bargaining position with the federal agencies concerned, some of which
we were certain would prefer that there be no such compact; further, we
could perhaps later on have forced upon us a Title II commission organized under the federal Water Resources Planning Act of 1965, previously
referred to. This would put Pennsylvania, in our view, in a worse position than could possibly be the case, even under the most adverse of
circumstances, if the Susquehanna compact became law in the form we
wanted. The request for such a meeting should come from Maryland
and New York, or at least one of them, and should be to the Speaker.
Goddard approved the idea. So did James and O'Donnell of Maryland,
and Montanari of New York. Lawrence was away and not reachable. His
secretary, Irene Sefcik, would get him on the phone when she could.
Meanwhile his alternate became his spokesman. However, before they
would send telegrams to Speaker Lee, he must give informal but binding
assurance that the requests would not be rebuffed, which was a matter of
diplomatic etiquette and of pride.

On June 14 I sent a memorandum to Goddard, O'Donnell, James,
Lawrence, and Montanari, transmitting suggested telegram language;
the memo also said Wise and others consulted believed we had nothing
to lose by the effort, and suggested who probably should attend the
conference if Lee was amenable.[6] About midday on Monday, June 17,
Goddard reached Lee by phone, then called me to say he had "bought

the thought without a quibble." This word was telephoned to Maryland and New York, after which James sent a telegram phrased much like the draft previously furnished; Montanari advised that his wire, in effect, said "Me, too."

Now the problem was to find a date mutually acceptable to the people who'd come to Harrisburg, and to the legislators. We had few options, since the meeting should be on one of the days the legislature was in session, and it then was closing down each week not later than Wednesday. After much telephoning—our long distance toll charges for that month probably were higher than in any other comparable period—it was decided the conference would be held on Monday, June 24. Our people gathered the evening before for a general discussion. Present were Senator Niles, Assemblyman Boland, and Montanari representing New York. The Maryland delegation consisted of O'Donnell and Everstine, with James to replace O'Donnell at the conference next day. (O'Donnell had to be in Baltimore on state business. When James arrived at the Statehouse, just ahead of the conference, Everstine gave him a quick briefing.) Goddard, Confair, Snare, and Wise represented Pennsylvania. Zimmermann, Wendell, and I completed the roster.

The amenities over, Wendell asked, "What is the root of the opposition?" There were several replies. Snare said that in view of the controversy that had built up in rural constituencies, any change in the compact's language would make its proponents look like saviors of Pennsylvania. Goddard referred to the state chamber's fears and the effect they had in arousing the opposition of the potent business and industrial lobby in the capitol. Wise and Confair followed this lead by saying "certain interests in the Pennsylvania Manufacturers Association" were fighting hard and had called attempts to strike the objectionable language as "ripper" actions, terminology used derogatorily.

In preparation for the meeting I had put in writing the chief arguments for and against the proposed amendments, using the parallel column technique for comparison reading. This material suggested that in at least two instances the amendments could be rephrased to apply only to Pennsylvania so they could go into the enabling area at the back of the bill and not disturb the body of the compact. The discussion disclosed how two more could be reworked to go in the enabler if Pennsylvania wanted them so badly that they were a prior condition of passage of the compact.

The first of the four was in reference to Section 12.5 and would provide that in case a Pennsylvania agency should give the commission technical assistance it would do so only under written contract except in some very minor case.

Next was that most objectionable change in Section 14.1 regarding the comprehensive plan. In House debate on the night of June 12, opposition members had protested that all they wanted was to assure that the commission would keep the Assembly fully informed of what it was doing. Very well, let it be abundantly informed; we would have the commission fill it to overflowing with information. We would write an enabler section to provide that each legislator would get copies of all commission meeting minutes. This would be supplemental to the various reports and documents the commission already was mandated to provide or make available under Sections 15.11, 15.12, and others, the scope of which we suspected the opponents had not fully grasped. I wondered how many legislators would read all that material—actually, how soon some might even come to consider it in the same category as junk mail—and if the whole thing would not fall of its own weight in a short time. At the moment, however, our thought was that if this would help ensure compact passage without body blows, we should go ahead and offer it.

Third was the matter of following duly prescribed budgetary processes, in Section 14.3 (c). Here all we considered necessary to meet professed desires was an enabler section specifying that, as an agency of Pennsylvania, the commission would follow budgetary processes customary to other agencies receiving appropriations from general tax revenues. New York had handled the subject in that fashion; Pennsylvania could do so in all propriety.

Finally, there was that pesky thing about the commission hiring watchmen who would have the same powers as peace officers. Here I had noted that Section 270 of the Pennsylvania Fish Code had for years made it possible for almost anyone who wore a badge to make arrests for fish law violations, which meant there already were several thousand potential "fish wardens" in the Commonwealth. However, if this was a sticking point, let an enabler section prohibit commission watchmen from arresting fishermen. We couldn't care less whether it was in or out of the enabler, but if it was in we just might pick up another vote or two.

This left two matters on which our conferees were adamant, the proposed voting change and the substitution of "shall" for "may" in Section 3.5-4. Our people flatly refused the first, and didn't see how the other could conveniently or practically be shifted from the body of the compact to the enabling area of the bill.

After the discussions ended, Zimmermann, Wendell, and I stayed behind for half an hour and put the suggested enabler sections in rough draft form. Most of the language was Wendell's. Next morning, early, my wife typed a number of clean copies—that is, errorless—which were distributed to Wise, Snare, and others of our people when I intercepted them at breakfast.

All chairs were filled in the small Appropriations Committee conference room when we met at 10 A.M. on the 24th. Present for our side were Boland, Confair, Everstine, Goddard, James, Montanari, Niles, Snare, Wendell, Zimmermann, and myself. For the other side were Lee, Appropriations Chairman Jack Seltzer, Bush, Representatives John Hope Anderson and Eugene Fulmer, Budget Secretary Martin Brackbill (an executive branch official appointed by the governor whose remarks aligned him with our—and the governor's—opposition), and Craig Truax, a former officer in Shafer's cabinet who had resigned to become assistant to the House leadership.

There were introductions and polite preliminaries, after which Bush stated his side's case for the proposed amendments. His group, he said, was unanimous in wanting a compact. The unanimous vote was the most important compact change from their point of view.[8] It would put all signatories on "an equal footing" and they would make it work "because of economic necessity." He stated his reasons, in turn, for each of the other compact alterations. When our turn came Wendell gave his views on legislative realities, in his typically studious, deliberate, reasoned style. He told the group that every subject that had been brought out could be handled to satisfy Pennsylvania in enabling sections except the unanimous vote and the "shall-may" matter, and described how and why it should be done that way if it was to be done at all. Bush brushed aside the subject of enabler sections; he didn't care to listen to them but wanted more discussion of the unanimous vote. He wasn't worried about a federal veto, on which several of our people had expounded at some length, since the federal government could withdraw at any time anyhow and in that way had a built-in veto. Wendell responded that this was true and if it wished the federal government could ride roughshod over the states; however, without the compact there was no restraint upon that government whatsoever. With the compact everyone would know who the spoilers were, and it was our only way to put and keep brakes on rampant federalism if such should become policy in Washington. He and Zimmermann—others of our group, too—emphasized that water projects badly needed in Pennsylvania or either of the other member states but that didn't completely meet federal agency wishes could be held up interminably by the unanimous vote provision.

One of Bush's associates (Fulmer) said quite forthrightly that without the veto the Pennsylvania member could connive with the others on a project detrimental to Pennsylvania and "look good back home" when the other three voted the project into effect. As he said it Zimmermann looked at me and slowly shook his head.

James said at one point that he could hardly believe his eyes when he read that Pennsylvania was willing to give Maryland a veto over commission action. It was too good to be true; Maryland, he said, had everything to gain by it.[9] (Fulmer later, in floor debate, twisted this into alleged approval of the proposed unanimous vote.) His state could stop New York, Pennsylvania, and even the federal government in their tracks any time they proposed to divert Susquehanna water or indicated they wanted to go easy on water polluters. Nevertheless, he opposed the unanimous vote and was confident the Maryland General Assembly would refuse to concur. The New York position was equally firm.

There was a good bit of rambling discussion. At one point the Appropriations Committee chairman, Seltzer, asked us for an explanation of the difference between the compact and its enabling sections—a most astonishing and revealing question. Later he complained that our side was trying to "railroad" the bill—an extraordinary declaration from the chairman of the committee that had sat on the Senate-passed bill for nine months and on its House companion still longer.

The upshot of the conference was that the two sides had become, as Bush put it, "polarized" on the matter of voting, and there could be no compromise agreement. Zimmermann closed for our side with the remark that any delay in getting the compact passed in identical form by the three states played into the hands of reluctant federal agencies. Our group left the room, Wendell to try to get to Madison, Wisconsin, in time for a speaking engagement, the others to go their respective ways. My immediate task was to get to Wise to report the situation so he and his fellow Democratic members could know where we stood and plan accordingly.

In customary course, under the existing parliamentary situation, the bill should have come up for definite action on Tuesday, June 24, but it didn't. The House went into session after 4 P.M., and began debate on the general appropriations bill—money to operate through the next fiscal year all the state agencies that were fed from the general fund. The debate was bitter at times, and quite extended, continuing without a break until after ten o'clock. Confair came into the gallery section, and toward the end of the action on the money bill he, Wise, Snare, and I discussed what we should do. Wise believed we should ask to have the compact bill laid over a day; many of our supporters had drifted out of the chamber. The opposition was glad to go along, for a glance at the numbers still present made it obvious neither side could muster a constitutional majority. It was agreed by the house leaders that the bill should be made a special order of business next day.

Sometime after 5 P.M. on the 26th the compact bill was called. Wise made a relatively brief speech telling about the conference on Monday and urging a vote in favor of striking out the six objectionable amendments. Laudadio called attention to the strength and numbers of the organized sportsmen on our side. Snare in a few words told of the years of effort that had gone into trying to produce good and needed legislation. Bush made what seemed at the time to be desperation remarks; my diary said he sounded that way, also that he still appeared uncertain as to the compact's true function and was convinced the commission would build and operate all water projects in the basin from that time forward. Wise said later he considered answering Bush but decided the time had come to get names on dotted lines and so abstained.

Our combined efforts had paid off. There were more Democrats in their seats than on June 12, and the work of Snare, Scott, and others had swung a few more Republicans into line with us. The vote to strike the obnoxious amendments was 100 to 77.

Wise immediately announced he wished to offer four amendments to the enabling part of the bill—the amendments we had agreed upon on June 23 and that had been brushed aside on the 24th—but Bush objected. He had been given copies of these proposals at the conference table but now protested there had not been time to study them; they had not gone through caucus consideration, and so on. So, in a smart parliamentary action, Wise simply withdrew the amendments. Bush was trapped. He had lost everything in trying to win everything, and now refused to accept enabler sections that he could have claimed as substantial "protective" language for Pennsylvania. I went home, since vote on final passage would have to be held over until next day at the earliest, but had hardly arrived before Wise telephoned to say Bush had come to him and asked if he now could have some of the amendments to the enabler; he'd seen his earlier mistake, and apparently wanted to salvage something from defeat. We were inclined to go along instead of being adamant about it. We agreed to meet in Wise's office next morning with the enabling sections material in hand, plus a collection of Delaware commission reports and other publications to show Bush what a mass of reading matter the legislators would receive if the enabler amendment should be adopted that would instruct the Susquehanna commission to send a wide variety of reports and other material to Pennsylvania legislators.[10] We hoped the exhibits from Delaware would cause Bush to change his mind and not ask for that one, but he did. All four were added without difficulty on June 27, with a few minor modifications of language requested by Bush, after which the legislature closed up shop for a long July 4 recess. It would reconvene on July 8.

My diary for that day contains the following entry:

> About 6:30 p.m. I phoned my wife from Snare's office and told her I'd be home in half an hour. As I drove to the carport I saw a square of red carpeting suspended from the eave, to which was appended a string of toy balloons. From the car to the front door were neatly spaced rectangles of the same red carpeting material, and just inside stood Billie with a long, cool drink in her outstretched hand.

That seems to tell the story of the final House action on the compact bill. It was passed by a vote of 146 to 45. There was no closing debate. There was one adverse speech by Representative Reynolds of Chester County, mentioned earlier as the booster for diversion from the lower Susquehanna. Wise didn't bother to answer. When the green and red lights flashed on the roll-call indicators on the chamber walls, they showed that Speaker Lee, Bush, the majority leader, and numerous other Republicans had swung over to the victory column. Only three House Democrats voted against the compact on final passage. Wise looked around and saw me already on my feet moving in his direction, and came back to the gallery area where we congratulated each other. Snare joined me in his office immediately afterward and said he and Wise had already agreed to meet on adjournment and down a couple of drinks in celebration.

One Pennsylvania hurdle remained to get over—Senate concurrence in the enabler amendments. They could have been voted on the following day, July 9, but when the Republican senators discussed the bill in caucus, Confair objected strenuously to some of the things being said by

The Susquehanna River Basin Compact was signed by Governor Raymond P. Shafer of Pennsylvania, right, on July 17, 1968. Chairman Goddard of the Interstate Advisory Committee is at the left. The author is the third person in the photo.

those on the other side. Davis feared votes were being lost and successfully moved for a week's delay. Confair phoned from his home that night to say, "I gave 'em hell," because "they needed it." He added that he still wasn't worried about the ultimate outcome. When Snare went to tell Governor Shafer the House vote on final passage, he forecast the bill would soon be on his desk for signature. Shafer's lingering pessimism showed in his reply: "I'll believe it when I see it."

The Senate debate on the 15th was largely a repeat of that of a year earlier, with one diverting variation. When Republican Senator William B. Lentz of the Dauphin County district began speaking about his obsessive fear that the commission could cut off Harrisburg's supplemental water supply from the river, Senator William G. Sesler, Erie Democrat, raised a point of order, holding that a motion to concur was not debatable. A flurry of activity followed. The parliamentarian, the majority leader, and nearly every lawyer on the Republican side clustered around the president pro tem. Minutes later they called Sesler up, and there was more discussion. The ruling that emerged was that at the request of the majority leader debate would continue, but only as to the merits of the amendments to the enabler, not on the compact. Lentz resumed, and Sesler stopped him for a question. Would Lentz be so kind as to tell him what was in the amendments? Lentz hesitated perceptibly, then replied that he hadn't read them. The vote to concur finally came, 28 to 13.

My reaction was not elation or jubilation, but release and relief. Snare, Confair, Davis, and a few other friends and I complimented each other and that was that.

A year earlier Governor Spiro T. Agnew of Maryland had suggested a ceremonial signing by the chief executives of the three states when all had passed the compact. The annual Governors' Conference was to be held the week after Pennsylvania passage, in Cincinnati, and a ceremony there was suggested, to be accompanied by a strong statement urging swift congressional action so the commission could be created and go to work. The proposal was rejected after deliberation, on the ground that the Cincinnati air would be filled with national political action—it was a presidential election year—and our Susquehanna compact-signing ceremony would be completely submerged. Consequently, Shafer signed in his reception room at the capitol on July 17.

I was given one of the pens, the one with which he put the "P" (for Philip) in his signature.

Part V

Through the Washington Maze

Chapter 1

Preliminaries in Washington

By late 1969 our people had had on-and-off discussions with water resources people in the federal executive branch for two and a half years without reaching agreement on what we considered the relatively simple matter of writing reservations to the Susquehanna compact acceptable to those concerned. The upshot of it was that in January, 1969, supporters of the Susquehanna compact introduced identical bills in the House and Senate that contained federal reservations language adapted from the previously enacted and highly regarded Delaware Compact. This chapter carries the story of the more significant happenings up to the point in late 1968 when, after much delay, partly our own, partly federal, we had not one but two sets of reservation proposals to mull over. We also faced a proposed executive order that looked to be devastating in effect.

All the reasons for the long delay cannot be set forth with certainty; some can only be surmised. My conclusion is that part of it was attributable to the simple fact that there's nothing spritely or nimble about the movements of Washington bureaucracy. Other reasons may have been many. Simple, old fashioned conviction on the part of certain civil servants that the whole idea of the authoritative federal–interstate compact is constitutionally wrong was in their case the activating force. They seemed as intransigeant as those Pennsylvania legislators who just didn't want a compact no matter how it was phrased. Another group wanted federal reservations—the conditions and exemptions under which the United States would become a party—phrased their way or they wouldn't have anything to do with the compact. At the other end of the line were some who were convinced, as we were, that the concept was beneficial and that reservations similar to those that had proved

workable in the Delaware basin were quite all right for the Susquehanna. Unfortunately for us, they apparently were a minority. Also,
delay was occasioned by the simple fact that the administration hadn't
made up its mind as to what it wanted.

The customary course in matters of diplomacy traditionally has been
for the several parties to confer until they resolve their differences or
decide to stand their ground, and put down roots. We who sought action
instead of stalemate eventually came to the conclusion that the only
course that could lead to a decision was to put something specific before
Congress. That, we believed, would force the issue, compel all concerned
to focus on specific language instead of, as we believed, writing substantive or merely semantic variations that settled nothing.

It would be nice to be able to say that the course from the beginning
to the present terminus was a fairly direct line, and to set forth the
successive actions in neat order. It didn't develop that way. The line of
march was not orderly. The narrative point of beginning has to be 1960,
and the locale another basin. At that time the Delaware Compact had
been put in initial draft form and laid before Dr. Walter Gellhorn,
Betts Professor of Law at Columbia Law School, and Dr. Frank P. Grad,
associate director of the Legislative Drafting Research Fund, also at
Columbia. Attorney William Miller of Princeton, New Jersey, who
headed the Delaware Compact drafters, furnished us with a copy of the
Gellhorn-Grad opinion.

It was known from the hearings on the Northeastern Compact, previously referred to, and other sources that questions of constitutionality of
the new intergovernmental mechanism would be raised. The essence of
the report of the specialists was that the compact should withstand such
attack without difficulty. This gave the Delaware advocates confidence
enough to press forward vigorously, with quick passage the result.

Between the passage of the Delaware Compact by the four state general assemblies early in 1961 and a "no contest" attitude on the part of
the federal agencies a few months afterward, however, much of significance had occurred. Chapter 3, Part I, tells how President Kennedy gave
Stewart L. Udall, Secretary of the Interior, the *ad hoc* assignment of
coordinating federal agency viewpoints on the Delaware Compact. This
was no easy task, for agency views diverged then fully as much as they do
today, possibly more so. Negotiations were conducted at a high level,
and there is a story, possibly aprocryphal, that at one point the President
referred to certain agencies holding out against agreement as "those

melancholy babies" and cracked the executive whip. However that may be, some twenty-three agencies were brought so well into line that the Delaware Compact passed handily in record time.[1] Without that unified federal approach it would have been necessary for the compact's proponents to try to win approval of the agreement and of federal reservations from all the agencies individually, a staggering undertaking in view of internal realities in Washington. (A high-level coordinator might have made a difference in the cases of the Missouri and Northeastern compacts.)

The demonstration of successful coordination of the agencies in the Delaware instance lent much support to a then budding effort to establish a federal agency whose chief mission would be day-to-day coordination of federal views on water matters. This became law in 1965 and created the federal Water Resources Council.[2] We welcomed its coming, believing this would simplify our task in going to Washington with our compact after it had been passed by the states of the basin. It was not to prove so simple, and the new law also contained a built-in question mark so far as compacts of our kind were concerned. Its Title II provided for forming federal–state water resources planning commissions, in which the federal voice could be powerful almost to the point of dominating. Beyond this, the Title II commissions were not empowered by law to go beyond planning water resources programs for river basins or groups of river basins. This factor left decision-making to the agencies and entities that had exercised it theretofore; these new commissions had no regulatory or enforcement authority. We began to wonder if the birth of the new type of commissions might not threaten establishment of any more administrative–regulatory type compacts and commissions of which the Delaware was the prototype and ours a reasonable facsimile. We considered it would be no more than natural for federal construction agencies to prefer an intergovernmental mechanism that left them a free hand to do much as they pleased, subject, of course, to the controlling hand of Congress, which has traditionally considered public works a favorite child. Affected regulatory agencies, too, likely would have similar sentiments.

However distracting the Title II commissions might be at moments when our minds had time for contemplation of their potential effect, we were for the most part concerned with the coordinating function of the Water Resources Council. We found that as regards the Susquehanna Compact the council could move as ponderously as any other federal bureau or collection of bureaus. At times I came to believe it could show agility mainly in postponing facing up to the issue until the last possible minute.

This is harsh and not entirely fair in hindsight. There were extenuating circumstances over the period under review, but I have learned nothing to account for certain earlier dilatoriness. Remember, as outlined in Part IV, Chapter 1, we had begun to communicate with the Water Resources Council in June, 1966, when our first draft was given out. Udall and WRC's Caulfield had appeared receptive, and our leaders felt approval in principle[3] would follow, after which serious negotiating could begin as soon as we had put the compact in final form. Indeed, we considered it not unlikely that we might receive from the council comments and suggestions that would help in the polishing and editing prior to laying the compact before the general assemblies of the basin states.

However, from that time through 1968 our communications with the council, from the IAC staff viewpoint at least, seemed to consist of little but frustration. Udall was the "summit" member of the Delaware commission and, after it had been in existence long enough to demonstrate a potential for good, he had frequently praised it. We felt he would use his prestige and his clout as chairman of the council to speed up its arriving at a point of determination with respect to the Susquehanna Compact. It didn't happen that way, but I don't know why.

One factor doubtless was the Potomac basin. Udall was given the responsibility of conducting a review of a survey of that basin that had been completed earlier by federal agencies under the leadership of the Corps of Engineers, and Udall and others high in Lyndon Johnson's official and personal family considered the Potomac as our "national river." Some time after the Susquehanna drafting began a Potomac River Basin Advisory Committee was organized by the governors and the District of Columbia, with a mission similar to ours, and it chose to draft a federal–interstate compact for that basin, one with strong regulatory features. The preliminary draft of the Potomac Compact was given to the public in October, 1967. It is possible that some of the WRC delay was occasioned by a wish to wait and see what the Potomac proposal consisted of. It was in some respects quite different from the Susquehanna; as one example, it put much more emphasis on natural beauty than we did. (The Potomac Compact was approved by Virginia in 1970 and Maryland in 1971.)

The internal turmoil of the later months of the Johnson years must be reckoned another factor that encouraged delay, especially by those who were not too enamored of the compact idea in the first place. If they held back strong enough and long enough a new administration would come into power and—who knew?—it just might agree with the foot-draggers.

Too, the problem we encountered in Pennsylvania in getting the compact through the General Assembly could be construed as protein and vitamins for an "anti" faction in the council.

The factors outlined—and there likely were others of which we could know or deduce nothing—were enough to leave us believing the going would get worse rather than better as time passed.

Four months after our conference with Udall we had completed our round of meetings with leaders of opinion in the three states and were ready to put the compact in final form for introduction in the legislatures. We had heard nothing from Udall or Caulfield, so an invitation was extended for council participation in our October 10, 1966, drafting session, at which we purposed to finish off our consideration of modifications. An "observer" from the council attended, but took no part in the deliberations. The council volunteered nothing. Late in October Goddard wrote Udall saying that since we'd had no adverse comment from the WRC we would assume that in general terms the compact language was agreeable to him. This brought a request on November 17 that we furnish the council with copies of the changes in the original draft that we had made in October. We complied. On December 6 Goddard received a letter from the staff executive saying a task force had been "meeting frequently and giving intensive study" to the compact and that "every effort" was being made to provide Goddard with comments "before the first of the year."

The first of the year came and went, and Goddard broke the silence on January 3, 1967, by sending Udall a nudging kind of inquiry in which he reminded that two of the states faced tight legislative schedules. Maryland was limited to seventy legislative days and New York's Assembly would have to quit by April to make room for a constitutional convention to occupy its chambers. Udall responded on January 27, 1967, but his letter was neither warming nor comforting to us who had espoused a Susquehanna Compact. He complained of the manner in which the Delaware Compact had been drafted (which was similar to our procedure and therefore by inference we considered we were being criticized as well). He said it was doubtful that the federal interest could be represented by adding reservations to the body of the compact (as had been done successfully in the case of the Delaware). The pace of our action should be slowed to allow the then still ongoing federal survey of the water resources of the basin to be completed so its report could, in essence, become the comprehensive plan or, at least, "fullfill planning requirements for some time." He spoke of possible "alternate" basin arrangements (which might mean Title II commissions). Finally, we should enlarge the scope of our compact to embrace the entire drainage area of Chesapeake Bay. In the closing sentence, he suggested a meeting.

The Udall letter contained much to disturb us, and brought sharp reaction from our people in all three states. Other than that long ago complaint to me in Harrisburg by the Soil Conservation Service man, McKeever, we had heard nothing directly to the effect that the federal people wanted to take part in the compact drafting. The council staff man who sat with us in drafting session the previous October had made it very clear that he was not there to participate but merely to observe and listen. The drafting technique that made federal reservations language an adjunct to the Delaware Compact, coupled with the positive passages preserving congressional and constitutional powers that had been written in the body of that compact, had caused no problems in the Delaware basin, and we had anticipated none in ours.

The "what's the hurry?" language was especially disconcerting, since it seemed the opposite of the federal attitude toward the Potomac Compact. Then, to have the entire Chesapeake Bay drainage thrown into the scene was simply too much. This was the first time that aspect of federal thinking had come to our attention, and we considered it totally unrealistic. The jurisdictions that would be involved in such an arrangement were as diverse as upstate New York, the Washington metropolitan district, and West Virginia's eastern hill country. In 1966 Congress had instructed the Federal Water Pollution Control Administration to conduct a water quality and economic study of the nation's coastal areas,[4] and it was just then getting in full stride, but that had nothing direct to do with the complexities of drafting compact language suited to the bay's drainage area. We would be starting a completely new undertaking. We would be forced to marry the Susquehanna and Potomac compacts, which already were different enough to make such a course cause extensive problems. Beyond that, we would have to bring in the State of Delaware, the source of some of the Chespeake's easterly tributaries, and that state had not participated in any of the work, extending over many months and ranging across a host of subjects, of the drafters of either the

Susquehanna or the Potomac compacts. Were the federal people serious about the bay, or was this a diversionary exercise, a red herring sort of maneuver? We had no way of knowing.

We had telephone and face-to-face consultations all over the Susquehanna basin, and with Wendell in Washington, and on February 13 Goddard sent Udall a reply the meaning of which was that we had had enough of nonspecifics and general complaints and comments. "There must be specific language under consideration, and suggestions of alternatives to that language, in order for negotiations to be meaningful," his letter said. "Certainly the council has had adequate time to indicate these views more specifically at an earlier date." The legislatures of all three states were already in session and bills were about to be introduced in two of them. Goddard's letter analysed that from Udall, he wrote, "to the degree its generality permits." It was difficult for Goddard to believe, he wrote, that there was sufficient difference between the Delaware and Susquehanna compacts "to cause Congress to prohibit for the Susquehanna basin what it approved for the Delaware." There was more, including an outright rejection of the Chespeake Bay ploy, but the above is enough to indicate the tone and tenor of the response.

The situation made it seem more urgent than ever that we should meet with the council, and for that reason Goddard left the way open for more communication and suggested alternate meeting dates. We did meet on March 3, in the council's conference room.

Before the meeting the letter exchange with Udall, accompanied by the text of the compact, went to all members of the House and Senate from the Susquehanna states. Compact legislation was introduced in the legislatures of New York and Maryland, so a start could be made toward passage there. Zimmermann drafted a variety of alternative federal reservations for consideration if the council people and our negotiators should come to nose-to-the-grindstone discussions. The alternatives didn't change our position on what we considered essentials, but modified terminology enough so they could be adopted by either side as facesaving compromises. Zimmermann also prepared a first draft of what became a Memorandum of Legislative Intent that we later used in Pennsylvania.

Goddard and Caulfield met in the latter's office on February 24 to firm up meeting time and arrangements. He returned with information to the effect that the questions now being raised by unnamed federal agencies were (1) why a compact is needed; (2) if one is needed, why must it be a federal–state arrangement; (3) why provide so many functions; and

(4) that matter of the Chesapeake Bay drainage area. These were to constitute the agenda for our meeting, and obviously had to be considered preliminaries; in themselves they didn't constitute negotiating substance, but discussion could lead to more productive talks concerning specific reservation language. So we believed.

Zimmermann brought a draft of a response to the first three items, and at a strategy meeting just head of our confrontation with Caulfield and his fellows we put in skeleton form several of our reasons why the Chesapeake Bay proposition seemed undesirable.

Zimmermann's statement called to mind the underdeveloped nature of the river, which urgently required intergovernmental planning to prevent haphazard construction that was single-project oriented and did not take into consideration the environmental realities of the whole. It spoke only of the existing diversion from the lower Susquehanna to Baltimore, but no one present could escape the implications that Baltimore's was just one of what could prove to be many out-of-basin demands for water from our river. For the geometrically minded, Zimmermann pointed out that the compact, as written, assured both vertical coordination between governmental levels, and horizontal coordination on each level.

Sommerville presented the Chesapeake Bay portions of our response. They included:

1. Riverine and estaurine conditions and problems differ greatly; they require different technologies and consequently a specialized staff with proper expertise would be needed in addition to that already contemplated for a Susquehanna commission.

2. The many and diverse jurisdictions involved made it questionable whether a compact could be devised that would be meaningful and satisfactory to all.

3. A separate Potomac Basin Compact embracing tidewater reaches had already been preliminarily drafted and was in the review stage.

4. Though the Potomac had been studied extensively, and the survey relating to the Susquehanna was in late stages, not even a start had been made toward a thorough study of the bay and its needs other than what was in the pollution-weighted survey under the aegis of the FWPCA.

Finally, the Susquehanna and Potomac compacts contained language protective of the bay and permitted coordination not only between federal–state commissions but also between commissions and riparian states.

Fresh fish from Chesapeake Bay on their way to the food markets of the country. *Ted Jones, Stuart Finley Films*

Discussion relative to the bay was brief. The federal people seemed more concerned over what they considered the possibility of the compact commission binding the federal government to a course of water resources action. This was reminiscent of the debate on the same subject raised back in 1960 when the Northeastern Compact was before a congressional committee.[5]

At the close Caulfield said, "We will move as fast as we can," which may have been realistic from his point of view, since none of his principals was present and in possession of the details that had been laid out on the table, but from our standpoint this was grossly unsatisfactory; it could only mean delay.

It would be almost two years before the two groups faced each other again, though it would be unfair to say all the postponements were initiated by the council. As earlier chapters have told, the compact was passed by New York and Maryland in the closing hours of their respective legislative sessions, and it got pigeonholed in Pennsylvania. When this happened in the summer of 1967, our leadership came to the conclusion that it would be unwise to insist on federal action before we had resolved our own dilemma. Our previous pressuring had been based on our faulty belief that all three state legislatures would act favorably and promptly. When the Pennsylvania legislative leadership balked, Goddard wrote Udall saying he believed it proper not to press for federal action until the obstacles at home had been overcome. Udall and the council people seemed happy to oblige.

Nevertheless, less formal communications were had. A month after our March, 1967, meeting Zimmermann and Wendell were told an *ad hoc* committee of agency lawyers had been formed in behalf of the WRC to write their own version of federal reservations to the compact and to suggest alternatives, but it was more than that. What was actually in the making was a formal statement of Water Resources Council policy with the formidable title of *Alternative Institutional Arrangements for Managing River Basin Operations,* published by the Council in 1967. When this booklet of federal guidelines arrived we weren't certain whether to embrace its encouraging words or look askance at passages that seemed to hint at a preference for something other than our kind of compact. In the foreword the pamphlet said that eight kinds of management arrangements had been studied, and the council had come to the conclusion that three "can be useful instruments in appropriate circumstances and under appropriate terms and conditions." The three listed were strictly interstate compacts, federal–interstate compacts, and the operations of "separate Federal and State institutions assisted by joint Federal–State planning bodies"; that is, the status quo coupled to the planning help that could be provided by Title II commissions.

The custom so prevalent of listing preferences in inverse order made it look to us as though we were in the middle, so to speak, and that the council would favor a Title II commission for the Susquehanna over our federal–interstate compact. The fact that the federal–interstate compact had been accorded second place in the ranking may be attributed in part to the obvious success the Delaware commission was enjoying. Its more visible accomplishments included resolution of the severe drought problems of 1965-66, coordination of pollution control criteria for the four states, and acting as agent for Pennsylvania to furnish water for use in New Jersey. The informal talks Zimmermann and Wendell had had with individuals connected with the Council served to lift our spirits.

Our thoughts were focused on our own river basin, as was natural, but our thinking was not entirely provincial. We could appreciate the fact that the council should view separate actions in the light of their relation to possible developments in other parts of the country. At one point Wendell reminded that the council was inclined to consider areas as small as the Susquehanna and Potomac basins as fragments for administrative purposes and the setting up of federal–interstate compacts for regions no larger than these as fragmentation of responsibility and operations. They had visions of expanding federalism. It is entirely possible that this may have motivated the council in suggesting that the entire drainage area of Chesapeake Bay should be considered as a unit for water resources management purposes. Wendell thought the bay issue was still very much alive; however, it was not pressed again by the council in connection with the Susquehanna Compact.

We had no way of knowing when, or whether, the Pennsylvania legislative problems might be surmounted, but it was obvious that if the break in our favor should come unexpectedly soon, we should be prepared for the next step—presentation of something to Congress. In my impatience I had suggested that our best strategy might be to go ahead and have our compact introduced in Congress, with our own federal reservations attached. These would be much like those enacted for the Delaware. Zimmermann agreed. Our executive committee agreed only that we should have the federal enabling legislation in ready form, and Zimmermann was assigned the drafting task.

Aside from casual individual encounters, there was relatively little official communication between our people and the council for many months. The council was intimately concerned with the revising of the first Potomac draft, and in mid-June, 1968, we came into possession of a work paper that had been prepared by the federal negotiating team in connection with the Potomac Compact. Despite our preoccupation with the climax of the legislative battle in Pennsylvania, the work paper was significant enough to cause considerable concern, as it contained the team's version of a substitute Potomac Compact draft. It indicated the federal people were thinking in terms of some rather radical changes in the compact concept. Perhaps the most significant was that the commission's power to approve or disapprove federal water projects would be thrown out the window. If that thinking should be applied to the Susquehanna Compact it would void the application to federal agencies of our Section 3.10 and Article 12. The first of these, it will be remembered, gave the commission the authority to review and approve categories of water projects that would have an actual or potential interstate effect; the second provided that federal water projects would not be deemed officially authorized without their prior inclusion by the commission in its comprehensive plan. Despite the positive language in those sections, the commission's hold would still be weak at best, by reason of the reservations, which as written for the Delaware and as we envisioned them would always give the President veto power to be exercised if he believed a commission action adverse to the national interest.

The total exclusion now advocated meant conditions would be little if any better than those which had caused the Delaware and the Susquehanna drafters to declare, in their preambles, that the water resources of the basins were being administered in a wholly uncoordinated manner that brought with it a splintering of authority and responsibility and other undesirable situations. We felt that the language of our compact plus the reservations of basic authority put in the enabling section gave the federal agencies ample protection against states trying to tell them what to do or not do. However, since the work paper was at that stage of direct concern only to people of the Potomac basin we filed its contents in memory and said nothing.

When our compact had finally been passed by Pennsylvania's lawmakers in the summer of 1968, Goddard wrote Udall that we were again ready to start negotiations.

This was a time of transition for the IAC. In March, 1968, I had given notice that I wished to resign at the end of the year. An earlier chapter noted that Wendell and Schwan had left the Council of State Governments, formed a consulting firm, and the two became the IAC representatives for negotiations with the agencies and to handle communications with members of Congress. Their employment signaled the transfer of primary attention from the state capitals to Washington.

Wendell began conversations with Caulfield within ten days, seeking a negotiating session with the council or, as an alternative, federal enabling language drafted by the council to which the IAC could address itself. The discussion resulted in Caulfield's asking Wendell to draft a set of reservations that the council's "Task Force on River Basins Management Institutions" could consider. A water resources conference which a number of people from the Susquehanna states would attend was to be held in Baltimore on August 21, and we set up a luncheon meeting for those who could be there to hear Wendell's assessment of the situation and to discuss the reservations proposal Caulfield had made to him.

Most of the council task force people were in third or fourth echelons from the top in the agencies they represented, and I gathered from Wendell's comments that these were the levels at which much of the federal opposition to our compact was concentrated. My impression was that Caulfield strained for good relations with his varied council clientele, and they were themselves much divided. I came to the conclusion that some of the federal people had so committed themselves to fixed positions that they might be willing to sacrifice the substance of the compact for the form of the reservations language to which they themselves had at some time given birth, no matter how picayune an individual issue might be.

On September 5 a Wendell draft of reservations was sent to Caulfield. It was largely a refinement of the Delaware Compact, which Udall, the chairman of the Water Resources Council, had approved in 1961 and which had worked well in that basin. Ten weeks later Udall transmitted the council's task force version of federal reservations for the Susquehanna. It contained the public power preference clause that Udall had testified the federal people wanted back in 1961 when Congress was considering the Delaware compact. (*cf.* Part II, Chapter 1.) Of greater concern was a provision that would give the federal commissioner veto power over any action that would affect a federal or a federally assisted water project or one in which the federal government had any kind of legal interest.

This was very bad. Wendell's draft had incorporated the Delaware's provision that the President could employ a federal veto if he came to the conclusion that the national interest was adversely affected. In our judgment, that was as far as the federal veto should go. At a conference in the IAC offices on December 9 our leadership agreed to this and otherwise prepared for our second meeting with the council people, which had been scheduled to be held in Washington on December 23.

We had something new to ponder at that conference on December 9. One of the friends of our compact had learned that a draft of a presidential executive order was being circulated among the water agencies for comment, and had obtained a copy. It would go even further than the November 13 reservations draft in the matter of a federal veto. The power to throw a block on the action of any commission to which the federal government would be a party would not only be given to the President, or to the federal commissioner, *but would also be vested in any affected federal agency.* If that executive order was signed, even in the dying days of an outgoing administration, it still would take time, effort, and much persuasion to bring about rescinding action by the new occupant of the White House, and before that might be achieved the new thinking could become ingrained and a devastating sticking point in any future negotiations. We took steps, but their telling comes later.

We met with the council group, which consisted of staff people and members of the federal task force previously mentioned and—as I saw it, we got nowhere. We came away deadlocked on the federal commissioner veto proposition, the public power preference clause, and other points. We also came away convinced we would gain nothing by waiting longer for the council's attitude to change to a meaningful extent. The indicated course was to go straight to Congress, to give Congress the compact and a reservations section the three states could agree to abide by, and let Congress, not the executive branch agencies, decide what the law should contain. There matters rested as the year ended and the new federal administration took over.

Chapter 2

Questions Multiply

The Interstate Advisory Committee had begun laying groundwork for action by Congress at the time the first draft of the Susquehanna Compact was written. From our office copies of the initial draft and of supporting information were sent to all members of the House and Senate from the three basin states early in June, 1966. The three states maintain offices in Washington, staffed by representatives of their respective governors.

Goddard and I were in touch with the Pennsylvania man, former Congressman Jimmy Van Zandt, and the IAC's New York leadership kept Daniel Ruge, Governor Rockefeller's staff representative, informed. After the Pennsylvania legislature passed the compact in the summer of 1968, Van Zandt was requested to arrange a luncheon meeting of the state's delegation. Goddard asked me to attend, along with his chief water engineer, C. H. McConnell.

We anticipated a twofold benefit from the luncheon. First was that we would exchange views regarding the compact with people who could have a vital role in its passage or failure in Congress. Second, we hoped to secure favorable publicity in the press back home in Pennsylvania. Indeed, a Washington correspondent for the Harrisburg newspapers did attend. However, someone wanted to know why communication had faltered between Pennsylvania and the delegation over the then pending Scenic Rivers System bills. The reporter interpreted the ensuing discussion as a "controversy"—and his story didn't even mention the compact that we had come to Washington to discuss!

One Pennsylvanian in Congress whom we made certain had all the information available to us that he wanted was Representative Daniel J.

Flood of Wilkes-Barre. Flood was keenly interested in the Susquehanna. He was especially concerned with regard to ways by which federal help could be had to rehabilitate the sadly maltreated portions of the basin in the anthracite coal region, much of which was in his district. Back in 1962 he had gone so far as to introduce a Susquehanna compact resolution that was virtually a carbon copy of the Delaware Compact, with only the name of the river changed. This was when the Delaware commission was just getting organized, long before we started our drafting. He did not push his bill when told the IAC had been formed.

When we faced the possibility that the executive order, referred to in the preceding chapter, might come before President Johnson, we turned to Flood for help. As a Democrat he had entrée, and we wanted him to intercede at the White House level, which he did. In a telephone conversation, Flood told me he had been promised a stop order would be issued that would hold up the proposal at least until January 20, when the new administration would take over. In addition, Flood said he had talked with Udall about it.

The order had to be of considerable concern for us to take the step of asking personal intercession at the White House and we believed "considerable concern" to be, if anything, an understatement. I had put what we considered the principal undesirable features of the proposed order in the form of a memorandum to Goddard, which was then distributed to a number of persons; a copy went to Flood. The objectionable features included:

1. The President's appointee [to a Susquehanna-type river basin commission] would be required to obtain and be guided by the views of designated representatives of interested federal agencies on all issues of substance. . . . If any one federal agency representative—whoever he might be—should oppose a . . . river basin action, whatever his reason for doing so, the President's appointed commissioner would have to be guided thereby.

2. Direct channels of communication between the President's appointee . . . and the Office of the President would seem to be lost. The proposed order would have the . . . representative . . . report to the President only through the Water Resources Council. The effect . . . would be to make the Federal Commissioner an errand boy of the council, of the council's member agencies, and perhaps of the Federal agencies represented at council meetings by observers and advisers. . . .

Finally—and this was stressed in conversations with Flood—"the proposal appears to be . . . an attempt to negate by executive order a specific act of Congress", the Delaware compact. In the case of the Susquehanna compact, the memorandum read, "the draft bill now being prepared will not retreat from present thinking that the functioning of the Presidential appointee shall be on the basis of a statute duly enacted into law by the Congress."

We learned later that a telegram sent jointly on behalf of the governors of the Delaware basin states had been effective; the authors exempted the Delaware from provisions of the proposal.

We thought the proposed order was a bold power-grab attempt by the Water Resources Council and I believe it at least a fifty-fifty bet that without prompt reaction on our part and the direct action taken by Representative Flood it might have succeeded.

The incident made us more determined than ever to go to Congress quickly with our own version of an appropriate and defendable set of federal reservations. Almost my last official act before leaving the Interstate Advisory Committee office at the end of December was to arrange to send to Wendell a number of duplicated copies of the compact in the form it had been passed by the states, with his own draft of federal reservations attached.

Shortly after the new Congress convened, Flood and a number of his Pennsylvania colleagues introduced the compact as House Joint Resolution 380. Immediately afterward H. J. R. 381 by Rep. Emanuel Celler and others of New York, and H. J. R. 382, by Rep. Rogers C. B. Morton and his colleagues of the Maryland delegation, were introduced. Later, two more identical bills, by Rep. Frank Horton and C. J. King of New York, were added. All were referred to the House Judiciary Committee, of which Celler was chairman. Senators Hugh Scott of Pennsylvania and Joseph D. Tydings of Maryland became the chief sponsors on the other side of the Capitol of S. 1079. Wendell's draft reservations were attached to all of them.

Securing the introduction of the compact legislation was a strategic step as well as a very necessary one. It seemed obvious that there would be little hope then of obtaining Water Resources Council concurrence, through negotiations, in a set of federal reservations in a reasonable length of time. The IAC advisers foresaw an indeterminate period in which there would be vacillation, possibly even outright refusal to undertake serious negotiations, and the introduction would have the effect —which it did—of forcing the executive branch people to concentrate their attention on something specific, however little they might relish what the bills provided. They might be reluctant to approve anything contained in the legislation, but they could hardly ignore the fact that it had been introduced. In this context it should be remembered that this was the period in which the Nixon administration was taking over from that of Johnson. There always is a degree of confusion and turmoil at such a time. The civil servants tend to put everything that is not strictly routine into the "hold" basket until the "new man" comes to head the department and revised sets of policy begin to take form. Too, the noncareer people who move into high level patronage positions need time to learn a few things before determining what courses to pursue in areas where they have discretionary authority.

Because of the changing situation the federal Water Resources Council principals held no meetings between early December, 1968, and late May, 1969. The executive director, Caulfield, was slated to go, and later was in fact replaced by Don Maughan, a Californian with water resources experience. Though Caulfield stayed on for several months in 1969, we could not be sure any accommodation that might be reached with him would be honored by his successor. Nevertheless, the Washington IAC team maintained communication with the council staff, and in the spring Schwan made it a point to visit the offices of all its members, most of whom were of cabinet rank. This strategy was sound. It was to try to assure that the new principals, the ultimate WRC decision makers, would at least keep open minds on the compact subject. The decision to seek out these WRC members had been made at a meeting of Interstate Advisory Committee members in Washington on March 27, 1969.[1] At its next meeting, on June 13,[2] Schwan reported that he had been received courteously by those he had seen—a majority of the members—and that responses ranged from noncommittal to a considerable understanding of the position taken by the states.

By the time of the June meeting Schwan sensed one modification of attitude favorable to the IAC viewpoint. It was that the council subofficials seemed to be retreating somewhat from the previously adamant holding that the federal member of the Susquehanna commission should have the right to veto any action that involved a federal interest. The IAC position, as it had been made abundantly clear to the WRC people at every opportunity, was that only the President should have that power, under limited, "national interest" circumstances.

Of greater concern then was Schwan's expressed conviction that there lingered a strong belief in the council that the federal water-related agencies should determine for themselves the extent to which they were bound by the compact; additionally, they themselves should judge how far they could stay outside any boundaries of action and activity in the Susquehanna basin that might be set by the commission. He also was of the opinion that the federal council people and the committee were still very much apart on the resolution of conflicts that might arise over the issuance, by the commission on the one hand and a federal agency on the other, of regulations, standards, licenses, and permits. As it turned out, certain aspects of the last-named controversy would linger until Congress settled the issue. Finally, in the background but nevertheless present, was the difference of position by the two sides on whether the public power preference clause, still seemingly viable and arguable long after its birth in the Great Depression era, should be incorporated in the reservations. Its omission had brought the only objection that Secretary Udall, speaking for the Kennedy administration in 1961, had voiced to the reservations written to accompany the Delaware compact through Congress. It seems now that Udall and his associates in 1961, the Water Resources Council workers and the Interstate Advisory Committee in 1969, were all unduly concerned. The House Committee on the Judiciary late in 1970 reported a finding to the effect that it didn't matter one way or the other whether there was reference to the perference clause in the compact bill, for the reason that the legislation would have no effect whatever on "existing statutory provisions which give perference to public bodies and cooperatives in the disposition of electric energy" that conceivably might be produced by the Susquehanna commission. The finding of the Judiciary Committee simply meant that since the commission would be a federal agency (even as it is an agency of each of the states) it could not escape having the preference clause apply unless the Congress specifically exempted it from applicable prevailing law.[3]

At the time of the June 13 meeting Wendell and Schwan were of the opinion that hearings on the bills could be had when the IAC considered it was ready for them, that the sponsors and committees would accommodate the states in that respect. Prior determinations should be reached, though, as to who would appear for the IAC and what sort of and how many supporting statements should be sought for hearing record. I attended this meeting as a guest, and was of the opinion as many as forty or more letters and statements could be had from Pennsylvania alone if they were wanted. The committee inclined to the view that oral testimony should be presented by only a few top-level persons representing the states. Flanked at the witness table by the vice-chairmen from the other states, Chairman Goddard would make the chief presentation. At the close of the state presentations, letters and statements of support, gathered from wherever they might be had, would be handed up for inclusion in the record, but not read. The solidarity usually found in the states west of the 100th Meridian in reclamation matters appeared much on Goddard's mind at the time. He said that as they stood together in seeking to secure federal reclamation projects and funds, so should the eastern states stand together and be counted in favor of this compact.

His comments pointed up a fact that I believe all familiar with the situation privately admitted but shied away from in public discussion. It was that we were far weaker in organized support when dealing with Washington than had been the proponents of the Delaware compact when it was ready for negotiation and definitive action. Then, as pointed out earlier, there was a solidly based citizen organization, the Water Resources Association of the Delaware River Basin, with excellent backing by the valley's financial, business, industrial, and cultural leadership. The Delaware basin's four-state delegation in the Senate had formed itself into an unofficial committee to use its collective influence on fellow members in behalf of the compact, and there had been outstanding assistance on the House side by the compact's guiding hand there, that of the late Representative Francis E. Walter of Pennsylvania. To all this was added the strategic place among President Kennedy's political counselors of Governor Lawrence of Pennsylvania. In the case of the Susquehanna Compact, Hugh Scott of Pennsylvania, the minority leader in the Senate, would be its leading supporter on that side of the Capitol. Representative Flood, from the Pennsylvania hard coal country, could surely be counted on in the House. There was no informal committee and no committed chairman. There was no Susquehanna counterpart of the Delaware's substantial citizen group. The IAC was largely on its own, as far as help of the kinds those had furnished in the Delaware effort was concerned, but this is not to say it was helpless.

Much of its strength lay in the knowledge and experience that Wendell and Schwan brought to their task. For years Wendell and Schwan, through their work on the staff of the Council of State Governments, had concentrated attention on intergovernmental relations, which is defined here as the interaction caused by or resulting from laws, regulations, and policies at one level of government that have impact on one or more other levels of government. The layman seldom has an encompassing concept of their great variety and scope. Wendell and Schwan had long since learned their way about and through the several labyrinths that are lumped under the label of Washington. They had become skilled in applying logic, reason, and gentle persuasion to the solution of problems arising in intergovernmental relations; they knew how to seek out, devise, and secure official approval of new and better ways by which the multiple levels of government in the United States might get along with each other and forward the interests of the people governed. The application of these skills took them to the far reaches of the country, so they well knew its geographic and cultural samenesses and differences. They were fully as familiar with the corridors, offices, and meeting rooms of the sprawling edifices of brick, stone, and concrete that house the executive branch. They were on first-name terms with high-level civil servants, career people whose jobs are not affected by the patronage system. They had equal acquaintance with the Capitol and its satellite office buildings, and the legislative and other assistants to members of Congress—which is of greater significance in the totality of the legislative process than being acquainted with the legislators themselves; the vagaries of the voters affect the longevity on Capitol Hill of the latter far more than they do the former.

To these skills and circumstances must be linked their familiarity with the compact route to improved intergovernmental relations. Wendell, it will be remembered, had teamed with Fred Zimmermann to write two publications about compacts for the Council of State Governments,[4] and alone or in association with others had written a number of compacts that had been enacted into law. Schwan's sixteen years in the Washington office of the Council of State Governments were predominately concerned with intergovernmental relations, and the compact device that in recent decades has grown to so prominent a place in guiding such relations.

These were the talents that a fortuitous set of circumstances had put at the disposal of the Interstate Advisory Committee. I am convinced that without them there would be no Susquehanna River Basin Compact as a result of action by the 91st Congress. This is not to say that over time others could not have accomplished a similar result, but I believe it must be conceded that few if any others in the entire contingent of Washington-based consultants, alone or in combination, could have brought to the undertaking their specific expertise.

It should not be inferred from these complimentary remarks about Wendell and Schwan that they alone were working affirmatively at the Washington level. IAC Chairman Goddard; Alan Sommerville, water resources coordinator on Goddard's staff; New York Vice-Chairman Lawrence; Maryland's Dr. Albert Miller; the governors of the basin states; key members of Congress and their staffs; all these, and more, too, went into the makeup of the smoothly functioning team that brought it off, each contributing what was required at strategic points in time. There were occasions when some of them were in virtually daily communication, exchanging views on the most appropriate moves to make or the best direction to travel toward the end objective. As one of their number put it on one occasion, the state IAC leaders and the Washington consultants were a dedicated group proud of their product and determined to see it through to enactment into law without crippling change and without diminution of the place the states considered rightfully theirs in the partnership.

The IAC believed the holding of hearings by the Senate and House Committees on the Judiciary as quickly as practical would serve the interests of the states in the matter of timing; none in the committee wanted the sort of eleventh-hour actions that secured passage of the compact in Maryland and New York, nor was anyone of the group eager to see another drawn-out legislative procedure such as that in Pennsylvania. Hearings also would force confrontation on a now basis with the federal agencies, and in one way or another bring end to uncertainty.

As the summer and early fall months of 1969 dragged on, efforts to obtain hearing commitments—earlier believed to be routine—seemingly were getting nowhere, and there was continued official silence in the executive branch. The Water Resources Council people remained noncommittal at times when there was communication with them. When legislation is introduced the committee to which it is referred routinely asks affected federal agencies to comment on it. This occurred in the case of the Susquehanna bills, but neither the council nor any of its constituent agencies had responded. Quite by accident it was learned in mid-November that the reason for this was that a study of federal–interstate relationships had been quietly undertaken at White House level with the objective of formulating a Nixon administration policy. This, then, was the root cause of what we had begun to consider bureaucratic dawdling. The Susquehanna Compact was understood to be among the subjects under study. A way was found through informal channels to send to the study group a statement saying that in weighing values the viewpoint of the states on the effectiveness of the Delaware and Susquehanna types of mechanism should be considered.

This brought a request that the IAC executive committee and its Washington advisers meet with a member of the study group, an assistant Secretary of the Interior. Following this the IAC was formally asked to submit its views. This was done[5] the first of the year, but for three months thereafter there seemingly was no change in the situation. When one came it was in the form of a statement at an April 14, 1970, meeting of the Delaware River Basin Commission by Walter J. Hickel, then Secretary of the Interior, who was the presidential appointee to that commission succeeding Udall.[6]

"It is my firm conviction," the Hickel statement read, "that the proposed Susquehanna River Basin Compact is a desirable intergovernmental arrangement for river basin planning, operation, and management."

This broke the official silence, and it gave strong backing to the compact itself. It did not, however, mention the federal reservations, which is where differences of consequence still lay, and it did not serve to bring accord in that aspect of the matter.

Three months and more of the second and final session of the 91st Congress had slipped away, and it still looked as though the compact was far from where its supporters wanted it to be. It was an election year and Congress, as always in those times, was eager to adjourn and get out of Washington for campaigning. There didn't seem much time left for affirmative action, considering that the Congress can move just as slowly and ponderously as the executive branch. Washington columnists and news commentators wrote and talked of adjournment in July or August, and not even a hearing by a subcommittee had been held. I visualized the several steps in the enactment process: hearings by subcommittees in both houses, subcommittee deliberations, submission of findings to each full committee for consideration, deliberation there, possibly, we hoped, favorable report to the floor in each house, eventual call-up of the legislation for debate and, at last, the voting, possibly followed by conferences to try to compromise any differences. How could all this take place in the remaining weeks? Why, the IAC still was at odds with the executive branch over reservations! A continuation of the drawn-out battle with the bureaucracy over the reservations language simply could not be countenanced, yet this looked inevitable, and under the circumstances of the moment it seemed to mean the compact had no more than a ghost of a chance of becoming law.

Wendell and Schwan were more sanguine.

Chapter 3

An End and a Beginning

Early in 1970 I received an answer to a question that had nagged me since before the writing of this account began in 1968. Other activities caused only casual inquiry to be made here and there and it had brought uncertain response. The question was how it came about that the federal reservations to the Delaware Compact had been drafted as an entity separate from the body of the document. Doing so was an excellent device. It brought great flexibility to the task of initiating and drafting interstate and federal–interstate compacts, a task that traditionally has been a function of the affected states. Their doing so seems appropriate since a compact is a binding contract for them whereas federal participation or impingement must be permissive and may be altered or stricken down at will by act of Congress. Placing the federal reservations in a separate portion of the legislative package offered to Congress permits the states to proceed to commit themselves fully and later negotiate with the federal executive branch as to reservation language; failing agreement there, then, Congress may be asked to become the ultimate arbiter as to what the reservation language should be.

My research, so far as I had gone with it, indicated that the Delaware was the first water-related compact in which the device had been employed, and this may be true as to compacts dealing with other subjects as well, though I did not inquire into that. In earlier compacts having to do with water resources, reservations or exceptions affecting the federal government and its specialized interests and responsibilities had been incorporated in the body of each agreement. That appeared to be the original intention of the drafters of the Delaware Compact. It will be recalled that its Section 1.4, which we duplicated in the Susquehanna, recognized the power of Congress to withdraw the United States as a member at any time, and specified that nothing in the compact was to be construed as relinquishing the functions, powers, or duties of the Congress with respect to the control of navigable waters in the basin or in derogation of its constitutional authority to regulate interstate and foreign commerce. A copy of a memorandum dated March 3, 1970, sent by William Miller, chief drafter of the Delaware Compact, to the secretary of the Delaware River Basin Commission, was relayed to me. (I had written W. Brinton Whitall, the Delaware Commission secretary, some time earlier, seeking enlightenment, and he relayed the request to Miller.) Miller wrote:

> As I recall, it was a two-step affair. We all realized that the [federal people concerned] might not swallow the entire Compact as the Advisory Committee agreed upon it, and I suggested that we could build in a provision, which later became Section 1.4, consenting in advance to Congressional modifications. The second step arose when we were negotiating in Washington after Udall had been designated to serve as spokesman for the various federal departments. His staff gathered together all manner of proposals to put before us. As I recall, I then took the position that we could not consider the various items piecemeal since we ought to know the total concessions that would be required in order to achieve agreement. It was therefore a natural consequence to prepare the entire agenda of federal "reservations," and to tack them on as an Article 15. This was possible because none of the reservations changed the relationship of the states among themselves, and all of the reservations dealt with the effect of the Compact on federal law and the federal agencies.

The originator of the idea was not named in the memorandum. However, the "natural consequence" became a procedure that appears now to be firmly established in its place. It is a simplifying device, despite the length and relative complexity it assumed in the case of the Delaware and as it was revised and extended in the Susquehanna; it is likely that it will be employed in other compacts of a broadly similar nature when they advance to a state–federal negotiating stage. When the Delaware Compact became law the federal reservations attached ran to nineteen subsections, all in addition to the compact's Section 1.4. The legislatures of the four Delaware basin states had passed the compact without change. If Congress, then, had enlarged Section 1.4 or put additional federal reservations somewhere else in the corpus of the agreement, the entire state legislative process would have had to be repeated so the compact language would have been identical in all affected jurisdictions. This may have taken years and, doubtless, entailed extensive deliberation and debate.

When we were drafting the Susquehanna compact we might well have omitted the language of Delaware's Section 1.4, and put the gist of it somewhere among the federal reservations to be appended later. That we did not do so stemmed largely from the desire, explained earlier, of the IAC members to conform rather closely to Delaware language for political reasons.

Now, with compact drafting far behind, with passage by the three Susquehanna state assemblies a reality, the IAC was following the reservations precedent established when the Delaware legislation was in process. However, it appeared to encounter much greater difficulty than its predecessor. This was caused mainly by the insistence of the executive branch people attached to or working with the Water Resources Council that control exercised by the Susquehanna commission in areas of federal interest should be substantially below the level envisioned by the states, far under what the Delaware provides. The IAC position was that without authority to act and to make its decisions stand up, including instances where federal agencies were involved, the compact would have little meaning and the commission's water management functions would be sharply restricted. The federal role in water-related undertakings has grown so pervasive it is hard to visualize a project significant enough for Susquehanna commission attention in which no federal agency that deals in any way with water resources would have an interest. The state officials and their counselors who had taken part in the endeavor for so many years were convinced of the need for jointly exercised controls and became committed to that proposition. Critical diminution of state influence could not be tolerated. The commission must not be just a rubber stamp for the agencies when a federal interest could be shown. Only an overriding national interest should take precedence, and it should do so then on the basis of official action by the President in the form of an executive order. The state firmness paid off.

The declaration by Hickel in Trenton in April, 1970, was taken as a signal that the executive branch would go along with the federal–interstate approach to water management in the Susquehanna basin and was willing to try to reach accommodation with the IAC on reservations language. Soon afterward Wendell and Schwan were provided a copy of the language the agencies wanted approved. When this was compared with the reservations in the Delaware legislation and those in the measures for a Susquehanna Compact introduced in Congress more than a year earlier, numerous differences showed up, some quite substantive. The agencies appeared to be retreating grudgingly from previous positions. New conditions had been inserted and added, the essence of which would be to let the federal regulatory agencies "proceed as they wished in the basin without regard to the management and control functions of the Susquehanna Commission."[1] Wendell and Schwan took a bold step. They arranged a May 15 meeting of the IAC leadership with members of the Water Resources Council staff, but also invited members of the staffs of the compact's sponsors in Congress and a high official from the office of Secretary Hickel. They wanted these people to be apprised by the IAC of the differences and their meaning and, they hoped, gain high level support. The assistant secretary from the Interior Department appeared surprised if not disturbed by disclosure that the WRC's suggested reservations consisted of considerably more than minor modifications of those attached to the Delaware Compact. One could surmise he may have gained a quite different impression at an earlier briefing.

The upshot was another meeting, hard on the heels of the first, but attended by only four persons, Schwan and Sommerville for the IAC, a representative of Secretary Hickel, and a man from the Bureau of the Budget. The end result was agreement on nearly all points of difference. Only two remained to the end, but they had what the IAC group considered critical aspects. Considering the fact that in all there were twenty-three primary reservation paragraphs, some with several subparagraphs, it may be said that getting thus far along toward total agreement was no small achievement. Nevertheless, the differences that remained were important, and the Congress was believed to be deep into its closing session. It was time to shut off debate outside its hearing rooms and offices or on the floor in open session.

A subcommittee of the House Committee on the Judiciary held the first hearing on June 4;[2] its schedule was so tight, though, that it then could only hear the views of spokesmen for the executive branch. A date convenient to all concerned for hearing the states and others could not be found before September 30. On the Senate side, Tydings of Maryland conducted a hearing at Bel Air, in his home state, on June 23. The presentations there were mostly by Maryland officials favorable to the compact. They were former Governor J. Millard Tawes, then Secretary of Natural Resources; Dr. Albert R. Miller, Jr., Maryland vice-chairman of the IAC; and Maryland Senate President William S. James, IAC member. A supporting statement was made by Mrs. Melvin W. Isenberg, representing the Susquehanna Inter-League Council of the League of Women Voters. Two Corps of Engineers officials spoke in favor of the compact; the principal statement, however, favored the WRC reservations. Chief spokesman was Thomas E. Burns of the legal staff of the Chief of Engineers. Col. W. J. Love, Baltimore District Engineer, in reply to questions, expressed support of the compact. There were no statements in opposition to the body of the compact.

When Senator Tydings decided to hold that hearing in the field, it brought up the possibility of a similar hearing being held somewhere in the Pennsylvania part of the basin. If that occurred the record likely would get all or most of the old arguments that we had to overcome when the compact was moving through the state legislature and, while they could be answered decisively they might cause disquiet and prevent a decision before final adjournment. Fortunately, Scott chose to hold the next Senate hearing in Washington, on August 20. I attended all but the hearing at Bel Air, Maryland, held by Senator Tydings. I made no oral statement but submitted for record letters supporting the views of the IAC.

As it happened, the debate at the Washington hearings was restrained. Both the principal spokesman for the executive branch, James Smith, Assistant Secretary of the Interior for Water and Power Development, and the compact's originators stressed the tremendous progress that had been made toward reaching accord. Smith advocated the Water Resources Council's version of the portions of the reservations still in dispute. I felt he was trying to make it appear that the IAC objections to them were of little import. Quite the contrary, said Goddard at the Senate hearing in August and Sommerville, speaking for Goddard, at the House hearing in September. They contended the two sticking points were of considerable moment.

In Reservation 2 (r)2 (ii)[3] the federal version would have stricken the applicability to federal water-oriented agencies of the compact's Section 3.10 and Article 12. The IAC pointed out that Section 3.10 constituted the heart of the control function that might be exercised by the Susquehanna commission over water undertakings proposed by either governmental or nongovernmental entities, and that Article 12 specifically declared neither federal nor state water projects might be considered authorized, or funded and built, without inclusion in the commission's comprehensive plan. Hence removal of the applicability references would mean the total exclusion of any measure of authority or control by the commission on projects having a federal interest.

In 2 (w) the WRC language would have excluded from commission purview the actions of federal regulatory agencies, mainly the Federal Power Commission and the Atomic Energy Commission. The IAC recognized that these agencies had responsibilities under law and agreed that commission actions should not seek to "supersede, impair, affect, compel, or prevent the exercise of any powers, rights, functions, or jurisdiction" of those agencies, nor should any commission action "conflict with any of the terms or conditions of any license or permit granted" by any of them. Its insistence was that the agencies should not have the power to "permit use of waters of the Susquehanna River Basin nor . . . endanger their quality without approval pursuant to the compact."[4] In that respect the committee refused to give any more ground—or water.

In all, six federal agencies submitted statements for the hearing records. One from Interior was signed by Hickel, who also was chairman of the Water Resources Council; and he signed a statement in behalf of the WRC to which was attached the council's arguments for reservations favored by its constituent agencies. The five agencies that supplemented the WRC statement with arguments in their own names were Commerce; Health, Education, and Welfare; Interior; Army; and the Federal Power Commission. The Department of the Army statement[5] went into considerable detail on WRC's version of (r). The most extensive statement was that of the Federal Power Commission.[6] It recited the chief contents of the compact and of the Federal Power Act,[7] then argued its case. The principal points set forth appeared to be these:

1. The full scope of this type of compact had not yet been demonstrated because of the, to date, "limited assertions of authority by the Delaware" River Basin Commission. The thought appeared to be that a more aggressive Susquehanna Commission might arrogate more authority in broader fields and in them impinge upon FPC prerogatives.

2. The FPC feared the "applicability of the safeguards and standards of the Federal Power Act" in regard to in-basin projects "could become obscured."

3. Without further clarification the compact "could serve to frustrate the purposes and functions" of both the FPC and the Susquehanna Commission.

4. There was some fear that Article 10 of the compact, relating to hydroelectric power, might lead to a dual rate-fixing situation.

Of "relative significance" was a reference to the possible destruction of the effectiveness of the Federal Power Act if another agency should be given "veto power" over the FPC. It was not openly asserted that the Susquehanna Commission would have such power; however, court decisions cited in the statement referred to such a situation and it certainly appeared as though the FPC was of the opinion that this might be the case here, perhaps if the Susquehanna Commission should become more aggressive than the Delaware had so far proved to be. For reasons such as the above the FPC wanted the WRC reservations, especially its version of 2 (w).

It appears to me to be significant that opposition to the compact proper was limited to one statement. This was at the time of Senator Scott's hearing, and it was presented for record without being read by the Pennsylvania affiliate of the Farm Bureau Federation. The statement was largely a reiteration of the allegations and opinions of the affiliate's people in earlier years, and it seemingly had no weight with either house of the Congress.

On the favorable side, in addition to presentations by the three basin states, were appearances or offerings by Chairman Emanuel Celler of the House Committee on the Judiciary, chief author of one of the compact bills, Representatives Daniel J. Flood of Pennsylvania, Howard W. Robinson of New York, Rogers C. B. Morton of Maryland, and others. The League of Women Voters was represented by Mrs. Edward Gallagher as proxy for Mrs. James M. O'Brien, secretary of the Susquehanna Inter-League Council. John W. Scott of the National Grange reiterated his approval; Joseph W. Penfold, conservation director of the Izaak Walton League of America, sent a letter of approbation. A statement of approval was submitted by Roger D. Ley in behalf of the group of investor-owned public utilities that operates in the basin. A number of letters and statements of support from Pennsylvania groups and individuals was handed up by Sommerville.

In the end, the committees of Congress came to the conclusion that the final set of federal reservations offered in behalf of the IAC, which were an admixture of the language in the bills as introduced originally, of Water Resources Council passages, of late compromises and alterations of both IAC and WRC terminology, and the portions of (r) and (w) insisted upon by the states, conferred adequate safeguards upon the affected agencies with respect to their activities and operations, and upon the states of the basin.

The text of the compact and the reservations attached by Congress are given in full in Appendix B. The principal elements of these reservations, as I construe them, are discussed in the following paragraphs, and differences between what the Water Resources Council wanted and what was ultimately enacted are pointed out where these were significant.

In Section 2 (a) Congress specified that no water project involving federal funds might proceed beyond the planning stage without full disclosure to Congress of all plans and cost estimates needed to evaluate it, plus details of apportionments of costs, benefits in relation to costs, and financing proposals. Reauthorization by Congress would be required in case of later changes involving water use; the WRC insisted on inclusion of this proviso as an outcome of a change in a Delaware water project to which the federal member of the Delaware River Basin Commission had objected. (This involved the addition of a proposed pumped storage feature to the dam and reservoir complex at Tocks Island, Delaware River.)

Section 2 (b) preserved federal prerogatives relating to charges for water uses and prohibited the commission from setting tolls for navigation in basin waters.

Section 2 (c) reiterated the executive authority of the President to act in emergency situations, and 2 (d) restated the powers resting in the President and Congress regarding appropriated federal funds.

Paragraph 2 (e) stipulated that if the commission should issue bonds they would not be exempt from Federal taxation "except to the same extent that state bonds are or may be" so excluded. Then, 2(f) was a disclaimer of federal responsibility to pay interest or principal on any commission-issued bonds.

Sections 2 (g), carrying a minimum wage provision for work done for the commission, and 2 (h) a nondiscrimination clause, were easily agreed upon. Contracts in excess of $10,000, said 2 (i), would be subject to the provisions of the Walsh-Healey Act (41 U. S. C. 35 *et seq.*).

The statutory powers of the Federal Water Quality Administration, successor to the Federal Water Pollution Control Administration, were preserved in 2 (j). Here the IAC previously had written a provision that the head of that agency should not issue water quality orders in the basin that were inconsistent with commission orders, but acceded to a request from the WRC that it be deleted.

In 2(k) it was made clear that the commission's authority would not extend to concessioners serving the public on federal facilities catering to recreation seekers.

Under 2(l) the commission would not be considered a federal agency in connection with tort claims. The IAC conferees agreed that a previously written exemption of a commission project from a Federal Power Commission license requirement should be stricken.

Section 2(m) stipulated that commission employes would not be covered under the federal civil service statutes.

In 2 (n) Congress specified neither the compact nor the attachments to it should be deemed to "enlarge the authority of any federal agency other than the commission to participate in or to provide funds for projects or activities" in the basin.

Section 2 (o) gave the federal district courts original jurisdiction in all cases of controversies arising under the compact and said nothing in the legislation "shall be construed as a waiver" of the immunity of the United States from suit.

In 2 (p) Congress retained the right to alter or amend the entire act, and gave its committees express power to require disclosure by the commission of any information wanted. It reserved to the President the fixing of compensation paid to the federal member, his alternate, and his adviser.

Section 2(r), one of the passages that caused much debate and little agreement during negotiations, had a number of subparagraphs. Its first provision was that nothing being enacted "shall impair, affect, or extend" the constitutional authority of the United States, nor might it or any commission action "supersede, impair, affect, compel, or prevent the exercise of the powers, rights, functions, or jurisdiction" of the federal establishment "in or over the area or waters" of the basin, "including projects of the commission." However, the commission would serve as the "principal agency for the coordination of federal, state, interstate, local, and nongovernmental plans" concerning "water and related land resources" in the basin. The significance of differences between the IAC and the WRC over the language of 2 (r)2 (ii) was indicated earlier in this chapter. This subsection also carries the important declaration that the President may "suspend, modify, or delete any provision of the comprehensive plan" if he finds and determines that "the national interest so requires"; his action, as indicated previously, would be by executive order. Then, 2 (r)2 (iii) requires that the commission shall be given full information in advance concerning federal water proposals covered by the compact's Section 3.10, and shall have the right to submit its views to Congress prior to any authorization or appropriation of funds. Finally, 2 (r)3 stipulated that with respect to the provisions of 2 (r)2(ii) the concurrence of the federal member in a commission action would be presumed unless within sixty days he filed notice of "no objection" or of nonconcurrence.

If the compact's Section 1.4 should be ruled unconstitutional, under 2 (s) the United States would withdraw as a signatory party, except that the President might continue federal participation to the extent considered necessary to "protect the national interest."

Section 2 (t) was written to amend any inconsistent federal statutes, and to say that no commission action might be construed as "repealing, modifying, or amending" federal law.

In 2 (u) the President was given the sole power to appoint and remove the federal member and his alternate, and 2 (v) spelled out the conditions under which federal services might be rendered to the commission.

Section 2 (w), concerning the relation of the commission and its activities to those of federal regulatory agencies, was discussed earlier. It and 2(r) produced irreconcilable differences at the time of the negotiations between IAC and WRC, but the end product in both instances tended to favor the views of the states rather than the federal agencies. Some may consider the inclination of the Congress toward the states' views as indicative of a trend away from expanding federalism; others likely would hold that view premature.

The Water Resources Council at one time proposed an additional reservation, labeled 2 (x) under which the commission would have been reduced to the status of a state in its relations with the regulatory bodies. It read: "The Susquehanna River Basin Commission shall have no greater authority respecting matters within the jurisdiction of the federal agencies referred to in Reservation (w) than a state would have under other existing or future legislation." This, too, was just too much to swallow. In a January 12, 1971, letter, Schwan wrote me, "Our arguments with respect to the . . . addition of (x) evidently were persuasive," and that "the federal people went along with us on them."

A Section 3 authorized the President to take needed steps to effectuate the compact so the commission could organize and go into business. It instructed other federal agencies to cooperate with the federal member, and authorized appropriations for the support of the federal member and his office. This authorization was phrased carefully to quiet fears of some of the members of the House Committee on the Judiciary that if left in "open end" fashion it could lead to excessive federal expenditures or abuse of funding processes. The committeemen wanted it clearly understood the authorization was for administrative routine only.

Some of the language in the reservations as ultimately enacted was more than the IAC and its advisers believed needed in order to protect fully all federal rights, privileges, and prerogatives without injury to the states, but in a corridor conversation at hearing time one of the advisers said "we can live with it"; the compromises, where made, were not excessive or burdensome to the states.

At their close my reaction was that the hearings had gone well. This is not to say, though, that I was mentally at ease. I was edgy, and I suspect I was not alone. There might be only two weeks or so between the last hearing at the end of September and final adjournment of the 91st Congress. If affirmative action could not be had in both houses before that occurred the outlook for the compact would be grave indeed. The chances of so swift a decision looked very slim.

Our spirits were given a tremendous lift when, on October 14, Senator Scott's bill, S.1079, containing reservations approved by the Interstate Advisory Committee, was passed by the Senate on the consent calendar. And there still remained an outside chance for action in the House, for the 91st was to take a long electioneering recess and then return for the first lame-duck session in many years. This would allow perhaps four or five weeks more, as we calculated it, for the compact to receive House approval, or die. There is no denying, though, that the situation was quite precarious, for many measures marked "urgent" were still pending, including large appropriations and other bills that were highly controversial. It would seem to be uphill going all the way.

That aspect of the matter, serious as it was, was complicated for the IAC by the time element. I was privy to certain internal affairs of the Interstate Advisory Committee, and knew the lame-duck session could very well mark a do-or-die opportunity for the compact. A rather closely guarded IAC secret was the condition of its treasury. It had been operating largely on carry-over funds for more than a year, money appropriated by the states in earlier sessions of their assemblies. We had been frugal in running the committee's affairs, and in earlier years, when funds were left over at the end of a fiscal period we invested in short-term government paper, usually Treasury Bills. We were not mandated to return carry-over funds to the states, as is often the case with appropriations from general revenue to departments. On maturity of our investments we either banked the proceeds or reinvested. Consequently, enough money had been squirreled away to pay IAC expenses at a moderate level of activities until about the end of the calendar year 1970. No provisions had been made for securing more funds when they should run out. Thus the adjournment of the 91st Congress without definitive action could likewise mean the closing down of the IAC, except perhaps on paper, and almost surely would mean the end of continuing, coordinated, and vigorous three-state support of the compact such as had been enjoyed since 1962. True, the state agencies participating might be in position to request emergency appropriations for 1971 and a regular schedule of funds as needed thereafter.

Unfortunately, money was only one aspect of the problem. It is noted elsewhere that the committee's permanent chairman, Goddard, was setting a record for longevity in his secretaryship of the Pennsylvania Department of Forests and Waters every day he reported for work. He might be asked to continue in office by the new governor elected in November; the odds were astronomically against it on the basis of past political history. If he went out of appointive office there would be at minimum a considerable break in the continuity of IAC leadership. Expertise gained through the life of the committee would be lost or not fully utilizable. This appeared to be more likely in Pennsylvania than in the other states, where IAC vice-chairmen were career officials. So it was that my feelings of unease rose as each day passed without word of affirmative action. (A letter from Sommerville dated January 28, 1971, informed me that Goddard had been appointed by Governor Milton Shapp as "acting" secretary of the newly organized Department of Environmental Resources, of which his former department became a part. Goddard served many months in the "acting" capacity without state Senate action on his appointment, was confirmed November 8, 1971.)

A half-dozen majestic old longleaf yellow pine trees stand in the yard of my winter home in southeast Georgia. I am sure that psychologically I was floating above the tallest of these when Sommerville telephoned from Harrisburg to tell me that the House, too, on December 7 had passed the IAC version of the compact and reservations by unanimous consent.

With the exhilaration came a feeling of intense relief that the long road had been traveled and the goal was within one step yet to be taken. Behind were the days and nights of drafting the compact, of debating various parts of it within our own circles, of answering critics in three states, of reassuring and counseling supporters, of cajoling waverers, of prodding legislators with all legitimate force and tactics, of trying to negotiate and eventually doing so with the federal executive branch, of countering opposition of official and unofficial nature in both governmental and private sectors. The combination of all supporting effort had succeeded in securing legislative approval by New York, Maryland,

and Pennsylvania of an intergovernmental agreement that bound them for a minimum of a century to what might become an awesome task in the "planning, conservation, utilization, development, management, and control of the water resources of the basin." The three state signatories had agreed to "apply the principle of equal and uniform treatment to all users of water and of water related facilities" in carrying out those undoubtedly difficult multiple procedures.[8] They had approved this binding contract in full faith and confidence that nothing harmful to its essentiality would be imposed upon them by the federal government. It had been the responsibility of the compact's sponsor, the Interstate Advisory Committee, its staff and counselors, to assure that what had to be done at the Washington level was in fact done there. The deed had been accomplished. Congress had acted, and in both houses without the need for floor debate.

Even as the House was acting on the compact bill on December 7, however, an action was taken in the same chamber that had all the marks of a clever end run to have the Corps of Engineers excluded entirely from provision of the compact's Article 12 and Section 3.10. It will be remembered that this was the thrust of the Department of the Army's argument for a change in Reservation 2 (r). The civil works aspects of the mission of the Corps is the Army's primary interest in the basin and in the basin compact.

Late in November a bill was introduced in the House to provide for a continuing Corps study of the waters of the Susquehanna basin.[9] This in itself would cause no problem, but the measure would have had the Corps report directly to the Congress, by-passing the Susquehanna River Basin Commission. The introduction of the bill in the lame-duck days of the session seemed to make little sense, since it was so late it obviously could not be considered in the usual way, but the IAC's advisers in Washington came quickly alert when they learned that the language of the new bill had been inserted as a section in the body of the Rivers and Harbors authorization bill. This perennial bill has traditionally been the repository of a very large share of the tax-bought meat packed in the congressional pork barrel. The Senate and House versions of the Rivers and Harbors bill differed, so as is custom they were referred to a joint conference committee to reconcile differences. Senator Scott and members of his staff worked smoothly on this from the inside, and Wendell and Schwan contributed assistance from outside the conference chamber. The result was that the conferees were persuaded to insert a neatly turned phrase in the bill that decreed the Corps could undertake the continuing study, but it would only report to the Congress "plans prepared pursuant to this section which are approved by the Susquehanna River Basin Commission in accordance with its comprehensive plan. . . ."[10]

Anyone familiar with the activities of the Corps of Engineers through the last forty-odd years will recognize that this was a tremendous accomplishment. The Corps has lost a few river basin skirmishes in its time, but seldom an encounter such as this. The Corps, which has been called "the lobby that can't be licked," has developed a pattern and technique that is a model of empire building and maintenance knowledge. I have sat in many an informal meeting and more formal public hearing and watched with reluctant admiration how deftly the Corps handled local interests and broader audiences. The Corps has been equally skillful in its relations with Congress. Geographic realities are kept in mind, and it seemingly is no accident that at least a majority of the members of Congress usually have at least one Corps public works project going in their districts. The result is that the well-padded periodic Rivers and Harbors bill ordinarily scoots through Congress with scarcely a hint of serious opposition to the projects it authorizes.

With passage of the compact legislation by the House, and the skillful blocking of the attempted end run, there now appeared to be nothing more to fear. We who were interested could sit back in satisfaction and at ease—or could we? The administration had committed itself to the sort of federal–interstate compact we had written. True, Hickel, who had voiced that commitment, was no longer in the Cabinet and spokesman for the executive agencies involved in water resources. But Representative Morton, who replaced him, had as a congressman sponsored one of the compact bills. We certainly didn't anticipate a presidential veto, yet once again we went through an agonizing eleventh-hour situation. Though short, it seemed real enough. We had endured one in Maryland and another in New York, the long months of delay and indecision in Pennsylvania, and in Washington the span of time from the visit with Udall in June, 1966 until Pearl Harbor Day, 1970. Now it was the turn of the White House to give us the shakes. The President had until midnight December 25 in which to follow one of three courses: to sign, to refuse to sign, or to pocket veto the measure by leaving it unsigned as the final hour of grace passed.

On the 24th all at the Wendell & Schwan office took their customary holiday except Charlie Schwan. He was at his desk, consulting by telephone between Capitol Hill and the White House and the three state capitols. He was on the phone to Sommerville and put him on "hold" for a long minute when I anxiously rang his number from South Georgia shortly before noon. I suspect there was much conferring in and between state capitol offices and homes that day, as well as between them and Washington. No doubt I was unnecessarily nervous, but I had visions of Capitol Hill and White House staffs being sufficiently distracted by holiday festivities and other activities to mislay, overlook, or ignore that one certain piece of paper that was hanging around somewhere, awaiting presidential attention. Whether this last flurry of IAC activity was needed is moot, for the bill was signed, along with a score or so of others, by President Nixon at his Christmas Eve hideaway, Camp David in Maryland's Catoctin Hills. The legislation had become P.L. (Public Law) 91-575. A jubilant memo was distributed by Goddard on the same date.

The Susquehanna River Basin Compact had been entered in the law books of the four signatory parties. It was time to close the books and end the activities of the Interstate Advisory Committee on the Susquehanna River Basin. Let it go quietly, without formality. Next would be the appointment of the members of the commission, recruiting of a staff, and commencement of the manifold water resources actions that will guide the future of those resources in a strategically located and sizable eastern America river basin. Each action will affect some or all of the basin's people, the quality of their environment and its material worth. Nor will the impacts be confined to the geographic boundaries of the basin itself. Much is riding on the words so laboriously drafted and eventually placed among the enacted statutes. What occurs will, of course, depend upon the administration of the compact by the commission, how it interprets its mission and performs thereunder. Over time the courts will be called upon for decisions stemming from commission action, or inaction. It is a bit sobering to look back across the years of drafting and legislating and all the rest. Did those who had a part in one phase or another perform at the best level of competence and prevision to be expected in view of the expertise brought to the task and of the technological and sociological conditions prevailing, or did we fall short? On balance I think we did pretty well and that the compact has great potential for high-grade water resources management in the basin. It covers most of the things it should, and it has teeth in nearly all the right places. Its chief weaknesses are in the fields of preservation of natural values and in flood-plain management, as detailed in Part III— yet even in these still politically sensitive areas we advanced beyond then existing boundaries.

A host of people consisting of a broad mix of realists, pragmatists, idealists, and others dreamed, labored, perspired and persevered to make the compact what it is and to safeguard it from avowed enemies and some who opposed less overtly or were simply dubious of its efficacy in this or that respect. Sometimes gently and by indirection, sometimes firmly and forthrightly, unnumbered steps were taken intended to lead to the culminations of enactment and effectuation. At how many points false steps could have been fatal to the compact in one or another of the states or in Washington I'll never know. Obviously not too many were taken or it would not have been possible to bring this narrative to the definitive point it has reached.

Henceforth the destiny of the compact and of the water resources of the Susquehanna River Basin will rest in the hands of the commission established. I speak only for myself, of course, but have little doubt that my sentiment is that of the overwhelming majority of all who had a hand, large or small, in the ultimate result. It is a fervent hope that performance under the compact will match or exceed the highest aims of the most dedicated in our group.

In the latter half of 1971 the chief executive of the three states decided to serve as members of the Susquehanna River Basin Commission instead of appointing "designees" as allowed in Article 2 of the compact. Unofficial but knowledgeable sources indicated that high level officials of the states persuaded their governors—Nelson A. Rockefeller of New York, Milton J. Shapp of Pennsylvania, and Marvin Mandel of Maryland— to do so in order that the President might be persuaded that he should appoint someone of the cabinet rank as his representative. This occurred; the federal member appointed was Secretary Robert C. B. Morton of Interior, a native of Maryland. In December, 1971, after long debate and consideration of a number of candidates, Robert Bielo, executive director of the Pennsylvania Fish Commission, was chosen as staff head of the commission, which was then, almost a year since enactment of the compact, ready to go into operation.

Appendixes

Appendix A

The Susquehanna Committee
and Compact Drafters

Careers of the Leaders, Interstate Advisory Committee

When an accomplishment considered worthy of more than passing note is brought about it is normal to ask who led in the doing, and to want to know something about the leaders. From 1962 forward into 1970 the committee had a total of twenty-four members and twenty-one alternates. It was organized on a basis of twelve members and twelve alternates; there were to be two representing the executive branches of government of New York, Pennsylvania, and Maryland, and two each from their legislative branches, a state senator and a member from the lower house. The greatest turnover from 1962 through 1970 was in New York, which had nine members and nine alternates. Pennsylvania had nine members and six alternates, and Maryland six each.

Here it is necessary for me to render judgment on the members and alternates, who were my employers, and separate those who played leading roles from those who were content to follow. There are many reasons why some appointees to committees do not find it feasible to become involved totally in a group's mission. Committee work usually is a sideline, occasionally something wished off on an individual whose occupation, plus other factors, make it impossible for him to plunge fully into the work to be accomplished. These points are brought out only half apologetically; it is to me obvious that each member and alternate cannot be given full biographical treatment in this narrative. Selections must be made of those to be mentioned by perhaps no more than name and dates of service. In a news story, these likely would be listed in a catchall paragraph that began, "Others present were. . . ." So must it be here.

The Interstate Advisory Committee

Maurice K. Goddard, Chairman, 1962—

From and after January, 1959, every day Maurice Goddard remained in office as Secretary of Forests and Waters of Pennsylvania he made a new record for the state's history books, for no other had previously served longer than the four-year term of the governor who appointed him. At the end of 1970 Goddard had served sixteen years in the same appointive office, and even that was not the end, for the new governor inaugurated in 1971, Milton J. Shapp, promptly appointed him Secretary of the Department of Environmental Resources, and Forests and Waters was a part of a reorganized aggregation of resource agencies given that name.

A forester by profession, Goddard was a graduate of the University of Maine. He received his master's degree at the University of California, and was awarded honorary doctorates by Waynesburg (Pa.) College, and by the University of Maine. In World War II he was awarded the Bronze Star and Legion of Merit, ending his service as executive officer, Military Personnel Division, AGS, SHAEF. He was director of the School of Forestry of the Pennsylvania State University when initially chosen for state office. In his appointive capacity he served as chairman of the Water and Power Resources Board, the State Forestry Commission, and the Geographic Board, and as a member of the Sanitary Water Board, the Governor's Executive Board, the Commission on Interstate Cooperation, State Planning Board, Soil and Water Conservation Commission, Land Reclamation Board, and numerous other boards and *ad hoc* groups. From 1961 forward he was the governor's alternate member of the Delaware River Basin Commission, and from 1963 through June, 1970, the Pennsylvania member of the Susquehanna River Basin Study Coordinating Committee. He was chosen permanent chairman of the IAC in June, 1963.

Dr. Harold G. Wilm, Vice-Chairman, 1963–66

Hal Wilm went westward from the Midwest to earn his degree in forestry at Colorado College, then came east to take his master's and doctoral degrees at Cornell University. For twenty-one years thereafter

Wilm was with the Forest Service, U. S. Department of Agriculture, in various ladder-climbing capacities, with experience in such varied regions of the country as California, the Rockies, the South and Southeast, and the Pacific Northwest. He was administratively responsible for USDA flood control surveys in the Northwest, and through the final two years was chief of the Division of Forest Influences Research and Flood Control Surveys, Washington.

In 1953 he became Associate Dean of Forestry at Syracuse University and six years later was appointed state Commissioner of Conservation. There, among other duties, Wilm took part in the drafting, passage, and administration of such natural resources statutes as the federal Water Resources Planning Act of 1965, and the Delaware River Basin Compact of 1961. In February, 1966, Wilm returned to Syracuse University as Director of the State University Water Resources Institute, and a year later went back to Washington to become Assistant Director for State Grants of the federal Water Resources Council. In 1970 he became associated with Wendell and Schwan as a consultant, and later moved to the faculty of the University of Vermont at Burlington.

Dr. W. Mason Lawrence, Vice-Chairman, 1966—

Mason Lawrence succeeded Wilm as New York's vice-chairman of the Interstate Advisory Committee upon the latter's departure from New York state government. A native upstate New Yorker, Lawrence received his bachelor's and doctor's degrees at Cornell University. His earlier career interests were in the fisheries field, and he has remained in the Conservation Department (later named Department of Environmental Conservation) of his home state from the time of his graduate student days forward.

Beginning in 1941 as a game research investigator, Lawrence progressively became a regional senior aquatic biologist, chief of the Bureau of Fish, assistant director, and then director of the Division of Fish and Game. In 1958 Lawrence was named Assistant Commissioner of Conservation, and Deputy Commissioner in 1964, the position held as this was written.

James J. O'Donnell, Vice Chairman, 1963–68

Jim O'Donnell is both a registered professional engineer and a member of the Maryland Bar. His higher schooling was at Loyola College, the U. S. Naval Academy, from which he was graduated in 1941, and the

University of Maryland School of Law. He holds a B. S. degree in engineering from the Naval Academy, and an LL. B. from the University of Maryland.

After service in the Navy in both the Atlantic and Pacific, O'Donnell resigned with the grade of lieutenant commander in 1946, and entered state service in 1947.

Following varied earlier state services, O'Donnell became successively the director of the State Department of Public Improvements and of the State Planning Department, joining the latter agency in 1959 and remaining until his resignation in October, 1968, to join the firm of J. Prentiss Browne Associates, Baltimore, in the field of architectural planning. He is a past president of the nationwide Association of State Planning and Developing Agencies, and has been honored in numerous other professional categories.

Dr. Albert R. Miller, Vice-Chairman, 1969—

Al Miller, an economics graduate of George Washington University, went on to Harvard to earn his MA and his PhD, both in economics. He was an assistant professor, in economics, at George Washington University for six years, and director of economic research of the National Foundation for Consumer Credit for almost six more years before joining the staff of the Maryland Department of State Planning in 1958; there he is director of development planning and research programs. He served as Maryland vice-chairman of the Potomac River Basin Advisory Committee and is alternate member from Maryland of the Ohio River Basin Commission. Miller became vice-chairman of the IAC for Maryland when O'Donnell left state government service.

Ronald B. Peterson, 1962–68

I believe even the file clerks in the New York Department of Commerce called its 1967-68 commissioner by his nickname "Ronnie." He was that kind of man, earthy, quick-witted, informal when possible but firm and businesslike when that was the appropriate stance to take. Peterson served as a member of the Interstate Advisory Committee from its beginning until his death in 1968. An industrial development specialist for most of his many years as a career employe of the state, Peterson approached the subject of a Susquehanna River Basin Compact from his special viewpoint; he wanted the agreement to assist, not retard, industrial development, and his often pungent comments reflected his convictions.

After ten years in mining and manufacturing, Peterson went in 1940 to the Division of State Planning, which evolved into the Department of Commerce, and stayed with it to the end except for an interlude in 1966-67 when, on request of Governor Nelson A. Rockefeller, he organized a new Office of Planning Coordination in the Executive Department. Peterson was First Deputy Commissioner of Commerce when appointed to the IAC in 1962, and became head of the department in 1967.

One of the accomplishments of which he was proud was the conception and organization early in World War II of a subcontracting program that enabled hundreds of the state's smaller manufacturers and fabricators, threatened with closure through lack of materials, to take part in and contribute to war production. This program was subsequently adopted by the Federal Government on a national basis.

William S. James, 1962—

The President of the Maryland Senate, Bill James has been a member of the Maryland Bar since 1937, after schooling at the University of Delaware and the University of Maryland Law School; his degree in law was granted at the latter. James was trial magistrate for two years in Havre de Grace, and from there went to the Maryland House of Delegates in 1947, serving continuously until 1955 when he was elected to the state Senate. In the Senate he became chairman of the Committee on Intergovernmental Cooperation in 1959, and in the same year was chairman of the Legislative Council Committee on Taxation and Fiscal Matters. He became President of the Senate in 1963 and has remained its chief officer to the present.

Elisha T. Barrett, 1962–66

A member of the New York Legislature from 1936 until his death in 1966, Senator Barrett was known better by his nickname of "June" than the biblical Elisha given by his parents. Barrett served in the Assembly until 1956, when he was elected to the Senate. He was for years the chairman, and in 1966 was secretary, of the New York Joint Legislative Committee on Interstate Cooperation, the committee that appeared to be his chief interest among many. In the course of his long tenure in the Assembly, Barrett served as vice-chairman of the Committee on Finance, and as a member of the Committees on Conservation and Recreation, Health, Insurance, Motor Vehicles and Transportation, Roads and Public Works, and Social Services. Through the Committee on Interstate Cooperation, Barrett was the prime mover in New York in the organization of the Interstate Advisory Committee on the Susquehanna River Basin, backed and egged on by Fred Zimmermann, then the research director of the Committee on Interstate Cooperation.

Other capacities in which Barrett served included executive membership on the Atlantic States Marine Fisheries Commission and the Board of Managers of the Council of State Governments.

Orvile E. Snare of Huntingdon, a member of the House of the Pennsylvania General Assembly, served as treasurer of the IAC throughout his membership.

A roster of the IAC members and alternates, complete through the winter of 1970, follows:

NEW YORK

Members

Executive Branch

Dr. Harold G. Wilm, Conservation Commissioner, Albany, vice chairman, 1962–66.
Dr. W. Mason Lawrence, Deputy Commissioner for Environmental Management, Albany, vice-chairman, 1966—.
Ronald B. Peterson, Deputy Commissioner (later Commissioner) of Commerce, Albany, 1962–68.*
Neal L. Moylan, Commissioner of Commerce, Albany, 1969—.

Legislative Branch

Senator Elisha T. Barrett, Bay Shore, 1962–66.*
Senator Dalwin J. Niles, Johnstown, 1967—.
Assemblyman Leo A. Lawrence, Herkimer, 1962–65.
Assemblyman James J. Barry, Syracuse, 1967–69.
Assemblyman Francis J. Boland, Binghamton, 1969—.

Alternate Members

Executive Branch

F. W. Montanari, Director of Water Resources, Albany, 1963–1970.
John Rhodes, Commerce Department, 1963–67.
William E. Seymour, Deputy Commissioner of Commerce, 1969—.
* Deceased.

Legislative Branch

Senator Frank E. Van Lare, Rochester, 1963–67.

Senator William T. Smith, Elmira, 1967—.

Assemblyman Daniel Dickinson, Binghamton, 1963–65.

Assemblyman George Ingalls, Binghamton, 1966–67.

Assemblyman Francis J. Boland, Binghamton, 1967–69.

Assemblyman Donald J. Mitchell, Herkimer, 1969—.

PENNSYLVANIA

Members

Executive Branch

Dr. Maurice K. Goddard, Secretary of Forests and Waters (later Secretary, Department of Environmental Resources), Harrisburg, chairman, 1962—.

John P. Robin, chairman, State Planning Board, Philadelphia, 1962–63.

John Tabor, Secretary of Commerce, Harrisburg, 1963–67.

Clifford L. Jones, Secretary of Commerce, 1967–69.

Legislative Branch

Senator George B. Stevenson, Jersey Shore, (Pa.), 1962–63.*

Senator Z. H. Confair, Williamsport, 1963—.

Representative Harris G. Breth, Clearfield, treasurer, 1962–63.

Representative Orville E. Snare, Huntingdon, secretary-treasurer, 1963–69.

Representative W. Brady Hetrick, Lewistown, 1970—.

Alternate Members

Executive Branch

Alan J. Sommerville, Department of Forests and Waters, Harrisburg, 1963—.

Clifford L. Jones, Deputy Secretary of Commerce, Harrisburg, 1963–67.

Edward D. Smith, Deputy Secretary of Commerce, Harrisburg, 1967–69.

Daniel B. Boyer, Jr., Department of Commerce, Harrisburg, 1969—.

Legislative Branch

Senator Preston B. Davis, Milton, 1963—.

Representative Stanley A. Meholchick, Ashley, 1966—.

* Deceased.

MARYLAND

Members

Executive Branch

James J. O'Donnell, Director, State Planning Department, Baltimore, vice-chairman, 1963–68.

Dr. Albert R. Miller, Jr., Chief, Bureau of Research and Special Studies, State Planning Department, Baltimore, vice-chairman, 1968—.

Thomas J. Hatem, Bel Air, 1962–67.

George Martinak, Baltimore, 1967—.

Legislative Branch

Senator William S. James, Bel Air, 1962—.

Delegate Marvin Mandel, Baltimore, 1962–67.

Alternate Members

Executive Branch

Paul W. McKee, Director, Department of Water Resources, Annapolis, 1964—.

Frank Harris, Perryville, 1965–67.

Werner Buchal, Bel Air, 1967–69.

Legislative Branch

Senator J. Albert Roney, 1963–65.

Delegate Chester W. Tawney, Baltimore, 1963–65.

Delegate Joseph Acker, Baltimore, 1965–69.

The Drafting Task Force

Three alternate members of the Interstate Advisory Committee were among the six members of the *ad hoc* Susquehanna River Basin Compact Drafting Task Force. They were Francis W. Montanari, then Assistant Commissioner of Conservation for Water Resources, New York; Alan J. Sommerville, Water Resources Coordinator, Pennsylvania Department of Forests and Waters; and Paul W. McKee, Director of the Maryland Department of Water Resources. Much background information on Task Force Chairman Zimmermann appears elsewhere in this book, as does career information on Dr. Mitchell Wendell, consultant to the group and to the parent IAC, so some duplication appears inevitable.

Frederick L. Zimmermann, Chairman, 1964–67

A native of Brooklyn and a graduate of Columbia, where he also earned his master's degree, Fred Zimmermann was a New Yorker for many years. He took an early interest in politics and was elected to the first of six terms to the New York Assembly in 1930, when he was twenty-two. In 1936 he became a member of the political science faculty at Hunter College, and while he remained there as a professor of political science until his retirement in 1971, he resigned his nine-year chairmanship of the department at the end of the 1968 college year.

His interest in interstate cooperation and intergovernmental relations began before he left the Assembly. In 1936 he was author of the legislation that resulted in establishment of the Joint Legislative Committee on Interstate Cooperation, which was the vehicle used by New York State for its part in the founding of the Council of State Governments. Zimmermann has been a job "moonlighter" for more than three decades, and became the research director of the interstate cooperation committee about the same time he joined the faculty at Hunter.

A simple listing of the consulting assignments and such that Fred Zimmermann has accepted and carried through to completion since 1936 requires three single-spaced typewritten pages, and the table of contents of his writings on intergovernmental relations and similar politico—scientific subjects is almost as long. The barest outline can be found by anyone interested in both *Who's Who in America* and *American Men of Science*. His home is at Catskill, New York.

Francis W. Montanari, New York, 1964–67

Monty Montanari is a graduate of Cornell, where he earned both his bachelor's and master's degrees in civil engineering; he earlier attended Northeastern University in Boston. In World War II he was a Sea Bee officer in the Pacific Theater.

For 10 years Monty's engineering was practiced in Brazil, Mexico, and Panama, 1946-56, on the staff of the Institute of Inter-American Affairs (now part of the Agency for International Development). In 1956 he went to the Ohio River Valley Water Sanitation Commission (OR-SANCO) as sanitary engineer, working principally on problems connected with mine drainage control, oil pollution control, evaluation of industrial wastes, and river studies.

Montanari holds licenses as a professional engineer in Ohio and New York and is a diplomate of the American Academy of Sanitary Engineers. He is a member of several associations in the water resources field. He moved from ORSANCO to the assistant commissionership for water resources, New York, in 1962. By virtue of his position there Monty was also director of the New York Water Resources Commission. He headed the Denver office of Parsons, Brenkerhoff, Quade, & Douglas, Inc., in 1970.

Paul W. McKee, Maryland 1964–67

Paul McKee has been involved in water resources, with many years of specialization in pollution control activities, since 1945. In that year he was executive secretary of a gubernatorial committee appointed to study pollution in Maryland, and became director of the state's Water Pollution Control Commission in 1947 upon enactment of legislation that resulted from the study. In 1964, when the commission was abolished and the new and broader-based Department of Water Resources was created, he became its director, and still holds that office.

McKee's undergraduate work was done at the University of North Carolina, where he majored in aquatic biology. This was followed by graduate study in chemistry at North Carolina and at Duke. In addition to being an alternate member of the IAC, McKee was a member of the Potomac River Basin Advisory Committee, which supervised the drafting of a federal–interstate compact for that basin similar to the one written for the Susquehanna.

Alan J. Sommerville, Pennsylvania, 1964–67

Alan Sommerville moved into water resource activities via flood forecasting in the U. S. Weather Bureau. After graduation from Pennsylvania State University with an A. B. degree, which was supplemented by three years of study in industrial engineering, Sommerville began his adult career as a junior draftsman for the Pennsylvania Department of Forests and Waters in 1939. He had a wartime tour of duty in the Weather Service of the Army Air Corps. After that he went on in turn to the Weather Bureau offices in New York City and St. Louis before returning to Pennsylvania as Chief Water Resources Development Engineer for Forests and Waters under Goddard, spending much time on intergovernmental relations matters. His title was changed to Water Resources Coordinator in 1967. He is co-author of U. S. Geological Survey Water Supply Paper 1526, *Hydraulic and Hydrologic Aspects of*

Flood Plain Planning and of numerous technical papers. He has been alternate member to Goddard on a half dozen river basin and regional coordinating committees and has worked closely with the commissioners and staff of the Delaware River Basin Commission since its inauguration in 1962.

Dr. Carl N. Everstine, Maryland, 1964–67

A Marylander from birth, Carl Everstine received his undergraduate schooling in liberal arts at the University of Maryland in 1930, and earned his doctorate at Johns Hopkins in 1938. Some years later he returned to the University of Maryland Law School at Baltimore for a law degree. He has spent his adult years in state service, starting as a research staffer for the Maryland Legislative Council, a permanent body whose chief activities are the interim study of legislation proposed for consideration by the general assembly. Everstine became director of the Department of Legislative Reference of Maryland and of the City of Baltimore in 1952 and has held those titles ever since. He is author of a history of the Grand Lodge of Masons of Maryland, and editor of twenty-four codes of public laws for counties in Maryland.

Robert J. Trace, Pennsylvania, 1964–67

Drafting legislation was no new thing to Bob Trace when he joined the compact writing team, for by then he had been doing it for close to twenty years. Trace was a product of Dickinson College (A.B.) and of the Dickinson School of Law (LL.B.), and had been chief counsel for the Pennsylvania Sanitary Water Board from 1948 through 1959. He was appointed as assistant attorney general, assigned to the Department of Forests and Waters, in 1963.

Trace's first contact with compact drafting came when the Ohio River Valley Water Sanitation Commission (ORSANCO) was in the making in the late 1940s. He represented the Commonwealth on the drafting task force. Later he gave counsel to Pennsylvania officials in the time the Delaware Compact was being drafted, and he was a member of the drafting task forces of both the Susquehanna and the Potomac basin compacts.

Dr. Mitchell Wendell, Washington, Consultant, 1964–70

After being graduated from Brooklyn College in 1943 with a liberal arts degree, Mitch Wendell went on to Columbia University to secure a law degree in 1945 and a doctorate in public law and government in 1949. While at Columbia, Wendell was editor of the *Columbia Law Review*. His first professional work was as a substitute instructor in political science at Hunter College. From there he went to Hamilton College as a political science instructor, but after one year he returned to New York and American International College, first as assistant professor of political science, from which he progressed to chairmanship of the department.

Wendell's biography, like that of Zimmermann, is so filled with the solid meat of accomplishment in his special field that it is difficult to determine where to start and stop cataloging, but for reasons of my own an attempt will be made. Since intergovernmental relations has been a principal love and concern, perhaps a simple listing of some of the more significant of his activities over the years in that field—from my viewpoint, not necessarily his—will be sufficient to indicate the professional stature of the man:

Counsel to the Interstate Sanitation Commission; member, Legal Advisory Committee, Atlantic States Marine Fisheries Commission; member, Special Committee on Flood Insurance, Council of State Governments; consultant to the Missouri Basin States Committee for the Council of State Governments; member, New York State Joint Committee on Revision of Water Law and Policy; member, Interstate Conference on Water Problems, chairman of its Policy Committee, and staff member; made study leading to New York's comprehensive oil and gas conservation law and drafted the legislation; drafted the Interstate Mining Compact, relative to restoration of mined lands and related matters; drafted a comprehensive State Air Pollution Control Act; participated in negotiation and some phases of drafting of the Delaware River Basin Compact; developed plan for and drafted Pest Control Compact; directed flood plain study for New York Joint Legislative Committee on Interstate Cooperation and drafted legislation; counsel of the same committee for four years; consultant, later counsel, Council of State Governments over a 10-year period; consultant to Parole and Probation Compact Administrators Association and of the Juvenile Compact Administrators Association for several years; and founder, in association with Charles F. Schwan, Jr., of the consulting concern of Wendell and Schwan, in Washington in 1968, later expanded and incorporated as Environments For Tomorrow, Inc.

Mitch Wendell's biography has run somewhat longer than those of other Susquehanna compact drafters, even of IAC committee leaders, and could have run on for several hundred additional words without repetition. This was deliberate on my part, for I have a tremendous admiration for a tremendous individual.

Appendix B

Text of the Susquehanna River Basin Compact

An Act

84 STAT. 1509

Consenting to the Susquehanna River Basin compact, enacting the same into law thereby making the United States a signatory party; making certain reservations on behalf of the United States, and for related purposes.

Be it enacted by the Senate and House of Representatives of the United States of America in Congress assembled,

Susquehanna River Basin Compact. Consent of Congress.

SUSQUEHANNA RIVER BASIN COMPACT

SECTION 1. The consent of Congress is hereby given to the Susquehanna River Basin compact in the form substantially as follows, and the compact is hereby enacted into law thereby making the United States a signatory party thereto:

"SUSQUEHANNA RIVER BASIN COMPACT

"PREAMBLE

"Whereas the signatory parties hereto recognize the water resources of the Susquehanna River Basin as regional assets vested with local, state, and national interest for which they have a joint responsibility; and declare as follows:

"1. The conservation, utilization, development, management, and control of the water resources of the Susquehanna River Basin under comprehensive multiple purpose planning will bring the greatest benefits and produce the most efficient service in the public interest; and

"2. This comprehensive planning administered by a basin-wide agency will provide flood damage reduction, conservation and development of surface and ground water supply for municipal, industrial, and agricultural uses, development of recreational facilities in relation to reservoirs, lakes and streams, propagation of fish and game, promotion of forest land management, soil conservation, and watershed projects, protection and aid to fisheries, development of hydroelectric power potentialities, improved navigation, control of the movement of salt water, abatement and control of water pollution, and regulation of stream flows toward the attainment of these goals; and

"3. The water resources of the basin are presently subject to the duplicating, overlapping, and uncoordinated administration of a large number of governmental agencies which exercise a multiplicity of powers resulting in a splintering of authority and responsibility; and

"4. The Interstate Advisory Committee on the Susquehanna River Basin, created by action of the states of New York, Pennsylvania, and Maryland, on the basis of its studies and deliberation has concluded that regional development of the Susquehanna River Basin is feasible, advisable, and urgently needed, and has recommended that an intergovernmental compact with Federal participation be consummated to this end; and

"5. The Congress of the United States and the executive branch of the Federal government have recognized a national interest in the Susquehanna River Basin by authorizing and directing the Corps of Engineers of the Department of the Army, the Department of Agriculture, the Department of Health, Education and Welfare, the Department of Interior, and other Federal agencies to cooperate in making comprehensive surveys and reports concerning the water resources of the Susquehanna River Basin in which individually or severally the technical aid and assistance of many Federal and state agencies have been enlisted, and which are being or have been coordinated through a Susquehanna River Basin Study Coordinating

275

Committee on which the Corps of Engineers of the Department of the Army, the Department of Agriculture, the Department of Commerce, the Department of Health, Education and Welfare, the Department of Interior, the Department of Housing and Urban Development and its predecessor Housing and Home Finance Agency, the Federal Power Commission, and the States of New York, Pennsylvania, and Maryland are or were represented; and

"6. Some three million people live and work in the Susquehanna River Basin and its environs, and the government, employment, industry, and economic development of the entire region and the health, safety, and general well being of its population are and will continue to be affected vitally by the conservation, utilization, development, management, and control of the water resources of the basin; and

"7. Demands upon the water resources of the basin are expected to mount because of anticipated increases in population and by reason of industrial and economic growth of the basin and its service area; and

"8. Water resources planning and development are technical, complex, and expensive, often requiring fifteen to twenty years from the conception to the completion of large or extensive projects; and

"9. The public interest requires that facilities must be ready and operative when and where needed, to avoid the damages of unexpected floods or prolonged drought, and for other purposes; and

"10. The Interstate Advisory Committee on the Susquehanna River Basin has prepared a draft of an intergovernmental compact for the creation of a basin agency, and the signatory parties desire to effectuate the purposes thereof; Now therefore

"The States of New York and Maryland and the Commonwealth of Pennsylvania, and the United States of America hereby solemnly covenant and agree with each other, upon the enactment of concurrent legislation by the Congress of the United States and by the respective State legislatures, to the Susquehanna River Basin Compact which consists of this Preamble and the Articles that follow.

"ARTICLE 1

"SHORT TITLE, DEFINITIONS, PURPOSES, AND LIMITATIONS

"SECTION 1.1—SHORT TITLE. This compact shall be known and may be cited as the Susquehanna River Basin Compact.

"1.2—DEFINITIONS. For the purpose of this compact, and of any supplemental or concurring legislation enacted pursuant to it:

"1. 'Basin' shall mean the area of drainage of the Susquehanna River and its tributaries into Chesapeake Bay to the southern edge of the Pennsylvania Railroad bridge between Havre de Grace and Perryville, Maryland.

"2. 'Commission' shall mean the Susquehanna River Basin Commission hereby created, and the term 'Commissioner' shall mean a member of the commission.

"3. 'Cost' shall mean direct and indirect expenditures, commitment, and net induced adverse effects, whether or not compensated for, used or incurred in connection with the establishment, acquisition, construction, maintenance, and operation of a project.

"4. 'Diversion' shall mean the transfer of water into or from the basin.

"5. 'Facility' shall mean any real or personal property, within or without the basin, and improvements thereof or thereon, and any and

276

all rights of way, water, water rights, plants, structures, machinery, and equipment acquired, constructed, operated, or maintained for the beneficial use of water resources or related land uses or otherwise including, without limiting the generality of the foregoing, any and all things and appurtenances necessary, useful, or convenient for the control, collection, storage, withdrawal, diversion, release, treatment, transmission, sale, or exchange of water; or for navigation thereon, or the development and use of hydroelectric energy and power, and public recreational facilities; or the propagation of fish and wildlife; or to conserve and protect the water resources of the basin or any existing or future water supply source, or to facilitate any other uses of any of them.

"6. 'Federal government' shall mean the government of the United States of America, and any appropriate branch, department, bureau, or division thereof, as the case may be.

"7. 'Project' shall mean any work, service, or activity which is separately planned, financed, or identified by the commission, or any separate facility undertaken or to be undertaken by the commission or otherwise within a specified area, for the conservation, utilization, control, development, or management of water resources which can be established and utilized independently or as an addition to an existing facility and can be considered as a separate entity for purposes of evaluation.

"8. 'Signatory party' shall mean a state or commonwealth party to this compact, or the Federal government.

"9. 'Water' shall mean both surface and underground waters which are contained within the drainage area of the Susquehanna River in the states of New York, Pennsylvania, and Maryland.

"10. 'Water resources' shall include all waters and related natural resources within the basin.

"11. 'Withdrawal' shall mean a taking or removal of water from any source within the basin for use within the basin.

"12. 'Person' shall mean an individual, corporation, partnership, unincorporated association, and the like and shall have no gender, and the singular shall include the plural.

"1.3—PURPOSE AND FINDINGS. That legislative bodies of the respective signatory parties hereby find and declare:

"1. The water resources of the Susquehanna River Basin are affected with a local, state, regional, and national interest, and the planning, conservation, utilization, development, management, and control of these resources, under appropriate arrangements for intergovernmental cooperation, are public purposes of the respective signatory parties.

"2. The water resources of the basin are subject to the sovereign rights and responsibilities of the signatory parties, and it is the purpose of this compact to provide for a joint exercise of these powers of sovereignty in the common interest of the people of the region.

"3. The water resources of the basin are functionally interrelated, and the uses of these resources are interdependent. A single administrative agency is therefore essential for effective and economical direction, supervision, and coordination of water resources efforts and programs of federal, state, and local governments and of private enterprise.

"4. Present and future demands require increasing economies and efficiencies in the use and reuse of water resources, and these can be brought about only by comprehensive planning, programming, and management under the direction of a single administrative agency.

277

"5. In general, the purposes of this compact are to promote interstate comity; to remove causes of possible controversy; to make secure and protect developments within the states; to encourage and provide for the planning, conservation, utilization, development, management, and control of the water resources of the basin; to provide for cooperative and coordinated planning and action by the signatory parties with respect to water resources; and to apply the principle of equal and uniform treatment to all users of water and of water related facilities without regard to political boundaries.

"6. It is the express intent of the signatory parties that the commission shall engage in the construction, operation, and maintenance of a project only when the project is necessary to the execution of the comprehensive plan and no other competent agency is in a position to act, or such agency fails to act.

"1.4—POWERS OF CONGRESS; WITHDRAWAL. Nothing in this compact shall be construed to relinquish the functions, powers, or duties of the Congress of the United States with respect to the control of any navigable waters within the basin, nor shall any provisions hereof be construed in derogation of any of the constitutional powers of the Congress to regulate commerce among the states and with foreign nations. The power and right of the Congress to withdraw the Federal government as a party to this compact or to revise or modify the terms, conditions, and provisions under which it may remain a party by amendment, repeal, or modification of any Federal statute applicable hereto is recognized by the signatory parties.

"1.5—DURATION OF COMPACT.

"(a) The duration of this compact shall be for an initial period of 100 years from its effective date, and it shall be continued for additional periods of 100 years if not less than 20 years nor more than 25 years prior to the termination of the initial period or any succeeding period none of the signatory states, by authority of an act of its legislature, notifies the commission of intention to terminate the compact at the end of the then current 100-year period.

"(b) In the event this compact should be terminated by operation of paragraph (a) above, the commission shall be dissolved, its assets and liabilities transferred in accordance with the equities of the signatory parties therein, and its corporate affairs wound up in accordance with agreement of the signatory parties or, failing agreement, by act of the Congress.

"ARTICLE 2

"ORGANIZATION AND AREA

"SECTION 2.1—COMMISSION CREATED. The Susquehanna River Basin Commission is hereby created as a body politic and corporate, with succession for the duration of this compact, as an agency and instrumentality of the governments of the respective signatory parties.

"2.2—COMMISSION MEMBERSHIP. The members of the commission shall be the governor or the designee of the governor of each signatory state, to act for him, and one member to be appointed by the President of the United States to serve at the pleasure of the President.

"2.3—ALTERNATES. An alternate from each signatory party shall be appointed by its member of the commission unless otherwise provided by the laws of the signatory party. The alternate, in the absence of the member, shall represent the member and act for him. In the event of a vacancy in the office of alternate, it shall be filled in the same manner as the original appointment.

84 STAT. 1513

"2.4—COMPENSATION. Members of the commission and alternates shall serve without compensation from the commission but may be reimbursed for necessary expenses incurred in and incident to the performance of their duties.

"2.5—VOTING POWER. Each member is entitled to one vote. No action of the commission may be taken unless three of the four members vote in favor thereof.

"2.6—ORGANIZATION AND PROCEDURE. The commission shall provide for its own organization and procedure, and shall adopt the rules and regulations governing its meetings and transactions. It shall organize annually by the election of a chairman and vice-chairman from among its members. It shall provide by its rules for the appointment by each member in his discretion of an advisor to serve without compensation from the commission, who may attend all meetings of the commission and its committees.

"2.7—JURISDICTION OF THE COMMISSION. The commission shall have, exercise, and discharge its functions, powers, and duties within the limits of the basin. Outside the basin, the commission shall act at its discretion, but only to the extent necessary to implement its responsibilities within the basin, and where necessary subject to the consent of the state wherein it proposes to act.

"ARTICLE 3

"POWERS AND DUTIES OF THE COMMISSION

"SECTION 3.1—GENERAL. The Commission shall develop and effectuate plans, policies, and projects relating to the water resources of the basin. It shall adopt and promote uniform and coordinated policies for water resources conservation and management in the basin. It shall encourage and direct the planning, development, operation, and subject to applicable laws the financing of water resources projects according to such plans and policies.

"3.2—POLICY. It is the policy of the signatory parties to preserve and utilize the functions, powers, and duties of the existing offices and agencies of government to the extent consistent with this compact, and the commission is directed to utilize those offices and agencies for the purposes of this compact.

"3.3—COMPREHENSIVE PLAN, PROGRAM AND BUDGETS. The commission in accordance with Article 14 of this compact, shall formulate and adopt:

"1. A comprehensive plan, after consultation with appropriate water users and interested public bodies for the immediate and long range development and use of the water resources of the basin;

"2. A water resources program, based upon the comprehensive plan, which shall include a systematic presentation of the quantity and quality of water resources needs of the area to be served for such reasonably foreseeable period as the commission may determine, balanced by existing and proposed projects required to satisfy such needs, including all public and private projects affecting the basin, together with a separate statement of the projects proposed to be undertaken by the commission during such period; and

"3. An annual current expense budget and an annual capital budget consistent with the commission's program, projects, and facilities for the budget period.

"3.4—POWERS OF COMMISSION. The commission may:

"1. Plan, design, acquire, construct, reconstruct, complete, own, improve, extend, develop, operate, and maintain any and all projects, facilities, properties, activities, and services which are determined by the commission to be necessary, convenient, or useful for the purposes of this compact.

"2. Establish standards of planning, design, and operation of all projects and facilities in the basin to the extent they affect water resources, including without limitation thereto water, sewage and other waste treatment plants and facilities, pipelines, transmission lines, stream and lake recreational facilities, trunk mains for water distribution, local flood protection works, watershed management programs, and ground water recharging operations.

"3. Conduct and sponsor research on water resources and their planning, use, conservation, management, development, control, and protection, and the capacity, adaptability, and best utility of each facility thereof, and collect, compile, correlate, analyze, report, and interpret data on water resources and uses in the basin, including without limitation thereto the relation of water to other resources, industrial water technology, ground water movement, relation between water price and water demand and other economic factors, and general hydrological conditions.

"4. Collect, compile, coordinate, and interpret systematic surface and ground water data, and publicize such information when and as needed for water uses, flood warning, quality maintenance, or other purposes.

"5. Conduct ground and surface water investigations, tests, and operations, and compile data relating thereto, as may be required to formulate and administer the comprehensive plan.

"6. Prepare, publish, and disseminate information and reports concerning the water problems of the basin and for the presentation of the needs and resources of the basin and policies of the commission to executive and legislative branches of the signatory parties.

"7. Negotiate loans, grants, gifts, services, or other aids as may be lawfully available from public or private sources to finance or assist in effectuating any of the purposes of this compact, and receive and accept them upon terms and conditions, and subject to provisions, as may be required by Federal or state law or as the commission may deem necessary or desirable.

"8. Exercise such other and different powers as may be delegated to it by this compact or otherwise pursuant to law, and have and exercise all powers necessary or convenient to carry out its express powers and other powers which reasonably may be implied therefrom.

"9. Adopt, amend, and repeal rules and regulations to implement this compact.

"3.5—DUTIES OF THE COMMISSION. The commission shall :

"1. Develop and effectuate plans, policies, and projects relating to water resources, adopt, promote, and coordinate policies and standards for water resources conservation, control, utilization, and management, and promote and implement the planning, development, and financing of water resources projects.

"2. Undertake investigations, studies, and surveys, and acquire, construct, operate, and maintain projects and facilities in regard to the water resources of the basin, whenever it is deemed necessary to do so to activate or effectuate any of the provisions of this compact.

"3. Administer, manage, and control water resources in all matters determined by the commission to be interstate in nature or to have a major effect on the water resources and water resources management.

"4. Assume jurisdiction in any matter affecting water resources whenever it determines after investigation and public hearing upon due notice given, that the effectuation of the comprehensive plan or the implementation of this compact so requires. If the commission finds upon subsequent hearing requested by an affected signatory party that the party will take the necessary action, the commission may relinquish jurisdiction.

"5. Investigate and determine if the requirements of the compact or the rules and regulations of the commission are complied with, and if satisfactory progress has not been made, institute an action or actions in its own name in any state or federal court of competent jurisdiction to compel compliance with any and all of the provisions of this compact or any of the rules and regulations of the commission adopted pursuant thereto. An action shall be instituted in the name of the commission and shall be conducted by its own counsel.

"3.6—Cooperative Legislation and Further Jurisdiction.

"(a) Each of the signatory parties agrees that it will seek enactment of such additional legislation as will be required to enable its officers, departments, commissions, boards, and agents to accomplish effectively the obligations and duties assumed under the terms of this compact.

"(b) Nothing in the compact shall be construed to repeal, modify or qualify the authority of any signatory party to enact any legislation or enforce any additional conditions and restrictions within its jurisdiction.

"3.7—Coordination and Cooperation. The commission shall promote and aid the coordination of the activities and programs of Federal, state, municipal, and private agencies concerned with water resources administration in the basin. To this end, but without limitation thereto, the commission may:

"1. Advise, consult, contract, financially assist, or otherwise cooperate with any and all such agencies;

"2. Employ any other agency or instrumentality of any of the signatory parties or of any political subdivision thereof, in the design, construction, operation, and maintenance of structures, and the installation and management of river control systems, or for any other purpose;

"3. Develop and adopt plans and specifications for particular water resources projects and facilities which so far as consistent with the comprehensive plan incorporate any separate plans of other public and private organizations operating in the basin, and permit the decentralized administration thereof;

"4. Qualify as a sponsoring agency under any Federal legislation heretofore or hereafter enacted to provide financial or other assistance for the planning, conservation, utilization, development, management, or control of water resources.

"3.8—Allocations, Diversions, and Releases.

"(a) The commission shall have power from time to time as the need appears, to allocate the waters of the basin to and among the states signatory to this compact and impose related conditions, obligations, and release requirements.

"(b) The commission shall have power from time to time as the need appears to enter into agreements with other river basin commissions or other states with respect to in-basin and out-of-basin allocations, withdrawals, and diversions.

"(c) No allocation of waters made pursuant to this section shall constitute a prior appropriation of the waters of the basin or confer any superiority of right in respect to the use of those waters, nor shall

281

any such action be deemed to constitute an apportionment of the waters of the basin among the parties hereto. This subsection shall not be deemed to limit or restrict the power of the commission to enter into convenants with respect to water supply, with a duration not exceeding the life of this compact, as it may deem necessary for the benefit or development of the water resources of the basin.

"3.9—RATES AND CHARGES. The commission, from time to time after public hearing upon due notice given may fix, alter, and revise rates, rentals, charges, and tolls, and classifications thereof, without regulation or control by any department, office, or agency of any signatory party, for the use of facilities owned or operated by it, and any services or products which it provides.

"3.10—REFERRAL AND REVIEW. No projects affecting the water resources of the basin, except those not requiring review and approval by the commission under paragraph 3 following, shall be undertaken by any person, governmental authority or other entity prior to submission to and approval by the commission or appropriate agencies of the signatory parties for review.

"1. All water resources projects for which a permit or other form of permission to proceed with construction or implementation is required by legislative action of a signatory party or by rule or regulation of an office or agency of a signatory party having functions, powers, and duties in the planning, conservation, development, management, or control of water resources shall be submitted as heretofore to the appropriate office or agency of the signatory party for review and approval. To assure that the commission is apprised of all projects within the basin, monthly reports and listings of all permits granted, or similar actions taken, by offices or agencies of the signatory parties shall be submitted to the commission in a manner prescribed by it.

"Those projects which also require commission approval pursuant to the provisions of paragraphs 2(ii) and 2(iii) following shall be submitted to the commission through appropriate offices or agencies of a signatory party, except that, if no agency of a signatory party has jurisdiction, such projects shall be submitted directly to the commission in such manner as the commission shall prescribe.

"2. Approval of the commission shall be required for, but not limited to, the following:

"(i) All projects on or crossing the boundary between any two signatory states;

"(ii) Any project involving the diversion of water;

"(iii) Any project within the boundaries of any signatory state found and determined by the commission or by any agency of a signatory party having functions, powers, and duties in the planning, conservation, development, management, or control of water resources to have a significant effect on water resources within another signatory state; and

"(iv) Any project which has been included by the commission after hearing, as provided in Article 14, Section 14.1, as a part of the commission's comprehensive plan for the development of the water resources of the basin, or which would have a significant effect upon the plan.

"3. Review and approval by the commission shall not be required for:

"(i) Projects which fall into an exempt classification or designation established by legislative action of a signatory party or by rule or regulation of an office or agency of a signatory party having functions,

282

powers, and duties in the planning, conservation, development, management, or control of water resources. The sponsors of those projects are not required to obtain a permit or other form of permission to proceed with construction or implementation, unless it is determined by the commission or by the agency of a signatory party that such project or projects may cause an adverse, adverse cumulative, or an interstate effect on water resources of the basin, and the project sponsor has been notified in writing by the commission or by the agency of a signatory party that commission approval is required.

"(ii) Projects which are classified by the commission as not requiring its review and approval, for so long as they are so classified.

"4. The commission shall approve a project if it determines that the project is not detrimental to the proper conservation, development, management, or control of the water resources of the basin and may modify and approve as modified, or may disapprove the project, if it determines that the project is not in the best interest of the conservation, development, management, or control of the basin's water resources, or is in conflict with the comprehensive plan.

"5. The commission, after consultation with the appropriate offices or agencies of the signatory parties shall establish the procedure of submission, review, and consideration of projects. And procedure for review and approval of diversions of water shall include public hearing on due notice given, with opportunity for interested persons, agencies, governmental units, and signatory parties to be heard and to present evidence. A complete transcript of the proceedings at the hearing shall be made and preserved, and it shall be made available under rules for that purpose adopted by the commission.

"6. Any determination of the commission pursuant to this article or any article of the compact providing for judicial review shall be subject to such judicial review in any court of competent jurisdiction, provided that an action or proceeding for such review is commenced within 90 days from the effective date of the determination sought to be reviewed; but a determination of the commission concerning a diversion, under Section 3.10–2(ii) with the claimed effect of reducing below a proper minimum the flow of water in that portion of the basin within the area of a signatory party, shall be subject to judicial review under the particular provisions of paragraph 7 below.

"7. Any signatory party deeming itself aggrieved by an action of the commission concerning a diversion under Section 3.10–2(ii) with the claimed effect of reducing below a proper minimum the flow of water in that portion of the basin which lies within the area of that signatory party, and notwithstanding the powers provided to the commission by this compact, may have review of commission action approving the diversion in the Supreme Court of the United States; provided that a proceeding for such review is commenced within one year from the date of action sought to be reviewed. Any such review shall be on the record made before the commission. The action of the commission shall be affirmed, unless the court finds that it is not supported by substantial evidence.

"3.11—ADVISORY COMMITTEES. The commission may constitute and empower advisory committees.

"ARTICLE 4

"WATER SUPPLY

"SECTION 4.1—GENERALLY. The commission shall have power to develop, implement, and effectuate plans and projects for the use of

283

the water of the basin for domestic, municipal, agricultural, and industrial water supply. To this end, without limitation thereto, it may provide for, construct, acquire, operate, and maintain dams, reservoirs, and other facilities for utilization of surface and ground water resources, and all related structures, appurtenances, and equipment on the river and its tributaries and at such off-river sites as it may find appropriate, and may regulate and control the use thereof.

"4.2—STORAGE AND RELEASE OF WATERS.

"(a) The commission shall have power to acquire, construct, operate, and control projects and facilities for the storage and release of waters, for the regulation of flows and supplies of surface and ground waters of the basin, for the protection of public health, stream quality control, economic development, improvement of fisheries, recreation, dilution and abatement of pollution, the prevention of undue salinity, and other purposes.

"(b) No signatory party shall permit any augmentation of flow to be diminished by the diversion of any water of the basin during any period in which waters are being released from storage under the direction of the commission for the purpose of augmenting such flow, except in cases where the diversion is authorized by this compact, or by the commission pursuant thereto, or by the judgment, order, or decree of a court of competent jurisdiction.

"4.3—ASSESSABLE IMPROVEMENTS. The commission may provide water management and regulation in the main stream or any tributary in the basin and, in accordance with the procedures of applicable state laws, may assess on an annual basis or otherwise the cost thereof upon water users or any classification of them specially benefited thereby to a measurable extent, provided that no such assessment shall exceed the actual benefit to any water user. Any such assessment shall follow the procedure prescribed by law for local improvement assessments and shall be subject to review in any court of competent jurisdiction.

"4.4—COORDINATION. Prior to entering upon the execution of any project authorized by this article, the commission shall review and consider all existing rights, plans, and programs of the signatory parties, their political subdivisions, private parties, and water users which are pertinent to such project, and shall hold a public hearing on each proposed project.

"4.5—ADDITIONAL POWERS. In connection with any project authorized by this article, the commission shall have power to provide storage, treatment, pumping, and transmission facilities, but nothing herein shall be construed to authorize the commission to engage in the business of distributing water.

"ARTICLE 5

"WATER QUALITY MANAGEMENT AND CONTROL

"SECTION 5.1—GENERAL POWERS.

"(a) The commission may undertake or contract for investigations, studies, and surveys pertaining to existing water quality, effects of varied actual or projected operations on water quality, new compounds and materials and probable future water quality in the basin. The commission may receive, expend, and administer funds, Federal, state, local, or private as may be available to carry out these functions relating to water quality investigations.

"(b) The commission may acquire, construct, operate, and maintain projects and facilities for the management and control of water quality in the basin whenever the commission deems necessary to activate or effectuate any of the provisions of this compact.

284

"5.2—POLICY AND STANDARDS.

"(a) In order to conserve, protect, and utilize the water quality of the basin in accordance with the best interests of the people of the basin and the states, it shall be the policy of the commission to encourage and coordinate the efforts of the signatory parties to prevent, reduce, control and eliminate water pollution and to maintain water quality as required by the comprehensive plan.

"(b) The legislative intent in enacting this article is to give specific emphasis to the primary role of the states in water quality management and control.

"(c) The commission shall recommend to the signatory parties the establishment, modification, or amendment of standards of quality for any waters of the basin in relation to their reasonable and necessary use as the commission shall deem to be in the public interest.

"(d) The commission shall encourage cooperation and uniform enforcement programs and policies by the water quality control agencies of the signatory parties in meeting the water quality standards established in the comprehensive plan.

"(e) The commission may assume jurisdiction whenever it determines after investigation and public hearing upon due notice given that the effectuation of the comprehensive plan so requires. After such investigation, notice, and hearing, the commission may adopt such rules, regulations, and water quality standards as may be required to preserve, protect, improve, and develop the quality of the waters of the basin in accordance with the comprehensive plan.

"5.3—COOPERATIVE ADMINISTRATION AND ENFORCEMENT.

"(a) Each of the signatory parties agrees to prohibit and control pollution of the waters of the basin according to the requirements of this compact and to cooperate faithfully in the control of future pollution in and abatement of existing pollution from the waters of the basin.

"(b) The commission shall have the authority to investigate and determine if the requirements of the compact or the rules, regulations, and water quality standards of the commission are complied with and if satisfactory progress has not been made, may institute an action or actions in its own name in the proper court or courts of competent jurisdiction to compel compliance with any and all of the provisions of this compact or any of the rules, regulations, and water quality standards of the commission adopted pursuant thereto.

"5.4—FURTHER JURISDICTION. Nothing in this compact shall be construed to repeal, modify, or qualify the authority of any signatory party to enact any legislation or enforce any additional conditions and restrictions to lessen or prevent the pollution of waters within its jurisdiction.

"ARTICLE 6

"FLOOD PROTECTION

"SECTION 6.1—FLOOD CONTROL AUTHORITY. The commission may plan, design, construct and operate and maintain projects and facilities it deems necessary or desirable for flood plain development and flood damage reduction. It shall have power to operate such facilities and to store and release waters of the Susquehanna River and its tributaries and elsewhere within the basin, in such manner, at such times, and under such regulations as the commission may deem appropriate to meet flood conditions as they may arise.

285

"6.2—REGULATION.

"(a) The commission may study and determine the nature and extent of the flood plains of the Susquehanna River and its tributaries. Upon the basis of the studies, it may delineate areas subject to flooding, including but not limited to a classification of lands with reference to relative risk of flooding and the establishment of standards for flood plain use which will promote economic development and safeguard the public health, welfare, safety, and property. Prior to the adoption of any standards delineating the area or defining the use, the commission shall hold public hearings with respect to the substance of the standards in the manner provided by Article 15. The proposed standards shall be available from the commission at the time notice is given, and interested persons shall be given an opportunity to be heard thereon at the hearings.

"(b) The commission shall have power to promulgate, adopt, amend, and repeal from time to time as necessary, standards relating to the nature and extent of the uses of land in areas subject to flooding.

"(c) In taking action pursuant to subsection (b) of this section and as a prerequisite thereto, the commission shall consider the effect of particular uses of the flood plain in question on the health and safety of persons and property in the basin, the economic and technical feasibility of measures available for the development and protection of the flood plain, and the responsibilities, if any, of local, state, and federal governments connected with the use or proposed use of the flood plain in question. The commission shall regulate the use of particular flood plains in the manner and degree it finds necessary for the factors enumerated in this subsection, but only with the consent of the affected signatory state, and shall suspend such regulation when and so long as the signatory party or parties, or political subdivision possessing jurisdiction have in force applicable laws which the commission finds give adequate protection for the purpose of this section.

"(d) In order to conserve, protect, and utilize the Susquehanna River and its tributaries in accordance with the best interests of the people of the basin and the signatory parties, it shall be the policy of the commission to encourage and coordinate the efforts of the signatory parties to control modification of the river and its tributaries by encroachment.

"6.3—FLOOD LANDS ACQUISITION. The commission shall have power to acquire the fee or any lesser interest in lands and improvements thereon within the area of a flood plain for the purpose of regulating the use or types of construction of such property to minimize the flood hazard, convert the property to uses or types of construction appropriate to flood plain conditions, or prevent constrictions or obstructions that reduce the ability of the river channel and flood plain to carry flood water.

"6.4—EXISTING STRUCTURES. No rule or regulation issued by the commission pursuant to this compact shall be construed to require the demolition, removal, or alteration of any structure in place or under construction prior to the issuance thereof, without the payment of just compensation therefor. However, new construction or any addition to or alteration in any existing structure made or commenced subsequent to the issuance of such rule or regulation, or amendment, shall conform thereto.

"6.5—POLICE POWERS. The regulation of use of flood plain lands is within the police powers of the signatory states for the protection of public health and the safety of the people and their property and shall not be deemed a taking of land or lands for which compensation shall be paid to the owners thereof.

"6.6—Cooperation. Each of the signatory parties agrees to control flood plain use along and encroachment upon the Susquehanna River and its tributaries and to cooperate faithfully in these respects.

"6.7—Other Authority. Nothing in this article shall be construed to prevent or in any way to limit the power of any signatory party, or any agency or subdivision thereof, to issue or adopt and enforce any requirement or requirements with respect to flood plain use or construction thereon more stringent than the rules, regulations, or encroachment lines in force pursuant to this article. The commission may appear in any court of competent jurisdiction to bring actions or proceedings in law or equity to enforce the provisions of this article.

"6.8—Debris. The signatory states agree that dumping or littering upon or in the waters of the Susquehanna River or its tributaries or upon the frozen surfaces thereof of any rubbish, trash, litter, debris, abandoned properties, waste material, or offensive matter, is prohibited and that the law enforcement officials of each state shall enforce this prohibition.

"Article 7

"watershed management

"Section 7.1—Watersheds Generally. The commission shall promote sound practices of watershed management in the basin, including projects and facilities to retard runoff and waterflow and prevent soil erosion.

"7.2—Soil Conservation and Land and Forest Management. The commission, subject to the limitations in Section 7.4(b) may acquire, sponsor, or operate facilities and projects to encourage soil conservation, prevent and control erosion, and promote land reclamation and sound land and forest management.

"7.3—Fish and Wildlife. The commission, subject to the limitations in Section 7.4(b) may acquire, sponsor, or operate projects and facilities for the maintenance and improvement of fish and wildlife habitat related to the water resources of the basin.

"7.4—Cooperative Planning and Operation.

"(a) The commission shall cooperate with the appropriate agencies of the signatory parties and with other public and private agencies in the planning and effectuation of a coordinated program of facilities and projects authorized by this article.

"(b) The commission shall not acquire or operate any such project or facility unless it has first found and determined that no other suitable unit or agency of government is in a position to acquire or operate the same upon reasonable conditions, or such unit or agency fails to do so.

"Article 8

"recreation

"Section 8.1—Development. The commission may provide for the development of water related public sports and recreational facilities. The commission on its own account or in cooperation with a signatory

287

party, political subdivision or any agency thereof, may provide for the construction, maintenance, and administration of such facilities, subject to the provisions of Section 8.2 hereof.

"8.2—COOPERATIVE PLANNING AND OPERATION.

"(a) The commission shall cooperate with the appropriate agencies of the signatory parties and with other public and private agencies in the planning and effectuation of a coordinated program of facilities and projects authorized by this article.

"(b) The commission shall not operate any such project or facility unless it has first found and determined that no other suitable unit or agency of government is available to operate the same upon reasonable conditions.

"8.3—OPERATION AND MAINTENANCE. The commission, within limits prescribed by this article, shall:

"1. Encourage activities of other public agencies having water related recreational interests and assist in the coordination thereof;

"2. Recommend standards for the development and administration of water related recreational facilities;

"3. Provide for the administration, operation, and maintenance of recreation facilities owned or controlled by the commission and for the letting and supervision of private concessions in accordance with this article.

"8.4—CONCESSIONS. The commission, after public hearing upon due notice given shall provide by regulation a procedure for the award of contracts for private concessions in connection with its recreational facilities, including any renewal or extension thereof, under terms and conditions determined by the commission.

"ARTICLE 9

"OTHER PUBLIC VALUES

"SECTION 9.1—INHERENT VALUES. The signatory parties agree that it is a purpose of this compact in effectuating the conservation and management of water resources to preserve and promote the economic and other values inherent in the historic and the scenic and other natural amenities of the Susquehanna River Basin for the enjoyment and enrichment of future generations, for the promotion and protection of tourist attractions in the basin, and for the maintenance of the economic health of allied enterprises and occupations so as to effect orderly, balanced, and considered development in the basin.

"9.2—PROJECT COMPATIBILITY. To this end, the signatory parties agree that in the consideration, authorization, construction, maintenance, and operation of all water resources projects in the Susquehanna basin, their agencies and subdivisions, and the Susquehanna River Basin Commission will consider the compatibility of such projects with these other public values.

"9.3—REGULATION STANDARDS. The commission may recommend to governmental units with jurisdiction within areas considered for scenic or historic designation minimum standards of regulation of land and water use and such other protective measures as the commission may deem desirable.

"9.4—LOCAL AREA PROTECTION. The commission may draft and recommend for adoption ordinances and regulations which would assist, promote, develop, and protect those areas and the character of their communities. Local governments may consider parts of their area which have been designated scenic or historic areas under the provisions of this article separately from the municipality as a whole, and pursuant to the laws of the state governing the adoption of those regulations generally may enact regulations limited to the designated area. In making recommendations to a local government which is partly in and partly out of such a scenic or historic area the commission may make recommendations for the entire municipality.

"ARTICLE 10

"HYDROELECTRIC POWER

"SECTION 10.1—DEVELOPMENT. The waters of the Susquehanna River and its tributaries may be impounded and used by or under authority of the commission for the generation of hydroelectric power and hydroelectric energy in accordance with the comprehensive plan.

"10.2—POWER GENERATION. The commission may develop and operate, or authorize to be developed and operated, dams and related facilities and appurtenances for the purpose of generating hydroelectric power and hydroelectric energy.

"10.3—TRANSMISSION. The commission may provide facilities for the transmission of hydroelectric power and hydroelectric energy produced by it where such facilities are not otherwise available upon reasonable terms, for the purpose of wholesale marketing of power and nothing herein shall be construed to authorize the commission to engage in the business of direct sale to consumers.

"10.4—DEVELOPMENT CONTRACTS. The commission, after public hearing upon due notice given, may enter into contracts on reasonable terms, consideration, and duration under which public utilities or public agencies may develop hydroelectric power and hydroelectric energy through the use of dams, related facilities, and appurtenances.

"10.5—RATES AND CHARGES. Rates and charges fixed by the commission for power which is produced by its facilities shall be reasonable, nondiscriminatory, and just.

"ARTICLE 11

"REGULATION OF WITHDRAWAL AND DIVERSIONS; PROTECTED AREAS AND EMERGENCIES

"SECTION 11.1—POWER OF REGULATION. The commission may regulate and control withdrawals and diversions from surface waters and ground waters of the basin, as provided by this article. The commission may enter into agreements with the signatory parties relating to the exercise of such power or regulation or control and may delegate to any of them such powers of the commission as it may deem necessary or desirable.

"11.2—DETERMINATION OF PROTECTED AREA. The commission, from time to time after public hearing upon due notice given, may determine and delineate such areas within the basin wherein the demands upon supply made by water users have developed or threaten to develop to such a degree as to create a water shortage or impair or conflict with the requirements or effectuation of the comprehensive plan, and any such area may be designated as a protected area, with the consent of the member or members from the affected state or states. The commission, whenever it determines that such shortage no longer exists, shall terminate the protected status of such area and shall give public notice of such determination.

289

"11.3—DIVERSION AND WITHDRAWAL PERMITS. In any protected areas so determined and delineated, no person shall divert or withdraw water for domestic, municipal, agricultural, or industrial uses in excess of such quantities as the commission may prescribe by general regulations, except (1) pursuant to a permit granted under this article, or (2) pursuant to a permit or approval heretofore granted under the laws of any of the signatory states.

"11.4—EMERGENCY.

"(a) In the event of a drought which may cause an actual and immediate shortage of available water supply within the basin, or within any part thereof, the commission after public hearing upon due notice given, may determine and delineate the area of the shortage and by unanimous vote declare a drought emergency therein. For the the duration of the drought emergency as determined by the commission, it thereupon may direct increases or decreases in any allocations, diversions, or releases previously granted or required, for a limited time to meet the emergency condition.

"(b) In the event of a disaster or catastrophe other than drought, natural or manmade, which causes or may cause an actual and immediate shortage of available and usable water, the commission by unanimous consent may impose direct controls on the use of water and shall take such action as is necessary to coordinate the effort of federal, state, and local agencies and other persons and entities affected.

"11.5—STANDARDS. Permits shall be granted, modified, or denied, as the case may be, to avoid such depletion of the natural stream flows and ground waters in the protected area or in any emergency area as will adversely affect the comprehensive plan or the just and equitable interests and rights of other lawful users of the same source, giving due regard to the need to balance and reconcile alternative and conflicting uses in the event of an actual or threatened shortage of water of the quality required.

"11.6—JUDICIAL REVIEW. The determinations and delineations of the commission pursuant to Section 11.2 and the granting, modification or denial of permits pursuant to Sections 11.3, 11.4, and 11.5 shall be subject to judicial review in any court of competent jurisdiction.

"11.7—MAINTENANCE OF RECORDS. Each signatory party shall provide for the maintenance and preservation of such records of authorized diversions and withdrawals and the annual volume thereof as the commission shall prescribe. Such records and supplementary reports shall be furnished to the commission at its request.

"11.8—EXISTING STATE SYSTEMS. Whenever the commission finds it necessary or desirable to exercise the powers conferred with respect to emergencies by this article, any diversion or withdrawal permits authorized or issued under the laws of any of the signatory states shall be superseded to the extent of any conflict with the control and regulation exercised by the commission.

"ARTICLE 12

"INTERGOVERNMENTAL RELATIONS

"SECTION 12.1—FEDERAL AGENCIES AND PROJECTS. For the purposes of avoiding conflicts of jurisdiction and of giving full effect to the commission as a regional agency of the signatory parties, the following rules shall govern Federal projects affecting the water resources of the

290

basin, subject in each case to the provisions of Section 1.4 of this compact:

"1. The planning of all projects related to powers delegated to the commission by this compact shall be undertaken in consultation with the commission.

"2. No expenditure or commitment shall be made for or on account of the construction, acquisition, or operation of any project or facility nor shall it be deemed authorized, unless it shall have first been included by the commission in the comprehensive plan.

"3. Each Federal agency otherwise authorized by law to plan, design, construct, operate or maintain any project or facility in or for the basin shall continue to have, exercise, and discharge such authority except as specifically provided by this section.

"12.2—STATE AND LOCAL AGENCIES AND PROJECTS. For the purposes of avoiding conflicts of jurisdiction and of giving full effect to the commission as a regional agency of the signatory parties, the following rules shall govern projects of the signatory states, their political subdivisions and public corporations affecting water resources of the basin:

"1. The planning of all projects related to powers delegated to the commission by this compact shall be undertaken in consultation with the commission;

"2. No expenditure or commitment shall be made for or on account of the construction, acquisition, or operation of any project or facility unless it first has been included by the commission in the comprehensive plan;

"3. Each state and local agency otherwise authorized by law to plan, design, construct, operate, or maintain any project or facility in or for the basin shall continue to have, exercise and discharge such authority, except as specifically provided by this section.

"12.3—RESERVED TAXING POWERS OF STATES. Each of the signatory parties reserves the right to levy, assess, and collect fees, charges, and taxes on or measured by the withdrawal or diversion of waters of the basin for use within the jurisdiction of the respective signatory parties.

"12.4—PROJECT COSTS AND EVALUATION STANDARDS. The commission shall establish uniform standards and procedures for the evaluation, determination of benefits, and cost allocations of projects affecting the basin, and for the determination of project priorities, pursuant to the requirements of the comprehensive plan and its water resources program. The commission shall develop equitable cost sharing and reimbursement formulas for the signatory parties including:

"1. Uniform and consistent procedures for the allocation of project costs among purposes included in multiple-purpose programs;

"2. Contracts and arrangements for sharing financial responsibility among and with signatory parties, public bodies, groups, and private enterprise, and for the supervision of their performance;

"3. Establishment and supervision of a system of accounts for reimbursement purposes and directing the payments and charges to be made from such accounts;

"4. Determining the basis and apportioning amounts (i) of reimbursable revenues to be paid signatory parties or their political subdivisions, and (ii) of payments in lieu of taxes to any of them.

"12.5—COOPERATIVE SERVICES. The commission shall furnish technical services, advice, and consultation to authorized agencies of the signatory parties with respect to the water resources of the basin, and each of the signatory parties pledges itself to provide technical and administrative service to the commission upon request, within the

291

limits of available appropriations, and to cooperate generally with the commission for the purposes of this compact, and the cost of such service may be reimbursable whenever the parties deem appropriate.

"ARTICLE 13

"CAPITAL FINANCING

"SECTION 13.1—BORROWING POWER. The commission may borrow money for any of the purposes of this compact and may issue its negotiable bonds and other evidences of indebtedness in respect thereto.

"All such bonds and evidences of indebtedness shall be payable solely out of the properties and revenues of the commission without recourse to taxation. The bonds and other obligations of the commission, except as may be otherwise provided in the indenture under which they were issued, shall be direct and general obligations of the commission, and the full faith and credit of the commission are hereby pledged for the prompt payment of the debt service thereon and for the fulfillment of all other undertakings of the commission assumed by it to or for the benefit of the holders thereof.

"13.2—FUNDS AND EXPENSES. The purposes of this compact shall include without limitation thereto all costs of any project or facility or any part thereof, including interest during a period of construction and a reasonable time thereafter and any incidental expenses (legal, engineering, fiscal, financial consultant, and other expenses) connected with issuing and disposing of the bonds; all amounts required for the creation of an operating fund, construction fund, reserve fund, sinking fund, or other special fund; all other expenses connected with the planning, design, acquisition, construction, completion, improvement, or reconstruction of any facility or any part thereof; and reimbursement of advances by the commission or by others for such purposes and for working capital.

"13.3—CREDIT EXCLUDED; OFFICERS, STATE AND MUNICIPAL. The commission shall have no power to pledge the credit of any signatory party or of any county or municipality, or to impose any obligation for payment of the bonds upon any signatory party or any county or municipality. Neither the commissioners nor any person executing the bonds shall be liable personally on the bonds of the commission or be subject to any personal liability or accountability by reason of the issuance thereof.

"13.4—FUNDING AND REFUNDING. Whenever the commission deems it expedient, it may fund and refund its bonds and other obligations, whether or not such bonds and obligations have matured. It may provide for the issuance, sale, or exchange of refunding bonds for the purpose of redeeming or retiring any bonds (including payment of any premium, duplicate interest, or cash adjustment required in connection therewith) issued by the commission or issued by any other issuing body, the proceeds of the sale of which have been applied to any facility acquired by the commission or which are payable out of the revenues of any facility acquired by the commission. Bonds may be issued partly to refund bonds and other obligations then outstanding, and partly for any other purpose of the commission. All provisions of this compact applicable to the issuance of bonds are applicable to refunding bonds and to the issuance, sale, or exchange thereof.

"13.5—BONDS: AUTHORIZATION GENERALLY. Bonds and other indebtedness of the commission shall be authorized by resolution of the commission. The validity of the authorization and issuance of any bonds by the commission shall not be dependent upon or affected in any way

292

by: (1) the disposition of bond proceeds by the commission or by contract, commitment or action taken with respect to such proceeds; or (2) the failure to complete any part of the project for which bonds are authorized to be issued. The commission may issue bonds in one or more series and may provide for one or more consolidated bond issues, in such principal amounts and with such terms and provisions as the commission may deem necessary. The bonds may be secured by a pledge of all or any part of the property, revenues, and franchises under its control. Bonds may be issued by the commission in such amount, with such maturities and in such denominations and form or forms, whether coupon or registered, as to both principal and interest, as may be determined by the commission. The commission may provide for redemption of bonds prior to maturity on such notice and at such time or times and with such redemption provisions, including premiums, as the commission may determine.

"13.6—BONDS, RESOLUTIONS AND INDENTURES GENERALLY. The commission may determine and enter into indentures providing for the principal amount, date or dates, maturities, interest rate, denominations, form, registration, transfer, interchange, and other provisions of the bonds and coupons and the terms and conditions upon which the same shall be executed, issued, secured, sold, paid, redeemed, funded, and refunded. The resolution of the commission, authorizing any bond or any indenture so authorized under which the bonds are issued may include all such covenants and other provisions other than any restriction on the regulatory powers vested in the commission by this compact as the commission may deem necessary or desirable for the issue, payment, security, protection, or marketing of the bonds, including without limitation covenants and other provisions as to the rates or amounts of fees, rents, and other charges to be charged or made for use of the facilities; the use, pledge, custody, securing, application, and disposition of such revenues, of the proceeds of the bonds, and of any other moneys of the commission; the operation, maintenance, repair, and reconstruction of the facilities and the amounts which may be expended therefor; the sale, lease, or other disposition of the facilities; the insuring of the facilities and of the revenues derived therefrom; the construction or other acquisition of other facilities, the issuance of additional bonds or other indebtedness; the rights of the bondholders and of any trustee for the bondholders upon default by the commission or otherwise; and the modification of the provisions of the indenture and of the bonds. Reference on the face of the bonds to such resolution or indenture by its date of adoption or the apparent date on the face thereof is sufficient to incorporate all of the provisions thereof and of this compact into the body of the bonds and their appurtenant coupons. Each taker and subsequent holder of the bonds or coupons, whether the coupons are attached to or detached from the bonds, has recourse to all of the provisions of the indenture and of this compact and is bound thereby.

"13.7—MAXIMUM MATURITY. No bond or its terms shall mature in more than fifty years from its own date, or on any date subsequent to the duration of this compact, and in the event any authorized issue is divided into two or more series or divisions, the maximum maturity date herein authorized shall be calculated from the date on the face of each bond separately, irrespective of the fact that different dates may be prescribed for the bonds of each separate series or division of any authorized issue.

"13.8—TAX EXEMPTION. All bonds issued by the commission under the provisions of this compact and the interest thereon shall at all times

293

be free and exempt from all taxation by or under authority of any of the signatory parties, except for transfer, inheritance and estate taxes.

"13.9—INTEREST. Bonds shall bear interest at a rate of not to exceed six percent per annum, payable annually or semi-annually.

"13.10—PLACE OF PAYMENT. The commission may provide for the payment of the principal and interest of bonds at any place or places within or without the signatory states, and in any specified lawful coin or currency of the United States of America.

"13.11—EXECUTION. The commission may provide for the execution and authentication of bonds by the manual, lithographed, or printed facsimile signature of officers of the commission, and by additional authentication by a trustee or fiscal agent appointed by the commission. If any of the officers whose signatures or countersignatures appear upon the bonds or coupons ceases to be an officer before the delivery of the bonds or coupons, his signature or countersignature is nevertheless valid and of the same force and effect as if the officer had remained in office until the delivery of the bonds and coupons.

"13.12—HOLDING OWN BONDS. The commission shall have power out of any funds available therefor to purchase its bonds and may hold, cancel, or resell such bonds.

"13.13—SALE. The commission may fix terms and conditions for the sale or other disposition of any authorized issue of bonds. The commission may sell at less than their par or face value, but no issue of bonds may be sold at an aggregate price below the par or face value thereof if such sale would result in a net interest cost to the commission calculated upon the entire issue so sold of more than six percent per annum payable semi-annually, according to standard tables of bond values. All bonds issued and sold for cash pursuant to this compact shall be sold on sealed proposals to the highest bidder. Prior to such sale, the commission shall advertise for bids by publication of a notice of sale not less than ten days prior to the date of sale, at least once in a newspaper of general circulation printed and published in New York City carrying municipal bonds notices and devoted primarily to financial news. The commission may reject any and all bids submitted and may thereafter sell the bonds so advertised for sale at private sale to any financially responsible bidder under such terms and conditions as it deems most advantageous to the public interest, but the bond shall not be sold at a net interest cost calculated upon the entire issue so advertised, greater than the lowest bid which was rejected. In the event the commission desires to issue its bonds in exchange for an existing facility or portion thereof, or in exchange for bonds secured by the revenues of an existing facility, it may exchange such bonds for the existing facility or portion thereof or for the bonds so secured, plus an additional amount of cash, without advertising such bonds for sale.

"13.14—NEGOTIABILITY. All bonds issued under the provisions of this compact are negotiable instruments, except when registered in the name of a registered owner.

"13.15—LEGAL INVESTMENTS. Bonds of the commission shall be legal investments for savings banks, fiduciaries and public funds in each of the signatory states.

"13.16—VALIDATION PROCEEDINGS. Prior to the issuance of any bonds, the commission may institute a special proceeding to determine the legality of proceedings to issue the bonds and their validity under the laws of any of the signatory parties. Such proceedings shall be instituted and prosecuted in rem, and the judgment rendered therein shall be conclusive against all persons whomsoever and against each of the signatory parties.

"13.17—RECORDING. No indenture need be recorded or filed in any public office, other than the office of the commission. The pledge of revenues provided in any indenture shall take effect forthwith as provided therein and irrespective of the date of receipts of such revenues by the commission or the indenture trustee. Such pledge shall be effective as provided in the indenture without physical delivery of the revenues to the commission or the indenture trustee.

"13.18—PLEDGED REVENUES. Bond redemption and interest payments, to the extent provided in the resolution or indenture, shall constitute a first, direct and exclusive charge and lien on all such rates, rents, tolls, fees, and charges and other revenues and interest thereon received from the use and operation of the facility, and on any sinking or other funds created therefrom. All such rates, rents, tolls, fees, charges and other revenues, together with interest thereon, shall constitute a trust fund for the security and payment of such bonds, and except as and to the extent provided in the indenture with respect to the payment therefrom of expenses for other purposes including administration, operation, maintenance, improvements, or extensions of the facilities or other purposes shall not be used or pledged for any other purpose so long as such bonds, or any of them, are outstanding, and unpaid.

"13.19—REMEDIES. The holder of any bond may for the equal benefit and protection of all holders of bonds similarly situated; (1) by mandamus or other appropriate proceedings require and compel the performance of any of the duties imposed upon the commission or assumed by it, its officers, agents, or employees under the provisions of any indenture, in connection with the acquisition, construction, operation, maintenance, repair, reconstruction, or insurance of the facilities, or in connection with the collection, deposit, investment, application, and disbursement of the rates, rents, tolls, fees, charges, and other revenues derived from the operation and use of the facilities, or in connection with the deposit, investment, and disbursement of the proceeds received from the sale of bonds; or (2) by action or suit in a court of competent jurisdiction of any signatory party require the commission to account as if it were the trustee of an express trust, or enjoin any acts or things which may be unlawful or in violation of the rights of the holders of the bonds. The enumeration of such rights and remedies, however, does not exclude the exercise or prosecution of any other rights or remedies available to the holders of bonds.

"13.20—CAPITAL FINANCING BY SIGNATORY PARTIES: GUARANTEES.

"(a) The signatory parties shall provide such capital funds required for projects of the commission as may be authorized by their respective statutes in accordance with a cost sharing plan prepared pursuant to Article 12 of this compact; but nothing in this section shall be deemed to impose any mandatory obligation on any of the signatory parties other than such obligations as may be assumed by a signatory party in connection with a specific project or facility.

"(b) Bonds of the commission, notwithstanding any other provision of this compact, may be executed and delivered to any duly authorized agency of any of the signatory parties without public offering and may be sold and resold with or without the guaranty of such signatory party, subject to and in accordance with the constitutions of the respective signatory parties.

"(c) The commission may receive and accept, and the signatory parties may make, loans, grants, appropriations, advances, and payments of reimbursable or nonreimbursable funds or property in any form for the capital or operating purposes of the commission.

295

"ARTICLE 14

"PLAN, PROGRAM AND BUDGETS

"SECTION 14.1—COMPREHENSIVE PLAN. The commission shall develop and adopt, and may from time to time review and revise, a comprehensive plan for the immediate and long range development and use of the water resources of the basin. The plan shall include all public and private projects and facilities which are required, in the judgment of the commission, for the optimum planning, development, conservation, utilization, management, and control of the water resources of the basin to meet present and future needs. The commission may adopt a comprehensive plan or any revision thereof in such part or parts as it may deem appropriate, provided that before the adoption of the plan or any part or revision thereof the commission shall consult with water users and interested public bodies and public utilities and shall consider and give due regard to the findings and recommendations of the various agencies of the signatory parties, their political subdivisions, and interested groups. The commission shall conduct public hearings upon due notice given with respect to the comprehensive plan prior to the adoption of the plan or any part of the revision thereof, except that public and private projects and facilities which, in the judgment of the commission, are not required for the optimum planning, development, conservation, utilization, management, and control of the water resources of the basin and which, in the judgment of the commission, will not significantly affect the water resources of the basin, may be added directly to the comprehensive plan at any time at the discretion of the commission without public hearing thereon. The comprehensive plan shall take into consideration the effect of the plan or any part thereof upon the receiving waters of Chesapeake Bay.

"14.2—WATER RESOURCES PROGRAM. The commission shall annually adopt a water resources program, based upon the comprehensive plan, consisting of the projects and facilities which the commission proposes to be undertaken by the commission and by other authorized governmental and private agencies, organizations, and persons during the ensuing six years or such other reasonably foreseeable period as the commission may determine. The water resources program shall include a systematic presentation of:

"1. The quantity and quality of water resources needs for such period;

"2. The existing and proposed projects and facilities required to satisfy such needs, including all public and private projects to be anticipated; and

"3. A separate statement of the projects proposed to be undertaken by the commission during such period.

"14.3—ANNUAL CURRENT EXPENSE AND CAPITAL BUDGETS.

"(a) The commission shall annually adopt a capital budget including all capital projects it proposes to undertake or continue during the budget period containing a statement of the estimated cost of each project and the method of financing thereof.

"(b) The commission shall annually adopt a current expense budget for each fiscal year. Such budget shall include the commission's estimated expenses for administration, operation, maintenance, and repairs, including a separate statement thereof for each project, together with its cost allocation. The total of such expenses shall be balanced by the commission's estimated revenues from all sources, including the cost allocations undertaken by any of the signatory par-

296

ties in connection with any project. Following the adoption of the annual current expense budget by the commission, the executive director of the commission shall:

"1. Certify to the respective signatory parties the amounts due in accordance with existing cost sharing established for each project; and

"2. Transmit certified copies of such budget to the principal budget officer of the respective signatory parties at such time and in such manner as may be required under their respective budgetary procedures. The amount required to balance the current expense budget in addition to the aggregate amount of item 1 above and all other revenues available to the commission shall be apportioned equitably among the signatory parties by unanimous vote of the commission, and the amount of such apportionment to each signatory party shall be certified together with the budget.

"(c) The respective signatory parties covenant and agree to include the amounts so apportioned for the support of the current expense budget in their respective budgets next to be adopted, subject to such review and approval as may be required by their respective budgetary processes. Such amounts shall be due and payable to the commission in quarterly installments during its fiscal year, provided that the commission may draw upon its working capital to finance its current expense budget pending remittance by the signatory parties.

"ARTICLE 15

"GENERAL PROVISIONS

"SECTION 15.1—AUXILIARY POWERS OF COMMISSION; FUNCTIONS OF COMMISSIONERS.

"(a) The commission, for the purposes of this compact, may:

"1. Adopt and use a corporate seal, enter into contracts, and sue and be sued in any court of competent jurisdiction;

"2. Receive and accept such payments, appropriations, grants, gifts, loans, advances, and other funds, properties, and services as may be transferred or made available to it by any signatory party or by any other public or private corporation or individual, and enter into agreements to make reimbursement for all or part thereof;

"3. Provide for, acquire, and adopt detailed engineering, administrative, financial, and operating plans and specifications to effectuate, maintain, or develop any facility or project;

"4. Control and regulate the use of facilities owned or operated by the commission;

"5. Acquire, own, operate, maintain, control, sell and convey real and personal property and any interest therein by contract, purchase, lease, license, mortgage, or otherwise as it may deem necessary for any project or facility, including any and all appurtenances thereto necessary, useful, or convenient for such ownership, operation, control, maintenance, or conveyance;

"6. Have and exercise all corporate powers essential to the declared objects and purposes of the commission.

"(b) The commissioners, subject to the provisions of this compact, shall:

"1. Serve as the governing body of the commission, and exercise and discharge its powers and duties, except as otherwise provided by or pursuant to this compact;

"2. Determine the character of and the necessity for its obligations and expenditures and the manner in which they shall be incurred,

297

allowed, and paid subject to any provisions of law specifically applicable to agencies or instrumentalities created by this compact;

"3. Provide for the internal organization and administration of the commission;

"4. Appoint the principal officers of the commission and delegate to and allocate among them administrative functions, powers and duties;

"5. Create and abolish offices, employments, and positions as it deems necessary for the purposes of the commission, and subject to the provisions of this article, fix and provide for the qualifications, appointments, removal, term, tenure, compensation, pension, and retirement rights of its officers and employees;

"6. Let and execute contracts to carry out the powers of the commission.

"15.2—REGULATIONS; ENFORCEMENT. The commission may:

"1. Make and enforce rules and regulations for the effectuation, application, and enforcement of this compact; and it may adopt and enforce practices and schedules for or in connection with the use, maintenance, and administration of projects and facilities it may own or operate and any product or service rendered thereby; provided that any rule or regulation, other than one which deals solely with the internal management of the commission, shall not be effective unless and until filed in accordance with the law of the respective signatory parties applicable to administrative rules and regulations generally; and

"2. Designate any officer, agent, or employee of the commission to be an investigator or watchman and such person shall be vested with the powers of a peace officer of the state in which he is duly assigned to perform his duties.

"15.3—TAX EXEMPTIONS. The commission, its property, functions, and activities shall be exempt from taxation by or under the authority of any of the signatory parties or any political subdivision thereof; provided that in lieu of property taxes the commission, as to its specific projects, shall make payments to local taxing districts in annual amounts which shall equal the taxes lawfully assessed upon property for the tax year next prior to its acquisition by the commission for a period of ten years. The nature and amount of such payment shall be reviewed by the commission at the end of ten years, and from time to time thereafter, upon reasonable notice and opportunity to be heard to the affected taxing district, and the payments may be thereupon terminated or continued in such reasonable amount as may be necessary or desirable to take into account hardships incurred and benefits received by the taxing jurisdiction which are attributable to the project.

"15.4—MEETINGS; PUBLIC HEARING; RECORDS, MINUTES.

"(a) All meetings of the commission shall be open to the public.

"(b) The commission shall conduct at least one public hearing in each state prior to the adoption of the initial comprehensive plan. In all other cases wherein this compact requires a public hearing, such hearing shall be held upon not less than twenty days' public notice given by posting at the offices of the commission, and published at least once in a newspaper or newspapers of general circulation in the area or areas affected. The commission shall also provide forthwith for distribution of such notice to the press and by the mailing of a copy thereof to any person who shall request such notices.

"(c) The minutes of the commission shall be a public record open to inspection at its offices during regular business hours.

298

"15.5—OFFICERS GENERALLY.

"(a) The officers of the commission shall consist of an executive director and such additional officers, deputies, and assistants as the commission may determine. The executive director shall be appointed and may be removed by the affirmative vote of a majority of the full membership of the commission. All other officers and employees shall be appointed or dismissed by the executive director under such rules of procedure as the commission may establish.

"(b) In the appointment and promotion of officers and employees for the commission, no political, racial, religious, or residence test or qualification shall be permitted or given consideration, but all such appointments and promotions shall be solely on the basis of merit and fitness. Any officer or employee of the commission who is found by the commission to be guilty of a violation of this section shall be immediately dismissed.

"15.6—OATH OF OFFICE. An oath of office in such form as the commission shall prescribe shall be taken, subscribed, and filed with the commission by the executive director and by each officer appointed by him not later than fifteen days after the appointment.

"15.7—BOND. Each officer shall give such bond and in such form and amount as the commission may require, for which the commission shall pay the premium.

"15.8—PROHIBITED ACTIVITIES.

"(a) No commissioner, officer or employee shall:

"1. Be financially interested, either directly or indirectly, in any contract, sale, purchase, lease, or transfer of real or personal property to which the commission is a party;

"2. Solicit or accept money or any other thing of value in addition to the compensation or expense paid him by the commission for services performed within the scope of his official duties;

"3. Offer money or any thing of value for or in consideration of obtaining an appointment, promotion, or privilege in his employment with the commission.

"(b) Any officer or employee who willfully violates any of the provisions of this section shall forfeit his office or employment.

"(c) Any contract or agreement knowingly made in contravention of this section is void.

"(d) Officers and employees of the commission shall be subject, in addition to the provisions of this section, to such criminal and civil sanctions for misconduct in office as may be imposed by Federal law and the law of the signatory state in which such misconduct occurs.

"15.9—PURCHASING. Contracts for the construction, reconstruction or improvement of any facility when the expenditure required exceeds ten thousand dollars, and contracts for the purchase of services, supplies, equipment, and materials when the expenditure required exceeds five thousand dollars shall be advertised and let upon sealed bids to the lowest responsible bidder. Notice requesting such bids shall be published in a manner reasonably likely to attract prospective bidders, which publication shall be made at least thirty days before bids are received and in at least two newspapers of general circulation in the basin. The commission may reject any and all bids and readvertise in its discretion. If after rejecting bids the commission determines and resolves that in its opinion the supplies, equipment, and materials may be purchased at a lower price in the open market, the commission may give each responsible bidder an opportunity to negotiate a price and may proceed to purchase the supplies, equipment, and materials in the open market at a negotiated price which is lower than the lowest rejected bid of a responsible bidder, without further observance of the provisions requiring bids or notice. The commission shall adopt rules and regulations to provide for purchasing from the lowest responsible bidder when sealed bids, notice, and publication are not required by this section. The commission may suspend and waive the provisions of this section requiring competitive bids whenever:

"1. The purchase is to be made from or the contract to be made with the Federal or any state government or agency or political subdivision thereof or pursuant to any open and bulk purchase contract of any of them;

"2. The public exigency requires the immediate delivery of the articles or performance of the service;

"3. Only one source of supply is available;

"4. The equipment to be purchased is of a technical nature and the procurement thereof without advertising is necessary in order to assure standardization of equipment and interchangeability of parts in the public interest; or

"5. Services are to be provided of a specialized or professional nature.

"15.10—INSURANCE. The commission may self-insure or purchase insurance and pay the premium therefor against loss or damage to any of its properties; against liability for injury to persons or property; and against loss of revenue from any cause whatsoever. Such insurance coverage shall be in such form and amount as the commission may determine, subject to the requirements of any agreement arising out of the issuance of bonds by the commission.

"15.11—ANNUAL INDEPENDENT AUDIT.

"(a) As soon as practical after the closing of the fiscal year an audit shall be made of the financial accounts of the commission. The audit shall be made by qualified certified public accountants selected by the commission, who have no personal interest direct or indirect in the financial affairs of the commission or any of its officers or employees. The report of audit shall be prepared in accordance with accepted accounting practices and shall be filed with the chairman and such other officers as the commission may direct. Copies of the report shall be distributed to each commissioner and shall be made available for public distribution.

"(b) Each signatory party by its duly authorized officers shall be entitled to examine and audit at any time all of the books, documents, records, files, and accounts and all other papers, things, or property of the commission. The representatives of the signatory parties shall have access to all books, documents, records, accounts, reports, files, and all other papers, things, or property belonging to or in use by the commission and necessary to facilitate the audit and they shall be afforded full facilities for verifying transactions with the balances or securities held by depositaries, fiscal agents, and custodians.

"(c) The financial transactions of the commission shall be subject to audit by the General Accounting Office in accordance with the principles and procedures applicable to commercial corporate transactions and under such rules and regulations as may be prescribed by the Comptroller General of the United States. The audit shall be conducted at the place or places where the accounts of the commission are kept.

"(d) Any officer or employee who shall refuse to give all required assistance and information to the accountants selected by the commission or to the authorized officers of any signatory party or who shall

300

refuse to submit to them for examination such books, documents, records, files, accounts, papers, things, or property as may be requested shall forfeit his office.

"15.12—REPORTS. The commission shall make and publish an annual report to the legislative bodies of the signatory parties and to the public reporting on its programs, operations, and finances. It may also prepare, publish, and distribute such other public reports and informational material as it may deem necessary or desirable.

"15.13—GRANTS, LOANS, OR PAYMENTS BY STATES OR POLITICAL SUBDIVISIONS.
"(a) Any or all of the signatory parties or any political subdivisions thereof may:
"1. Appropriate to the commission such funds as may be necessary to pay preliminary expenses such as the expenses incurred in the making of borings, and other studies of subsurface conditions, in the preparation of contracts for the sale of water and in the preparation of detailed plans and estimates required for the financing of a project;
"2. Advance to the commission, either as grants or loans, such funds as may be necessary or convenient to finance the operation and management of or construction by the commission of any facility or project;
"3. Make payments to the commission for benefits received or to be received from the operation of any of the projects or facilities of the commission.
"(b) Any funds which may be loaned to the commission either by a signatory party or a political subdivision thereof shall be repaid by the commission through the issuance of bonds or out of other income of the commission, such repayment to be made within such period and upon such terms as may be agreed upon between the commission and the signatory party or political subdivision making the loan.

"15.14—CONDEMNATION PROCEEDINGS.
"(a) The commission shall have the power to acquire by condemnation the fee or any lesser interest in lands, lands lying under water, development rights in land, riparian rights, water rights, waters and other real or personal property within the basin for any project or facility authorized pursuant to this compact. This grant of power of eminent domain includes but is not limited to the power to condemn for the purposes of this compact any property already devoted to a public use, by whomsoever owned or held, other than property of a signatory party. Any condemnation of any property or franchises owned or used by a municipal or privately owned public utility, unless the affected public utility facility is to be relocated or replaced, shall be subject to the authority of such state board, commission, or other body as may have regulatory jurisdiction over such public utility.
"(b) The power of condemnation referred to in subsection (a) shall be exercised in accordance with the provisions of the state condemnation law in force in the signatory state in which the property is located. If there is no applicable state condemnation law, the power of condemnation shall be exercised in accordance with the provisions of Federal condemnation law.
"(c) Any award or compensation for the taking of property pursuant to this article shall be paid by the commission, and none of the signatory parties nor any other agency, instrumentality or political subdivision thereof shall be liable for such award or compensation.

301

84 STAT. 1536

"15.15—Conveyance of Lands and Relocation of Public Facilities.

"(a) The respective officers, agencies, departments, commissions, or bodies having jurisdiction and control over real and personal property owned by the signatory parties are authorized and empowered to transfer and convey in accordance with the laws of the respective parties to the commission any such property as may be necessary or convenient to the effectuation of the authorized purposes of the commission.

"(b) Each political subdivision of each of the signatory parties, notwithstanding any contrary provisions of law, is authorized and empowered to grant and convey to the commission, upon the commission's request, any real property or any interest therein owned by such political subdivision including lands lying under water and lands already devoted to public use which may be necessary or convenient to the effectuation of the authorized purposes of the commission.

"(c) Any highway, public utility, or other public facility which will be dislocated by reason of a project deemed necessary by the commission to effectuate the authorized purposes of this compact shall be relocated and the cost thereof shall be paid in accordance with the law of the state in which the facility is located; provided that the cost of such relocation payable by the commission shall not in any event exceed the expenditure required to serve the public convenience and necessity.

"15.16—Rights of Way. Permission is hereby granted to the commission to locate, construct, and maintain any aqueducts, lines, pipes, conduits, and auxiliary facilities authorized to be acquired, constructed, owned, operated, or maintained by the commission in, over, under, or across any streets and highways now or hereafter owned, opened, or dedicated to or for public use, subject to such reasonable conditions as the highway department of the signatory party may require.

"15.17—Penalty. Any person, association, or corporation who violates or attempts or conspires to violate any provisions of this compact or any rule, regulation, or order of the commission duly made, promulgated, or issued pursuant to the compact in addition to any other remedy, penalty, or consequence provided by law shall be punishable as may be provided by statute of any of the signatory parties within which the violation is committed; provided that in the absence of such provision any such person, association, or corporation shall be liable to a penalty of not less than $50 nor more than $1,000 for each such violation to be fixed by the court which the commission may recover in its own name in any court of competent jurisdiction, and in a summary proceeding where available under the practice and procedure of such court. For the purposes of this section in the event of a continuing offense each day of such violation, attempt, or conspiracy shall constitute a separate offense.

"15.18—Tort Liability. The commission shall be responsible for claims arising out of the negligent acts or omissions of its officers, agents, and employees only to the extent and subject to the procedures prescribed by law generally with respect to officers, agents, and employees of the government of the United States.

"15.19—Effect on Riparian Rights. Nothing contained in this compact shall be construed as affecting or intending to affect or in any way to interfere with the law of the respective signatory parties relating to riparian rights.

"15.20—Amendments and Supplements. Amendments and supplements to this compact to implement the purposes thereof may be adopted by legislative action of any of the signatory parties concurred in by all of the others.

302

84 STAT. 1537

"15.21—Construction and Severability. The provisions of this compact and of agreements thereunder shall be severable and if any phrase, clause, sentence, or provision of the Susquehanna River Basin Compact or such agreement is declared to be unconstitutional or the applicability thereof to any signatory party, agency, or person is held invalid, the constitutionality of the remainder of such compact or such agreement and the applicability thereof to any other signatory party, agency, person, or circumstance shall not be affected thereby. It is the legislative intent that the provisions of such compact, be reasonably and liberally construed.

"15.22—Effective Date; Execution. This compact shall become binding and effective thirty days after the enactment of concurring legislation by the Federal government, the states of Maryland and New York, and the Commonwealth of Pennsylvania. The compact shall be signed and sealed in five identical original copies by the respective chief executive of the signatory parties. One such copy shall be filed with the Secretary of State of each of the signatory parties or in accordance with the laws of the state in which the filing is made, and one copy shall be filed and retained in the archives of the commission upon its organization."

RESERVATIONS

Sec. 2. In the exercise of the powers reserved to the Congress, pursuant to section 1.4 of the compact, the consent to and participation in the compact by the United States is subject to the following conditions and reservations: Ante, p. 1512.

(a) Notwithstanding any provision of the Susquehanna River Basin compact the Susquehanna River Basin Commission shall not undertake any project (as defined in such compact), other than a project for which State supplied funds only will be used, beyond the planning stage until— Project plans, submittal to Congress.

(1) such commission has submitted to the Congress such complete plans and estimates for such project as may be necessary to make an engineering evaluation of such project including—

(A) where the project will serve more than one purpose, an allocation of costs among the purposes served and an estimate of the ratio of benefits to costs for each such purpose.

(B) an apportionment of costs among the beneficiaries of the project, including the portion of the costs to be borne by the Federal Government and by State and local governments, and

(C) a proposal for financing the project, including the terms of any proposed bonds or other evidences of indebtedness to be used for such purpose, and

(2) such project has been authorized by Act of Congress: *Provided*, That when a project has been authorized by Congress, such additional or changed uses of storage therein as the commission may desire shall require project reauthorization, with reallocation of project costs to all project purposes served.

(b) No provision of section 3.9 of the compact shall be deemed to authorize the commission to impose any charge for water withdrawals or diversions from the basin if such withdrawals or diversions could lawfully have been made without charge on the effective date of the compact or to impose any charges with respect to commercial navigation within the basin, jurisdiction over which is reserved to the Federal Government: *Provided*, That this paragraph shall be applicable to the extent not inconsistent with section 1.4 of this compact. Water withdrawals or diversions, charges, prohibition. Ante, p. 1516.

303

(c) Nothing contained in the compact shall be deemed to restrict the Executive powers of the President in the event of a national emergency.

(d) Nothing contained in the compact shall be construed as impairing or in any manner affecting the applicability to all Federal funds budgeted and appropriated for use by the commission of such authority over budgetary and appropriation matters as the President and Congress may have with respect to agencies in the executive branch of the Federal Government.

Bonds, taxation.

(e) Except to the same extent that State bonds are or may continue to be free or exempt from Federal taxation under the internal revenue laws of the United States, nothing contained in the compact shall be construed as freeing or exempting from internal revenue taxation in any manner whatsoever any bonds issued by the commission, their transfer, or the income therefrom (including any profits made on the sale thereof).

(f) Nothing contained in the compact shall be construed to obligate the United States legally or morally to pay the principal or interest on any bonds issued by the Susquehanna River Basin Commission.

Wages.

(g) All laborers and mechanics employed by contractors or subcontractors in the construction, alteration or repair, including painting and decorating of projects, buildings and works which are undertaken by the commission or are financially assisted by it, shall be paid wages at rates not less than those prevailing on similar construction in the locality so determined by the Secretary of Labor in accordance with

49 Stat. 1011.

the Davis-Bacon Act, as amended (40 U.S.C. 276a–276a–5), and every such employee shall receive compensation at a rate not less than one and one half times his basic rate of pay for all hours worked in any workweek in excess of eight hours in any workday or forty hours in any workweek, as the case may be. A provision stating the minimum wages thus determined and the requirement that overtime be paid as above provided shall be set out in each project advertisement for bids and in each bid proposal form and shall be made a part of the contract covering the project. The Secretary of Labor shall have, with respect to the administration and enforcement of labor standards specified in this provision, the supervisory, investigatory and other authority and functions set forth in Reorganization Plan Numbered 14 of 1950 (15 F.R. 3176, 64 Stat. 1267), and section 2 of the Act of June 13, 1934, as amended (48 Stat. 948, as amended, 50 U.S.C. 276(c)).

Discrimination, prohibition.

(h) The commission shall insure that there is no discrimination on the ground of race, color, religion, sex, or national origin in (1) the programs and activities of the commission, (2) the employment practices of the commission, and (3) the employment practices of parties entering into contracts with the commission, including construction contracts and contracts for private concessions in connection with recreational facilities.

Contracts.

(i) Contracts for the manufacture or furnishing of materials, supplies, articles and equipment with the commission which are in excess of $10,000 shall be subject to the provisions of the Walsh-

49 Stat. 2036.
Water pollution.

Healey Public Contracts Act (41 U.S.C. 35 et seq.).

(j) Nothing contained in this Act or in the compact shall be construed as superseding or limiting the functions, under any other law, of the Secretary of the Interior or of any other officer or agency of the United States, relating to water pollution: *Provided*, That the exercise of such functions shall not limit the authority of the commission to control, prevent or abate water pollution.

84 STAT. 1539

(k) The provisions of section 8.4 of article 8 of the compact shall not be construed to apply to facilities operated pursuant to any other Federal law. Ante, p. 1522.

(l) For the purposes of the Federal Tort Claims Act, of June 25, 1948 (62 Stat. 982), as amended (28 U.S.C. ch. 171 and sections 1346(b) and 2401(b)) and the Tucker Act of March 3, 1887 (24 Stat. 505), as amended (28 U.S.C. 1346(a)(2), 1402, 1491, 1496, 1501, 1503, 2411, 2412, 2501), and the Administrative Procedure Act of June 11, 1946 (60 Stat. 237), as amended (5 U.S.C. 551–558, 701–706), and the Federal Power Act of June 10, 1920 (41 Stat. 1063), as amended (16 U.S.C. 791–823), the commission shall not be considered a Federal agency.

(m) The officers and employees of the commission (other than the United States member, alternate United States member, and advisers, and personnel employed by the United States member under direct Federal appropriation) shall not be deemed to be, for any purpose, officers or employees of the United States or to become entitled at any time by reason of employment by the commission to any compensation or benefit payable or made available by the United States solely and directly to its officers or employees.

(n) Neither the compact nor this Act shall be deemed to enlarge the authority of any Federal agency other than the commission to participate in or to provide funds for projects or activities in the Susquehanna River Basin.

(o) Notwithstanding paragraph 7 of section 3.10 of the compact, the United States district courts shall have original jurisdiction of all cases or controversies arising under the compact and this Act, and any case or controversy so arising initiated in a State court shall be removable to the appropriate United States district court in the manner provided by section 1446 of title 28, United States Code. Nothing contained in the compact or elsewhere in this Act shall be construed as a waiver by the United States of its immunity from suit. Jurisdiction.
Ante, p. 1517.

62 Stat. 939;
79 Stat. 887.

(p) The right to alter, amend, or repeal this Act is hereby expressly reserved. The right is hereby reserved to the Congress or any of its standing committees to require the disclosure and furnishing of such information and data by the Susquehanna River Basin Commission as is deemed appropriate by the Congress or any such committee.

(q) The provisions of sections 2.4 and 2.6 of article 2 of the compact notwithstanding, the member and alternate member appointed by the President and adviser there referred to may be paid compensation by the United States, such compensation to be fixed by the President at the rates which he shall deem to prevail in respect to comparable officers in the executive branch. Ante, p. 1513.

(r) 1. Nothing contained in this compact or in this Act shall impair, affect, or extend the constitutional authority of the United States.

2. Nothing contained in this compact or in this Act and no action of the commission shall supersede, impair, affect, compel, or prevent the exercise of any of the powers, rights, functions, or jurisdiction of the United States under other existing or future legislation in or over the area or waters which are the subject of the compact, including projects of the commission: *Provided*, That—

(i) The commission shall serve as the principal agency for the coordination of Federal, State, interstate, local, and nongovernmental plans for water and related land resources in the Susquehanna River Basin.

(ii) Except as provided in reservation (j), whenever a comprehensive plan, or any part or revision thereof, has been adopted with the concurrence of the member appointed by the President, the exercise of any powers conferred by law on any officer, agency, or instrumentality

84 STAT. 1540

of the United States with regard to water and related land resources in the Susquehanna River Basin shall not substantially conflict with any such portion of such comprehensive plan and the provisions of section 3.10 and article 12 of the compact shall be applicable to the extent necessary to avoid such substantial conflict: *Provided further*, That whenever the President shall find and determine that the national interest so requires, he may suspend, modify, or delete any provision of the comprehensive plan to the extent necessary to permit action by the affected agency or officer in accord with the national interest. Such action shall be taken by executive order in which such finding and determination shall be set forth.

Ante, pp. 1516, 1524.

Federal project proposals, review by commission.

(iii) To insure consideration by Congress or any committee thereof of the commission's views, proposals for Federal projects which come within one or more of the classes requiring commission review under section 3.10 of the compact shall be submitted to the commission for review and recommendation for a period of ninety days or such longer time as may be requested by the commission with the concurring vote of the member appointed by the President; and the recommendations and views of the commission thereon, if any, shall be included in any report submitted by the sponsoring Federal agency to the Congress or to any committee thereof in connection with any request for authorization or appropriations therefor.

Report to Congress.

Comprehensive plan, adoption.

3. For the purposes of paragraph 2(ii) hereof, concurrence by the member appointed by the President shall be presumed unless within sixty days after notice to him of adoption of the comprehensive plan, or any part or revision thereof, he shall file with the commission notice of (i) no objection, or (ii) nonconcurrence. Each concurrence of the member appointed by the President in the adoption of the comprehensive plan or any part or revision thereof may be withdrawn by notice filed with the commission at any time between the first and sixtieth day of the sixth year after the initial adoption of the comprehensive plan and of every sixth year thereafter.

Withdrawal, notice.

Ante, p. 1512.

(s) In the event that any phrase, clause, sentence or provision of section 1.4 of article 1 of the compact, is declared to be unconstitutional under the constitution of any of the signatory parties, or the applicability thereof to any signatory party, agency or person is held invalid by a court of last resort of competent jurisdiction, the United States shall cease to be a party to the compact: *Provided*, That the President may continue United States participation in the activities of the commission to the extent that he deems necessary and proper to protect the national interest.

(t)(1) All Acts or parts of Acts inconsistent with the provisions of this Act are hereby amended for the purpose of this Act to the extent necessary to carry out the provisions of this Act.

(2) No action of the commission shall have the effect of repealing, modifying, or amending any Federal law.

(u) Notwithstanding the provisions of section 2.2 and 2.3 of the compact, the Federal member of the commission and his alternate shall be appointed by the President of the United States and shall serve at the pleasure of the President.

Technical services.

(v) Notwithstanding the provisions of section 12.5 or any other provision of the compact, the furnishing of technical services to the commission by agencies of the executive branch of the Government of the United States is pledged only to the extent that the respective agencies shall from time to time agree thereto or to the extent that the President may from time to time direct such agencies to perform such services for the commission. Nothing in the compact shall be deemed

84 STAT. 1541

to require the United States to furnish administrative services or facilities for carrying out functions of the commission except to the extent that the President may direct.

(w) Nothing contained in this Act or in the compact shall supersede, impair, affect, compel, or prevent the exercise of any of the powers, rights, functions, or jurisdiction of the Federal Power Commission, Federal Communications Commission, Atomic Energy Commission, Interstate Commerce Commission, or other such Federal independent regulatory agency under existing or future legislation. Accordingly, no action of the Susquehanna River Basin Commission shall conflict with any of the terms or conditions of any license or permit granted or issued by the aforementioned Federal agencies. This reservation shall not be construed as a basis for noncompliance with the requirements of the compact or this Act; nor shall it be construed to permit use of waters of the Susquehanna River Basin or to endanger their quality without approval pursuant to the compact.

EFFECTUATION

SEC. 3. (a) The President is authorized to take such action as may be necessary and proper, in his discretion, to effectuate the compact and the initial organization and operation of the commission thereunder.

(b) Executive departments and other agencies of the executive branch of the Federal Government shall cooperate with and furnish appropriate assistance to the United States member. Such assistance shall include the furnishing of services and facilities and may include the detailing of personnel to the United States member. Appropria- Appropriation. tions are hereby authorized as necessary for the support of the United States member and his office, including appropriations for the employment of personnel by the United States member.

Approved December 24, 1970.

O

LEGISLATIVE HISTORY:

HOUSE REPORT No. 91-1643 (Comm. on the Judiciary).
SENATE REPORT No. 91-1333 (Comm. on the Judiciary).
CONGRESSIONAL RECORD, Vol. 116 (1970):
    Oct. 14, considered and passed Senate.
    Dec. 7, considered and passed House.

Notes

Notes

PART I

Chapter 1

1 Boston: Christopher Publishing House, 1949, pp. 27–44.

2 Bulletin G9, *The Geomorphology of the Wyoming-Lackawanna Region,* by Harry A. Itter, Pennsylvania Topographic and Geologic Survey, 1938, p. 7.

3 *Coal in Pennsylvania,* Education Series No. 7, State Topographic and Geologic Survey, 1968, Fig. 3, p. 9.

Chapter 2

1 U.S. Geological Survey Circular 44, May 1949, Table 2, p. 5.

2 Gordon Trembley, assistant executive director, Pennsylvania Fish Commission, personal communication as to commission activities, 1968.

3 Joint Resolution 29, 1967 Maryland legislative session, urged Pennsylvania and New York to allow no further diversions of Susquehanna water prior to the enactment and effectiveness of the basin compact. Cf. Part I, Chapter 3.

4 *Pennsylvania's Coal Industry,* Gettysburg Historical Society publication, 1954, says soft coal mining began in the West Branch and Juniata subbasins in the 1830s.

5 An early reference is "Oxidation of Sulfides," by V. H. Gottschalk and H. S. Buehler, in *Economic Geology,* 1910, Vol. 5, pp. 28–35, in which the air–water–sulfur interaction is described.

6 Act of June 22, 1937, P. L. 1987.

7 Act of May 8, 1945, P. L. 435.

8 Act of August 23, 1965, P. L. 372.

9 *Coal in Pennsylvania,* state Topographic and Geologic Survey bulletin, Education Series No. 7, 1968, p. 10.

10 *Ibid.,* p. 8.

11 The bore hole and gravity outfall data were supplied by the Mine Drainage Section, Department of Environmental Resources.

12 Pennsylvania Coal Company vs. Sanderson, 113 Pa. 126, 149, 6 ATL. 453, 459 (1885). In that case the court quoted still earlier rulings—which may not have referred specifically to coal mining—saying "to encourage development of the great natural resources of a country, trifling inconveniences to particular persons must sometimes give way to the necessities of a great community." In *Public Health Laws of Pennsylvania,* School of Law, University of Pittsburgh, 1958, p. 460, David Stahl, editor, said "the court held the pollution caused by drainage from a coal mine was an injury

for which the law provides no redress to an individual lower riparian owner." In its brief in the case cited the coal company referred to a still earlier decision, Swett vs. Cutts, 11 Am. Law Reg., N. S. 24: "It must be conceded . . . that the right of landowners to deal with surface water and all water mixed with the soil, or coming from underground springs, in any manner they may deem necessary for the improvement or better enjoyment of their own land is almost unquestionable."

[13] The shut-down notice to the state Sanitary Water Board was dated September 30, 1967, but the actual closing came somewhat later.

[14] Pennsylvania Department of Environmental Resources, personal communication.

[15] 79 Stat. 902.

[16] *Legislative Bulletin,* Pennsylvania Farmers Association, Feb. 14, 1967, is typical.

Chapter 3

[1] *The Nation's Water Resources,* an assessment of national conditions and needs, 1968, pp. 6–1–7, 8.

[2] *Water Resources Data for Pennsylvania, Part 1, Surface Water Records, 1967* (U. S. Geological Survey in cooperation with the Pennsylvania Department of Forests and Waters). The maximum flow was gauged in March, 1936, the minimum in September, 1932.

[3] Letter from F. W. Montanari, Director, Division of Water Resources, New York Conservation Department, March 26, 1969.

[4] Bureau of Business Services, Statistical Division, daily use figures.

[5] Letter, Mayor Theodore McKeldin of Baltimore to Maryland Senate President William S. James, March 13, 1967.

[6] Calculated from *Maryland Water Supply and Demand Study, Part I, Vol. 2, Susquehanna River Basin* (Maryland State Planning Department), 1965.

[7] The 2020 figures supplied by FWPCA were in conjunction with the federal-state survey of the basin, and were as of May, 1968. It should be noted that they do not agree with projections made by the North Atlantic Regional Office, Corps of Engineers, in its Type I study of the territory from Maine to North Carolina authorized by the Rivers and Harbors Act of 1965, P. L. 89-298, 79 Stat. 1073, which are for far greater demands on Susquehanna water. The NAR Water Resources Study's Table 1, Area 17 (Susquehanna basin) projects 2020 needs for public municipal and industrial, self-supplied industrial, rural uses other than irrigation and power cooling uses will aggregate 12,815 cfs. Without the whopping irrigation needs projected, and the smaller rural-other-than-irrigation, which are given as 3,646 and 305 cfs respectively, the total for municipal and industrial uses in 2020 comes to 8,864 cfs, which is 5,726 MGD, or 2089.9 billion gallons a year. This is about two and a half times as much as was estimated in the Susquehanna basin's study, which was conducted in considerably greater depth than the NAR study. No doubt technologists in both camps would vigorously defend their statistics and methods of arriving at them.

[8] *The Nation's Water Resources, supra.,* p. 6–1–8.

[9] Approved by the Pennsylvania Water and Power Resources Board, May, 1962, and the Delaware River Basin Commission, August, 1962. Applicants may take up to one billion gallons a year at a rate not to exceed 3 MGD. No water has been diverted in recent wet years.

[10] Footnote 6, *supra. Cf.* Part II, Vol. 1, p. 247.

[11] A southeastern Pennsylvania group has enlisted Delaware and Maryland support for a so-called "Mason-Dixon Plan" to pipe 150 MGD eastward from the Susquehanna, most of which would go into the Delaware after use, and another 150 MGD westward. Part of the latter would return to the river via Codorus Creek in York County and the

rest would enter the Potomac drainage via the Monocacy River Basin for the benefit of Greater Washington. The proposal was still in promotional stages as this was written.

12 *Cf.* Part I, Chapter 2.

13 Though estuarine studies have not produced answers to all questions of environmental specialists, it does appear that a certain degree and perhaps timing of fluctuations in Susquehanna flow is beneficial to the bay, or so conversations with Maryland technologists indicate. Maryland's concern seems to have to do with extremes of flow, perhaps prolonged, whose results would be provably detrimental. As this was written, Maryland water officials were disturbed over the potential effects on the bay of the deepening of the Chesapeake and Delaware Canal to accommodate larger vessels. Because of the difference in elevation of the two bodies of water it was anticipated that about 3,600 cfs of upper Chesapeake water would flow into Delaware Bay. The regimen of the lower Chesapeake and the rich aquatic nursery waters of its upper reaches might be changed drastically.

14 *Cf.* Preamble, Delaware and Susquehanna basin compacts.

15 The federal act is P. L. 87-328, 75 Stat. 688.

PART II

Chapter 1

1 Communication from Legislative Reference, Library of Congress, October 18, 1968, reported 190 compacts as of September 6, 1963; doubted if "as many as a dozen" had been enacted since then.

2 Colorado vs. Kansas, 320 U. S. 383, 392 (1943). Washington vs. Oregon, 214 U. S. 205, 217 (1909); Minnesota vs. Wisconsin, 252 U. S. 273, 283 (1920); and New York vs. New Jersey, 256 U. S. 296, 313 1921) contain similar statements.

3 P. L. 87-328, 75 Stat. 688.

4 An example is the Interstate Commission on the Potomac River Basin, 54 Stat. 748 (1940). Amendments have recently strengthened this compact.

5 The Ohio River Valley Water Sanitation Commission (ORSANCO), 54 Stat. 752 (1940), which became effective in 1948, was created by this type of compact.

6 A federal commissioner is permanent chairman of the Upper Colorado River Basin Commission, 63 Stat. 31 (1949); federal commissioners observe and participate in ORSANCO discussions but do not vote; the District of Columbia representation on the present Potomac commission is federal and has voting privileges.

7 In his foreword to *The Law and Use of Interstate Compacts*, a manual written by Zimmermann and Wendell, published by the Council of State Governments in 1961, Brevard Crihfield, council executive director, wrote that "perhaps the two most significant pioneering developments in the compact field at the present time are the federal-interstate compact and the use of compacts for agreements among local governments in states. The authors . . . have played the leading role in originating and developing both these concepts."

8 Information relative to career activities of Zimmermann and Wendell is from biographical sketches they furnished, and from personal communications, oral and written, 1964–1969. See Appendix A for career details.

9 A September 20, 1968 letter from Zimmermann said, in part, that when the Delaware River Basin Compact was enacted in 1961 and the Interstate Commission on the Delaware River Basin (INCODEL) was to be dissolved, "the attorneys in Albany told me I had confronted them with the insuperable task of repealing a statute that had never been enacted."

10 *Cf.* footnote 6.

[11] By Felix Frankfurter and James M. Landis, *Yale Law Review*, Vol. 34, 1924–1925, pp. 685–758.

[12] U. S. Constitution, Art. 1, Sect. 10, Clause 3.

[13] At a meeting of the Susquehanna River Basin Study Coordinating Committee on July 29–30, 1969, representatives of each basin state put forward their views on all projects proposed and indications were that state wishes would be complied with in each case involving divergent opinion.

[14] *The Law and Use of Interstate Compacts, supra.*, was a logical extension of their first manual but is of incidental importance in the present context.

[15] September 20, 1968, letter, *supra*.

[16] *The Interstate Compact Since 1925*, p. ix (preface).

[17] *Ibid.*, p. 8.

[18] *Ibid.*, p. 60.

[19] The Pick-Sloan Plan was embodied in the Flood Control Act of 1944, 59 Stat. 10.

[20] Richard G. Baumhoff, *The Dammed Missouri Valley*, New York: Knopf, 1951, p. 182. The formal name of the governors' group was "The Missouri Basin States Committee."

[21] Letter, Brevard Crihfield, executive director of the council, to the writer, July 8, 1969.

[22] *Ibid.*

[23] The commission was created by Executive Order 10095. The study report, titled *A Water Policy for the American People,* was published in three volumes in 1951 by the Government Printing Office, Washington. *Cf.* Vol. I, pp. 10–11.

[24] *Missouri: Land and Water,* report of the Missouri Basin Survey Commission, Washington, 1953.

[25] "Representation of the Region in Missouri Basin Organization," by Zimmermann and Wendell, *American Political Science Review*, Vol. XLVIII, No. 1, March, 1954, pp. 152–165.

[26] Crihfield letter of July 8, 1969, *supra.*, and *Missouri: Land and Water, supra.*, p. 249.

[27] Revised draft, *Missouri Basin Compact,* 1953, Art. 7, Powers, pp. 8–9.

[28] *Ibid.*, Arts. 4 and 5, pp. 5–6.

[29] September 20, 1968, *supra*.

[30] Senate Document 14, 85th Congress, 1st Session.

[31] Hearings on H. R. 9999 and H. R. 10022, House Committee on Public Works, March 30–31, 1960, House Document 86-18; *cf.* statement of Senator Elisha T. Barrett, chairman, New York Joint Legislative Committee on Interstate Cooperation, p. 44.

[32] Zimmermann and Wendell communications, *supra*.

[33] House Document 86-18, *supra*.

[34] *Ibid.* There is evidence elsewhere that an upper New England senator feared lower states might be put in position to claim more than their fair share of Connecticut River water.

[35] The Delaware River Basin Advisory Committee approved a final draft of the compact on February 1, 1961; on November 2, 1961, effectuating documents were ceremonially signed by the President and the governors of the four states.

[36] The 1954 decision is New Jersey vs. New York, 347 U. S. 995.

[37] *Cf.* Legislative journals, 1953 sessions, of New York, New Jersey, Delaware, and Pennsylvania. Zimmermann, *supra.*, attributes the compact's failure in Pennsylvania to opposition by Governor John S. Fine.

[38] Some of this is supposition, for INCODEL records have eluded me. They were traced through Pitkin's former secretary to the Pennsylvania State Planning Board, where I was told they were at one time stacked in cartons in a hallway en route to

the State Archives Building. It is possible a janitor assumed they were to be removed and destroyed.

39 Some of this organization information came from the files of Paul M. Felton, executive director of the Water Resources Association of the Delaware River Basin (WRA/DRB), the citizens group, which formally came into existence in 1959.

40 By Martin, Burkhead, Burkhead, and Munger, Syracuse University Press.

41 There is evidence that the compact proposal drafted by Zimmermann and Wendell for INCODEL came to Martin's attention. Further, it is inconceivable that capable researchers such as Martin and his associates would have overlooked such obvious source material as the Missouri and Northeastern compacts. A more tenable hypothesis is that Martin was influenced to favor a TVA-like mechanism by his long association with TVA. The compact proposal in the book appears to have been a second and subordinate choice.

42 Conversation, August 20, 1969, *supra.*, and biographical sketches, Appendix A.

43 Flood Control Act of 1944, 59 Stat. 10, *supra.*

44 *Cf.* Part V, Chapter 3. When the Susquehanna legislation was before the House Committee on the Judiciary, it was ruled that the compact had no adverse reference to, nor did it supersede or invalidate, the statutes concerning the preference clause.

45 P. L. 89-80. These commissions, for planning only, have a permanent federal chairman and a vice chairman who represents all the member states. Efforts are made to achieve agreement on issues through concensus, which avoids direct voting confrontations.

Chapter 2

1 From conversations with Zimmermann and Breth.

2 Recorded interview with Breth September 3, 1968; the legislation referred to was House Resolution 68, May 8, 1961.

3 House and Senate resolutions in 1961, by Rep. Daniel J. Flood and Senator Joseph Clark.

4 Files of the Joint State Government Commission, Harrisburg.

5 *Ibid.*; from transcripts of the hearings.

6 Personal communications and files of Interstate Advisory Committee.

7 Personal communications.

8 Personal communications.

9 *Record, Interstate Advisory Committee on the Susquehanna River Basin,* published by the Joint State Government Commission, Harrisburg, 1963.

10 *Ibid.,* pp. 32–47.

11 The reference was to a map accompanying a paper on water pollution, "The Luxury We Can't Afford," that I had presented at the Sixth Annual Clean Streams Conference, Pennsylvania State Chamber of Commerce, Harrisburg, May, 1958.

12 *Record, Interstate Advisory Committee . . ., supra.*

13 *Ibid.*

14 *Ibid.* The record does not reflect the basis for the proration but was supplied by principals attending.

Chapter 3

1 Personal communication.

2 "Staff Study Proposals," mimeo; presented to the IAC December 16, 1963.

3 It carried the cumbersome title of *Resources—Responsibilities and Coordination Related to the Comprehensive Survey of the Susquehanna River Basin.* We published 3,000, nearly all of which had been distributed by the end of 1968.

PART III

Chapter 1

[1] With respect to water projects, the conditions precedent to commission action in these articles must also be consistent with the restrictive provisions of Section 1.3-6, which see.

[2] From June, 1964, through January, 1967.

Chapter 2

[1] Biographical sketches of the members of the drafting task force are found in Appendix A.

[2] John Starr, key civilian in the district office of the Corps of Engineers at Baltimore, relays to me the following conversation he had early in 1966 with Col. Frank Rhea, then the district enngieer:

> *Rhea:* Do you know what's in that compact?
>
> *Starr:* No, I've had no information from the committee or anyone else.
>
> *Rhea:* Hmmm. That damn' compact has had better security than the Manhattan Project!

Chapter 3

[1] Delaware compact's Article 14; Susquehanna's 15.

[2] This duplicates in part and supplements provisions found in Section 3.4-9.

[3] Articles 3 and 10.

[4] Section 3.11.

[5] Article 13.

[6] Section 3.4-2.

[7] Preamble, Paragraph Number 3.

[8] Section 3.4-3.

[9] Section 3.4-4.

[10] Section 3.4-5.

[11] Section 3.4-6.

[12] At the time this was written I was an active member of the Public Relations Society of America, so it could be called self-criticism.

[13] Section 3.4-7.

[14] Section 3.4-9. *Cf.* footnote 2, this chapter.

[15] Section 3.7.

[16] Section 3.3 and Article 14.

[17] See Article 12, Sections 12.1 and 12.2, and Part III, Chapter 4, *The Comprehensive Plan.*

[18] *Ibid.*

[19] Delaware Article 11.

[20] Delaware Section 3.8; its major clause says "No project having a substantial effect on the water resources of the basin shall hereafter be undertaken by any person, corporation, or governmental authority unless it shall have been first submitted to and approved by the commission . . ."

[21] Section 11.2.

[22] Section 11.3.

[23] Section 11.4 (a).

[24] Article 4.

[25] Section 4.1.

[26] Section 4.5.

[27] A further reference to the provisions of Article 11, which see, seems appropriate.

[28] Delaware Section 5.1.

29 Section 5.1 (b).

30 Section 5.2 (a).

31 Section 5.2 (c) and (d).

32 Section 5.2 (e).

33 Section 6.2 (a) and (b).

34 Section 6.2 (c).

35 Section 6.4.

36 Section 6.5.

37 Transcript of IAC meeting of April 9, 1965, in Harrisburg.

38 Section 6.2 (c) *supra*.

39 Section 6.8.

40 Section 7.4 and 8.2.

41 Section 7.3.

42 The IAC deleted such references late in 1966 when legislative members feared they'd frighten the rural element.

43 Section 9.2.

44 Section 9.3.

45 Section 9.4.

46 Delaware Article 9.

47 Section 10.1.

48 Sections 10.2 and 10.3.

49 Section 10.4.

50 Section 10.5.

51 This was raised by Stewart L. Udall, Secretary of the Interior, at hearings before Senate and House committees on bills to approve the Delaware compact. *Cf.* transcript of hearing, August 24, 1961, before "Subcommittee of the Senate Public Works Committee" on S. 856, 87th Congress, First Sesstion.

52 The earliest were York Haven, below Harrisburg in 1905, Warrior's Ridge above Huntingdon in 1907, Holtwood below Harrisburg in 1910, and the first Raystown near Mount Union, in 1911. All are in Pennsylvania.

53 The existing plant is known as Muddy Run, and is operated with water from Conowingo pool. The other will be located above Stony Creek just north of Harrisburg; the question of exchanging adjacent land for state game land, on which the upper reservoir would be situated, was resolved in favor of the project by the State Game Commission in January, 1969.

Chapter 4

1 Section 1.2.

2 Delaware Compact Section 13.1.

3 Section 14.1.

4 Section 2.7, Jurisdiction of the Commission.

5 This is not written in derogation of the Delaware commission. So far as I have been able to learn, no one wishing to be heard by that commission has been denied opportunity.

6 At Safe Harbor, Holtwood and Conowingo, all downstream from the U. S. Highway 30 crossing.

7 *Water Resources Development by the U. S. Army Corps of Engineers* is the title of a report issued annually for each state. Corps projects—their statutes, location, nature, cost and other pertinent factors—can be found for the Susquehanna basin in the reports under the above title for New York, Pennsylvania, and Maryland. The flood control structures for the most part were authorized after devastating floods were experienced in March, 1936.

[8] P. L. 89-298 (79 Stat. 1037).

[9] Information not published at that time but obtained informally in a visit to the New York Division office, Corps of Engineers, in November, 1967, by the writer.

[10] The reference is chiefly to the diversion by New York City of up to 800 MGD of Delaware water for its municipal supply system, and to the long drawn out court battles that resulted in Supreme Court decrees in New York's favor. *Cf.* 347 US 995 (1954).

[11] David C. Coyle, *Conservation,* New Brunswick, N.J.: Rutgers University Press, 1957, p. 148.

[12] Irving K. Fox, associate director, University of Wisconsin Water Resources Center, Madison, as quoted in "The Drive for Breadth in River Basin Planning," ad hoc committee report to the Fourteenth National Watershed Congress, Boston, June 18–21, 1967, p. 28.

[13] From a personal file copy of a paraphrase of my oral statement, written on or about April 14, 1967, from pencilled notes.

[14] Section 14.1, last sentence.

[15] Section 3.10-7.

Chapter 5

[1] Sections 1.2-11 and 1.2-4 respectively.

[2] Section 1.3.

[3] This is discussed at length in Part IV, Chapters 1, 2, 4, and 5.

[4] Delaware River Basin Compact, Section 2.7.

PART IV

Chapter 1

[1] Mimeographed; in IAC files.

[2] Mimeographed memorandum to IAC of March 22, 1966.

[3] P. L. 89-80, *supra.*

[4] Early in 1966 Dr. W. Mason Lawrence, New York deputy commissioner of conservation for water resources, succeeded Wilm, who resigned to return to Syracuse University.

[5] News release, for PMs, June 14, 1966, by Caulfield, on Water Resources Council paper.

Chapter 2

[1] P. L. 89-80, *supra.,* Title II.

[2] Scott became Master of the National Grange and moved to Washington late in 1968.

[3] South Carolina vs. Katzenbach, 383 U. S. 301, re Act of August 6, 1965, P. L. 89-110, 79 Stat. 437.

[4] Charles Slaton and Jared Miller, respectively.

[5] Dated June 27, 1966, addressed to IAC members and alternates.

[6] Section 1.3-6. In all we made 44 changes in language, some large, mostly small, when the compact was reprinted in January, 1967, prior to introduction in the state assemblies.

[7] The Law Division, Document Section, of the Pennsylvania State Library was provided copies of all significant IAC printed material in June, 1969, along with copies of minutes of meetings held and other mimeographed material.

[8] Section 3.11.

[9] Section 15.3.

10 Section 15.14.
11 Section 15.19.

Chapter 3

1 A "quick" call may be used in New York—and in other states as well—on legislation where no opposition is evident. When it is, the clerk usually calls the first one or two names of the alphabetical list of Senate or House members, then the last one, after which the presiding officer announces unanimous passage or passage without dissent.

2 Chapter 785, *supra.*

3 As reported in the Baltimore *Sun* of March 15, 1967.

4 Letter to Senator James, March 13, 1967.

5 The request for a meeting was by Senator James, perhaps in consort with Mr. O'Donnell. My records are not specific on the subject.

6 No minutes of the meeting were kept. This account is based on oral statements in 1968 by Everstine and James.

7 Oral communication, James to Voigt.

8 Baltimore *Sun*, March 29, 1967.

9 *Cf.* Part I, Chapter 3.

10 The originals are in the files of the Interstate Advisory Committee.

Chapter 4

1 For details, *cf.* Pennsylvania Senate Journal, July 31, 1967.

2 The account of this meeting is based on memory reinforced by notes pencilled at the time, from which a diary entry was typed next day.

3 IAC "Restraints and Limitations," Mimeo, July 26, 1967.

4 From my diary. Our information was that the company feared the commission would force it to higher degrees of treatment of factory wastes.

5 Part IV, Chapter 2.

6 Chapter 345, New York Laws of 1966.

Chapter 5

1 Section 2.5 would be changed to require four instead of three affirmative votes.

2 The reference here is to the small watershed work of the Soil Conservation Service in headwater and tributary stream areas, and the main stem or large tributary work in which the Corps of Engineers is chiefly engaged.

3 New York Laws of 1967, Chapter 785, Section 835-h.

4 "Report on the Amendments to the Susquehanna Compact," undated but distributed in behalf of the House Appropriations Committee and received by us on or about June 6, 1968.

5 *Cf.* Pennsylvania House Legislative Journal, June 12, 1968.

6 IAC Memorandum, "Proposal for Meeting with Pennsylvania Legislators," June 14, 1968.

7 Section 15.11 provided for an annual independent audit of commission books and for anytime examinations of the books by the "duly authorized officers" of the signatories, the results to be public information. Section 15.12 directed the commission to "make and publish an annual report to the legislative bodies of the signatory parties and to the public." Also, Section 15.4(a) said "All meetings of the commission shall be open to the public," and Section 14.2 provided for formulation annually of a water resources program that would be a public document.

8 From my June 25 diary entry. I wrote pencilled notes at the meeting.

⁹ *Cf.* House of Journal, June 26, 1968.

¹⁰ Relative to Sections 14.1, 15.11, 15.12, 15.4(a), and 14.2, *supra.*

PART V

Chapter 1

¹ *Cf.* Delaware River Basin Compact, transcript of hearing on S. 856, before a sub-committee of the Senate Committee on Public Works, August 24, 1961, for testimony by Udall and others, and letters from the affected agencies.

² P. L. 89-80. The Council of State Governments had a leading role in the effort, working largely through its Interstate Conference on Water Problems.

³ Unless otherwise noted, the contents of this chapter are based on personal recollections bolstered by copies of official documents and correspondence, plus diary entries.

⁴ Water Pollution Control Act, 33 U. S. C. Sec. 466 *et seq.*

⁵ *Cf.* Part II, Chapter 1.

Chapter 2

¹ "Summary of Notes of Meeting," IAC mimeo, April 8, 1969.

² "Summary of Notes of Meeting," IAC mimeo, June 13, 1969.

³ From Report No. 91-1643, December 1, 1970, of the House Committee on the Judiciary, p. 6.

⁴ *Cf.* Part II, Chapter 1.

⁵ *Ibid.*

⁶ News release, Department of the Interior, "Secretary Hickel Endorses Susquehanna River Basin Commission."

Chapter 3

¹ IAC mimeo, June 22, 1970, *supra.*

² Subcommittee No. 3. A transcript was published under the title of *Susquehanna River Basin Compact, Hearings . . . Ninety-First Congress, Second Session, on H. J. Res. 380 . . . June 4 and September 30, 1970. Serial No. 31.*

³ The text is in Appendix B, Section 2, Reservations.

⁴ *Ibid.*

⁵ Hearings transcript, *supra.,* pp. 171–179.

⁶ *Ibid.,* pp. 182–203.

⁷ 16 U. S. C. 791a, *et seq.*

⁸ Susquehanna Compact, Section 1.3-5.

⁹ H. R. 19863, by Fallon of Maryland, chairman of the House Public Works Committee (He co-sponsored Morton's H. J. Res. 382.).

¹⁰ Section 215 of H. R. 19877, Section 235 of the bill as reported by the conference committee. See Congressional Record of December 17, 1970, pp. H 11973 and H 11975. All other information relative to what I have termed the "end run" attempt was obtained from unofficial sources that I believe well informed.

Index

Office, 38, 154, 246; Office, Chief of, 246; bill to let Corps by-pass commission, 254; bill killed in conference, 254; mentioned, 42–222 *passim*

Council of State Governments: Publishes Missouri Compact draft, 60; Board of Managers of, 266; Wendell consultant to, counsel for, 272; special committee on flood insurance, 272; mentioned, 54, 55, 57, 68, 78, 96, 99, 230, 239, 289

Cowanesque River, 10

Coyle, David C., 132

Cumberland County, 26

Dams, inflatable, 37

Dauphin County, 26, 205, 216

Davis, Preston, 163, 188, 189, 215, 216, 267

Deer Creek, 29, 36; spawning area, anadromous species, 29

Delaware: Early compact passed by, 63; stake in basin water, 69; mentioned, 37, 197, 224

—River, Branches of, 6; mentioned, 36, 37, 65, 68

—River Agency for Water (DRAW), 64

—River Basin: States of, 56, 69; conflict over water, 63; water for New York City, 63; survey ordered, 63; governors of, 65; water conditions in, 69; compared with Susquehanna, 69; mentioned, 12, 62, 64, 68, 70, 81, 131, 166, 170, 181, 201, 224, 225, 239, 249

—River Basin Advisory Committee, 64, 65, 73, 81

—River Basin Commission: Significance of memberships, 66–67; its task, 69; short term achievement, 97; long term promise, 98; mentioned, 37, 47, 96, 157, 173, 197, 214, 222, 228–271 *passim*

—River Basin Compact: First of a kind, 47; quick enactment, 62, 98,

220; governors as members, 66; first considered "oddball," 67; a guide to Susquehanna drafters, 100; substantial change from, 110; its constitutionality, 220; how federal reservations evolved, 242; mentioned, 54–245 *passim*

—River Port Authority, 206

—University of, 265

Denison, Richard, 156

Denver, 270

Determinations: By the commission, alarm over, 185

Dickinson, Daniel, 267

Dickinson College, 271; School of Law, 271

Disaster area, 111–112

District of Columbia, 39, 222

Diversion, water: Discussion of, 33–40; compact definition of, 36; where done now, 36; caution over, 37; possible points of, 37–37; possible destinations, 37–38; Mason-Dixon proposal, 37, 181, 186, 187, 214; economics a factor, 38; interest alignments, 131; as a bitterly debated question, 131–132; when Chesapeake Bay is affected, 132–133; differs from "withdrawal," 135

Drafting task force. *See* Task force

Drainage, coal mine. *See* Coal

Driftwood Branch, 29

Drought, 31, 111–112

DuBois, Pennsylvania, 36

Duryea, Borough of, 19

Duryea Gravity Outfall, 19

Earthquake Lake, 4

Easton, Pennsylvania, 65

Ecenbarger, William, 185

Economic Research Service, 151

Eisenhower, Milton, 164

Eisenhower, President David Dwight, 164

Electric utilities. *See* Hydroelectric power and energy

Elk County, 21

*The text of this book was set in Baskerville Linotype
and printed by offset on P & S Special Book manu-
factured by P. H. Glatfelter Co., Spring Grove, Pa.
Composed and printed by Rae Publishing Co., Cedar
Grove, New Jersey. Bound by A. Horowitz & Son,
Clifton, New Jersey.*

About the Author

William Voigt, Jr., was a journalist from 1925 to 1942, working for several large newspapers and for six years with the Associated Press. Throughout World War II he was a historical writer for the Army Ordnance Department and thereafter he was associated with the Isaac Walton League of America and the Pennsylvania Fish Commission.

From 1963 to 1968 Mr. Voigt was executive director of the Interstate Advisory Committee on the Susquehanna River Basin and his experiences in that position are detailed in this volume. Now semiretired, he divides his time between homes near Mechanicsburg, Pennsylvania, and Blackshear, Georgia, and is engaged chiefly in writing and consulting.

Mr. Voigt is the author of *National Fishing Guide* (1946), he has served as editor of *Outdoor America* and editorial director of *Pennsylvania Angler,* and he has contributed articles to a number of nature and field sports periodicals.

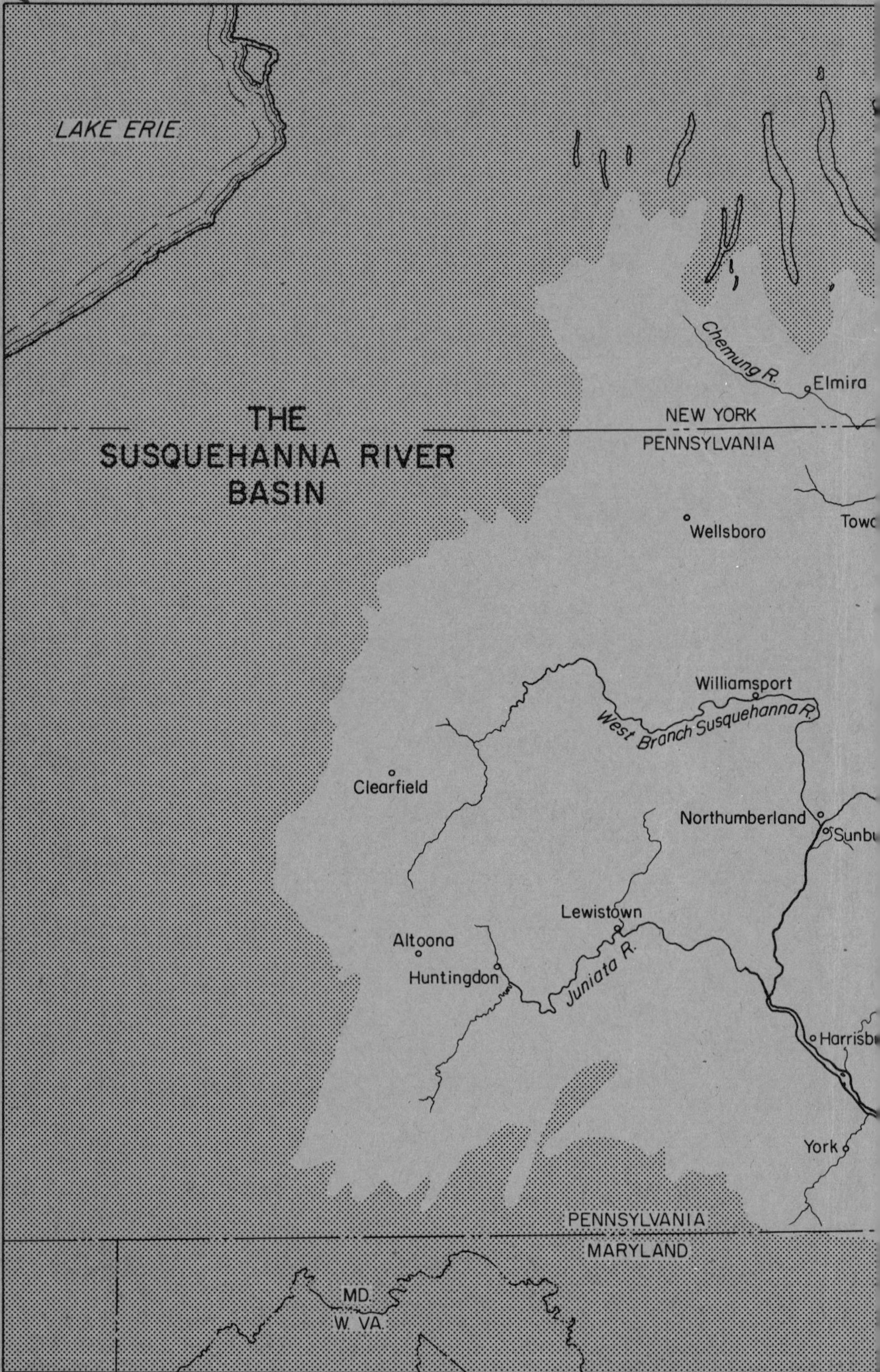

THE SUSQUEHANNA RIVER BASIN

LAKE ERIE

Chemung R.

Elmira

NEW YORK
PENNSYLVANIA

Wellsboro

Towa

Williamsport

West Branch Susquehanna R.

Clearfield

Northumberland

Sunb

Lewistown

Altoona

Juniata R.

Huntingdon

Harrisb

York

PENNSYLVANIA
MARYLAND

MD.
W. VA.

 SO-AXU-955

Welcome

to MMA's Living Stewardship Series!

As a church-related organization dedicated to helping people live lives of Christian stewardship, MMA is pleased to provide this resource as part of the *Living Stewardship Series.*

MMA exists to help Christians answer God's call to care for and cultivate the gifts God has given them. To accomplish this, we offer products, services, and resources – like this study book. Our goal is to help you understand biblical principles of stewardship while, at the same time, providing real world ways you can incorporate those principles into your everyday living.

The Bible tells us we are to seek wholeness in our lives. In the Gospel of Matthew (5:48) Jesus said in his Sermon on the Mount to *"Be perfect, therefore, as your heavenly Father is perfect."* But, who among us can ever be perfect?

Actually, the Greek word traditionally translated as "perfect" in that verse is *teleios* – which means, "to be whole." *Living Stewardship* is not a series for perfect people, but for people like you who are seeking wholeness. People who don't want to leave their faith in Christ at the church door after Sunday worship. People who want that faith to color how they relate to family and friends, how they work at their jobs, how they spend their money, how they take care of themselves – essentially, how they live.

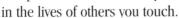

At **MMA**, "holistic" refers to the essential interconnectedness of all the elements of Christian stewardship. For the sake of simplicity, we've identified the crucial elements as time, relationships, finances, health, and talents. Integrating all five, and nurturing the relationships between them, produces a healthy life of holistic stewardship. **MMA** feels strongly about holistic stewardship – so strongly, in fact, that we have reoriented our approach to stewardship to recognize this interconnectedness of all parts of our lives.

On the stewardship path of your life, you will find the journey easier if you pay attention to all of these areas of your life and recognize how they work together to lead you to the wholeness of God. If one of these elements becomes unbalanced, broken, or disconnected, you experience a lack of wholeness. However, with a strong core (faith) connecting each area, and careful attention to each area as needed, God's love can flow through you and produce wholeness in your life – and in the lives of others you touch.

What is MMA?

MMA helps people manage resources in ways that honor God through its professional expertise in insurance and financial services.

Rooted in the Anabaptist faith tradition, MMA offers practical stewardship education and tools to individuals, congregations, and organizations.

MMA helps you pursue stewardship solutions through insurance and financial services, charitable giving, and other stewardship resources as well as with our educational resources, such as this study book, and stewardship education events through Stewardship University.

MMA wants to help you live a holistic life of stewardship centered on Christ – and become the best steward of God's resources you can.

This is why we believe *holistic stewardship* involves much more than just the products and services MMA provides. Holistic stewardship looks at the *interconnectedness* that weaves through the areas of our lives. And, as Christians, it's all filtered through our faith in Christ. This faith is what drives the search for wholeness.

How good a steward you are in your finances, can affect your health and your relationships. If you are having trouble with your health, that can affect how you are able to use your talents or your time each day. If you're overcommitted and your day feels too full, you may opt to give short shrift to your children or your job. And on it goes. There are countless ways our search for wholeness is affected by our shortcomings in these areas.

MMA®

Stewardship Solutions

Practical tips to keep you moving!

This study book is on the stewardship of your health – but in this study you won't find the diet or exercise plan perfect for you and you won't learn about the ins and outs of MMA's health insurance plans. What you'll study in these pages is how your health, and your stewardship of it, affect your life and the lives of those around you – even into your community. Each of us has been given the gift of life by God. We live in various stages of "good" health. Maybe you feel health, maybe you don't. But if you're not taking care of the health you do have, what does that say to the God who created you?

Because of the holistic nature of stewardship, don't be surprised when we also talk about your talents, time, finances, and relationships – specifically as they relate to your health.

We'll give you practical ways to implement the suggestions we make here – not just open-ended theories! Each chapter ends with discussion questions you can answer as a group, or individually, that will help you identify areas where you may need to do some repair work.

There's more!

If you like what you learn here, look for other study guides in the *Living Stewardship Series*.

If you want to learn more about us, visit MMA-online, our home on the Web (www.mma-online.org). There you can find more information and tools to help you on your stewardship journey. You'll also find connections to the MMA partners in your area who can help you achieve the stewardship goals you have for your life.

Body Talk
Speaking the Words of Health

by Ingrid Friesen Moser

MMA®

Stewardship Solutions

Goshen, Indiana

Co-published with Herald Press

Body Talk

LivingStewardship Series

Copyright © 2007 by MMA, Goshen, Ind. 46527. All rights reserved.
Co-published with Herald Press, Scottdale, Pa. 15683
Printed in the United States of America

    Library of Congress Cataloging-in-Publication Data
Moser, Ingrid Friesen, 1970-
    Body talk : speaking the words of health / by Ingrid Friesen Moser.
    p. cm.
ISBN 978-0-8361-9370-1 (pbk. : alk. paper)
1. Health–Religious aspects–Christianity. 2. Church work with the sick.
3. Stewardship, Christian. I. Title.
BT732.M67 2007
261.8'321–dc22

                                                2006102528

Cover design by Tom Duckworth
Edited by Michael Ehret

MMA®

Stewardship Solutions

1110 North Main Street
Post Office Box 483
Goshen, IN 46527

Toll-free: (800) 348-7468
Telephone: (574) 533-9511
www.mma-online.org

Acknowledgements

To Levi Nelson and Peter Millard who came to life alongside this book.

You inspire new awe and admiration of our physical bodies,

and greater appreciation for the body of Christ

that surrounds us in life.

Contents

First Word: A Unique Message

Search Amazon.com for books on health and you get close to half a million possible options.

Why another book on health?

In some ways it seems absurd to add yet another book on health to the glut already out there. Yet when I consider MMA's unique message of health in the light of biblical stewardship, I do believe you will find something different here.

As stewards of God's gifts, and certainly one of those gifts is our health, we are consciously choosing a different path – a path where we have a responsibility and opportunity to show gratitude to God and to make choices about living that reflect our faith. According to Lynn Miller, MMA's stewardship theologian, stewardship is a response to God's extravagance. This message of goodness and love is at the heart of this book's unique message. How do we respond as wise and faithful stewards to God's extravagant gift of health?

The stewardship wisdom we desire can be attained through a three-part process.[1] As you embark on this journey toward becoming a steward of health, keep three things in mind.

First, be sure to experience God's grace and goodness. I pray you have a renewed sense of your goodness and God's redeeming grace in your life as a result of reading this book and engaging in each chapter's activities.

The activities are an important part of the book and will engage both your heart and head. Many of us feel comfortable engaging one or the other, but not both. I should warn you that, because of this double engagement, some of the activities may push the limits of your comfort level. If this happens to you, ask yourself why you're feeling resistance. *What in me is being asked to stretch and grow?* Sometimes the uncomfortable places we have courage to explore yield significant and vital growth.

Second, learn to tell the story of God's action in our lives. Hearing the biblical stories of God's faithfulness and love and telling the story of God's action in our lives are both vital to our development as stewards. As a result, I share with you in this book stories from the Bible, my own life, my experience of living and working in a variety of places, including clinical and community health settings as a Registered Dietitian, and from my background as a trained spiritual director. Unless stated otherwise, names have been changed to protect identity.

I have been blessed with the opportunity to get to know many people and their stories. I have lived, worked, and worshiped in at least six communities as an adult. As a child, my family lived overseas and made our home in several places due to my parents' work as missionaries and pastors. The variety of people I have come to know throughout my lifetime has made my life richer and taken me to deeper places of knowing God's extravagant love despite sickness, suffering, trials, and pain. These complex and blessed stories have brought me to the place I am today and are the inspiration for the work I do.

I pray this book encourages you to know your own health story in a more intimate way, and that it also encourages you to share your story with others in ways that feel comfortable and led by the Spirit.

Third, I hope you will be moved to take action. You will soon discover this book is not filled with lots of health "information." There are plenty of other resources out there that offer instruction on how to be healthy – sleep better, lose weight, lower your cholesterol, manage your stress, prevent cancer. You name it, there is a book on it. After all, there are close to half a million health books out there!

Don't get me wrong, we need to be adequately informed, and these instructional resources play an important function in meeting that need. But, if information alone had the power to change us, we would all likely be well on our way to attaining the perfect weight, having normal cholesterol and blood pressure readings, and adequately lowering our cancer risk factors. Many of us know what we need to do or "should" do to improve our health. Actually doing it, and finding genuine pleasure in the doing, is a totally different story for most of us.

My hope and prayer for you is that you are able to connect your heart, mind, and spirit in ways that inspire you to live out some of those health "shoulds" in your life with joy.

Living a joy-filled, disciplined life is about living in a way that shapes and molds us more into the image of Christ. May you see changes in your body, and the body you belong to, as a result of reading and engaging with this book that draws you closer to Jesus the healer.

Sources

1   Mark Vincent's stewardship manifesto, available to download at www.designforministry.com.

Listen to What the Spirit Says

*And a voice came from heaven: "You are my Son, whom I love;
with you I am well pleased." (Luke 3:22)*

Being a good steward of your health starts by listening to the Spirit. Those words from the Gospel of Luke are addressed to Jesus, but are for us as well: we are deeply loved. This is the first and most important message the Spirit wants us to hear.

James, like many of us, needed to hear that message. Two months after his diabetes diagnosis, he still struggled with controlling his blood sugar. All the changes he needed to make overwhelmed him. Worst of all, he could not shake the oppressive feeling he was now marked by his condition and in some way he had failed.

During the fellowship hour at church one Sunday, someone asked him how he was as they stood next to the coffeepot and a big tray of doughnuts. Rather than answer the usual, "Fine, and how are you?," James took a risk and answered truthfully. He was struggling. Dealing with his diagnosis of diabetes was difficult. The friend who had asked simply listened, and when James was done said, "Take heart, my friend. God loves you, diabetes and all. You'll find your way through this. I'm glad I now know how I can be praying for you."

The response James got didn't take away the difficult journey of learning to live with diabetes, but it did help him reframe his situation in the light of God's love and care.

The goal of this study is to help you do that – to help you look at your health in the light of God's love and care. *How do we live in our bodies as fully loved beings?* That is a central question of this book. We understand "our bodies" in this question to be somewhat of a paradox, referring both to our personal body, as well as to the body – the community – we belong to.

Health can mean different things to different people, so beginning with a common definition will be helpful. For purposes of this book, health means not so much the absence of disease, but rather living fully in the body we *do* have in spite of disease. Not the body we *wish* we had, or the body we *hope* to have, but the body we have *right now*. Practicing good stewardship of health starts here.

Each day we live we are given the gift of health – the opportunity to live as fully as possible in the physical body we have. But also, the opportunity to participate as fully as possible in the body of Christ manifested in the communities where we live, work, and worship.

This gift of health is not the promise of a perfect body, or that the body of believers will be perfect – at least not in this life! God's gift of health is a promise that we are loved and our needs for each day will be provided (Matthew 6:25-34). The perfection we strive toward will be ours in the life to come.

The gift of health is not the promise of a perfect body.

It may also be helpful to delineate what being a good steward of your health is *not*. It is not about finding the perfect diet and exercise plan. It is not about discovering one right way to make health care decisions. And it is not about finding "the" solution to our country's health care crisis – or even our own personal crises. Again, being a good steward of your health starts by listening to what the Spirit is calling you to do in response to the gift of health you have been given.

For each of us, this will mean something different. For some, it may mean making a significant lifestyle change, such as starting a more healthy diet, or making a commitment to exercise more, or getting serious about the need to get more sleep. To others, it might mean reprioritizing your health care decision making, or changing how you respond to the health care needs of others. What the Spirit is saying to you about your health is unique and special.

Group questions

1. How does having an orientation toward the future, and the promises for the life to come, change how we think and act as Christians about our health?

2. How might this kind of orientation affect your daily choices that influence health and well-being or your health care decision making?

3. How might you be called to live a more faithful and abundant life in your physical body?

How do we listen to the Spirit?

In the first chapters of the book of Revelation, the book's author, John, is sharing an important message from Jesus to the seven churches in Asia about listening and the rewards of being faithful. Christians in these places were living in a time of uncertainty and trial. In each of the letters, John tells the body of believers who are faced with challenging situations, "Let anyone who has an ear listen to what the Spirit is saying." (Revelation 2:7, NRSV) Listen. Be faithful. Be guided by the Spirit, for the reward is great!

Faithful people listen. After listening, faithful people engage in careful and thoughtful reflection – and they *take action*! They are sensitive to how God's Spirit may be leading them and are courageous. In the face of adversity, faithful people persevere, not alone, but as a united whole guided by the Spirit.

> *After listening, faithful people engage in careful and thoughtful reflection – and they take action!*

The reward for living a life guided by the Spirit is a full and abundant life. In Revelation, Jesus, through John, promises to each of the churches that faithful servants of God will be rewarded. Let's look at those rewards. Some will:

- Eat from the tree of life;

- Be given the crown of life, or hidden manna, and a new name;

- Receive the morning star;

- Have their names written in the book of life;

- Be made as a pillar in the temple of God; or

- Receive a place on the throne of God.

All amazing promises for a full and blessed life to come! These promises are not necessarily promises that will make life today easier and more prosperous. Instead, they give us a hope and an orientation.

The author of Revelation wrote with a prophetic voice. He shared words of support and issued words of challenge. Given the growing incidence of lifestyle-related health conditions such as heart disease, diabetes, and some types of cancer, as well as the rising costs of health care combined with the lack of access to adequate care many Americans face, we need listening people who can speak with prophetic voices about health in our country. And we need listening people who can take action and propose some solutions with hope.

Remember James? Sharing his story with a friend at church and that friend's active listening didn't suddenly heal his diabetes or make things easier for him. He still had to check his blood sugar and make different choices about food and exercise.

What did change for James was his perception of his situation. Rather than feeling sorry for himself, he started looking at all the possibilities and opportunities before him. He also realized he was not alone, and that nothing could separate him from the love of God. God's promises for him were still for a full and blessed life. This hope helped change James' perspective and gave him a new motivation to get control of his blood sugar. He also gained confidence to start speaking more openly about his health struggles. Sharing his story, and listening to other people's stories, motivated James to think about what he could do in his community to help others struggling with diabetes.

> *Realize you are not alone, and nothing can separate you from the love of God.*

Overview of the book

As you participate in this study, you will have the opportunity to read and reflect on several aspects of health. In Chapter 2, we'll examine our current orientation and motivations for pursuing health and wellness. This may help you discover where you are on your health journey.

Then, in Chapters 3 through 9 we'll focus on how we can be better stewards of our personal health. We'll look at the following topics:

- What does it mean to be "created good"? (Chapter 3)

- Living fully in the body we have been given. (Chapter 4)

- Determining what good health looks like. (Chapter 5)

- Taking advantage of the biblical formula for success with health. (Chapter 6)

- The importance of naming our suffering. (Chapter 7)

- The role of attitude and humor in health. (Chapter 8)

- How our attitudes and approach to death influence our living and keep us from trusting God. (Chapter 9)

In the last three chapters, we'll start thinking about our life and health in the context of community. As Christians, this is an important shift and a critical step in our stewardship journey. We'll look at what happens as we rise to new life in

Christ and are born into the community of believers and how this impacts our health and health care decision making. (Chapter 10) We will also look at the role of life-giving discipline in the context of a loving relationship and how the community of believers plays a critical role in shaping and supporting us as we seek to be healthy, whole, and well. (Chapter 11) Finally, we'll end with some instructions and encouragement for the community of believers as they journey toward greater health and wholeness for all of God's people. (Chapter 12)

Draw closer to the heart of God that you may be able to say with Samuel, who heard God's call in the night, "Speak, for your servant is listening." (1 Samuel 3:10)

Prayer:

Lord, teach me to quiet my heart

that I may listen to the gentle movement

of the Holy Spirit within me

and sense the depths that are of God.

– Elijah De Vidas

Blessings and challenges

1. Name three things you sense God is pleased with about you on your journey toward greater health and wholeness.

2. Name three areas where the Spirit is challenging you to be more loving with how you care for yourself and/or others.

3. Share, as you feel led, about the blessings and challenges you are facing on your health journey.

End questions

1. *What message do you think needs to be shared today about health and health care issues?*

2. *To whom are you listening when it comes to your health and health care decision making? Is this the authority you want to listen to?*

3. *How might you be called to live more faithfully in the context of the body you live, work, and worship in?*

Motivated by Love?

*"God is love. Whoever lives in love lives in God, and God in him.
... There is no fear in love. But perfect love drives out fear."*
(1 John 4:16, 18)

When we place loving God and allowing God to love us as the guiding
and motivating factors in our lives, we become one with God. In this space
there is no room for fear, and fear can no longer control us. Love has the power
to put our actions and decisions about health and wellness, and about health
care, into a different light.

The following story is not necessarily a success story in terms of the outcome
for the patient. I share it, however, because it was instrumental in helping
me understand the difference our source of motivation can make in our lives
and health.

> *When we place loving God and allowing God to love us as the guiding and motivating factors in our lives, we become one with God.*

Bruce came to me for several months for nutritional counseling regarding his
weight. He was successful at weight loss and actually made changes in his diet
that also improved his blood cholesterol levels. At our meetings, I would look
over his food records and give him feedback on ways he could continue to
modify his eating habits, and I encouraged him in the ways I saw him making
wonderful changes. After several meetings, I suggested he was on the right track
and we could afford to have more time between our meetings. At his very next
appointment, however, Bruce had regained some of the weight he had lost. We
scheduled another meeting, but I never saw him again.

There are lots of explanations for what may have happened with Bruce, but as I look back on it, I realize that fear of my disapproval was likely a significant motivating factor for keeping him on track. Possibly, over time, he grew less and less afraid of my disapproval because I didn't become progressively more strict or severe with him. Or perhaps the lengthened time between our appointments gave him more time to escape his fear of my disapproval, and he slipped into old behaviors. Why he ultimately decided not to come in and face me, I will never know. I do wonder what might have happened if I had worked with Bruce on being motivated out of love rather than fear.

For Bruce, and for you, there is the promise that, abundance, not scarcity exists in the kingdom of God. "Because of the Lord's great love we are not consumed, for his compassions never fail. They are new every morning; great is your (God's) faithfulness." (Lamentations 3:22-23) It is precisely this kind of love, overflowing in abundance and steadfast, that we want to sink our roots into. It is this love that enables and empowers us to take on the radical mind frame, attitude, and actions we are called to.

Our source of motivation can make all the difference

When it comes to your health, what motivates you? Do you strike out in search of a closer relationship with God, others, and the created world? Are you trying to make your doctor happy? To get a spouse or parent off your back? To look good for the next big event in your life like a wedding, high school reunion, or vacation? To avoid death? To keep up with your neighbors, friends, or cultural expectations of beauty and health?

According to the Media Awareness Network, we are exposed to more than 3,000 advertisements each day.[1] Many of these ads are for products or services related to our health or our bodies. Often these advertisements prey on our fears and insecurities about our bodies in order to sell us something that promises to improve our health or make us look better. Almost without realizing it, this bombardment can become a driving force for how we make decisions about our bodies, our health, and our use of health care resources.

Ads can become a driving force for how we make decisions about our bodies and our health.

What are you afraid of? Below is a list of some of the common fears we can fall subject to if we're not careful. As you read through the list, ask yourself if these things sound familiar. Have you ever been caught believing them? I know I have.

Fear of rejection – If I'm not thin enough or don't look right, I won't be loved and will be rejected. I won't get the job I want, the mate or friends I desire, or the opportunities I deserve.

Fear of disapproval – If I don't do what the people in my life recommend or value (these people could include a doctor or other health care provider, a boss, peers, a spouse, a parent, etc.), then I won't be a good patient, employee, friend, spouse, child, etc.

Fear of losing control – I could do everything right and still die young (or suddenly) or be left with a disability or disease I have to live with for the rest of my life. I wish there were something I could do to guarantee I will avoid illness, suffering, and pain.

Fear of being alone – I am all alone with my health problems. Nobody cares about me. I have to take things in my own hands because nobody will be there for me. I will have no one to help me in my time of greatest need.

Fear that there won't be enough – When I need health care resources, they won't be there for me. I won't be able to afford the care I need/deserve. My employer doesn't care about me, the medical system and pharmaceutical companies are just trying to get rich, the government can't be depended upon to provide for my needs, I can't ask people in my community to help me.

If fears such as these are what is motivating you to exercise, watch what you eat, or practice stress management, you can become hostage to them. However, for them to be effective, they have to continue to make you afraid.

Kayla was a college student I learned to know. She had seen her mother struggle with low self-esteem related to her weight and watched her mom go on and off diets all her life. Kayla was afraid of having similar struggles, so she carefully watched what she ate. When she went to college, she was no longer around her mother daily and found she enjoyed eating in the cafeteria and going out with friends. Food and eating, for the first time in her life, were actually enjoyable. At the end of the first semester, her weight had gone up five pounds.

We can choose to be rooted in the biblical story of love that tells us we … are created good and loved unconditionally.

Freaked out by her weight gain, Kayla came to talk to me. In the course of our conversation, we discovered she had never really learned to listen to her own internal eating signals of hunger and fullness. She had always relied on having an image of something she was afraid of becoming as her motivation and indicator of when and how much to eat. For Kayla, the answer was a process of learning to listen to her body's internal signals of hunger and fullness and develop some eating behaviors that were not based in fear.

Like Kayla, we all have choices to make. We can choose to be rooted in a fear-based scenario that tells us our bodies are not lovable as they are and can't be trusted to know what they need. Or we can choose to be rooted in the biblical story of love that tells us we can trust our bodies because they are created good and loved unconditionally.

Group questions

1. *What does it mean for us today if we are going to take Lamentations 3:22-23 seriously when we consider our health and health care decisions?*

2. *What would it take for you to believe this promise of abundance is true? Or if you find yourself living in this promise already, how have you been able to do it?*

3. *How would we go about our day differently in taking care of ourselves if we were truly living in the promise of God's love?*

The difference love makes

Fear has the power to make us suspicious and give us an inward focus – effectively closing us down. Love, on the other hand, helps us trust and gives us an outward focus – creating openness to others. In turn, our increased receptivity applies not just to our own bodies, but naturally draws us out into the larger body we are a part of as well.

> *Love ... helps us trust and gives us an outward focus – creating openness to others.*

When we approach our health from the perspective of love, we embrace a way of living that is positive and joy-filled. Just as eating became enjoyable for the first time in Kayla's life when she stopped letting fear rule her food choices, so we can experience the fullness of living God intends for us when we stop letting fear rule *our* choices. To be rooted in love means we trust our bodies and listen to them so they can thrive and function as God created them. Ideas for how to do this will be discussed in the next two chapters.

To be rooted in love also requires the leap of faith that each of our bodies – exactly as they are – are loved by God. It's true. Right now, no matter what you weigh, no matter what your physical abilities are or are not, no matter what your cholesterol level is, regardless of what you have or haven't done as a steward of your health – you are loved by God and your body is loved by God.

> *God does not provide extra love to those who eat well and he does not withhold love from those who don't exercise daily.*

God does not provide extra love to those who eat well and he does not withhold love from those who don't exercise daily. Don't misunderstand. God is pleased when we care for our bodies and use the gifts and resources we have wisely, but doing so does not earn us more love and failing to do so does not cause God to remove his love.

Strangely, this idea may make some of us feel uncomfortable. You may think, for instance, that if you are loved just the way you are, then won't you (and others you think need to make changes!) settle for things as they are and not want to change? Won't you simply be tempted to accept those health behaviors that are hurtful, such as poor eating habits, smoking, or living a sedentary lifestyle, because 'that's just the way I am'?

This is unlikely if we truly believe we are loved. Because then what develops in us is a deep desire for our body to reflect God's love. It is out of that space that we begin to really care for our body and for others, not from a place of fear, guilt, shame, or even from a drive to earn love, but from a place of joy and a place of abundance.

When we are motivated by love, our health goals naturally change from having the most fit and perfect earthly body, to making choices that draw us closer to the heart of God. Unlike some aspects of our health and bodies, such as our genetics, or how tall or short we are, this is a choice we have complete control over!

Prayer:

Lord, you have created life, and you breathe life

into all living things. May my life reflect yours.

Help me find in Jesus the way to you

and to more abundant life.

Amen.

Activity

Key health ideas

For each of the categories listed in the far left-hand column, identify three or four key ideas promoted by each of the groups named in columns 1, 2, and 3.

	Societal/Cultural	Medical/Scientific	Biblical/Theological
Body			
Exercise			
Food and Eating			
Death and Dying			

End questions

1. *What differences do you notice among the messages we receive in each of the columns?*

2. *Which column do you spend the most time "listening" to for messages about food and eating, exercise, your body, and death and dying? Is this where you want to be listening? Are there other places you need to spend more or less time listening?*

3. *How might our health and lifestyle decisions be different if we believed in the promise of love and abundance?*

Sources

1   Media Awareness Network. http://www.media-awareness.ca/english/parents/marketing/advertising_everywhere.cfm.

My Body – Created Good

"For you created my inmost being; you knit me together in my mother's womb. I praise you because I am fearfully and wonderfully made; your works are wonderful, I know that full well." (Psalm 139:13-14)

For some of us, the idea of being "fearfully and wonderfully made" may be easy to believe. Chances are, however, that all of us at one point or another will struggle with the question of how do we fully embrace being "created good?" (Genesis 1:27-28a, 31) How do we even begin to talk about "the gift of health," when the body we have has many "unique" qualities we wish it didn't have or is less than perfect due to illness, injury, genes, or aging?

One way to begin thinking about this is to consider creation. As you observe the whole of creation, it becomes clear that God loves and admires variety and variation. How else do you explain what you see when you walk in the woods or go snorkeling in the ocean? There are more types of plants and animals than you can name and more ways for things to grow and thrive than you can imagine. If you haven't taken a walk in the woods for a while, try going out and looking with God's eyes. The Celtic monk, Saint Columbanus, once said, "If you want to understand the Creator, study creation." Creation speaks loudly of God, who created it.

> *"If you want to understand the Creator, study creation." Celtic monk, Saint Columbanus*

The variation we see in nature is confirmation that God does not make mistakes in the creating process. Even when we are born with, or develop through the normal aging process, a physical body that doesn't look like or work like everyone else's or has genetic traits that are variations on what is considered normal or acceptable, we are a part of what God has created good.

Remembering the truth that, in creating each of us, God made no mistakes can be helpful. Christ lives in each of us (Galatians 2:20) no matter what our physical body looks like or how it functions. Christ doesn't just live in those of us who "look" healthy or engage in all the right practices when it comes to our health.

Helen Keller, a well-known and respected 20th century author and lecturer, was born with sight and hearing, but after falling seriously ill as a young child was left both blind and deaf. Stories from the years immediately following her illness describe an angry and out-of-control child. Some accounts even describe relatives who saw her as a "monster" that needed to be institutionalized.

Helen could easily have spent the rest of her life angry and trapped, not only in her body, but behind the closed doors of an institution. Fortunately, through the love and care of her family and a wonderful teacher, Anne Sullivan, Helen discovered how to overcome her body's physical limitations. She learned to communicate using sign language and Braille and went on to become an internationally known and learned woman who was a powerful advocate for equal rights and opportunities for all, especially people with disabilities. Helen Keller's life story demonstrates what can happen if we don't let the imperfection that befalls our physical bodies limit or define us.[1]

We *all* were destined for a beautiful life. It was never God's desire or intent for the human suffering that often accompanies bodies that are less than "perfect." God's plans are always for good and not harm (Jeremiah 29:11). When we suffer with our imperfect bodies, we can take comfort in knowing God is continually working at restoring to wholeness what was broken when sin entered the world. "I am making everything new!" (Revelation 21:5)

The incarnation of Jesus helps us better understand how God views the body. In the Gospel of John we are told, "And the word became flesh and lived among us, and we have seen his glory, the glory as of a father's only son, full of grace and truth." (John 1:14)

The choice God made to come to earth in the human . . . form of Jesus is an indicator of the good God sees in our physical form and being.

The choice God made to come to earth in the human, bodily form of Jesus is an indicator of the good God sees in our physical form and being, and a reminder that God longs to redeem our earthly bodies. God became known to us in a human body, therefore we need to consider what it means to truly be in our bodies. Chapter 4 will focus more on this, but for now it is enough to know that God created us and loves us in our fully human state, as flawed as we are.

Group questions

1. Share a story of someone who has been an inspiration to you for living fully in a body that is less than perfect by society's standards.

2. What does God's promise to make "all things new" in Revelation mean to you when you think about your body?

3. As you think about the stories of Jesus recorded in the Gospels, what inspires you about how Jesus lived in his body and treated the bodies of others?

The life and teachings of Jesus help us glimpse what living fully in a physical body can be like. The Gospel stories don't include many details about how Jesus lived, but from what is included we can get an overall picture of the lifestyle Jesus led and what some of his daily activities must have been. We know Jesus lived fully in his body – feasting, fasting, and enjoying basic meals of bread and fish with friends and strangers. He walked a lot, talking and teaching on the way. He rested and prayed and often engaged with the disciples and crowds who flocked to see him. He wept, he loved others, he enjoyed life through his body. Jesus prayed that the physical suffering he would endure be taken from him – and yet he took it on. Though we can't fully understand or explain the details of how it happened, his body conquered death.

We know Jesus lived fully in his body … he wept, he loved others, he enjoyed life through his body.

The biblical story tells us our bodies are created good, and that God longs to redeem and bless our bodies. The language we use to describe our bodies, however, often does not reflect this sacred view of the body. Often our language is filled with derogatory words that speak harshly about the body. Here are a few examples. I'm sure you can add others to the list.

- Gut

- Flab

- Beer belly

- Thunder thighs

- Love handles

- Age spots

- Lazy lump

- "Having a bad hair day"

A list like this leaves me wondering what words we might use instead if we were able to see ourselves the way God sees us. Psalm 103:1 tells us to bless God: "Praise the Lord, O my soul; all my inmost being, praise his holy name." Words like these are anything but a blessing offered to God! When we use phrases like this to describe our bodies that are "fearfully and wonderfully made," does it make God feel sad?

Studies show kind words make a difference in how children, animals, and even our household plants respond.

Just as our kind words about God's creation are a blessing to God, studies show kind words make a difference in how children, animals, and even our household plants respond. Surely kind words can do amazing things for our bodies as well! The words we choose to use about our bodies, and the bodies of those around us, can make a big difference in how we live and feel.

These words can especially affect our children — how they grow and develop. These days, it is common to overhear young children repeating negative comments about their bodies based on comments they have heard adults in their lives or on television say. These messages teach us at an early age to distrust our bodies. They teach that, instead of the body being a sacred place where we encounter God and God's goodness, our bodies can become places where we feel judged and inadequate.

> *Instead of the body being a sacred place where we encounter God … our bodies can become places where we feel judged and inadequate.*

When it comes to honoring the goodness of our bodies, one of the most important things adults can do for themselves, as well as for the children in their lives, is resist the cultural temptation to talk about our bodies in ways that are disparaging or negative. There is a difference in saying out loud or to ourselves "my body is _____" (fill in a disparaging comment) and choosing to say, "I praise you for I am fearfully and wonderfully made."

A good spiritual discipline for anyone who wants to honor God is to repeat this phrase from Psalm 139 often, especially when negative thoughts about our bodies spring up. The more often we say it, the more likely we are to start believing it and living it and reflecting it in how we look to others.

Prayer:

Gracious God, thank you for the gift of today.

May my living reveal your goodness.

Amen.

Activity

Body Blessing²

This blessing is designed for use with groups, inviting those present to each find a partner to bless. However, it could also be used by just two people, with one blessing the other. When used with groups, partners should face each other and then ask about the other person's comfort level with being touched. If he or she prefers a non-touch blessing, the other person can simply hold his or her hand near the part of the body being blessed, rather than touching it. As the leader prays each blessing out loud, the partners silently bless one another at the same time. For the last part, each phrase or sentence is repeated after the leader.

Forehead: May you have keen insights and clear thoughts. May your thoughts be kind and wise. May you resolve anything in your mind that keeps you from being your true self.

Ears: May you listen to the inner voice of the beloved and act on the word of God. May you hear the melodies of your own goodness and treasure who you are.

Eyes: May you have inner vision to see more clearly the path that is yours. May you look upon others with love as you search for your way home.

Mouth: May you speak with love, proclaim the truth, and make your needs known. May you laugh at the absurdities of life and taste life with joy and enthusiasm.

Nose: As you inhale and exhale, may you be reminded of the cycle of life with its dying and rising, its emptying and filling. May you breathe in the aroma of goodness and breathe out what needs to be let go.

Hands: May you use your hands to touch all of life with reverence and gratitude. May these hands reach out with care to others. May these hands be willing to receive care from others.

Skin: May you not be too thick-skinned or too thin-skinned as you journey. May you reverence and protect the dignity of others no matter what color of skin they have.

Heart: May you develop awareness of what stirs deep within you. May you have a vibrant, compassionate heart, one that is filled with generosity and kindness.

Feet: As you travel though the many ups and downs of life, may all the places your feet take you lead you to greater transformation and inner freedom. May you develop an ever firmer foundation for your spiritual path.

Leader: I invite you to repeat what I say as words of blessing to your partner.

May the Shelter of God embrace you in your difficult moments. (repeat)

May the Dance of God play in your joyful moments. (repeat)

May the Peace of God be with you wherever you are on your journey of life. (repeat)

Amen! (repeat)

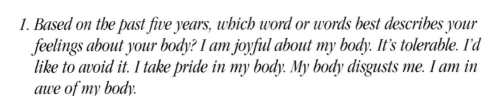

1. *Based on the past five years, which word or words best describes your feelings about your body? I am joyful about my body. It's tolerable. I'd like to avoid it. I take pride in my body. My body disgusts me. I am in awe of my body.*

2. *What words do you hope to use to describe your body in the next five years?*

3. *How has the language you use to describe your body made a difference in how you feel about it and take care of it? Or does it?*

Sources

1   Sources: http://www.afb.org (American Foundation for the Blind), http://www.bartleby.com/65/ke/Keller-H.html, http://www.rnib.org.uk/xpedio/groups/public/documents/publicwebsite/public_keller.hcsp.

2   *Out of the Ordinary: Prayers, Poems, and Reflections for Every Season,* Joyce Rupp. Notre Dame, Ind. Ave Maria Press, 2000.

Be in Your Body

"Do you not know that your body is a temple of the Holy Spirit, who is in you, whom you have received from God?"
(1 Corinthians 6:19)

The verse that opens this chapter is quoted frequently when it comes to health and faith. Often it is used to encourage people to care for their bodies, but far too often the fact that you can't glorify God with your body *if you're not in it* is neglected or overlooked.

We can get disconnected from our bodies in many ways. Our busy North American lifestyles often inhibit us from being intentional and reflective about the activities and choices we make every day.

For some, multitasking has become a way of surviving in this fast-paced world. We drive and eat. We talk on the phone and do just about anything and everything. We watch TV while we work on a project.

> *Doing multiple activities at the same time inevitably means nothing gets our full attention – including our bodies.*

Doing multiple activities at the same time inevitably means nothing gets our full attention – including our bodies. For some, the disconnection may be the result of a body that has been a source of physical or emotional pain. It is a natural human tendency to avoid pain. At times, pain avoidance is an acceptable, temporary method of coping. But if over time avoidance becomes your primary coping strategy, it becomes dangerous. Being a good steward of your health ultimately requires getting back inside your body and facing the pain – or slowing life down to a pace where you can notice what your body may be trying to tell you.

Being a good steward of your health ultimately requires getting back inside your body and facing the pain.

For those who have experienced pain and hurt related to their bodies, facing that pain is especially important and not something you can easily do yourself. Getting help from a trusted friend, pastor, counselor, or spiritual director may be necessary to begin healing.

Whether you feel disconnected from your body or not, you need to be more aware of this issue because we live in a culture that encourages disconnection. We are bombarded by products, pills, diets, and health plans that alter our bodies without addressing the issues that are causing the responses and reactions we're experiencing.

A popular diet and health magazine in America ran an article on intuitive eating. The helpful article encouraged people to listen to their bodies and gave tips and advice on ways to do so, including eating only when you are hungry and stopping when you are full. Ironically, on the page immediately following the article, a photograph of thin and supposedly happy people appeared in an advertisement for appetite-suppressing diet pills. With one picture and less than 30 words, the advertisement contradicted everything written in the three-page article and created an impossible double standard. You cannot know when you are hungry or feel a natural sense of fullness when you are medicated to not have those feelings!

In the last chapter, we noted that God came and lived among us as Jesus (John 1:14), giving us an example of how to live well in our bodies. Jesus walked, taught, feasted, and fasted with others in intentional and meaningful ways. He took time for rest and prayer, and ultimately, when it came to his body, he was willing to give it in sacrifice for the greater good of all humanity. Jesus revealed God's plan for the redemption of the world through his physical body.

Jesus revealed God's plan for the redemption of the world through his physical body.

We, too, are to live fully in our bodies during the time we are given. But we also need to be willing to let go of our earthly bodies when the time comes. It is possible that God's greater purpose for each of us involves a plan where our death is in some way the greatest gift we give to others. Earthly bodies are important, but the biblical story is clear — our earthly bodies are not where we have our hope, nor are they the end of the story. Embracing death is a part of living well (we'll explore this further in Chapter 9).

Group questions

1. What are some of the products, pills, or advertisements you have seen recently that, through their use, encourage a disconnection from our bodies?

2. What impact does our culture and the media have on you personally as you think about your ability to be in your body in a healthy way? How would watching less TV or paying less attention to advertisements influence your ability to pay attention to your body?

3. Imagine yourself spending a day with Jesus. What new awareness of your body would you gain during that day?

Since living in our earthly bodies is an important part of living in this world, we need to know how to do so – or how to get back inside them if need be, so we can go about the business of glorifying God. Psalm 139:23-24 may hold a clue: "Search me, O God, and know my heart; test me and know my anxious thoughts. See if there is any offensive way in me, and lead me in the way everlasting."

"Search me, O God, and know my heart; test me and know my thoughts. See if there is any wicked way in me, and lead me in the way everlasting." (Psalm 139: 23-24)

This prayer acknowledges God in the deepest parts of our being and asks God to lead us from the deepest parts of our being in ways that are good for us. The psalmist asks God to search him – and we too must do our part to search ourselves and engage in intentional acts of awareness to get to know our bodies. When we do this, we can help our bodies function as they are intended.

A client, Diane, helped me learn this lesson. Diane came to see me for help in lowering her cholesterol. While chatting, I asked her about the activities and exercises she did. Diane informed me that she didn't do anything for exercise – and, further, that she wasn't that interested in exercise because it was not enjoyable. After pointing out that exercise can help lower cholesterol levels and promote better health in general, I suggested several things she might try.

Diane was still not interested. From what I could tell, her diet did not need many changes. I suspected she would see the greatest impact on her heart health by doing some sort of regular exercise. But how to get her to do it – that was the challenge! All my questions and suggestions went nowhere. Finally, I asked her what she enjoyed doing when she was little. That she could answer. Diane loved skipping, swimming, and taking walks with her grandfather. Just remembering what her body felt like when it moved, and that there was a time in her life when she enjoyed moving her body, was encouraging to her – and yes, to me, too! Through the years Diane and her body had lost touch. Her challenge now became getting reacquainted with her body and learning from it so she could take better care of it – and enjoy it more!

Our challenge is becoming reacquainted with our bodies and learning from them so we can take better care of them – and enjoy them more!

The most tangible ways I know to talk about or engage in intentional acts of awareness related to our bodies involve experiencing the world through our five senses: tasting, touching, seeing, smelling, and hearing.

Young children, without needing to learn how to do it, explore the world through their five senses from birth. In fact, some experts claim babies recognize who their mother is more by smell, at the very beginning of their life, than by any other sense. In those first few weeks of life, babies are comforted most by being wrapped tightly and held close. And without anyone teaching them how, they root around trying to suckle at the breast for nourishment.

> *Being in bodies and glorifying God with them simply means living with the curiosity of a child.*

As babies grow and develop, they become more adept and complex in their exploring. Because they haven't yet learned to filter or censor themselves, you get the straight-up truth as they taste a sour pickle for the first time, touch a scratchy beard, smell a goat at the fair, hear a blender buzz in the kitchen, or startle at the sight of the large, red brushes in the car wash.

Being in bodies and glorifying God with them simply means living with the curiosity of a child. As we allow ourselves to remember the awe and appreciate the wonder of what it is like to really see, taste, touch, hear, and smell things, our bodies will age and thrive as they were designed to.

Prayer:

Breathing in, I am aware of my heart.

Breathing out, I am aware of my heart.

I vow to eat, drink, and work in ways that preserve

my health and well-being.

– Thich Nhat Hanh

Activity

Celebrating our five senses

This activity is designed to help you slow down, notice, and appreciate your body and all it can do. In our everyday life, we aren't used to doing something like eating a cracker with so much intentionality, so it may feel awkward. If you are able to give yourself some grace and approach it with the curiosity of a child, who knows? You might learn something amazing about your body and how to glorify God with it!

Supplies: Soda crackers (enough so each person has one)

If doing this as a group, one person should be designated the leader. This person will introduce each of the steps and keep the activity focused by reading the questions for each step out loud.

Pass out a cracker to everyone with the instruction to do nothing with it until directed.

Once everyone has a cracker, pause to be grateful, and bring your self into the present moment. The leader might offer a short prayer, or you can simply sit for a few moments in silence.

Step One: Touch the cracker. What does it feel like? Rub your fingers over it. Rub it against your arm or face. Does it feel the same on all sides? (pause for reflection)

Step Two: Look at the cracker. What do you see? What do you notice? How are the sides different? What do the edges look like? (pause for reflection)

Step Three: Smell the cracker. What does it smell like? Does it smell different if you smell if through one nostril or the other or with both? What happens in your body when you smell it? Does it trigger a memory? Does smelling it make you salivate? Can you already start to taste it? (pause for reflection)

Step Four: Listen to the cracker. Using your hands, break the cracker in two. What do you hear? What does the noise make you think of? Experiment with the sound of crackers breaking. Break the cracker in half again, this time listening to the sound of a single cracker breaking compared to the sound of several at once. (pause for reflection)

Step Five: Taste the cracker. Take a bite of the cracker and hold it on your tongue. What happens in your mouth and body? (pause) Slowly start to chew the cracker. What is happening in your mouth? (pause) Now swallow the cracker. Where does the cracker go, and how does your body know how to get it down? (pause for reflection)

Step Six: Finish eating the rest of the cracker, noticing how all five of your senses are engaged in the process.

Discuss what you learned about your body from this experience.

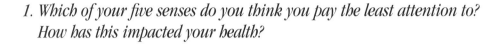

End questions

1. Which of your five senses do you think you pay the least attention to? How has this impacted your health?

2. When was the last time you noticed something unique or special about your body and how it was created?

3. Share an experience you have had watching a young child learn about his or her body and the world through the five senses. What lesson might you learn from this child to help you on your health journey?

What Does Good Health Look Like?

"By contrast, the fruit of the Spirit is love, joy, peace, patience, kindness, generosity, faithfulness, gentleness, and self-control. There is no law against such things." (Galatians 5:22-23, NRSV)

Most of us have been taught to judge our health and the health of others two different ways. The first and most common way we judge how healthy we are (or someone else is) is by how we look or feel. This is easy to do and doesn't cost anything.

The second way is by the report we get from our doctor or other health care provider. This assessment is usually more complex than just how we look or feel. It often involves some medical testing and requires making an appointment and paying a fee.

> *The first and most common way we judge how healthy we are … is by how we look or feel.*

Both of these ways of judging our health have their benefits – and both of them have limitations as well. Neither of them, interestingly enough, offers an assessment of health that is fully adequate based on the definition of health we are using in this book: living fully in the body we have.

Evaluating health based on how we look or feel

For years, I took a magazine advertisement for bottled water with me to the health education classes I taught. It was a black and white picture of a thin, beautiful model in a swimsuit on the beach. She was dressed to look like she had just been exercising, but she was still fresh and lovely in the photo, not sweaty and tired. The caption read, "Another day, another chance to be healthy." I would hold up the advertisement and ask, "How do we know she is healthy?"

The only measure we have to go by from a photo is what the model looks like. Therefore, one could conclude if you looked good, you were healthy. But who knows what her cholesterol level was or her blood sugar? Who knows what activities she was engaged in to maintain her thin figure? There are plenty of unhealthy things people do just to be thin, not to mention diseases that cause people to maintain a sometimes dangerously low body weight. Was the model in the picture happy and satisfied? What was her stress level? Did she belong to a meaningful community or have family support? Was she growing spiritually?

> *There are plenty of unhealthy things people do just to be thin*
> *… to maintain a sometimes dangerously low body weight.*

After some thoughtful reflection, the ad helps make clear that you cannot tell how healthy someone is just by looking. Too often we judge health (and people) in this superficial way, assuming that all thin people are healthy and all heavy people are not.

So, is judging our health by how we feel the answer? It is important to note that our feelings are always real, but they can be influenced by our perceptions and how we view a situation or circumstance. What feels bad to one person can feel good to another. The exact same situation can cause a variety of feelings, depending on the person experiencing it. Listen to your feelings for clues, but don't give them the final say when it comes to your health.

The opportunity to participate in a 5K walk is one example of how our feelings can influence our decisions. Some would say, "Great. Sounds like fun," while others would dread even the thought of it. The person who thinks it would be fun still may have to say no to the opportunity due to knee strain. Meanwhile, the person who dreads the thought of it may just need to be challenged to try something for the first time. It could end up being an enjoyable way to be active when done with a group of friends and to support a cause they feel passionate about. Both examples show the reality that our feelings should be only one part of any health decision we make. (See Appendix for a Wellness Self-check that can help you evaluate your feelings, values, and beliefs about health.)

> *…our feelings should be only one part of any*
> *health decision we make.*

At times, how we look or feel may be good indicators of our health – for instance, if you notice a mole growing in a strange or different way or if you realize that frequent headaches seem to be connected to particular activities or times of the day or month. If you are really living in your body, like we discussed in Chapter 4, you will have a sharper awareness of when things aren't quite working the way they should. These observations remain important indicators to listen to.

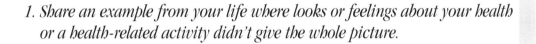

Group questions

1. *Share an example from your life where looks or feelings about your health or a health-related activity didn't give the whole picture.*

2. *Speculate on how that example might have turned out differently if the whole picture was known and/or celebrated.*

Evaluating health based on labs and tests

In a medical context, measures like your weight as compared to your height, body mass index, blood pressure, or laboratory testing levels for cholesterol, blood sugar, or triglycerides, are used to help health care professionals determine someone's level of health. These are all helpful measures in a physical assessment and it is important to have these things monitored by trained medical professionals. We can learn a lot about our risk factors for developing diseases by careful monitoring and basing interventions on the results of these kinds of health screenings and tests. (See Appendix for a listing of recommended health screenings and tests that are important for promoting health and disease prevention.)

> *… medical tests, while quantifiable and measurable, still give only one vantage point for measuring and encouraging health.*

But medical tests, while quantifiable and measurable, still give only one vantage point for measuring and encouraging health. These tests only guess about behaviors and how someone is living. They give possible clues, but say nothing for certain. Not all skinny people exercise daily or eat foods that help prevent disease. Not all people with high cholesterol levels eat high-fat diets.

A temptation also exists to make the test result the sole focus and to use it as the primary motivator in encouraging lifestyle change. When having as goals the desire to reach normal blood sugar numbers or a cholesterol level under 200, my experience as a health educator has taught me that it works for some people, some of the time, but rarely works for anyone over the long term.

A third way to evaluate health

If, as we've stated here earlier, our definition of health is living fully in the body we have, then we need an additional way to evaluate health that reflects the biblical and physical "fullness" we have been talking about. We need a way to assess our health that tells us something more about our lifestyles, what we value, and where we will find the motivation that can sustain lifestyle choices for the long term.

> *We need a way to assess our health that tells us something more about our lifestyles, what we value, and where we find the motivation to sustain lifestyle choices.*

The fruits of the Spirit found in Galatians 5 offer us a great checklist for such an evaluation. Someone who is healthy is sure to reflect these characteristics: love, joy, peace, patience, kindness, generosity, faithfulness, gentleness, and self-control. (Galatians 5:22-23, NRSV)

One of the healthiest people I know reflects these characteristics – and he has incurable cancer. How can I describe Dan as one of the healthiest people I know if he has such a devastating disease? Because more than anyone else, Dan embodies the fruits of the Spirit. It is not something he set out to do on purpose, but it is something I am certain he discovered helped him live well with his diagnosis.

The reality is any of us could die tomorrow. Dan is just more aware that he might be the one who does. In response, he chooses to fully live each day he is given. Dan is someone who tells people when they have touched him in a special way, asks forgiveness when he has done wrong, and notices when something is done well. He appreciates a really good burrito, laughs often, shares his story openly, and is willing to be the first to speak a kind word in a difficult situation. Dan resists the urge to indulge a bad habit for instant gratification and gives hugs to friends and family freely.

> *Why not simply choose to use the fruits of the Spirit as your guide for daily living and evaluation for how you are doing?*

I did not know Dan before his diagnosis, but from what others have said about him, the Dan I now know is the same Dan he was before his diagnosis. Living with an acute awareness of death can be a motivator for how we live. But rather than placing yourself in that shadow day after day to motivate you, why not simply choose to use the fruits of the Spirit as your guide for daily living and evaluation for how you are doing? Chances are you will experience a new vitality and sense of well-being if you do!

Prayer:

Fill me with the fruits of your Spirit, Lord.

Fill me with love, so that I seek to understand and appreciate

the rich variety and diversity of life that surrounds me.

Fill me with joy, so that I celebrate your presence in

each and every moment I am on this earth.

Fill me with peace, so that I know how to ease those

angry urges that well up inside me.

Fill me with patience, so that I stop rushing long enough to witness

your miraculous works taking place all around and within me.

Fill me with kindness, so that I take the extra time to help the

one in need, even when it isn't convenient for me.

Fill me with faithfulness, so that I place my mind, heart, and

all that I do in the service of your gospel.

Fill me with gentleness, so that others know I believe in a God

who loves and cares for all people.

Fill me with self-control, so that I act not on my impulses and urges,

but rather on my beliefs and values, which are rooted in you.

Fill me with these fruits of your spirit, Lord.

Amen.[1]

Activity

Embodying the fruits of the Spirit

Think again about the magazine advertisement mentioned earlier in this chapter. If you were to determine the "healthiness" of that model based on the fruits of the Spirit, what would be the measurable indicators you would be looking for? In other words, what does it mean to live a life that embodies love, joy, peace, patience, kindness, generosity, faithfulness, gentleness, and self-control?

Below, identify ways you can tell if a person embodies each quality. For example, you may want to list the types of behaviors and activities he or she would engage in on a regular basis or the kinds of things you might overhear other people saying about him or her.

Love:

Joy:

Peace:

Patience:

Kindness:

Generosity:

Faithfulness:

Gentleness:

Self-control:

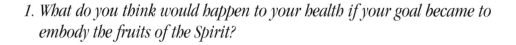

End questions

1. *What do you think would happen to your health if your goal became to embody the fruits of the Spirit?*

   a. *What might happen to the labs and measures your doctor and health care providers monitor?*

   b. *What effect would it have on how you feel?*

   c. *What would it do to the picture of you that everyone sees?*

2. *Which of the fruits of the Spirit do you feel particularly drawn to work on?*

3. *Which of the fruits of the Spirit seem particularly important at this time for improving the health of those in your community?*

Sources

1   Taken from *Caregiving Chronicle,* Editor Beverly John-Driver. November/December 2004, Vol. 2, Issue 6.

Formula for Success –
Sabbath and Shalom

"Remember the Sabbath day by keeping it holy. Six days you shall labor and do all your work, but the seventh day is a Sabbath to the LORD your God. On it you shall not do any work." (Exodus 20:8-10)

God desires us to live with a healthy rhythm in our lives that includes work, play, eating, exercise, worship, prayer, rest, and service. This healthy rhythm helps us observe Sabbath in our lives. God also desires that we see our existence as interconnected, not compartmentalized. This is evident in the biblical concept of shalom. This chapter will look at both of these concepts and why they are needed for good health. When it comes to our health, I can almost imagine God saying, "Take these two seriously and call me in the morning."

> *A healthy rhythm in our lives that includes work, play, eating, exercise, worship, prayer, rest, and service ... helps us observe Sabbath.*

Sabbath

From the beginning of Genesis, we are instructed about healthy life rhythms. "And God blessed the seventh day and made it holy, because on it he rested from all the work of creating that he had done." (Genesis 2:3)

The children of Israel remembered the example God set in the creation story and sought to follow it. The instructions are clear:

Remember the Sabbath day by keeping it holy. Six days you shall labor and do all your work, but the seventh day is a Sabbath to the Lord your God. On it you shall not do any work, neither you, nor your son or daughter, nor your manservant or maidservant, nor your animals, nor the alien within your gates. For in six days the Lord made the heavens and the earth, the sea, and all that is in them, but he rested on the seventh day. Therefore the Lord blessed the Sabbath day and made it holy. (Exodus 20:8-11)

We are to be engaged in the work and activities of living, but we are also to rest.

The same pattern of engagement and rest is found in Jesus. After a big day of teaching and feeding a crowd of 5,000, Jesus is clear about what he needs. "Immediately Jesus made his disciples get into the boat and go on ahead of him to Bethsaida, while he dismissed the crowd. After leaving them, he went up on a mountainside to pray." (Mark 6:45-46) Jesus modeled how to be actively engaged with his work and people, while still taking time out for rest and prayer.

Jesus modeled how to be actively engaged with his work and people, while still taking time out for rest and prayer.

I know a dean at a seminary in Ohio, who routinely powers off all the computers in his office during the weekend because he read that even machines need a full rest. In my own limited experience with using a computer, I know sometimes all you can do to get things up and working again is to turn it off and let it rest a minute. Somehow when you turn it back on, it works. Rebooting can do wonders for computers – and us!

However, Sabbath is not just about resting and rebooting. Sabbath is about trusting God to take care of what must be done, and not falling into an exaggerated sense of our own importance that says if we don't do it, the world will fall apart. When we learn to let go and allow God to be in control, it is the first step in learning to make choices that allow us to live fuller lives.

Sabbath is not just about resting and rebooting. Sabbath is about trusting God to take care of what must be done.

It can be tempting to say yes to everything that feels important in our lives, but when we say yes to everything that presents itself we are actually saying no to a lot of things – things that may be more important to us, but just aren't presenting themselves as urgently. Think of it like a phone that keeps ringing. We continue to answer it, even though it has voice mail, until we've worked right through lunch, our window of time to exercise, or the opportunity to get to bed at a decent hour.

Making room for Sabbath in our lives has to be intentional. Activities, tasks, and responsibilities can take over and crowd out important parts of our lives – like our health – unless we draw some boundaries. One sign that someone is successful at being a good steward of his or her health is that healthy boundaries have been established with the different parts of life.[1]

Jean was never able to eat a balanced breakfast in the morning. More times than not, she would stop by fast food restaurants on her way to work or eat high-fat, high-sugar snacks at her first morning break. It wasn't that she didn't have wholesome things to eat at home or that she was getting up late. The problem was the lack of healthy boundaries with her family about what she could – and could not – do to help them get out the door on time in the morning.

After discovering this connection between her choices in the morning, Jean decided to make some changes. She decided to take 15 minutes every morning to sit down in a calm and quiet manner and eat breakfast, instead of spending that time looking for lost school books, ironing a shirt required for the day that was not hung up like it should have been, or trying to solve whatever the current crisis for the day was. It was painful at first, but eventually her family learned.

After a few tears and a few missed breakfasts themselves, they learned that if they wanted to make it out the door on time and eat breakfast, they needed to be more prepared the night before or get up earlier to get what they needed done. By creating a healthy boundary for herself of what she would be able to help with in the mornings, Jean changed from reacting to things and "putting out fires" to living a life with more intentionality and purpose. She got breakfast and a few minutes of calm at the start of her day. Eating breakfast at home also saved her both calories and money. After instituting that one change in her morning routine, she discovered a month later she had lost four pounds and calculated a monthly savings of at least $25.

By creating a healthy boundary for herself … Jean changed from reacting to things … to living a life with more … purpose.

As Christians, we can fall into the trap of justifying our busy schedules or denying our own needs for the sake of serving others. The reality is that this type of living actually isn't about what is good for us or others. It reinforces a way of living and being that doesn't promote health. This style of living is not about others – it's about making ourselves feel important. It's about believing our families, churches, work, and friendships can't go on without us. But, if we are the ones trying to hold all things together, then we're trying to take God's job!

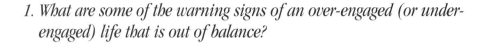

Group questions

1. What are some of the warning signs of an over-engaged (or under-engaged) life that is out of balance?

2. What are some examples of some boundaries you could set in your life that could have direct or indirect influence on your health?

Shalom

Frequently, shalom gets translated as peace. But it is more than that. Living with a biblical awareness of shalom is about realizing the deep interconnectedness that exists in life and how all our lifestyle choices are related. Our physical health is not a separate part of us that can be changed, fixed, or altered without taking into account the whole of our lives and our environment. Sabbath is about finding and establishing a healthy rhythm, or balance, in our lives.

Living with a biblical awareness of shalom is about realizing the deep interconnectedness that exists in life.

The biblical vision of shalom speaks to the conditions that allow all living things to reach their highest potential of wholeness. Therefore, you could say, true health is about being in right relationship with the entire created world.[2] In other words, we can't pollute our environment and not expect to see rises in cancer rates. Or, we can't consistently work 50-60 hour workweeks and not expect our relationships and exercise habits to be affected.

Leviticus may not be a book of the Bible many of us turn to often, but it is a book concerned with living in right relationship with God. In it we find a beautiful vision of a new Eden where God will again live and walk among us if we keep God's commandments. Leviticus 26:2-13 (*The Message*) describes a vision of shalom where all needs are met and illness and suffering are no more:

2 Keep my Sabbaths; treat my Sanctuary with reverence. I am God.

3-5 If you live by my decrees and obediently keep my commandments, I will send the rains in their seasons, the ground will yield its crops and the trees of the field their fruit. You will thresh until the grape harvest and the grape harvest will continue until planting time; you'll have more than enough to eat and will live safe and secure in your land.

6-10 I'll make the country a place of peace—you'll be able to go to sleep at night without fear; I'll get rid of the wild beasts; I'll eliminate war. You'll chase out your enemies and defeat them: Five of you will chase a hundred, and a hundred of you will chase ten thousand and do away with them. I'll give you my full attention: I'll make sure you prosper, make sure you grow in numbers, and keep my covenant with you in good working order. You'll still be eating from last year's harvest when you have to clean out the barns to make room for the new crops.

11-13 I'll set up my residence in your neighborhood; I won't avoid or shun you; I'll stroll through your streets. I'll be your God; you'll be my people. I am God, your personal God who rescued you from Egypt so that you would no longer be slaves to the Egyptians. I ripped off the harness of your slavery so that you can move about freely.

Psalm 85 is another place to go in your Bible to get a glimpse of the shalom that is possible for God's faithful people. Where your Bible may use the word "peace" in Psalm 85, it can also be translated "shalom." When you read this Psalm using the word shalom, you realize God has a much more comprehensive view of our human condition and desires more for us than we can begin to imagine in our fragmented understanding of life.

¹ You showed favor to your land, O Lord;
   you restored the fortunes of Jacob.
² You forgave the iniquity of your people
   and covered all their sins. Selah.
³ You set aside all your wrath
   and turned from your fierce anger.
⁴ Restore us again, O God our Savior,
   and put away your displeasure toward us.
⁵ Will you be angry with us forever?
   Will you prolong your anger through all generations?
⁶ Will you not revive us again,
   that your people may rejoice in you?
⁷ Show us your unfailing love, O Lord,
   and grant us your salvation.
⁸ I will listen to what God the Lord will say;
   he promises peace to his people, his saints –
   but let them not return to folly.
⁹ Surely his salvation is near those who fear him,
   that his glory may dwell in our land.
¹⁰ Love and faithfulness meet together;
   righteousness and peace kiss each other.
¹¹ Faithfulness springs forth from the earth,
   and righteousness looks down from heaven.
¹² The Lord will indeed give what is good,
   and our land will yield its harvest.
¹³ Righteousness goes before him
   and prepares the way for his steps. (Psalm 85)

These Scriptures teach us that shalom can be achieved when we are faithful to God's commands. We will discuss these commands further in Chapter 11. Psalm 85 also suggests in the relationships of love and faithfulness meeting, righteousness and shalom kissing, and faithfulness coming up from the ground to meet righteousness coming down from the sky (verses 10-11), that you can't be broken in one part of your life and not have it affect all the other parts of your life. The hopeful side of this is that you can make a positive difference in multiple areas of your life by simply being more intentional in one area. I learned the power of this interconnectedness when I made a commitment to eat with my grandparents every Monday night.

Shalom can be achieved when we are faithful to God's commands.

A number of years ago, I found myself not eating very well despite my background and training as a dietitian. At the time, I was living by myself and did not enjoy cooking and eating alone. I discovered my grandparents were having a difficult time with meals, too, but for a different reason. Their advancing age was keeping them from cooking and eating a variety of foods. I decided to start taking a meal to their house once a week and eating dinner with them. As it turned out, it did much more for all of us than just getting us to eat better.

The best part of our meals together was not that our stomachs ended up full, but that our times of sharing food together also left us feeling more emotionally, socially, and spiritually satisfied. This regular discipline of eating with my grandparents taught me how interconnected my eating habits were with the social, emotional, and spiritual parts of my well-being. I am grateful for the opportunity to eat with them and for the knowledge I gained about my own health.

Prayer:

Teach me my God and King,
in all things Thee to see
and in what I do in anything,
to do it as for Thee.

– George Herbert, 17th century

Activity

Wellness wheel

Each of the spokes on this wellness wheel represents a part of your health and wellness. Place a dot on each of the spokes indicating where you see yourself.

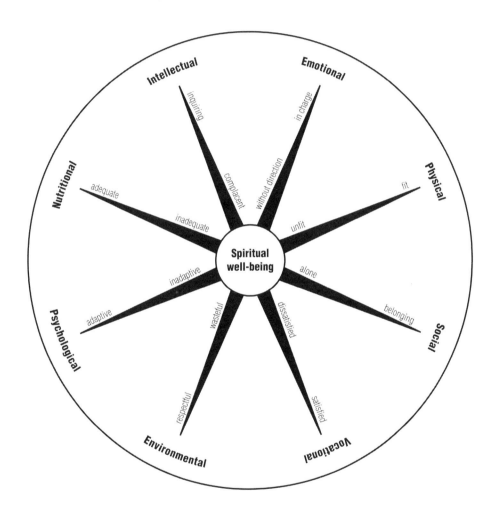

When you have placed all the dots, draw a line to connect the dots.

In the center, where it says spiritual well-being, write a number between one and 10, with "one" meaning as far away from God as you can imagine and "10" being as close to God as you can imagine.

Activity (cont.)

List the characteristics of a well-working wheel.

What is the purpose of the hub of a wheel?

Evaluate your wheel

What does your wellness wheel look like? Does it make a circle? Or is it lopsided? Does it have a flat spot? How big is your circle? How many of the characteristics of a good wheel does your wheel have? A bigger, rounder wheel rolls further with less effort. Do you have a strong and well-working hub? What happens if your wheel has a weak hub?

If you find your wheel is in need of repair, there are several ways to go about fixing it. Sometimes the best way is to take a direct approach and target the area where you are struggling or weak. And sometimes, due to the interconnectedness of all life that the biblical concept of shalom suggests, you can make a difference in one area simply by being more intentional in another area.

Select one spoke on your wheel of health where you would like to see changes. What is one thing you could do this week to strengthen this spoke?

End questions

1. *How might thinking about your health in the context of shalom change how or why you do something?*

2. *Describe someone you know who you think is living a life following the biblical prescription of Sabbath and shalom?*

   a. *How do you think they got to that place?*

   b. *What kinds of choices do you observe them making that help them do this?*

Sources

1   A good resource for learning how to create healthy boundaries in your life is the book, *Boundaries: When to Say YES, When to Say NO, to Take Control of Your Life,* by Christian authors Dr. Henry Cloud and Dr. John Townsend.

2   Definition according to Erland Waltner. "Health and Wholeness in Christ" Health Assembly presentation at Mennonite World Conference, Strasbourg, France, 1984.

Naming Our Suffering, Finding Healing

"Then the woman, knowing what had happened to her, came and fell at his feet and, trembling with fear, told him the whole truth. He said to her, 'Daughter, your faith has healed you. Go in peace and be freed from your suffering.'" (Mark 5:33-34)

"Then the woman, seeing that she could not go unnoticed, came trembling and fell at his feet. In the presence of all the people, she told why she had touched him and how she had been instantly healed. Then he said to her, 'Daughter, your faith has healed you. Go in peace.'" (Luke 8:47-48)

These two accounts of the biblical story of the woman who touches Jesus and is healed are similar enough that we know it must be the same story, but Mark and Luke each offer something significant worth noting. Mark highlights the telling of the "whole truth" while Luke highlights that "in the presence of all the people" she made her confession of why she touched Jesus and the healing that took place when she touched him. Perhaps both of these elements are necessary to our own healing process?

When we can honestly name our pain and suffering in the presence of God and others, we arrive at a place God already is and can then begin to see God at work healing and transforming our lives. The story of the woman who risked everything to touch Jesus and was healed because she dared to seek healing, shows what can happen if we choose to speak the truth and believe healing is possible.

> When we can honestly name our pain and suffering … we arrive at a place God already is and can then begin to see God at work healing … our lives.

The unnamed and unclean hemorrhaging woman from the Gospels took a serious religious and social risk just to touch Jesus. And then, as if that wasn't enough, Jesus boldly calls out into the crowd asking her to identify herself as the one who touched him. Instead of running or hiding, she falls to her feet trembling – and speaks the truth. To her surprise, and the crowd's astonishment, Jesus responds in love. When we risk being honest with God, we will be met with love. Wouldn't it be nice if all of life's risks were guaranteed to have such an outcome!

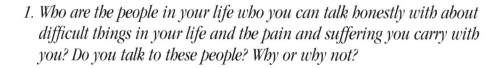

Group questions

1. *Who are the people in your life who you can talk honestly with about difficult things in your life and the pain and suffering you carry with you? Do you talk to these people? Why or why not?*

2. *How does being able to name and acknowledge the larger suffering and sin that exists in the world change how we live our personal lives and our sense of health and well-being?*

Truth telling

One of the ways the church has encouraged people to practice this kind of honesty is through healing prayers and anointing with oil. The church takes its instruction for doing this from James 5:14-16. Some churches do this once a month, others once a week, or as a part of a communion service. If you have not had the opportunity to be part of a healing service with anointing, it is something worth requesting from your church leadership.

> *We all have this need to be part of a healing Christian community.*

No matter what your current state of health is, you still have a reason and need to be part of a service of healing and wholeness that prays for forgiveness and petitions God for healing on behalf of our broken sinful world and ourselves. We all have this need to be part of a healing Christian community.

Key components of a healing service based on the James text include:

• Call together the elders of the church.

• Pray together.

• Anoint with oil.

• Confess sin and name suffering.

• The Lord raises up the sick and forgives sins.

Confession of sin is named in James as an important component of our suffering and request for healing. This is because all illness and suffering is connected to sin. However, please note, not all sin that causes disease, illness, suffering, or trial comes from *personal* sin. Naming what is broken in us personally, what is broken in us as part of the larger human family, and what is broken in our world should be considered as part of our quest for healing and wholeness.

The cause of our illness is as likely to come from collective sin that is part of being from a broken world touched by the results of original sin as it is from a personal sin we have committed. We live in a broken world. All of us are vulnerable to illness, disease, and physical trial as a result, and we all need healing. Consider the child born with a heart defect, or the person with lung cancer who never smoked a day in her life and has no family history of cancer, or the growing number of children in this country who are more vulnerable to developing diabetes because of the culture they were born into.

We live in a broken world. All of us are vulnerable to illness, disease, and physical trial as a result, and we all need healing.

In our broken, wounded, diseased, and less than perfect state, we frequently keep God and others shielded from the truth of our hurting, wounded, and dying selves. We go about our lives thinking as long as we are happy and good people and don't draw attention to our brokenness we are being loving toward God and others. But ironically, the way we truly love God and others is by letting them love us – the real us. That means living honestly and facing the unnamed skeletons in our lives, families, and communities and risking naming the full, non-exaggerated truth.

Another part to our truth telling is being able to clearly identify what in us needs healing. In Mark we have the story of Bartimaeus, a blind beggar, who cries out to Jesus to have mercy on him. After getting Jesus' attention, Bartimaeus hears Jesus say, "What do you want me to do for you?" Bartimaeus replies, "Rabbi, I want to see." And Jesus answers saying, "Go, your faith has healed you." (Mark 10:46-52)

What do you think would have happened if Bartimaeus had instead said to Jesus, "I don't like sitting by the roadside. I'm tired of people walking by and ignoring me. I don't like sleeping on the hard dirt, and I never get anything good to eat. I'm fed up with this life, I deserve a better one."

Instead of complaining about the consequences of being blind and blaming his troubles on someone else, Bartimaeus asked for healing where he needed it, and Jesus responded with mercy.

While naming the truth in our lives will always have healing potential and power, it doesn't guarantee our pain and suffering will be taken from us. We can, however, be assured that God hears and answers our prayers (Psalm 65:2, 5). Just because we ask for healing doesn't mean we will receive it the way we think, or the way we wish. God answers prayer in God's way. This means we may live in a body that, despite our prayers, continues to carry with it illness, disability, or pain.

Just because we ask for healing doesn't mean we will receive it the way we think, or the way we wish.

In 2 Corinthians 12:9-10, we are invited to be united with Christ in our suffering. "'My grace is sufficient for you, for my power is made perfect in weakness.' Therefore I will boast all the more gladly about my weaknesses, so that Christ's power may rest on me. That is why, for Christ's sake, I delight in weaknesses, in insults, in hardships, in persecutions, in difficulties. For when I am weak, then I am strong." Through joining with Christ, we are made strong and are no longer alone. Our suffering joins us in solidarity with all who suffer.

Frank, a man I knew from church, lived with terrible pain. The pain continued despite seeking advice from doctor after doctor. Frank was often down and frequently asked for prayers for his pain to be taken away. When his pain was controlled, it was easier for Frank to see God loved him and cared for him. But when the pain came back with a fury, God felt distant and Frank felt abandoned. One day Frank made a significant spiritual breakthrough when someone else at church shared a tragic story of pain and suffering.

During prayer time, Frank offered to pray for Ed since pain was something Frank knew well. Frank prayed a beautiful prayer, and I was reminded of the suffering Christ who came to be with us in our pain and who strengthens us in our suffering. I imagine Frank still lives with pain. I don't go to church with him anymore, but I trust God is still working in his life for healing and I hope he has continued in his prayer ministry for those who live with pain.

> *Our God is a God who was willing to take on human form and human suffering to show us how much we are loved.*

One of the unique marks of Christianity is that our God is a God who was willing to take on human form and human suffering to show us how much we are loved. A favorite quote of mine comes from French poet and writer Paul Claudel: "Jesus did not come to do away with suffering or remove it. He came to fill it with His presence." I like this quote because it addresses the temptation to expect Jesus to be the kind of Savior who keeps us from suffering. We often set ourselves up to test God's love for us by how pain-free our lives are, but that is not how God works. The painful parts of our lives are also times of drawing closer to the heart of God.

Prayer:

Lord, we pray for courage…

courage to name the wounded and broken parts

of our lives and in our world.

We ask for healing and trust in your redeeming power.

Amen.

Activity

Speaking truth

The reflection for this activity can be done as a private pen and paper activity or, depending on the comfort level of group participants with each other, sharing out loud may feel appropriate. Be sure everyone has paper and something to write with.

Sit quietly with your eyes closed while the leader reads the following paragraph:

Imagine yourself in a safe and comfortable space. A favorite place, perhaps. A place where you feel loved. (pause) Now imagine Jesus coming to join you in this place. The two of you are just "hanging out" enjoying all that makes this place a good place to be. (pause) After awhile you find a comfortable place to sit in a quiet and private area. (pause) When you are resting comfortably, Jesus turns to you and says, "What is the whole truth you need to speak?"

Spend 5 to 10 minutes resting in that question.

Write down what comes to you. You may choose to keep this truth between you and Jesus right now, or you may choose to share it with people in your study group, your pastor, spouse, friend, or family member.

At the close of this activity, speak the words of Jesus aloud that he said to the hemor-rhaging woman, but are also for you: "Go in peace and be healed."

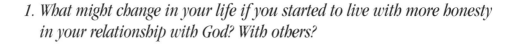

End questions

1. What might change in your life if you started to live with more honesty in your relationship with God? With others?

2. What is the difference between complaining and naming your suffering?

3. What difference can it make in our prayers for healing when we are able to name honestly and accurately the healing we need and desire from God?

Attitude and Humor

"A cheerful heart is good medicine, but a crushed spirit dries up the bones." (Proverbs 17:22)

Unlike machines, God has gifted humans with the ability to choose our responses to life. This gift makes it possible to take ourselves and life lightly, especially when faced with situations beyond our control. While God created the world good, God did not create the world, or us, perfect. Instead, God created us with a sense of humor and gives us the opportunity to choose how we respond to stressful and painful situations. Attitude and humor are gifts from God that make it possible to live a rich and blessed life despite the imperfections, stresses, and struggles we face each day.

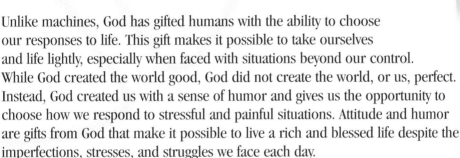

God created us with a sense of humor and gives us the opportunity to choose how we respond to stressful and painful situations.

Attitude

Charles Swindoll, pastor and writer, is well known for these words on attitude:

"The longer I live, the more I realize the impact of attitude on life. Attitude is more important than facts. It is more important than the past, than education, than money, than circumstances, than failures, than successes, than what other people think, say, or do.

"It is more important than appearance, giftedness or skill. It will make or break a church ... a home. The remarkable thing is we have a choice every day regarding the attitude we will embrace for that day. We cannot change our past ... we cannot change the fact that people will act in a certain way. We cannot change the inevitable.

"The only thing we can do is play on the one string we have, and that is our attitude ... I am convinced that life is 10 percent what happens to me and 90 percent how I react to it. And so it is with you ... we are in charge of our attitudes."

Choosing gratitude

One practice that will help you develop an attitude of gratitude is practicing the spiritual discipline of keeping a gratitude journal. It doesn't need to be a time-intensive or complicated thing to do. Just simply name and record five things you are grateful for each day. You can either select a small notebook to write in (and keep it somewhere handy, especially at first), or take advantage of some online opportunities to journal. A simple search on the Internet will result in several Web sites that offer a place to record the five things you are grateful for each day.

Name and record five things you are grateful for each day.

The regular practice of this discipline of developing an attitude of gratitude can do several things for you:

- Change your perspective.

- Draw attention to the positive.

- Point to the reality that every day includes both bad and good moments.

- Over time, provide you with a wonderful and encouraging record of all the blessings and ways God has been faithful in your life.

As a child, I remember taking turns around the dinner table or at bedtime prayers when we were little, sharing our "happy moment" for the day. I can remember times when I was not in a particularly good mood, and when it came my turn to share, I struggled to think of one good thing from the day. My response on days like those was often, "Today is almost over!" Not exactly a happy declarative, but it was my perception of reality and was graciously received by my parents. Having to name something, even if it was that the day was almost over, taught me an important lesson: There is always something to be grateful for!

I went off to college, started life on my own, and drifted away from that particular family routine. It wasn't until later when I was a seminary student and a teaching assistant for a college-level course on spiritual care and healing that I encountered the gratitude discipline again. The professor required all students to keep a gratitude journal for the semester, and I decided to do it, too, as the teaching assistant in the class. It was tedious at first. I discovered at times, just like when I was a child, the only things I could be grateful for was that the day was over or that the coffee had been hot that morning. But the more the weeks went by, the more I appreciated being drawn into that space where, no matter what awful or challenging things had happened that day, I was making a choice to look at the whole of my life from the perspective of gratitude.

> *No matter what awful or challenging things had happened that day, I was making a choice to look at the whole of my life … with gratitude.*

At the end of the course, I thanked the professor for the assignment. I didn't have to do it as the teaching assistant, but the fact that it was part of the course requirements inspired and challenged me to return to a childhood discipline in a helpful adult way. The professor was not surprised by my comments. She shared with me that of all the assignments she covered in this class designed to help students going into healing and caregiving careers, the gratitude journal assignment was the one she received the most consistent positive feedback about. She noted it was not uncommon to have former students come up years later and thank her for that assignment.

Through the years, my work in health care has given me many opportunities to see how people respond to illness, injury, and disease – particularly through the attitudes they choose. While working at a cancer center, I got to know Vickie, whose husband had died of lung cancer. Shortly after his death, she was diagnosed with breast cancer. Like other cancer patients, Vickie faced several options upon hearing this news. Unlike many others, Vickie chose to view her cancer through a positive attitude. She called it a blessing.

A blessing? I admit Vickie's attitude is one I would be challenged to choose were I in her shoes. But Vickie was serious. On more than one occasion, I remember her saying, "I thank God for my cancer daily and what it has taught me." Her remarkable attitude made an impact on the life she was living, and I know it also made a powerful impact on the staff who cared for her and the other patients she interacted with when she came in for treatments.

Her choice didn't make her life a bed of roses. There were still days when Vickie was down and depressed. But she played beautifully the one string she did have control over – her attitude – and it made music all could hear. Several years later, Vickie's story continues to inspire me to practice an attitude of gratitude and to continue working on cultivating this discipline on a daily basis.

Group questions

1. What is your typical response to difficult or challenging situations?

   a. Where, or from whom, do you think you learned this?

   b. If this is not how you'd like to respond to challenging situations, what would you like to change?

2. Have you ever kept anything similar to a gratitude journal?

   a. If yes, how did the practice change you or help you?

   b. If no, what is the most challenging part of keeping a gratitude journal for you and how might you be able to overcome this challenge?

A prescription for humor

Biblical wisdom literature has long told us what modern science is now proving: "A cheerful heart is good medicine ..." (Proverbs 17:22). If laughter is such an essential and universal prescription, you had better check to be sure your health plan covers it, because a regular, daily dose is required for general good health and healing.

Laughter affects the body, mind, and spirit. Mark Twain captured the relationship between them succinctly in this quote attributed to him from a variety of sources, "The human race has only one really effective weapon, and that's laughter. The moment it arises, all our hardnesses yield, all our irritations and resentments slip away, and a sunny spirit takes their place." Our health and wholeness depend on our choice of attitude and being able to laugh.

"A cheerful heart is good medicine ..." (Proverbs 17:22).

Laugh yourself well?

Researchers claim young children laugh an average of 300 to 400 times a day. By the time we're adults, we laugh (on average) only 12 to 15 times a day. Apparently, as we age we start to take life too seriously and forget to be playful and to look at life's funny side. Need help remembering that playful, funny side of life? Try this prescription: Spend 15 minutes with some diluted dishwashing detergent, a bubble wand, and a small child.

Research on laughter and health claims the 15 minutes you spend laughing while you blow and chase bubbles isn't just for fun. It stimulates both the respiratory and cardiovascular systems, relaxes your muscles, reduces your blood pressure, and strengthens your immune system. It can also aid in combating depression and anxiety.

Laughing stimulates the respiratory and cardiovascular systems, relaxes your muscles, reduces your blood pressure, and strengthens your immune system.

So why aren't you laughing more? If you have forgotten how to laugh, or if you sense laughing more would help you heal on your wellness journey, then surround yourself with people who know how to laugh! "Laughter begets laughter." So even if you have to fake it a bit at first, it won't be long before you'll likely be experiencing hearty and genuine laughter. Not everything this contagious is good for you, but laughter is – and thank God!

> *Not everything ... contagious is good for you, but laughter is – and thank God!*

Probably the best known biblical story of laughter is found in the Old Testament story of Sarah. In Genesis, Chapter 18, we learn about Sarah's struggles with infertility. Her story is a painful one that led her to do some extreme things. It wasn't until late in life, long after her child-bearing years seemed to be past that she finally gave birth to Isaac. When she heard God was going to make this happen for her, her first response was to laugh.

Have you ever been in a situation where something you have wanted – and long ago given up on – is about to come true? In these situations, many of us can only shake our heads and laugh in disbelief. I imagine Sarah shaking her head in this kind of joyful disbelief. The absurdity and awe of what God was promising was almost too much. Out of fear she denied her laughter, but God is persistent and faithful and brought a child into Sarah and Abraham's lives.

God longs for us to have the desires of our hearts (Psalm 37:4) and continually works at bringing about our healing and wholeness. Because of this our desires are sometimes fulfilled in unexpected ways. God's sense of humor in this story about Abraham and Sarah, and the birth of a child in old age, is expressed in doing what seemed impossible. I can imagine God saying, "See, I can do shocking and marvelous things. Just watch me!"

This story also suggests that laughing with God requires openness. If God is always working at bringing healing and wholeness into our lives, then we need to be prepared for the strange and unexpected ways it may enter our lives and be willing, like Sarah, to laugh along with God – even when we are afraid.

Prayer:

God grant me the serenity

to accept the things I cannot change;

courage to change the things I can;

and wisdom to know the difference.

Living one day at a time;

enjoying one moment at a time;

accepting hardships as the pathway to peace;

taking, as He did, this sinful world

as it is, not as I would have it;

trusting that He will make all things right

if I surrender to His Will;

that I may be reasonably happy in this life

and supremely happy with Him

forever in the next.

Amen.

– Reinhold Niebuhr

Activity

Practice laughing

Set aside at least 15 minutes to share jokes and funny stories. If you think you may have trouble getting the humor rolling, try this: Buy a bag of Laffy Taffy candies and start out reading aloud the jokes submitted by children printed on the wrappers.

Other possible resources to get the giggles going:

• *Menno-Lite: A Humorous Look at Mennonite Life,* by Merle Good, Rebecca Good, and Kate Good.

• Christian comedians, like Ted (Swartz) and Lee (Eshleman). Their theatrical comedy sketches are available on video/DVD from the MMA Bookstore (www.bookstore.mma-online.org).

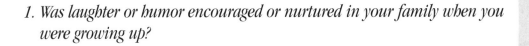

End questions

1. *Was laughter or humor encouraged or nurtured in your family when you were growing up?*

   a. *If yes, what place does play, laughter, and humor have in your life now?*

   b. *If no, how might this be impacting the degree of health you are currently experiencing?*

2. *Share about a time in your life where God worked in an amazing or unexpected way to bring healing that left you speechless or laughing.*

Death and Dying

"For as in Adam all die, so in Christ all will be made alive."
(1 Corinthians 15:22)

We are all born human like Adam – therefore death and dying
are part of the human experience. Yet, in Christ, we know death
is not the end of the story.

Friends sent me photos of their two-month-old daughter after going on a
family outing in the woods to look for wild, edible mushrooms. While there,
their baby's foot brushed up against a wild raspberry bush, and she ended up
with a small cut. They took a picture of it and sent it along with others from
their outing. The only thing in the picture was a precious little foot with a wee
small scratch, but that picture spoke loudly of the reality of this world. It was a
picture of new life, but you could also see it as a picture of death or a reminder
of our mortality.

Being born into this world means we will experience pain and suffering – and
eventually death. My friends instinctively noticed something significant had happened to their little girl who had not yet been touched by the pain of this world,
and they took a photo of it. Even the most careful and loving parents cannot protect their children from pain, suffering, and death. Freedom from death can be
achieved only in the life to come that is promised through Jesus.

> *Freedom from death can be achieved only in the life to come
> that is promised through Jesus.*

The losses we experience in this world may take on different forms. They
may be personal, relational, or physical. Death ends existence as we know it.
Grieving, though painful, is a normal part of life. Managing to escape death and
suffering are not marks of a successful Christian. In contrast, some of the marks

of people who are living a faithful life (and being a good steward of their health) are more likely to reflect an understanding that God is our companion and an acceptance of death as the culmination of our earthly life.

Recognizing God as our companion

The first mark of living a faithful life with one's health is the ability to see God as being with you, even in – *especially* in – times of trial. Psalm 23 is one of the most loved psalms because of the promise that *even in our darkest valley we are not alone*. There is nowhere we can go and be separated from the love and comfort of God (see Psalm 139). The image of God as the loving shepherd who is our protecting companion is a hopeful and restful image we can cling to in times of trial and hardship.

"Even though I walk through the valley of the shadow of death, I will fear no evil, for you are with me; your rod and your staff, they comfort me." (Psalm 23:4)

When a young college student died in a car accident, the campus community was shocked. Instead of death, they had wished for healing for her broken and damaged body. As the student body processed the death, it was amazing to see ways the Spirit had been moving on campus preparing them for tragedy. A special speaker that spring spoke on fear, and overcoming the fear of death was part of his talk. Several chapel services had focused on where God is in the midst of horrible suffering, focusing on the tragic tsunami in Asia. These chapel services had the campus community thinking and praying about death and suffering.

Finally, long before the car accident, two student groups from the college had been booked to perform at churches in the home area of the student who had died. These performances, when they actually happened on their scheduled dates in the shadow of her death, were important times of healing for everyone. Jesus the faithful shepherd was indeed walking alongside.

The image of God as the loving shepherd who is our protecting companion is a hopeful and restful image we can cling to.

Accepting death as the culmination of life's journey

A second mark of a faithful life is the ability to look at death as a positive. This is often tough. While intellectually I comprehend death and desire to face it with the hope of future glory, emotionally I find it terribly difficult to accept and struggle to find myself in this space daily. I find consolation, however, in understanding that even Jesus struggled with this. In the garden of Gethsemane, Matthew's Gospel tells us Jesus was agitated and, grieving, even threw himself on the ground and prayed, "My Father, if it is possible, may this cup be taken from me. Yet not as I will, but as you will." (Matthew 26:39) Death is not easy to accept! Since it was difficult for Jesus, we can anticipate it will be difficult, but not impossible, for us as well.

> *Read Romans 8:18-30. "I consider that our present sufferings are not worth comparing with the glory that will be revealed in us." (Romans 8:18)*

Pope John Paul II died in the same week as Terri Schiavo — both very public deaths. Terri Schiavo was a young woman who had been kept alive on life support for years — and whose family was painfully divided on whether to keep her alive with a feeding tube or allow her to die by removing that tube. The difference in these two public deaths was striking. Granted, the death of an older person who has lived a full life will always feel more natural and acceptable than the ending of the life of a young person who seems to have been robbed of living at an early age, but we can still learn something from these examples.

We make choices about how to say goodbye and how to let go. How we embrace death, no matter what stage of life we are in, speaks volumes about where we have our hope. Terri Schiavo's family was divided and conflicted as they argued about whether to keep her on life support or not. The way medical resources are used and how medical technology that is supporting life is used became a widely and hotly debated issue among people nationwide, not just in Terri's family. As people and politicians argued about how to proceed, the pain in this family came out, and it touched on pain and fears about death we carry collectively.

How we embrace death, no matter what stage of life we are in, speaks volumes about where we have our hope.

Pope John Paul II, on the other hand, made a public statement about his life and faith. He chose not to go to the hospital for more aggressive measures when the end of his earthly life approached. His choices about using health care resources, and prolonging life in this world, seemed to be more about embracing death as part of living rather than trying to fight it at all costs. His decision to use or not use medical technology is not the issue I want to highlight here. Rather, let's think about the peaceful environment he was able to create around himself as he breathed his last breaths. Through the choices he made, he continued in his role as a spiritual leader by modeling a way of dying that was not filled with fear.

Group questions

1. *What are your stories of God's presence in the dying process?*

2. *Share about a time when you were in the presence of someone or something that was dying.*

3. *Share about a situation from your personal life, or that you know of, where there was challenge or conflict about the death and dying process.*

Fear and death

We live in a culture that seeks to avoid death. Our culture is willing to pour large amounts of money and resources into developing medical technology that can keep us alive regardless of quality of life. We have turned death into something we do in a sterile environment. How does this distancing ourselves from death influence our human struggle with fears related to death and dying? The unknown qualities of a situation or circumstance are usually what scare us the most. The known parts are simply facts. What we *don't* know is what makes us feel afraid.

Generations ago we lived much closer to death. People knew firsthand the cycles of life from witnessing the birth and butchering of animals for food. In addition, most people did not escape childhood or early adulthood without experiencing the death of someone they knew and loved. Now, fewer people are farming and it is normal to live longer. Therefore, we may not encounter death until midlife or later. Life has gotten easier and better, but our lack of familiarity with death makes life even more of an unknown.

Life has gotten easier and better, but our lack of familiarity with death makes life even more of an unknown.

The commercialization of death has increased our fear of it. For the most part, we no longer die in our own homes as people once did. Neither do we keep the dead in our homes before burial. Now, most people die in hospitals or nursing homes, and when they die their bodies are taken to funeral homes. It is rare for us to touch, let alone see, a dead body. In fact, in some circles it has become common practice to have only photos of the deceased at a visitation. Likewise, instead of a funeral where the body is present, we have memorial services after the body has been buried. There are good and logical reasons for these choices, and when a family or loved ones have made these choices it is right and appropriate to respect those choices.

But I think we need times of being near death. Why? So that when it is our time to die – or when someone we love dies – the experience is not unfamiliar. The more we can remove the unknown from the dying process, the less we will fear death. The facts of death are simply facts – dead bodies are cold. It is the unknown that is scary. Allowing ourselves to become more familiar with death in healthy, affirming ways can release some of the paralyzing hold fear can have on us.

We need times of being near death ... so that when it is our time to die ... the experience is not unfamiliar.

As Christians, our familiarity with Christ's resurrection gives us another piece of information that can free us from the fear of the unknown. The Resurrection story still leaves mystery about what exactly will happen when we die, but it is clear that death is not our end or a final separation.

Set free from our bondage to decay (Romans 8:21)

In my office is a copy of a drawing a talented artist friend gave me. It is a lovely picture of a lush green vine with big wide leaves reflecting the bright sun's rays. It was a gift given to me during a difficult time in my life when I was grieving a painful loss. As I thanked my friend, I inquired about the vine she had chosen to draw. She was somewhat embarrassed to admit that it was just a vine she had seen in her back yard – growing out of her compost pile.

After learning about the origins of the vine, the picture became more dear to me. Here was proof that life – beautiful new life – really does come out of dead things. As someone grieving, that realization was a comfort. It has been years since I was given the picture, but I keep it still as a reminder that my life is made strong and secure in the hope of resurrection.

Before the next class

At the end of this book are some questions for a Health Autobiography. Before the next class meeting, it would be helpful if you have completed at least part of that assessment. Chapter 10 begins looking at the stewardship of health in our communities and your reflections will be helpful for the discussion of Chapter 10.

Prayer:

Prayer of Maria van Beckum, Anabaptist martyr who died in 1544

To you, O Christ,

I have given myself;

I know that I shall live with you forever.

Therefore, O God of heaven,

into your hands do I commend my spirit.

Amen.[1]

Activity

Sitting close to death

If proximity and the weather allow it, do this activity in a cemetery. If this is not possible, surround yourself with items that remind you of people in your life and community who have died. You may want to create a list and read aloud the names of people who have died in the last few years whom you have known.

As you sit close to death, read and reflect on poems that deal with death. Some suggestions are, "To be of the earth is to know" by John Soos and two poems, or what he called heartsongs, by Mattie Stepanek, "Eternal Roll Call" and "About Living (Part II)." Mattie died in 2004 of a rare form of muscular dystrophy. He was just shy of his 14th birthday. John Soos' poem is available on the Internet and Mattie's are in his book, *Celebrate Through Heartsongs*. While reading these poems, consider your response to this question: What are some of the characteristics of a life that is not ruled by death or the fear of death?

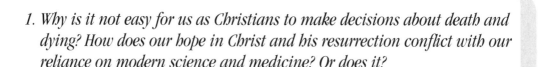

End questions

1. *Why is it not easy for us as Christians to make decisions about death and dying? How does our hope in Christ and his resurrection conflict with our reliance on modern science and medicine? Or does it?*

2. *How does fear of death make a difference in how we live and how we make choices about health care?*

3. *How might our willingness to let go of life be related to our feeling of "not being done" with life? What might you need to do before you can say you are ready and willing to trust God's timing?*

Sources

1   *Praying with the Anabaptists*, Marlene Kropf and Eddy Hall, Faith and Life Press, November 1994, p. 109.

Born to New Life in the Body of Believers

"Therefore, if anyone is in Christ, he (or she) is a new creation; the old has gone, the new has come!" (2 Corinthians 5:17)

Up until now, we have discussed health and being good stewards of our health, primarily as it relates to our personal bodies. This understanding is important. However, to be people who are striving to integrate our health into an understanding of stewardship, we have to look beyond our personal experiences alone. After all, as members of the body of Christ, our bodies, our selves, belong to the body of believers as well.

> As members of the body of Christ, our bodies, our selves, belong to the body of believers as well.

Dying to self and being born anew

In the last chapter, we talked about our physical death, but there is another kind of death and birth important to Christians – the dying to self and being born new in the body of believers as a new creation. The new life we are born into is our invitation to participate in the life of Christ and to join our lives with others who have also been born into new life with Christ. As Paul suggests in Ephesians, "Instead, speaking the truth in love, we will in all things grow up into him who is the Head, that is, Christ. From him the whole body, joined and held together by every supporting ligament, grows and builds itself up in love, as each part does its work." (Ephesians 4:15-16)

Glorify the individual

In North America, we live in a society that glorifies and promotes the *opposite* of a joined life in Christ. In our society, the needs, wants, and desires of the individual take priority. We live in homes that have multiple televisions so each member of the family can watch the show he or she wants to watch. We download hundreds of our personal favorite musical selections so we can listen exclusively to "our" music whenever and wherever we want. Food is packaged in single-serving containers so we can each eat what we want when we want.

> *We live in a society that ... promotes the opposite of a joined life in Christ. In our society, the needs, wants, and desires of the individual take priority.*

In many ways, this pervasive individualism touches our faith journeys as well. A common phrase expressed among Christians has to do with having a "personal relationship with Jesus." The ability to know and be intimate with God personally is one of the wonderful and revolutionary things about Christianity, and I am truly grateful for that access. But I am also left to ponder what kind of spiritual insight we need to hear about our personal relationship with Jesus in the context of our individualistic society, especially as it relates to health.

Individualism, faith, and health

Just as individualism is endorsed by the entertainment, food, and religion facets of our lives, individualism is encouraged with our health and health care decisions as well.

Do these statements about health and health care sound familiar?

- If I have the money and insurance necessary, I deserve whatever treatment I want.

- Health care decision making is private. It's my decision to make – not my family's or my pastor's or my church's.

- I get frustrated, and sometimes angry, when I can't get the health care I need because the system is overtaxed meeting others' needs or I can't afford the cost.

- I have difficulty following through with the health recommendations I have been given, because they sometimes require lifestyle changes, medication protocols I'm not comfortable with, and therapy appointments that interrupt my schedule.

In each of these examples, the needs or desires of the individual are the focus, and the element of community sharing, support, and accountability are absent.

Group questions

1. Give some examples demonstrating how our culture glorifies the needs, desires, and faith of the individual over the corporate.

2. What are some of the ways your personal relationship with Jesus draws you into the wider community?

3. What spiritual insight, based on prayer, searching the Scriptures, and discussion with others, would you offer our individualistic society as we work at issues of health?

We are all in it together

A biblical perspective found in 1 Corinthians 12 notes, beginning at verse 14, that "Now the body is not made up of one part but of many." Then in verse 26, Paul expands on this idea from the previous verses: "If one part suffers, every part suffers with it; if one part is honored, every part rejoices with it." This biblical message, which is counter to the message from our culture, tells us our individuality is not the sum total of who we are. We are part of something larger. Something we both suffer and rejoice with.

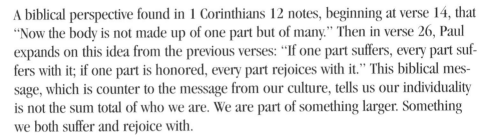

"If one part suffers, every part suffers with it; if one part is honored, every part rejoices with it." (1 Corinthians 12:26)

As much as we may want to think we are on our own with our health care decisions, every decision we make affects someone else. There is both tremendous blessing – and tremendous responsibility – in this. The biblical challenge is clear about the role of self and the responsibility we have for the needs of others. Here are a couple of examples:

> *Then he called the crowd to him along with his disciples and said: "If anyone would come after me, he must deny himself and take up his cross and follow me. For whoever wants to save his life will lose it, but whoever loses his life for me and for the gospel will save it." (Mark 8:34-35)*
>
> *Jesus answered, "If you want to be perfect, go, sell your possessions and give to the poor, and you will have treasure in heaven. Then come, follow me." (Matthew 19:21)*

The gospel message of healing, hope, and wholeness is for everyone. But the only way any of us will experience it completely is if we are pursuing it collectively. This means being willing to think and act for the good of the whole – not just the good of ourselves. Michelle's story is an example of how a community helped bring healing, hope, and wholeness to an individual and how, over time and in the context of love and support, healing was returned.

As much as we may want to think we are on our own with our health care decisions, every decision we make affects someone else.

Michelle had a rocky life as a youth. Among other trials, her parents divorced when she was in her teens. Now on her own and struggling with depression and suicidal thoughts, Michelle remembered the church of her childhood days and wandered into a local church to ask for help.

Someone from the church's elders and from the pastoral staff met with Michelle to see how they could help. From that conversation, it became clear Michelle needed help taking her medications as prescribed. Plus, maintaining access to her prescription medications was also an issue. With her compromised health in the last few months had come decreased job performance, and she was in jeopardy of losing her job.

To maintain her health insurance benefits, Michelle needed to be healthy enough to perform her job – and be able to maintain that health. Given her prescription medication needs, this was a significant concern. The elders and pastoral staff members who met with Michelle also had a profound sense that she also needed to feel loved and part of a safe and secure community.

> *The elders and pastoral staff members … had a profound sense that she also needed to feel loved and part of a safe and secure community.*

With Michelle's permission, the elders shared her health needs with the larger church community. Out of this, one family committed themselves to inviting Michelle to their home once a week for a meal, and a retired nurse volunteered to help Michelle figure out a schedule for taking her medications. She also committed to call or check in with her regularly to see how she was doing. Did this automatically fix things for Michelle? Of course not. Our lives are not as simple as television sitcoms. But, though things were not easy for several years, over time significant healing took place in the context of community – and is continuing to happen.

Now at midlife Michelle has learned to thrive. She continues to need medications to keep her life running smoothly and has learned to be faithful in taking them. She now recognizes the signs that indicate things are taking a turn for the worse and knows where to get help when she needs it. Michelle also has learned how to give love.

Seeing a member of her church community displaying all the marks of depression, Michelle lovingly confronted that person, offering her support and encouragement. She then challenged the person to get help. Michelle also has discovered she has a ministry through her poetry. Through her poems, she is able to tell her story and experience with mental illness in powerful and healing ways.

Michelle is an example of someone who is practicing the holistic stewardship of health. She knows and cares for her body – her personal body as well as the larger body of believers she is a member of. We can all do the same.

In another example, an institution I am familiar with had several leaders experience significant health events within a relatively short period. Two of the three subsequently died. This was shocking and distressing – but it led this work community to respond in an unusual way. They paused to reflect on what their role may have been in these events, and to brainstorm what they could do to protect and promote the health of their community. As a result they restructured their leadership model and offered a course in CPR for staff.

The individual lives represented in this story, of course, had their own risk factors which contributed to the health events they experienced, but the involvement of the community in owning this as a part of their collective story did something important for the health of all current and future leadership.

These are stories we can all learn from.

Prayer:

We bring before you, O Lord,

the troubles and dangers of people and countries,

the sighing of prisoners and oppressed,

the sorrows of the grieving,

the needs of strangers,

the helplessness of the weak,

the depression of the weary,

the failing abilities of the aged.

O Lord, draw near to each; for the sake of Jesus Christ our Lord.

– St. Anselm, 11th Century, Adapted

Activity

Health autobiography

At the end of this chapter, you learned how Michelle's church pulled together to support her. In return, she was made stronger to support someone else. You also heard the story of how one institution responded to the health needs of their community.

As a part of this book study you have the opportunity to write a health autobiography (see Appendix). This is a chance to reflect on the past and present story of your health and the health of those around you. With some simple sleuthing you can uncover vital health information to help you better understand your health story. During this process, you will talk with:

• Relatives who can give you a good idea of what illness or conditions people in your family are likely to face.

• Your church wellness committee, or similar group, which can give you an idea of the common illnesses and conditions found at your church.

• The human resources staff where you work to gain an understanding of the illnesses and conditions common to people you work with.

• Your local health department to learn about the commonly reported diseases and illnesses in your community. This information may be available online.

Knowing which illnesses and conditions people in your family, church, workplace, and community are most prone to can help you influence the future. Take the information you gain from this health autobiography and evaluate your current lifestyle for triggers that may make you more susceptible to developing these conditions and illnesses. Then, focus your efforts to decrease your risk in these areas.

This exercise may lead to a dramatic life change or confirm what you already know. Regardless, it should lead to a greater understanding of the past and the present, as well as ways our personal lives intersect with the lives of others – and that means a future with more possibilities for making a difference.

1. *How might your use of health care resources or decisions about self-care in the last year make it easier (or more difficult) for someone else in your community to achieve optimal health?*

2. *What are some of the blessings that come from not being alone in our quest for health? What are some of the responsibilities?*

3. *Share a story from your life where individuals in a community made a difference in the health of the broader community.*

Forming and Defining the Community

"I am the Lord your God; consecrate yourselves and be holy, because I am holy." (Leviticus 11:44a)

Living by laws and rules for "right living" were part of the day-to-day reality for the children of Israel – and for Jesus. These laws and rules were important in terms of community identity and as guides for daily living. What does it mean to live with a degree of restriction and restraint in our daily lives? And what might this ancient wisdom offer us today in relationship to our health – and the people with whom we live and share life?

God's laws for living are a gift, not a punishment.

First off, it is important to recognize that God's laws for living are a gift, not a punishment. They are instructions for how to live a full and abundant life within the context of community. They are an invitation to be in a loving, growing relationship with God and to protect the gift of life and health God has given.

Parents make "laws for living" (we call them rules) all the time to protect both their children and the collective family sanity and property. "No jumping on the furniture" is not mean or punitive. Instead, it is a means to fend off potential broken limbs, keep the beds and couches in good condition, *and* keep noise levels in the home from getting out of hand!

How these laws for living form and define community

You don't have to go too far back in Anabaptist history to find a time when the obvious marks of a more simple life identified the majority of people of this faith tradition. The plain dress, rural lifestyle, and separateness from the world were easy indicators of who the Anabaptists were. These behaviors also said something about their values and relationship with God. Some Anabaptists, by their dress and choice of vehicle, still honor these "laws for living" simply. By doing so, they make it easy for others to identify their religious affiliation.

> *Being a people who desire to be recognized by their actions as followers of Jesus Christ … continues to be a hallmark of all Anabaptists.*

Being a people who desire to be recognized by their actions as followers of Jesus Christ, whether the dress is plain or not, continues to be a hallmark of all Anabaptists. Being able to recognize someone through his or her faith, actions, and deeds as being part of a particular group of people is creating an intentional community. Think back to our "no jumping on the furniture" example. If you are in a furniture store with children who were NOT raised with this rule, chances are good you could easily identify that fact by their behavior.

The laws found in Leviticus, the Ten Commandments, and other laws in the Old Testament would have identified the children of Israel to all their neighbors as people who were faithful to God alone. Many of these laws would have continued to identify Jews in Jesus' day and even today.

The laws were given by God to Moses for the people of Israel – to help them form a community and give them a sense of identity. But the laws also provided a focus for living that was about all of life being sacred and striving to be holy. Leviticus 11:44 states, "I am the Lord your God; consecrate yourselves and be holy, because I am holy." The language about being holy because God is holy is about God loving us and longing to be in relationship with us.

> *The laws were given by God … to help [the Israelites] form a community and give them a sense of identity.*

Lessons from the laws

One of the key lessons we can learn from those Old Testament laws – and one we can apply to our lives today – is what it means to be the people of God. What does it mean to choose to live with discipline that is good for us and for our communities? What does it mean to willingly accept restraints and restrictions in our lives to achieve a fuller and healthier community life?

For example, in the book of Leviticus, the children of Israel were instructed to do certain things if they had sores that appeared to be leprosy. Further instructions were given in chapter 14 for what to do if you actually have leprosy so you don't infect and spread the disease in the community. Today, we have different methods and techniques for diagnosis of disease and different methods employed to stop the spread of the disease. But the need to protect and provide leadership to the community remains the same.

Choosing to live with laws in life, because it is part of God's grace and love promising a fuller life if you do, is not just an Old Testament message. In the New Testament (Matthew 7:13-14), Jesus calls us to enter through the narrow gate that leads to life. Jesus also tells us he came not to replace the law, but to fulfill it (Matthew 5:17). This is an important distinction. We are freed from following the letter of the law, but not freed from the purpose and rationale of the laws.

1. *What has been your experience, positive and negative, of living in ways that mark you as different from others around you?*

2. *When you think about choosing to give up something (such as smoking or talking on your cell phone while driving), does it change how you feel to think about it in terms of your choice being a way for you to give and receive love?*

A closer look

The Ten Commandments are probably the most familiar of all the Old Testament laws for right living – and we can still learn much about healthy living from them today. One of the first things I noticed is that these ancient laws address health in a broad manner. The Ten Commandments address not just our physical health, but our emotional, spiritual, and mental health as well. Health is so much more than just the state of our physical existence.

The Ten Commandments (Exodus 20:1-21)

1. Serve no other gods besides me.

2. Have no graven images.

3. Do not take the name of the Lord God in vain.

4. Keep the Lord's Day (Sabbath) holy.

5. Honor your father and mother.

6. Do not kill.

7. Do not commit adultery.

8. Do not steal.

9. Do not bear false witness against your neighbor.

10. Do not covet.

It is important to notice that the focus in all 10 is relational. The first four commandments are about our relationship with God. The last six are about human relationships with family, friends, and neighbors. If we follow the Ten Commandments, we are being intentional about the health and vitality of our relationships with God and with others.

> *If we follow the Ten Commandments, we are being intentional about the health and vitality of our relationships with God and with others.*

When we look at the Old Testament commandments with fresh eyes, we often realize that the messages we receive in the communities where we live, work, and worship, may be quite opposite. Below are some thoughts on what those opposite messages may be. As you read through them, consider how they resonate with your own experience.

- We are frequently lured into worshiping "gods" such as beauty, thinness, modern medicine, or people we believe have great power (such as our doctors).

- We live in a world where God is trivialized in our language and through our lack of reverence for holy things, such as our bodies and the earth.

- The concept of a Sabbath day has been nearly eliminated. Every day is now a work day. We push our bodies to live without a healthy balance between work and rest.

- Increasingly, we lack respect for our elders, even our parents. Our culture values youth to such an extreme that our young people have few incentives to grow up and take responsibility, and older people have less and less impact on society as valuable, contributing members.

- Our relationships, marriage and others, lack healthy boundaries and communication. Divorce rates continue to soar as we struggle with maintaining healthy intimate relationships. The sexual, physical, and verbal abuse happening even among Christians and people of faith are telling signs.

- Creating a spin (or "sound bite") of a half-truth carries more weight and gets more attention than honesty and truth-telling. Our politicians, political systems, and news media are known for this.

- We do not value all life equally. Some lives are treated as if they have more value than others.

As you consider these opposite messages, I challenge you to go back to the Ten Commandments and do some work to re-establish a right relationship with our loving God who desires health and wholeness for everyone.

When less is more: Frank's story

Frank thought he was fine, but his wife began to notice that he often needed an extra nap in the afternoon just to get through the day. Finally, after some nudging from his wife, Frank went to see a doctor about his fatigue. Test results showed Frank had severe heart blockage. He would need to make dramatic lifestyle changes and have a stent placed to open up a blocked artery.

Frank had the surgery and made a serious effort to change his diet and exercise habits. As he shared his story, other people in his church came forward saying they too had been advised to cut back on saturated fats, increase fiber in their diets, and exercise more. As a result, they formed an accountability group that shared helpful tips and checked in on each other regularly to see how they were doing.

Consider forming an accountability group to share helpful health tips – and check in on each other regularly to gauge progress.

This decision meant living with more discipline about eating and exercise than any of them were used to, but they found doing it as a group made it easier. As they lost weight and made different choices at potlucks, other people (who were not part of their group) started to notice and ask about what they were doing and whether they could join their efforts at healthier living.

Unfortunately, even though Frank had been working diligently at changing his lifestyle, at his next appointment his cardiologist told him he should have more stents. Frank had been shocked by the bill for his first stent, and in consultation with his family and his pastor, decided that while he was going to continue with the lifestyle changes he had made, he was not going to have any more stents. Remembering the years he spent as a missionary in Mexico with people who had inadequate basic medical care, as well as seeing an adult child struggling to pay an overdue emergency room bill for one of his grandkids, contributed to his decision.

While Frank's choice was difficult for his family to accept, Frank felt he had lived a full life. He did not want to spend the last years of his life in and out of the hospital spending money that could be better spent in other places. In the context of their church community, Frank and his family felt supported and loved in the decision. They are living with the uncertainty of the future, but understanding God's promise to be with them no matter what.

God promises to be with us – no matter what!

Frank's choice will not be right for everyone. But his example is a good starting point for discussions with our families and communities about how to make health care choices. Community helps us identify and keep central who we are and where our hope lies. In addition, our communities provide us with support and accountability – both for living faithfully and for the uncertainties of life. In this context we have more options for living a full and blessed life.

Just as a poet can sometimes be even more creative within the boundaries of the rules for writing a sonnet, haiku, or limerick, living with some limits and restrictions that define who we are, can actually be freeing to us on our health journeys.

Prayer:

God of Grace,

Thank you for your love and mercy.

May we thrive with abundance within your laws

and follow in your ways with a grateful heart.

Amen.

Activity

Your health signature

In this activity, work with your group to create a stewardship of health "signature" for your faith community. Why a signature? Because a signature is an identifying mark in our culture. It is how we know who someone is. Common laws and rules of a community identify us and help define our relationship with God. A shared health signature can do the same.

First, identify the ways you and your community can be recognized as stewards of health in each of the following areas (remember to think of health holistically):

1. The health and healing services we offer are ...

2. The health-related functions we support/sponsor are ...

3. Our building says we care about health in the following ways ...

4. The grounds of our church say we care about health in the following ways ...

5. Our committees (and organizational structures) that pay attention to health-related matters are ...

6. Some of the ways we offer accountability and support to people in areas related to health are ...

Second, ask yourselves this question. If someone who knew nothing about our congregation spent a day as a part of our community, what are the top three ways they would know this community cares about the health of its members?

1.

2.

3.

End questions

1. *Are there places where you personally, and as a community, could be more faithful in following the Ten Commandments?*

2. *If you think about health in terms of living in "right relationship" with God, what are some of the changes you sense you might need to make in your life to re-establish a right relationship?*

Charge to the Community

"The King will reply, 'I tell you the truth, whatever you did for one of the least of these brothers of mine, you did for me.'"
(Matthew 25:40)

There are three markers for success by which any community engaged in health care discernment and working at being stewards of health can, in some way, measure their success:

1. Members are living in a context of mutual love and support.

2. Members are living in ways that are good for their physical bodies.

3. Members are using the resources and gifts they have wisely and generously.

Do you see these markers in your church community? If not, do not be discouraged. You are taking a great step forward just participating in a study of this nature. Now be encouraged – and challenged – to use what you're learning to create a healthier congregation. But there is also something important to learn from the order they are in. Let's look back to the early church.

> *Be encouraged – and challenged – to use what you're learning to create a healthier congregation.*

Mutual aid brought many people into the family of faith. First century Christians took literally Jesus' instruction to his disciples, "When you enter a town and are welcomed ... Heal the sick who are there and tell them, 'The kingdom of God is near you.'" (Luke 10:8-9). In the context of community, the sick and the lame became strong, and the community grew in strength and numbers.

Then, once people in the community were strong and believed, they felt loved. Consequently, when you feel loved it becomes natural to take better care of yourself. If you try to do this before you feel that sense of belonging, trust, and support, you may become frustrated and find it difficult. Many times we jump in and want to start working here first, both in our individual lives as well as in our communities. Jesus' instruction, however, was never to go and make people better at caring for themselves. Rather, better self-care is a natural result of being part of a loving and compassionate community.

> *Better self-care is a natural result of being part of a loving and compassionate community.*

Finally, once we know we're loved and cared for and are therefore taking better care of ourselves naturally, only then can we move on to the third step where we begin to think critically and carefully about our resources and gifts and how both are used. This thinking naturally leads to the intersection of your needs with others' needs.

Getting to this critical third step is important since part of the final judgment we will all face one day includes accounting for how we've used the resources and gifts we've been given. Matthew 25:31-46 tells us that whenever we have used resources and distributed kindnesses to the least of these, we have done it to the Lord.

"But we appeal to you, brothers and sisters …"

Given that these three characteristics identify a healthy body of believers, how does your church get there? What exactly are we supposed to do? Fortunately, Paul gives us some helpful instructions we can take as both a challenge and an opportunity.

In 1 Thessalonians 5:12-28, Paul reinforces his earlier teachings about how Christians should live in the face of the imminent return of Jesus. He makes a point to encourage us to strengthen one another in life together. At the close of his letter, Paul instructs us on how to be a healthy, wise, and discerning community:

- Respect those who labor among you and have charge over you.

- Be at peace.

- Admonish idlers.

- Encourage the faint-hearted.

- Help the weak.

- Be patient with everyone.

- Do not repay evil with evil.

- Seek to do good.

- Rejoice always.

- Pray without ceasing.

- Give thanks in all circumstances.

- Do not quench the Spirit.

- Do not despise the words of prophets.

- Test everything.

- Hold fast to good.

- Abstain from every form of evil.

As you work together to become part of a discerning community concerned about health and health care, use these characteristics from Paul's letter to guide you. This list can easily become a checklist used when faced with health issues and health care decisions. We may find ourselves looking at a particular situation from only one vantage point. This list challenges us to think differently. It encourages us to draw away from making health decisions in isolation and instead embrace a context of mutual love and support that will make it easier to care for and love our bodies.

To be able to give – or receive – support …
requires good listening skills.

A list like this may make some people feel uncomfortable. Choosing to live this way invites others into our personal space. North American Christians, in many cases, are used to operating within an individualistic context. With a list like this, someone in my community could confront me about being idle in an area of my health I need to work on. Or I may need to be the one who admonishes a brother or sister. To be able to give – or receive – support of this nature requires good listening skills, first and foremost.

Group questions

1. *Do you agree or disagree with the ordering of the three markers of success for a community working at being stewards of health stated at the beginning of this chapter? Share examples that make your point.*

2. *As you feel led, share one of the health challenges facing you. How can you represent more of the love-filled and sustaining body of Christ to each other as you seek health, healing, and wholeness?*

The value of listening – again

At the beginning of this book, we looked at the importance of listening. Let's look there again, because to live by Paul's list, and to be able to interact with others in our community, we need to listen. Why? So we can truly sense the needs of others in our community, listen for the Spirit's leading, and hear the prophetic voices around us that may be challenging us to grow. This holy listening enhances our sensitivity to others, helps us live in ways good for our physical bodies, and inspires us to use our resources wisely and generously.

Holy listening enhances our sensitivity to others, helps us live in ways good for our physical bodies, and inspires us to use our resources wisely.

In my life, one person who exemplifies listening is Renee. Renee is in her late 40s and is married with three active children. For most of her working career she was a nurse. In addition, she was involved with church life, teaching Sunday school, and volunteering as part of her congregational wellness committee.

Recently, an injury from a long-ago horseback riding accident has made it difficult for her to walk and has forced her to quit her job and scale back her commitments. When I met Renee, her doctor had presented her with an option for a new surgical technique that seemed hopeful in helping her walk again without pain and in helping her return to work.

Because she lived in chronic pain, Renee struggled to listen to and remain present in the parts of her life that were still positive. To help her decide what to do, Renee consulted with several medical experts and gathered her trusted friends, family, and spiritual director, who had been working to help her understand where God was in the midst of her pain and suffering. It was a tedious process — full of difficult questions — but finally Renee came to a place of peace, and she knew what she needed to do.

Yet the possibility of walking pain-free, going back to work she enjoyed, and participating fully (including financially) with her family, added up to a dangling carrot she could not ignore. Prayerfully, she underwent the surgery, spending more than a month in the hospital. The surgery did wonders for her physical pain, but unfortunately was not able to correct her injury. Now, three years later, Renee is dependent on a wheelchair to get around. This created depression and isolation.

When Renee's community noticed, they took action. Members of her small group built ramps into their homes so she could continue to attend weekly meetings. They encouraged the church to upgrade its handicapped accessibility. At the coaxing of a close friend who knew exercise could help Renee fight off depression and weight gain, as well as make it possible for her to be active with her family again, Renee looked into buying a bicycle.

God and God's people stand before and around us as the body of Christ filled with a compassion that sustains and maintains our health.

Unfortunately, with her medical bills and limited work capabilities it was out of the question, at least for a while. However, others in her church family were listening to the desires of Renee's heart. A generous gift from the benevolent fund made it possible to purchase a bicycle she could ride right away.

Life has not been easy for Renee the last several years. But there was never a promise it would be. Each day presents challenges, but Renee has learned we never have to be alone in them. God and God's people stand before and around us as the body of Christ filled with a compassion that sustains and maintains our health.

Prayer:

Loving God,

who sees in humankind nothing

that you have not given to us yourself,

make my body healthy and nimble,

my mind acute and clear,

my heart happy and content,

my soul loyal and loving.

And surround me with a crowd of people and angels

who share my devotion to you.

Above all let me live in your presence,

for with you all fear is banished,

and there is only concord and peace.

Let every day combine

the beauty of spring,

the brightness of summer,

the harvest of fall,

and the sleepy quietness of winter.

At the end of my life on earth,

grant that I may come to see and know you in the fullness of your glory.

– St. Thomas Aquinas, 13th Century, Adapted

Activity

Discerning community

Think of a recent health care situation in your life or community. Recall the story and the details. When you have done this, go back through Paul's list of characteristics of a discerning community from 1 Thessalonians 5:12-28 (see pages 136-137). Identify how the situation could be influenced by acting in each of the ways Paul suggests.

End questions

1. *Which of the qualities from Paul's list would you personally find most challenging to do when faced with a health dilemma?*

2. *Why are some "jobs" on Paul's list easier or more difficult for us? What might this tell us about ourselves and how we relate to our communities?*

3. *Are there qualities of a discerning community from Paul's list you sense are absent or especially needed in the context where you live, work, and worship?*

Blessing

"May God himself, the God of peace, sanctify you through and through. May your whole spirit, soul and body be kept blameless at the coming of our Lord Jesus Christ. The one who calls you is faithful and he will do it." (1 Thessalonians 5:23-24)

Final Word: Stewardship of Health

At MMA, I have thought about and worked with many of the principles embedded in the stewardship of health concepts presented in this book. Even so, Ingrid has provided me with a more complete understanding of the three central concepts of MMA's vision. She has clearly presented:

1. The importance of making the most of the health we enjoy.

2. The significance of mutual love and support from and for those in our community.

3. The wise and generous use of the resources and gifts we have all been given.

This study helped me realize again the blessings I have received. One of the most significant blessings in my life has been my mother, Celeste. My mother lived these simple, yet profound ideas.

Mom had severe knee arthritis since her late 40s. She finally had surgery to correct the problem when she was 62. One of her knees never fully healed, thus forcing her to use crutches until she died at age 83.

My mother often had severe discomfort and pain in her knee, but she always carried a positive attitude. Many people commented to me about her example both before and after she died.

When she was 70, Mom moved 100 miles from her home community to be closer to our family. It did not take long for her to connect with our church community, and she became an integral part of it, both giving and receiving support.

Mom expressed concern about using health care resources to cure her knee problem – even though Medicare and Medicare supplement insurances fully covered her expenses. Finally, she agreed to a major knee surgery when she had all but lost the ability to walk, even with her crutches. The surgery helped for several years, allowing her to continue an independent life, but she still needed the help of crutches. My mother, however, determined to live her life to the fullest and often spent time in person or on the phone with her family and friends.

Near the end of her life on earth, she developed pancreatic cancer and intentionally chose no extreme curing treatments. Instead, she enrolled early in the local hospice program to access measures that would increase her comfort level. We were able to care for her in her home until she peacefully passed into the next life. During this difficult time, the community she built also supported and encouraged her (and us).

Now when I think of an example of someone living out the stewardship of health, my mother comes to mind. Hopefully you were able to select a role model as you studied this book – someone to keep you inspired as you journey through this life stewarding the various and valuable gifts of health and health care. God's blessings to you.

– Steve Garboden, Senior Vice President of Health Services

Recommended Health Screening and Tests

Adapted From: The Pocket Guide to Good Health for Adults,
U.S. Department of Health and Human Services
Agency for Healthcare Research and Quality
www.ahrq.gov

Checkup and Tests	Timing	Age	Other
Teeth and Gums	Once or twice a year	All ages	
Hearing	If straining or needing to turn up volume of TV or radio	Risk increases after age 50	
Vision	Based on symptoms	More problems seen after age 45. By 65, regular eye exams recommended.	
High Blood Pressure	Based on risk factors	People over the age of 45 more likely to have problems	More common in African-Americans
High Cholesterol	Every 5 years, or more often if it is high or you have risk factors	Males 35 and older. Females 45 and older.	If you have risk factors for heart disease (tobacco use, diabetes, high blood pressure, family history) it is recommended you start earlier

Checkup and Tests	Timing	Age	Other
Diabetes	Based on risk factors	As soon as there is reasonable cause to suspect	You will want to be tested more often if you are: • overweight • American Indian • Alaska native • Hispanic • African-American • had diabetes during pregnancy • have a family member with diabetes
Osteoporosis	Regularly	All women over the age of 65. Over the age of 60 if risk factors.	Risk factors: • people weighing less than 155 pounds • poor calcium intake • smoking • lack of weight bearing exercises
Tuberculosis (TB)	If reason to suspect exposure	Based on exposure	
Colorectal Cancer	Regularly	Males and females starting at age 50 or earlier based on risk factors	Risk factors: • history of polyps • family member with colorectal cancer, breast cancer, cancer of the ovaries or uterus
Breast Cancer	Every 1-2 years	Mammogram starting at age 40 or earlier if risk factors	Risk factors: • sister or mother with breast cancer

Checkup and Tests	Timing	Age	Other
Cervical Cancer	Pap test at least every 3 years	All currently or formerly sexually active women, unless uterus is removed. After age 65 testing not recommended unless there is an increased risk factor	Risk factors: • history of a sexually transmitted disease • more than one sex partner • previous abnormal Pap tests
Prostate Cancer	Regularly	After age 50 or earlier if you have increased risk factors	Risk factors: • father or brother with prostate cancer • more common in African-Americans
Oral Cancer	Regularly	After age 40 in people who have used tobacco or alcohol	

Give yourself a point for each statement you answer "Yes":

	Yes	No
I experience inner peace and harmony, even during times of misfortune.	☐	☐
I express my emotions in ways that tell others how I feel.	☐	☐
I know how to build and keep healthy relationships with others.	☐	☐
I recognize the needs of others and can think of ways to meet them.	☐	☐
I engage in meaningful activities that match my values and beliefs.	☐	☐
I know my physical body: its needs, rhythms, and signals.	☐	☐
I see life as an opportunity for growth and service, rather than seeing it as full of problems.	☐	☐
I believe I have the strength and ability to grow and serve.	☐	☐
I know I am an interesting, vital person with freedom to act and enjoy life.	☐	☐
I am in charge of my life, choosing to act rather than react, to situations I face.	☐	☐
I take responsibility for my personal health.	☐	☐
I have a sense of purpose that guides me as I make decisions.	☐	☐
I recognize how others can help me, both individually and in groups.	☐	☐
I have a plan to continue working at my personal well-being.	☐	☐
I keep faith in God as central in my activities and relationships.	☐	☐

15	Excellent
12-14	Doing great
8-11	Good job
4-7	You're on your way
0-3	Don't give up

Adapted from MMA Congregational Wellness

1. What is the first illness or injury you remember experiencing as a child? Who cared for you? What were the expectations for your recovery? What, if any, lasting effects of that experience do you carry with you today?

2. What do you remember about your body and your health from your teen years? Do you still feel the same way? If not, how have your thoughts or emotions changed with regard to your body and your health?

3. Name three beliefs you were raised to believe concerning health and the use of health care resources.

4. The five most frequent illnesses or body ailments you are likely to experience are:

5. You are currently under medical care for the following conditions:

6. List the people genetically related to you (grandparents, parents, aunts, uncles, siblings, cousins, children, etc.) and the illnesses or conditions they have, or have had (include physical as well as mental and emotional illnesses):

7. List the people in your immediate family (spouse or children) and/or people you live with and the illnesses or conditions they have, or have had, in the last two years (include physical as well as mental and emotional illnesses):

8. Name the top three illnesses or conditions people you relate to in each of these settings seem to come down with or are frequently diagnosed with (Note: Your company human resources department and/or county health department may share this information without personally identifying who has had what illnesses or conditions.)

    a. Place of employment:

    b. Church/faith community:

    c. Neighborhood:

    d. City or town:

9. What role, if any, do the communities you relate to have in helping you meet your health and wellness needs and processing health care decisions?

    a. Family:

    b. Place of employment:

    c. Church/faith community:

    d. Neighborhood:

    e. City/Town:

Bringing stewardship to life

If you enjoyed *Body Talk: Speaking the Words of Health*, you will want to consider the other books in MMA's *Living Stewardship* study series, including **Time Warped: First Century Time Stewardship for 21st Century Living.**

In *Time Warped*, Steve Ganger, MMA's director of stewardship education, provides:

- Twelve flexible, interactive lessons on how to "do less" yet create a more fufilling relationship with God.

- Practical Scriptural applications that ground each lesson in God's Word.

- Personal time chart and planning documents that help you take immediate action.

- Helpful group discussion questions that encourage deep, personal reflection.

- Encouragement and ideas that will motivate you to make lasting life changes now!

MMA's *Living Stewardship* study series examines holistic stewardship from the inside out in the areas of time, talent, money, health, and relationships. Each book deals with one area of stewardship – but in a holistic way.

You will think about stewardship in new ways as you work through these titles – and more books are in the planning stages now! Visit MMA-online (www.mma-online.org) to learn more about holistic stewardship.

Living Stewardship books and other educational resources, are available in the MMA Bookstore (www.bookstore.mma-online.org) or call (800) 348-7468, Ext. 269.

Bringing stewardship to life

If you enjoyed *Body Talk: Speaking the Words of Health*, you will want to consider the other books in MMA's *Living Stewardship* study series, including **Money Mania: Mastering the Allure of Excess.**

In *Money Mania*, Mark L. Vincent, a consultant with Design for Ministry, provides:

- Twelve flexible, interactive lessons that take readers beyond budgeting to visit various intersections in life where money plays a significant role.

- Practical Scriptural applications that ground each lesson in God's Word.

- Pointers to help you be earnest about your faith and organize your finances in ways that honor God.

- Helpful group discussion questions that encourage deep, personal reflection.

- Encouragement and ideas that will motivate you to make lasting life changes now!

MMA's *Living Stewardship* study series examines holistic stewardship from the inside out in the areas of time, talent, money, health, and relationships. Each book deals with one area of stewardship – but in a holistic way.

You will think about stewardship in new ways as you work through these titles – and more books are in the planning stages now! Visit MMA-online (www.mma-online.org) to learn more about holistic stewardship.

Living Stewardship books and other educational resources, are available in the MMA Bookstore (www.bookstore.mma-online.org) or call (800) 348-7468, Ext. 269.

Bringing stewardship to life

If you enjoyed *Body Talk: Speaking the Words of Health*, you will want to consider the other books in MMA's *Living Stewardship* study series, including **Talent Show: Your Faith in Full Color.**

In *Talent Show*, Bob Lichty, MMA's director of sales, provides:

- Twelve flexible, interactive lessons on how to discover and use your gifts, talents, and passions in service to God, your community, and your family.

- Practical scriptural applications that ground each lesson in God's Word.

- Personal spiritual gifts inventory.

- Helpful group discussion questions that encourage deep, personal reflection.

- Encouragement and ideas that will motivate you to make lasting life changes now!

MMA's *Living Stewardship* study series examines holistic stewardship from the inside out in the areas of time, talent, money, health, and relationships. Each book deals with one area of stewardship – but in a holistic way.

You will think about stewardship in new ways as you work through these titles – and more books are in the planning stages now! Visit MMA-online (www.mma-online.org) to learn more about holistic stewardship.

Living Stewardship books and other educational resources, are available in the MMA Bookstore (www.bookstore.mma-online.org) or call (800) 348-7468, Ext. 269.